# Advance Praise for The Project Management AI Handbook

"Practical, insightful, and timely, *The Project Management AI Handbook* is a must-read for project professionals navigating the intersection of AI and project management. Dr. Prasad Kodukula and Guz Vinueza masterfully bridge the gap between theory and practice, offering actionable tools and real-world examples for both waterfall and agile methodologies. This book is not just a guide—it's a roadmap for leveraging AI to transform how projects are managed and value is delivered."

—**Antonio Nieto-Rodriguez**, Thinkers50, HBR Author, PMI Fellow, CEO

"I could write a book about the profound insights found in this groundbreaking publication! The holistic approach taken keeps the reader eager to turn each page, uncovering not only 'truths' about AI but also its transformative and practical applications in project management. This book is a must-read for professionals seeking actionable strategies to integrate AI into their workflows effectively."

—**Lee Lambert**, A Founder of PMP, PMI Fellow, CEO

"This pathfinding book provides project managers with a thorough guide to incorporating AI and ML into project workflows, enhancing risk management, and maximizing efficiency. Whether for the seasoned professional or the novice, this book will equip you to navigate the complexities of modern project management."

—**Dr. Gregory Baecher**, G.L. Martin Institute Professor of Engineering, University of Maryland; Member, National Academy of Engineering

"Packed with insights, this handbook is a game changer for leveraging Generative AI tools across project and portfolio management, spanning both agile and waterfall environments. What truly sets it apart is its bold focus on the 'how'—showing real-world applications of GenAI instead of just hyping its capabilities. Whether your approach is predictive, adaptive, or hybrid, this is the ultimate resource for anyone ready to harness AI's potential in any industry."

—**Joe Campa**, PMO Leader, Strategic Excellence Office, Ontario Power Generation

"Knowing one of the authors (Guz) well, I knew that if he wrote a book, it had to be a good one! It is very hard to capture how to apply a fast-moving innovation like AI into day-to-day work and projects, as either: 1) it becomes too conceptual, or 2) it is too dense. The authors have managed to give us a pragmatic and very useful approach to understand the way new technology is completely changing the world of work and how we can capitalize on it. For many of us who are unsure how to keep on the pulse and create value in a hyper-fast and confusing world, I want to deeply thank the authors for their wonderful contribution via this book and wish them all the success they deserve."

—**Balvinder Singh Powar**, Co-author of *Going Digital*, Entrepreneur and Academic

"*The Project Management Al Handbook* is a timely collection of Al topics in the project management profession. The focus is on how to apply Al tools effectively in project management. I have been waiting for a book like this that focuses on the practical applications of Al in project management. I plan to put forward the knowledge from this book to provide successful AI PM solutions in my organization."

—**Dr. Michael O'Connor**, Senior Research Program Director, Medtronic; Adjunct Professor, Purdue University and University of Maryland

"*The Project Management AI Handbook* is an essential guide for professionals looking to harness the power of generative AI in both agile and traditional waterfall project environments. Dr. Prasad Kodukula and Guz Vinueza bring decades of expertise to demystify AI's role in project and portfolio management, offering a practical, hands-on approach filled with real-world use cases. This book stands out to me as it bridges the gap between AI theory and actionable application, enabling project managers to leverage AI for smarter decision making, risk mitigation, and enhanced productivity. With clear explanations, case studies, and prompt engineering techniques, it provides an indispensable roadmap for integrating AI into everyday project tasks. Whether you're a seasoned professional or new to AI, this book is a must-read for staying ahead in the rapidly evolving landscape of project management."

—**Jeff F. Zircher**, Senior Program Implementation Manager, Burns & McDonnell

"We live in an era of unprecedented volatility, where AI is reshaping industries in a way we've never seen before. *The Project Management AI Handbook* offers a timely and practical guide to integrating generative AI into both agile and waterfall environments. Prasad Kodukula and Guz Vinueza provide an entirely transformative perspective on how AI can enhance decision making, streamline processes, and elevate project management to new levels of efficiency. A must-read for any project leader looking to stay ahead in the AI-driven future!"

—**Dr. Ricardo Vargas**, PMI Fellow, Founder of PMOtto.ai, Former Chairman of PMI

"The field of project management is experiencing extraordinary influence and growth. This book captures the essence of the impact of artificial intelligence on project management, in all its subtleties and nuances. Both authors share backgrounds with rich expertise in both domains, so readers will benefit from their extraordinarily insightful observations. As AI marches relentlessly forward to transform multiple domains, this is the only book I know that masterfully and comprehensively captures that transformation story for project management."

—**Professor Siva K. Balasubramanian**, Harold L. Stuart Chair in Business, Stuart School of Business, Illinois Tech

"Revolutionary and insightful, *The Project Management AI Handbook* is an indispensable resource for project professionals eager to harness the power of AI. The authors provide a masterful blend of theory and practical application, offering tools and real-world examples that span both waterfall and agile methodologies. This book is more than a guide—it's a strategic blueprint for transforming project management through AI, ensuring projects are not only managed but optimized for success. Having real cases makes it very understandable for readers and professionals from different areas."

—**Juan Pablo Guerrero Daw**, Head of Tax & Legal, KPMG, Chile

"As a business leader and scholar, I am always on the lookout for resources that bridge emerging technology with practical application. *The Project Management AI Handbook* by Dr. Prasad S. Kodukula and Guz Vinueza does exactly that. It provides an accessible yet comprehensive guide to leveraging AI in project management, offering real-world use cases across both waterfall and agile methodologies. It moves beyond theory to show how AI can enhance decision making, streamline workflows, and automate critical project management tasks. The authors do a remarkable job of making AI practical and actionable for today's project professionals. For anyone looking to stay ahead in the evolving landscape of project management—whether a student, practitioner, or executive—this book is an invaluable resource. I highly recommend it as a must-read for those who want to integrate AI into their project management toolkit."

—**Fernando Yepez**, Adjunct Faculty in Project Management, University of Chicago

"Propel your project management skills with the power of AI! This book provides you with practical applications and real-world case studies on AI-powered project management, which will help you to deliver more efficient, effective, and reliable projects. Dr. Prasad Kodukula and Guz Vinueza's know-how shines through on every page of the book, illustrating us with practical applications of Gen AI to better predict project outcomes, develop project management plans, streamline work processes, or simply automate routine tasks. A valuable resource for project managers and teams looking to thrive in a rapidly changing world. A must-read for any project management professional looking to stay ahead of the game."

—**Jose Beuses**, PMO Director, Dow Inc.

"In a rapidly evolving landscape where countless books explore what generative AI can do, *The Project Management AI Handbook* by Prasad S. Kodukula and Guz Vinueza is a game changer because it stands out by focusing on how to apply it effectively. This book bridges the gap between theoretical AI concepts and practical, actionable applications in project management. The authors go beyond theory, presenting more than 50 practical use cases of AI in both waterfall and agile environments, offering actionable insights for real-world project execution. A key differentiator is that this book does not just cover AI applications; it also provides a primer on project management methodologies, making it an invaluable resource for both seasoned professionals and newcomers to the field. For any project management practitioner looking to harness AI to enhance efficiency, decision making, and strategic execution, this book is an essential read."

—**Vijay K. Verma**, PMI Fellow, The PMI David I. Cleland Project Management Literature Award Winner

"*The Project Management AI Handbook* is a delightful, down-to-earth guide on how project managers can navigate the hype around generative AI and instead discover how they can use it to improve their productivity. It provides practical guidance from real-world examples and addresses concerns and shortcomings head-on. Highly recommended."

—**Kyle Brown**, IBM Fellow, Vice President, CTO to the CIO, IBM

# The Project Management AI Handbook

## Leveraging Generative Tools in Waterfall and Agile Environments

Dr. Prasad S. Kodukula, PMP, PgMP, DASSM
and Guz Vinueza, M.S., MBA

J.ROSS PUBLISHING

ISBN: 978-1-60427-205-5
e-ISBN: 978-1-60427-859-0

Printed and bound in the U.S.A. Printed on acid-free paper.

10 9 8 7 6 5 4 3 2 1

**Library of Congress Cataloging-in-Publication Data**
Names: Kodukula, Prasad author | Vinueza, Gus, 1974– author
Title: The project management AI handbook : leveraging generative tools in waterfall and agile environments / Dr. Prasad S. Kodukula, PMP, PgMP, DASSM, Gus Vinueza, M.S., MBA.
Description: Plantation, FL : J. Ross Publishing, [2025] | Includes bibliographical references and index. | Summary: "The Project Management AI Handbook: Leveraging Generative Tools in Waterfall and Agile Environments is an essential guide for project and portfolio management professionals, business leaders, and anyone interested in using generative AI to enhance project management. Packed with use cases and prompts, this book illustrates how AI tools can be applied through real-world case studies that mirror actual projects and portfolios. Whether you are managing projects using waterfall or agile methods, this book demonstrates how generative AI can automate tasks, streamline documentation, generate project plans, forecast risks, and optimize project performance with greater efficiency and accuracy"— Provided by publisher.
Identifiers: LCCN 2025025743 (print) | LCCN 2025025744 (ebook) | ISBN 9781604272055 hardcover alk. paper | ISBN 9781604278590 epub
Subjects: LCSH: Project management | Artificial intelligence—Industrial applications
Classification: LCC HD69.P75 K6564 2025 (print) | LCC HD69.P75 (ebook) | DD 658.4/04—dc23/eng/20250725
LC record available at https://lccn.loc.gov/2025025743
LC ebook record available at https://lccn.loc.gov/2025025744



Direct all inquiries to J. Ross Publishing, Inc., 151 N. Nob Hill Rd., Suite 476, Plantation, FL 33324. For EU safety/GPSR concerns, email: gpsr@mare-nostrum.co.uk or contact: Mare Nostrum Group B.V., Mauritskade 21D, 1091 GC Amsterdam, The Netherlands.



Phone: (954) 727-9333
Fax: (561) 892-0700
Web: www.jrosspub.com

# Dedication

*To my beloved mother and late father—your unwavering authenticity, generosity, and simple way of life have been my greatest inspirations. Your kindness and selflessness continue to guide me, and I am forever grateful for the values you instilled in me.*

*To my wife, Padma—the most patient and supportive person I know. Your encouragement and understanding have been my greatest source of strength. I deeply appreciate your unwavering support through every challenge.*

*To my brother, Mahesh, and my sisters, Suryam, Vani, and Durga—our strong bond means everything to me. We are more than siblings; we are a deeply connected family, always there for one another through every chapter of life.*

*With love and gratitude, this book is for you.*

—Prasad

*To my beloved wife, Cori—always by my side through every challenge and triumph, thank you for your love and infinite patience.*

*To my greatest treasures, Oli and Feli—your laughter, curiosity, and boundless energy make every day brighter. Being your dad is my greatest privilege.*

*You are my heart, my drive, and the reason I wake up every day with purpose and joy. This book is a dream come true, but even more special because I get to share it with you.*

*With all my love, always.*

—Guz

# CONTENTS

# FOREWORD

We stand at the dawn of something extraordinary. As I write these words, artificial intelligence (AI) and generative AI (Gen AI) are not just transforming project management—they are redefining what we believe is possible. What began as simple automation tools has evolved into sophisticated systems capable of creative problem-solving, strategic thinking, and even autonomous decision making. The revolution unfolding before us is not just another technological shift; it is a fundamental reimagining of how we conceive, execute, and deliver projects.

As someone who has spent over two decades working at the intersection of technology, innovation, and global business strategy, I have witnessed the transformative potential of AI firsthand over the last ten years. My career has spanned global IT consulting, entrepreneurial ventures, and leading digital transformation initiatives across industries and geographies. I have been leading teams of up to 200 people focused on data analytics and AI. This breadth of experience underpins my perspective on AI's role in shaping the future of project management. From advising Fortune 500 companies and governments to leading high-growth global organizations, I have seen how AI-driven innovation can unlock new levels of efficiency, resilience, and strategic value. It is with this lens that I wholeheartedly endorse the principles and use cases presented in this book.

I remember using AI in project management in the early days—when we witnessed AI systems drafting project plans and risk assessments. Many were skeptical, viewing these as mere novelties. Yet here we are today, watching these systems evolve at a breathtaking pace, learning from every interaction, and growing more sophisticated by the day. Yesterday's rudimentary project documentation generators have blossomed into sophisticated partners capable of crafting nuanced stakeholder communications, predicting complex risk scenarios, and proposing innovative solutions to age-old project challenges.

The evolution has been nothing short of remarkable. Early AI systems could handle basic scheduling and resource allocation, but today's advanced algorithms can process vast amounts of historical project data to identify patterns invisible to the human eye. They can predict potential roadblocks months before they materialize, suggest optimal team compositions based on past performance metrics, and even anticipate stakeholder concerns before they arise. This is not just automation—it is augmented intelligence at its finest.

Perhaps most intriguing is the emergence of semi-autonomous project management systems. While we are still in the early stages, the possibilities are staggering. Imagine AI systems that not only support project managers but can independently monitor project health, adjust resources in real time, and orchestrate entire workflows while maintaining continuous alignment with strategic objectives. These are not distant dreams—they are emerging realities that are already taking shape in pioneering organizations.

We are witnessing early examples of Gen AI systems that can automatically rebalance project portfolios in response to changing market conditions, generate detailed project documentation that adapts to different stakeholder perspectives, and even facilitate virtual team collaboration by identifying potential communication gaps and suggesting interventions. The potential for fully autonomous project management may seem like science fiction, but the building blocks are already here.

This book arrives at this pivotal moment to serve as your guide throughout this transformation. Through four carefully crafted sections, it takes you on a journey from the fundamentals of AI to its most advanced applications in portfolio management, traditional waterfall environments, and modern agile management practices. But more than just a technical guide, this book is a vision of what is possible when human ingenuity meets AI.

Let me be clear: the rise of AI in project management does not signal the twilight of human project managers—quite the opposite. As AI handles increasingly complex tactical aspects of project execution, human project managers are free to focus on what they do best: leading with empathy, navigating complex stakeholder relationships, and making nuanced decisions that require emotional intelligence and cultural awareness. The future belongs to those who can masterfully orchestrate this symphony of human and artificial intelligence.

The potential applications are boundless. Consider how Gen AI is already revolutionizing requirements gathering by analyzing stakeholder feedback and automatically generating comprehensive user stories. Think about AI systems that can simulate thousands of project scenarios in seconds, helping teams prepare for virtually any contingency. Imagine project status reports that write themselves, not just compiling data but providing insightful analysis and recommendations in natural language that resonate with each stakeholder's specific interests and concerns.

The challenges ahead are significant, yes. Questions about data quality, ethical AI use, and governance frameworks, among others, demand our attention. How do we ensure AI systems make decisions that align with organizational values? How do we maintain transparency and accountability in AI-driven project management? How do we protect sensitive project data while leveraging the power of machine learning? Yet, these challenges pale in comparison to the opportunities before us. We are not just improving project management—we are reimagining it from the ground up.

Integrating Gen AI into project management also raises fascinating questions about the future of professional development in our field. The project managers of tomorrow will need to be both technologists and humanists, capable of working seamlessly with AI systems while maintaining the human touch that makes project management as much an art as a science. This book addresses these evolving skill requirements, helping you prepare for a future where technical expertise and emotional intelligence are equally crucial.

As you turn these pages, you will discover practical insights drawn from the front lines of this revolution. You will learn how organizations are already deploying AI to achieve what was once thought impossible, and you will gain the knowledge needed to lead this transformation in your own organization. Whether you are a seasoned professional or new to the field, this book offers a roadmap to not just survive but thrive in this new era.

This book is not solely a technical guide to AI applications in project management; it also serves as a primer for key project management disciplines, including portfolio management, waterfall methodologies, and agile practices. It ensures that even readers new to project management will benefit from a solid foundation, while seasoned professionals can explore advanced AI applications to elevate their practices. This dual-purpose approach makes the book accessible to a broad audience, bridging the gap between AI enthusiasts and project management practitioners.

The actionable tools and strategies provided in this book transcend specific AI tools, making them relevant across a range of project environments and challenges. Whether the reader is focused on agile, waterfall, or portfolio management, they will find methodologies and use cases that offer immediate practical value, helping them address real-world challenges with AI-powered solutions. The case studies and examples presented here are not just theoretical exercises—they are real-world applications that demonstrate the tangible benefits of AI integration.

Dr. Prasad Kodukula and Gustavo Vinueza bring decades of experience in project management and cutting-edge AI applications, making this book an authoritative guide. Their shared vision to bridge AI and project management practices is evident in every chapter of this insightful work. Together, they offer a rich blend of theoretical depth and practical guidance. This book is the result of their relentless pursuit of knowledge and their commitment to advancing the field.

While advancements in AI, particularly in Gen AI, will inevitably accelerate after the publication of this book, the principles and methodologies presented herein remain timeless. Frameworks like GAE (Gen AI Engagement) and PRIME (a methodology for AI application) have been crafted to adapt to new tools and techniques, ensuring that readers are equipped to thrive as AI technology evolves. This adaptability is a hallmark of the book, making it a long-term resource for professionals.

We are witnessing the birth of a new age in project management—one where the boundaries between human capability and AI blur, creating possibilities we are only beginning to understand. This is not just about adopting new tools—it is about embracing a fundamentally new way of thinking about project management. It is about imagining a future where projects are not just managed but are orchestrated through a perfect harmony of human wisdom and AI.

This foreword serves as an invitation for you—project managers, leaders, stakeholders, team members, and other project professionals—to view this book as your launchpad into the world of AI in project management. It encourages you to embrace AI, not as a replacement for human expertise but as a transformative enabler that enhances collaboration, decision making, and project outcomes. With this book, you can confidently take the first steps—or accelerate your journey—into AI integration.

The future is calling, and it is more extraordinary than we ever imagined. Let this book be your guide as you step into this brave new world, where the impossible becomes routine and the boundaries of project management extend far beyond what we once thought possible. The journey ahead is exciting, challenging, and filled with opportunity for those bold enough to embrace it.

Together, let us embrace this revolution and shape a future where project management transcends its traditional limitations to become something truly extraordinary. The pages that follow are not just a roadmap—they are an invitation to be part of one of the most significant transformations in the history of project management.

*—Kumar R. Parakala*

Kumar R. Parakala is a distinguished CEO, founder, investor, and board director with over 25 years of experience building global technology and consulting firms. A pioneer in digital transformation and AI since the early 2000s, he has advised Fortune 500 companies and governments across 30 countries on technology innovation and growth strategies. Currently, he is the CEO of Tabhi North America, an AI-enabled travel company with nearly $3 billion in revenue across six countries. Kumar previously founded GHD Digital, which expanded to 700 professionals across nine countries, achieving a valuation exceeding $400 million. Earlier, he founded Technova, which was acquired by GHD in 2017. Kumar spent 15 years at KPMG, where he co-founded its $3 billion technology advisory practice and held senior roles, including Senior Partner and Regional Managing Partner. A USA Today best-selling author of two leadership books and a keynote speaker, he has advised leaders at JP Morgan, Microsoft, Dell, and Shell.

# PREFACE

Have you ever felt the excitement of returning from a professional conference, your mind buzzing with newfound insights and possibilities? That's exactly how I felt when I returned from the Project Management Institute's (PMI's) 2023 Global Summit in Atlanta. Artificial intelligence (AI) was the talk of the town—in conference settings and cocktail hours alike. It was exhilarating, but also somewhat overwhelming.

Attending numerous technical presentations, I noticed a fascinating trend. The sessions explored the expansive landscape of AI, delving into its definitions, ethics, and broader implications. Many thought leaders, academics, and consultants provided valuable insights into the vast AI panorama. This coverage was enlightening, providing a comprehensive understanding of AI's theoretical aspects. This was beneficial for setting the stage, yet, for practitioners, there was a palpable eagerness for more direct guidance on the practical implementation of AI within project management. I observed an opportunity for additional focus. There seemed to be room for more discussion on how project managers and teams could effectively utilize AI tools in their day-to-day work to boost productivity and manage projects with greater efficiency.

On the flight back from Atlanta, I found myself engaged in an enriching conversation with a fellow attendee of the same conference. Our discussion, which spanned from the airplane to baggage claim, revolved around AI. We shared thoughts and experiences, finding common ground in our reflections. Both of us acknowledged a widespread desire, one that seemed to resonate in the conference halls—a wish for more concrete advice on how to apply AI tools effectively in the realm of project management.

Just a fortnight before this conference, I had been discussing the idea of developing a workshop on generative AI (Gen AI) for project managers with my friend Gustavo, who is now my coauthor of this book. The day after I returned, I couldn't resist calling him to share the excitement and insights from the conference. It didn't take long for us to realize that there was a pressing need for a book on this subject, complementing the workshop we had envisioned.

Gustavo and I are no newcomers to the world of AI, let alone the realm of project management. Gustavo has spent over a decade teaching and consulting in project quantitative risk analysis. His expertise extends from Microsoft Project applications to Monte Carlo Simulations, which he has not only mastered but also taught numerous times. With a decade of experience both as a data scientist and as an analytics leader, Gustavo's familiarity with algorithms and proficiency in data exploration and visualization tools are nothing short of impressive. In 2021, he fortified his experience by obtaining a specialized credential in AI/ML from the University of Texas at Austin.

As for me, my experience in project management spans over 40 years, during which I've also taught the discipline extensively. My journey with AI began in 1988, when, as a senior engineer in a chemical manufacturing company, I developed two AI-based expert systems in environmental engineering, earning a corporate technical achievement award. In the late 1990s, my business partner, Chuck Stack, and I created an innovative AI-based smart system for water, sewage, and industrial wastewater treatment facilities. This system was designed to detect malfunctions and failures in advance, providing alerts to management and government authorities while also recommending and, in some cases, automatically triggering preventive actions. It integrated emerging technologies like neural networks, IoT, and cloud computing—long before these concepts gained widespread attention—alongside optimization algorithms, pattern recognition, and encryption/decryption techniques. In 2005, we were granted a United States patent for this innovation, which was later licensed to leading companies in process control and automation. This work, along with other advancements, contributed to our recognition as the most innovative environmental technology company in Illinois. Today, many AI-driven water and wastewater treatment systems reflect the foundational principles outlined in our patented approach to real-time monitoring, advanced failure detection, and proactive response.

While working on a book about project portfolio management (PPM) in the late 2000s, I had an unexpected spark of inspiration: the realization that key aspects of the PPM process—project evaluation, prioritization, and selection—could potentially be automated using AI algorithms. Motivated by this idea, I explored the possibility of patenting it. However, after consulting with my legal counsel, I was advised that evolving patent laws and the significant legal costs made pursuing a patent impractical. Undeterred, I redirected my energy into completing the book on PPM, allowing me to share my vision and insights in a different way.

As my interest in AI took a back seat due to other priorities, the tides shifted during the COVID era. In 2021, fate would have it that I heard about Gustavo receiving his AI/ML credential from the University of Texas at Austin. I reached out to congratulate him and expressed my interest in collaborating on AI and project management. By some twist of digital fate, my message seemed to vanish into a cyber black hole.

However, serendipity would once again play its role just a few days before that PMI conference. Just as I was rekindling my interest in AI and considering the development of teaching materials, Gustavo reached out to me, renewing our conversation about AI and project management.

So, let's talk about what this book is and what it isn't.

This book is not about AI in general, nor is it about the broader implications of Gen AI. It's not another book on how the world is changing due to AI or high-level insights. There are plenty of those books available, and they serve their purpose well.

Our book is exclusively focused on the *practical applications of Gen AI in the domain of project management*. We dive into the tools that project managers, schedulers, cost estimators, planners, controls professionals, and team members use daily. We've focused on real-world case studies and use cases to illustrate each application. While our examples may be specific to certain industries, the principles and tools we discuss are universally applicable. Our aim is simple: to enhance your productivity in managing projects and teams by demonstrating how you can leverage Gen AI to create key project management documents, plans, and artifacts.

What sets this book apart is that it's probably the first of its kind in the project management space to focus on practical applications. Furthermore, we don't limit ourselves to just one project development approach. We explore applications for both traditional waterfall and modern agile methods, providing a comprehensive understanding of how Gen AI can benefit your projects, regardless of their nature.

This book ventures beyond merely discussing AI use cases within project management; it serves as an educational platform for novices and seasoned professionals. We have included concise primers on fundamental project management principles, covering both waterfall and agile practices. This dual focus (AI use cases and project management principles and tools) ensures that even those new to project management can gain a solid foundation in the field's core principles while simultaneously learning how to integrate AI tools into their project management practices.

As we penned this handbook, we harnessed the capabilities of ChatGPT, one of the most popular Gen AI tools today, not only for research but also in composing many sections of the book. This collaboration with AI underscores a crucial theme of our discourse: the creative partnership between human insight and AI. Far from detracting from our creative contributions, ChatGPT has extended our capabilities, enabling us to process and synthesize vast amounts of information at unprecedented speeds. This partnership illustrates a powerful use case of Gen AI in creative writing and research, demonstrating how professionals—not just in project management but in any field—can enhance their creative output. Employing AI in this manner allows us to focus on the art of storytelling and the conveyance of complex ideas in accessible ways, ensuring that the content is not only informative but also engaging. By embracing AI as a coauthor, we aim to show that Gen AI is an ally in the creative process, opening new avenues for innovation and efficiency. This book stands as a testament to the potential of AI to not only support but also inspire and expand the horizons of professional practice.

Just as we were completing the manuscript, reflecting on whether our effort would resonate or fulfill the burgeoning interest in AI within project management, we took our work into the world to test the waters. Following the writing phase, we presented a paper featuring selected AI use cases from the book at PMI's Global Summit in 2024. The reception was overwhelmingly positive, providing us with the validation we hoped for.

A month later, we extended our engagement with the community through a one-day workshop cosponsored by the PMI Chicagoland chapter and the Stuart School of Business at Illinois Tech, where I serve as an adjunct industry professor in project management. The success of this event went beyond our expectations, confirming the demand and need for practical AI applications in project management.

This enthusiastic reception has been both humbling and exhilarating. It has reinforced our belief that there is a keen and growing interest in exploring how AI can be effectively integrated into the project management discipline. With this book, we aim to bridge the gap between theoretical AI concepts and practical, actionable applications in project management. We invite you, our readers, to engage with us, share your thoughts, and apply these insights in your professional environments.

But this is just the beginning. Knowing that AI is progressing at every blink of the eye, we've established a website for this book, where we plan to continually update content, share more application scenarios, and foster a community of like-minded professionals. We hope that the website will help you stay current as the practice of AI in project management evolves, while our book provides the foundation.

As you read through these pages, understand the use cases, and start applying them in your projects, we invite you to share your feedback and insights. Let's learn from each other's experiences and collectively explore the endless possibilities that AI can bring to the world of project management. You can find us at pmaihandbook.com.

So, fasten your seatbelts and get ready for a transformative journey into the world of AI-powered project management. Your adventure begins now!

*—Prasad S. Kodukula*
(with *Gustavo "Guz" Vinueza*)

# ACKNOWLEDGMENTS

Writing *The Project Management AI Handbook* has been an incredible journey, and we are deeply grateful to those who supported and contributed to this endeavor.

First and foremost, we extend our heartfelt thanks to Stephen Buda at J. Ross Publishing. Steve's unwavering guidance through the book-writing process, the editorial journey, and the production phase has been invaluable. His expertise and encouragement ensured that this book reached its fullest potential. We are also profoundly grateful to Jackie Lininger, our diligent copy editor, whose meticulous attention to detail significantly enhanced the manuscript.

A special thanks goes to Jonathan Lee for his thorough review and constructive input. His insightful feedback and engaging discussions were instrumental in refining the manuscript and elevating its quality. Similarly, we thank Professor Shankar Sankaran for his critical review of the entire manuscript. His thought-provoking comments and suggestions further improved the depth and clarity of this book. We are deeply indebted to Kumar Parakala for writing the Foreword to this book. His thoughtful and insightful words set the perfect tone for our work, and we are honored to have his contribution.

On a personal note, Guz extends his deepest gratitude to his wife, Corina, and his children, Olivia and Felipe, for their constant love, support, and encouragement throughout the writing process. Prasad wishes to thank his wife, Padma, for her incredible patience and unwavering support. Balancing the demands of this book alongside teaching at two universities and managing numerous other projects would not have been possible without her understanding and encouragement.

To all our readers, colleagues, and supporters who have been a part of this journey, "Thank you." Your belief in the potential of AI in project management inspires us to continue exploring and sharing this exciting field.

# ABOUT THE AUTHORS

**Dr. Prasad S. Kodukula**, PMP, PgMP, PMI-ACP, DASM, DASSM, BCES, is a globally recognized speaker, management coach, best-selling author, award-winning entrepreneur, and innovative inventor with over 40 years of professional experience. As the founder and CEO of Kodukula & Associates, Inc., a project management training and consulting firm based in Chicago, Illinois, he has delivered impactful insights to audiences across nearly 50 countries. Dr. Kodukula specializes in project, program, and portfolio management; leadership; and creativity and innovation. He has trained and coached thousands of professionals from more than 40 Fortune 100 companies, as well as prestigious organizations like the World Bank, the United Nations, and the U.S. government. Most recently, he has been working with NASA, focusing on strategies to recover troubled projects. Some of the major corporations he has collaborated with include Abbott Labs, Boeing, BP, Caterpillar, Cisco, Corning, Dow Chemical, Ericsson, IBM, Medtronic, and Volkswagen. Dr. Kodukula is also an adjunct industry professor of project management at Illinois Tech and teaches at the University of Chicago.

As the CEO and cofounder of NeoChloris, Inc., a Chicago-based green technology company, Dr. Kodukula leads a team developing patented technologies that convert carbon dioxide to renewable energy. His previous roles include R&D director at a bio-environmental startup, senior engineer at a multinational petrochemical corporation, and senior project manager at a global engineering consulting firm. Additionally, he taught senior/graduate environmental engineering and science courses at institutions like Illinois Tech, West Virginia University, and the University of Kansas.

Dr. Kodukula has received several prestigious accolades from the Project Management Institute (PMI), including the 2020 PMI Fellow Award, the highest honor in project management. He was also honored with the 2016 PMI Eric Jenett Project Management Award of Excellence and the 2010 PMI Distinguished Contribution Award. In 2025, he received Project Control's Excellence Award from the Project Control Academy. His contributions to environmental science and engineering have been recognized by the U.S. Environmental Protection Agency and the Kansas Department of Health and Environment. Under his leadership, Constant Compliance, Inc., an environmental technology company he cofounded, was recognized as Illinois' most innovative small business in the environmental category. Similarly, NeoChloris received the University of Arizona Center for Innovation Startup Award.

Dr. Kodukula holds baccalaureate degrees in chemistry, biology, and education, an M.S. in environmental science from Rutgers University, and an M.S. and Ph.D. in environmental engineering from Cornell University and the Illinois Institute of Technology, respectively. He also earned a master's certificate in project management from George Washington University. A prolific author, he has coauthored or contributed to 12 books and more than 50 technical articles. He co-owns four U.S. patents, including a groundbreaking invention patented in 2005 that utilized AI technologies such as neural networks and machine learning to predict and prevent process upsets and failures in water and wastewater treatment systems. This early innovation highlights his visionary approach to adopting AI systems for practical applications, solidifying his role as a pioneer in leveraging AI for solving real-world challenges.

Dr. Kodukula's extensive, multidisciplinary expertise spans collaborations with organizations across all 11 industrial sectors of the S&P 500, encompassing industries as diverse as healthcare, technology, energy, finance, and consumer goods. This breadth of experience underscores his ability to apply project management principles and innovative solutions to a wide range of challenges. With his global reach and groundbreaking contributions in project management and environmental technology innovation, Dr. Kodukula continues to inspire professionals and organizations to achieve excellence in their endeavors.

**Gustavo (Guz) Vinueza** is a recognized expert in data analytics, machine learning, and quantitative risk solutions, with over 25 years of experience driving business growth through advanced technology strategies.

As the consulting director at The Ferryfield Group, a boutique consulting firm specializing in quantitative risk software, he has played a pivotal role in expanding the company's footprint across different industries and countries. Previously, Gustavo served as data director at Betterfly, Latin America's first social unicorn, overseeing the company's data architecture, analytics, and machine learning initiatives. His leadership helped scale the organization's data capabilities, increasing adoption and efficiency across multiple regions.

During his tenure as director of consulting and analytics solutions at Palisade Corporation, he transformed the consulting division into an agile software factory, expanding revenue 3x and delivering dozens of software and consulting projects annually across Latin America, the United States, and the Middle East. His strategic approach to data-driven decision making and risk quantification has influenced key industries, making him a sought-after consultant and speaker at PMI, AACE, SPE, and INFORMS events.

He has trained thousands of professionals from prestigious organizations like Amway, the U.S. Army Corp of Engineers, Ontario Power Generation, and DEWA. Major corporations he has collaborated with include AMGEN, Mitsubishi Pharmaceuticals, SEMPRA Energy, Borg Warner, and Network Rail.

Gustavo is also a seasoned academic. He has served as an adjunct professor in analytics and business intelligence at institutions such as Universidad de San Andrés in Argentina, Universidad de Cuenca, Escuela Politécnica Superior del Litoral in Ecuador, and EALDE in Spain, where he has trained hundreds of professionals in data science, agile methodologies, and project management.

His diverse experience spans leadership roles in investment banking, insurance, and technology. He has also driven major AI and machine learning initiatives, reducing model deployment times and enhancing predictive capabilities across multiple business applications.

Gustavo holds an MBA from Universidad Torcuato Di Tella, an M.S. in financial direction from Universidad Adolfo Ibáñez, and a Postgraduate Certificate in AI and machine learning from the University of Texas at Austin (USA). With a passion for bridging the gap between cutting-edge technology and strategic business decisions, Gustavo continues to shape the future of data analytics and risk management, empowering organizations to navigate uncertainty with confidence.

Web Added Value™

This book has free material available for download from the Web Added Value™ resource center at *www.jrosspub.com*

At J. Ross Publishing we are committed to providing today's professional with practical, hands-on tools that enhance the learning experience and give readers an opportunity to apply what they have learned. That is why we offer free ancillary materials available for download on this book and all participating Web Added Value™ publications. These online resources may include interactive versions of material that appears in the book or supplemental templates, worksheets, models, plans, case studies, proposals, spreadsheets and assessment tools, among other things. Whenever you see the WAV™ symbol in any of our publications, it means bonus materials accompany the book and are available from the Web Added Value Download Resource Center at www.jrosspub.com.

Downloads for *The AI Project Management Handbook* include the prompts used in the book's use cases and information about the book's companion website: pmaihandbook.com.

# SECTION 1

## *AI in Project Management: Basics*

# 1

## INTRODUCTION

In the ever-evolving landscape of project management, the introduction of artificial intelligence (AI) has been akin to the dawn of a new era. AI has emerged as a transformative force, fundamentally altering how projects are planned, monitored, and executed. This paradigm shift is not just about automating routine tasks or crunching large datasets; it is about redefining the very essence of project management. AI technologies, with their ability to learn and adapt, bring to the table unparalleled predictive prowess and decision-making capabilities. For the project manager, this means an ability to plan efficiently and effectively, anticipate challenges well before they become evident, allocate resources with a level of efficiency that human foresight might not match, and maintain a project's course with a steady, informed hand. By leveraging AI, organizations can transition from traditional ways of managing projects to more dynamic, data-driven approaches, ensuring projects are delivered on time, within budget, and with optimal quality while also generating promised value.

The advantage of AI is its capacity to sift through and analyze vast amounts of data to find patterns and correlations that escape the human eye. It can predict project risks with a high degree of accuracy and recommend mitigation actions, identify the optimal mix of skills needed for project teams, and even suggest the most effective communication channels for stakeholder engagement. Moreover, AI-driven analytics can provide project managers with real-time insights into the health of their projects, enabling proactive interventions that can save time, costs, and, often, the project itself.

Building on the foundation of analytical AI, generative AI (Gen AI) stands as the next frontier in project management. This breed of AI goes beyond analysis and into the realm of creation, generating novel solutions and strategies that can revolutionize the approach to project tasks. Gen AI can synthesize new project plans, draft potential risk mitigation strategies, and even devise comprehensive communication plans tailored to the unique dynamics of each project. It is like having a forward-thinking collaborator that not only understands the past and present but can also anticipate and construct possible futures, empowering project managers to innovate and lead with confidence.

Today's project managers are custodians of complexity, steering multiple projects through the choppy waters of change, risk, and uncertainty. Generative tools powered by AI are the compasses and sextants in this metaphorical journey, offering navigational aids that no project manager can afford to be without. These tools do more than automate—they innovate. They generate content, images, and computer code. You can converse with them like human beings and produce the desired information in the form of text, a picture, or even a video. Upon receiving your requests in the form of so-called prompts, they can produce common tools used by project professionals.

For example, consider the crafting of a meticulous stakeholder matrix and communication plan. By analyzing previous project data and current stakeholder interactions, Gen AI can assess stakeholder influence and interest levels with remarkable acuity. This enables the creation of a dynamic stakeholder matrix that not only categorizes stakeholders according to their relevance and impact on the project but also suggests customized communication strategies for each group or individual. Such an approach ensures that every communication is impactful, addressing stakeholders' concerns and expectations proactively, thus fostering a more engaged and supportive project environment.

When it comes to risk management, Gen AI stands out in its ability to construct and maintain a robust risk register. By ingesting data from numerous sources—including past project archives, market trends, and even social media sentiment—AI can identify potential risks that might otherwise go unnoticed. It can populate the risk register with the identified risks, assigning probabilities and potential impacts and suggesting mitigation strategies. AI can also identify and analyze early signs of significant risks, alert the project team, and suggest preventive actions, all at the same time. This proactive risk identification and assessment process allows project managers to address potential issues before they manifest, effectively safeguarding the project against unforeseen complications.

In the realm of software development, Gen AI demonstrates a keen utility in the creation of user stories. Through the analysis of user feedback, requirements, and behavior patterns, AI can automate the creation of user stories that are precisely aligned with end-user needs. This ensures that the development team can focus on delivering features that directly enhance the user experience, guided by a backlog of well-defined and validated user stories. This results not only in a product that meets user expectations but one that resonates with them on a more intuitive level.

These examples underscore how Gen AI, when applied with thoughtful intention, can be a powerful ally in the quest for project management excellence, bringing forth efficiency, foresight, and a level of personalization that is simply unmatched by traditional methods. Gen AI can swiftly generate an initial *draft* response, serving as a solid foundation that users can refine and enhance by incorporating their expertise, contextual understanding, and human judgment.

In this book, our focus will be on the breadth of Gen AI applications within project management, each selected for their potential to forecast and shape the future trajectory of the field. Through detailed case studies and a survey of industry best practices, we aim to illuminate the significant role Gen AI plays in enhancing aspects of project management, including stakeholder engagement, risk assessment, and the crafting of user stories for software development. While acknowledging the variety of AI tools at one's disposal, our discourse will center predominantly on Gen AI, probing its unique capabilities and the transformative ways it can be applied within various industries and project management methodologies.

## THE BOOK'S INTENT

This book is crafted to address a critical gap in the current literature on AI in project management. While there is a wealth of information heralding the capabilities of AI—enumerating its potential to revolutionize industries and redefine roles—there is a noticeable void when it comes to the *how*. It is one thing to know what AI can do; it is another to understand how to put AI to work effectively within the nuanced context of managing projects. This book aims to transcend the theoretical and enter the practical, moving beyond the *what* of AI's possibilities to the *how* of its application.

We focus on use cases, bringing the concepts to life with practical examples and case studies that demonstrate tangible ways to apply Gen AI for enhanced efficiency and productivity in the workplace. The focus is on empowering project managers with the ability to deploy Gen AI for the administrative and procedural aspects of projects—such as scheduling, risk assessment, requirements documentation, stakeholder communication, and resource allocation. By doing so, project managers can reallocate their valuable time and energy toward project leadership. This shift from management to leadership allows for a deeper engagement with the team's creative and strategic endeavors, fostering innovation and driving the project to new heights.

In addition to project management, the book also addresses project portfolio management (PPM), a critical discipline for aligning projects with organizational strategies and goals. Whether the projects within a portfolio follow a waterfall or agile methodology, they must be evaluated, prioritized, and selected to optimize the allocation of limited resources. This book illustrates how AI tools can enhance PPM by streamlining project selection, ranking, and categorization processes while ensuring alignment with strategic objectives. By integrating portfolio management into the discussion, we connect project-level activities with the broader context of organizational success, underscoring the importance of strategic decision making.

An added bonus of this book is its comprehensive coverage of foundational project management principles. We not only present AI use cases; we also provide a primer on the essentials of project management, a brief overview of key tools, and a rundown of best practices within the field. Whether you are a novice with limited knowledge of project management or a seasoned expert, this book stands alone as a self-contained guide to understanding and applying project management and AI techniques effectively. This ensures that, regardless of your experience level, you can find valuable insights and tools to enhance your project management skills and adapt to new challenges in the AI era.

The book's intent is clear: to provide you with the know-how to harness Gen AI in a way that will create a powerful ally in project execution. The goal is to enable project professionals to delegate the routine yet critical tasks of project management to AI, ensuring that projects run smoother, risks are mitigated effectively, and decisions are informed by the most comprehensive data analysis available. In doing so, project leaders can focus on steering their projects with vision and foresight, cultivating an environment where strategy, creativity, and leadership thrive. This is not just about keeping pace with technological advances but about leveraging them to become pioneers of project leadership in the AI era.

This book reflects the knowledge available at the time it was written; however, the world keeps moving forward faster than ever. Competition—there is an abundance of it—fosters innovation, and breakthroughs will likely emerge in the Gen AI arena between now and this book's final release. As of today, OpenAI's ChatGPT remains the clear leader in Gen AI, and we have used ChatGPT's 4o model for all the prompts presented in this book. This does not mean you can only use ChatGPT to apply the principles and tools presented herein. Any major Gen AI tool will likely be as effective.

## WHY WATERFALL AND AGILE ENVIRONMENTS?

Given the subtitle of this book, *Leveraging Generative Tools in Waterfall and Agile Environments*, it is only natural to delve into why these two environments are central to our exploration. Waterfall and agile represent more than just project management philosophies. They embody distinct approaches, referred to as project development approaches, to managing projects in today's dynamic industries. Development approaches serve as guiding strategies for how projects are planned, executed, and controlled. Broadly categorized into predictive, adaptive, and hybrid, each offers strategies for tackling varying levels of complexity and uncertainty:

- *Waterfall models* are the hallmark of predictive approaches, characterized by linear and sequential progression through distinct project phases, such as initiation, planning, execution, and closeout. This approach thrives in environments with high levels of certainty, where requirements are well-defined early in the project life cycle. Frameworks like the PMBOK® Guide (PMI, 2021) and PRINCE2 (AXELOS, 2017) embody waterfall principles, emphasizing meticulous up-front planning and strict control mechanisms.
- *Agile*, by contrast, exemplifies adaptive approaches, prioritizing flexibility, collaboration, and iterative progress over rigid adherence to predetermined plans. Agile is particularly effective in dynamic environments where requirements evolve and uncertainty is high. Frameworks like Scrum and Kanban support this iterative and incremental approach, enabling teams to adapt quickly to changing circumstances while delivering continuous value.
- *Waterfall and agile* approaches each offer distinct advantages, yet projects often require a combination of structure and adaptability, giving rise to *hybrid* approaches that blend predictive and adaptive strategies. However, this book does not treat hybrid contexts as a separate discussion, as hybrid approaches inherently integrate principles from both waterfall and agile.

Waterfall and agile environments dominate the project management landscape, representing two ends of the spectrum in how projects are approached. By focusing on these two widely adopted paradigms, this book addresses the most common industry practices, ensuring relevance to a broad audience. Waterfall's methodical structure and agile's dynamic adaptability serve as ideal backdrops to illustrate the transformative potential of Gen AI tools in real-world settings.

Moreover, the tools discussed in this book apply not only to distinct waterfall or agile projects but also extend to hybrid contexts. For example, a hybrid approach might apply waterfall principles to hardware components while leveraging agile techniques for software development. Gen AI tools can be seamlessly adapted to these blended approaches because they are rooted in the core principles of predictive and adaptive management.

## INTEGRATING PROJECT PORTFOLIO MANAGEMENT

Whether projects are managed using a waterfall or agile approach, they are often part of a broader project portfolio. Portfolio management focuses on evaluating and aligning projects to achieve strategic organizational goals. Regardless of the approach chosen, they must be selected, prioritized, and resourced in a manner that aligns with the organization's overarching goals. The chosen development approach—be it waterfall or agile—plays a significant role in shaping the project's resource needs, timeline, and risk profile, all of which are critical considerations for portfolio-level decision making. For instance, waterfall projects typically require a substantial up-front investment in planning and longer lead times, whereas agile projects may call for iterative resource allocation and greater adaptability to change.

Gen AI tools can enhance portfolio management by supporting these critical activities. For instance, AI can assist in analyzing large amounts of data to assess project feasibility, evaluate strategic fit, recommend optimal resource allocation, and even simulate different portfolio scenarios to maximize overall returns. By integrating AI into the portfolio management process, organizations can make more informed decisions about project selection, termination, portfolio optimization, and balancing risks and opportunities across the portfolio. By leveraging AI across both the portfolio and project levels, organizations can create a cohesive strategy that drives success across their initiatives.

## PRACTICAL APPLICATIONS

This book places a strong emphasis on the practical application of Gen AI in project and portfolio management. A key feature is its focus on real-world applications, showcasing over 50 use cases of Gen AI across waterfall and agile project environments as well as portfolio management. These use cases are designed to bridge the gap between theoretical knowledge and practical execution, offering project managers actionable insights into how AI can enhance decision making, efficiency, and effectiveness.

To provide deeper context and illustrate these applications, the book introduces case studies that replicate real-world scenarios. These include Project Omega, Project Pinot, and Project Victor as project management use cases, as well as the GeneMatrix portfolio for portfolio management scenarios. Through these examples, you can observe how Gen AI tools address common challenges faced by project teams, from resolving conflicts to improving risk management and decision making. The case studies serve as microcosms of real-world projects, helping you grasp the principles of AI application regardless of the project's size or complexity.

While the book does not include the extensive documentation typically associated with large- or even medium-scale projects, the simulated scenarios are enriched with sufficient detail to make the concepts transferable. By following the case studies, you will learn how to apply AI tools in your own projects, appreciating both the transformative potential and inherent limitations of Gen AI. For instance, while the book demonstrates the impressive capabilities of Gen AI even with limited data, it also highlights the added value of using project-specific and organizational data to achieve superior outcomes.

## COMPANION WEBSITE: pmaihandbook.com

We created a website, *pmaihandbook.com*, which serves as an essential companion to the book, extending its value beyond the printed pages. This dynamic platform offers you access to a wealth of supplementary resources, creating an interactive and evolving hub for project management professionals, trainers, and AI enthusiasts. By providing materials and tools that could not be accommodated in this book due to space limitations, the website enhances the practical utility of the book's content.

Key features of the website include expanded AI-generated outputs for the use cases presented in this book since some responses were too extensive for inclusion in the print version. Additionally, the website features new case studies and use cases, illustrating further applications of Gen AI in project and portfolio management. It is designed to foster a collaborative community where users can share their experiences, lessons learned, challenges, and innovative approaches to applying AI to real-world project management scenarios.

The website also serves as a platform for staying up-to-date on the latest AI developments relevant to project and portfolio management, ensuring that readers remain informed as the technology evolves. For academics and trainers, the website offers tailored questions and exercises tied to the book's chapters, making it a valuable resource for classroom use and professional training. Other offerings may include templates, curated articles, video tutorials, and opportunities for direct engagement with the authors through webinars or Q&A sessions.

By bridging the gap between theory and practice, *pmaihandbook.com* not only complements the book but also builds a vibrant learning and sharing ecosystem for leveraging AI in project management.

## WHAT IS THIS BOOK *NOT* ABOUT?

The *Project Management AI Handbook* is a practical guide to leveraging Gen AI tools in project and portfolio management. However, it is important to set clear boundaries regarding its scope and what it intentionally omits.

This book is not a technical manual on AI. Foundational concepts like machine learning (ML), neural networks (NNs), and Gen AI are briefly introduced to provide context, but detailed discussions on technical algorithms, programming, mathematical models, or advanced topics such as AI agents and agentic AI are beyond its scope. The latter, known for its ability to autonomously perform tasks and make decisions, represent an exciting frontier, but their technical intricacies and broader implications lie outside the practical focus of this book. Instead, the emphasis here is on usability and the practical application of Gen AI for project professionals.

This book does not attempt to cover every AI application in project management. The focus remains on practical use cases in waterfall and agile environments, such as cost estimation, risk management, and sprint planning. Portfolio management is addressed through a few illustrative use cases rather than an exhaustive exploration.

The book also does *not* go in depth on some of the project management knowledge areas outlined in PMI's PMBOK® Guide but does emphasize scope, schedule, cost, and risk management. Value management, program management, and the role of AI in leadership are not included.

Finally, the rapid evolution of AI means new developments will likely emerge between the manuscript's submission and the book's release. While these advancements may introduce new tools, the principles and frameworks presented—such as the PRIME methodology (prepare, relay, inspect, modify, execute) and generative AI engagement principles—are adaptable and long-lasting, offering a durable foundation for future applications.

## HOW IS THIS BOOK ORGANIZED?

This book is methodically segmented into four main sections, each dissecting distinct but interrelated aspects of AI's role in project management. The first section, *AI in Project Management:*

*Basics*, serves as an educational and contextual foundation; the second, *AI in Portfolio Management*, explores AI's capabilities applied to project portfolio strategies and support on decision making; the third section, *AI in a Waterfall Environment*, navigates AI's integration in more structured traditional and predictive project environments; and the fourth, *AI in an Agile Environment*, explores AI's contributions to more flexible, agile practices. This logical organization not only facilitates a gradual buildup of knowledge but also caters to a diverse readership ranging from novices to seasoned project management professionals, providing valuable refreshers and introducing core concepts in project management that tie seamlessly into AI applications.

## Section 1: AI in Project Management: Basics

The first section functions as both an introduction to AI for newcomers and a substantive review for experienced practitioners, addressing the why, what, and how of AI in project management. *Chapter 1* (this chapter) opens the dialogue on why AI is an indispensable tool for modern project managers, along with a transparent discussion of the book's scope. *Chapter 2* expands on the technical aspects, breaking down AI into digestible definitions and categories, covering key facets from ML to NNs, and revealing how these concepts converge within the domain of project management. *Chapter 3* delves into Gen AI, discussing its historical context, ethical considerations, and distinctions from other AI technologies. *Chapter 4* introduces a new concept that we call *Gen AI Engagement*, emphasizing the interactive nature of these systems and illustrating their application through real-world examples. Completing this foundational section, *Chapter 5* brings AI into the daily grind of project tasks, showing how AI can enhance routine activities through prompt engineering—writing emails, creating presentations, summarizing documents, and analyzing data. This section ensures readers are not just passively learning about AI but are equipped with the knowledge to actively begin integrating it into their project management practice.

## Section 2: AI in Portfolio Management

This section is designed to educate project and portfolio managers on how AI can greatly enhance the PPM practice. *Chapter 6* starts from the top, with an introduction to PPM and the opportunities AI brings to its practice. *Chapter 7* explores a set of AI use cases for PPM, from strategic fit analysis to project categorization, ranking, and selection, then finishes with the construction of a portfolio efficient frontier—everything generated with the support of ChatGPT, a leading Gen AI model.

## Section 3: AI in a Waterfall Environment

Section 3 is tailored to align AI with the typical sequential phase-gate model of the waterfall approach. *Chapter 8* revisits the core principles of project management, laying a common groundwork by explaining development approaches (ranging from waterfall to agile). This is to ensure that regardless of your familiarity with these concepts, you can appreciate their subsequent AI integration. *Chapters 9 to 12* walk you through the typical waterfall project phases—initiation, planning, execution, and closeout—infusing each with AI-driven insights and tools. This section illuminates how AI can enrich the waterfall model, from building work breakdown structures and automating business case documentation to refining risk management strategies, ultimately illustrating AI's value in enhancing predictability and control in project management. It is a resource for project managers entrenched in waterfall methodologies who seek to elevate their practices with AI, ensuring efficient project progression.

## Section 4: AI in an Agile Environment

In the fourth and final section, the focus shifts to integrating AI within the flexible framework of agile project management. *Chapter 13* sets the stage with an exploration of the agile framework, contrasting various agile methodologies and focusing on the principles and practices of Scrum. *Chapters 14* and *15* then delve into the specific enhancements AI can provide, from creating backlogs to facilitating Scrum ceremonies and augmenting reporting processes. This section is a guide for agile practitioners, detailing how AI tools can be adapted to support the iterative cycles of Scrum, enhance team collaboration, and bring predictive power to sprint planning and review processes. It illustrates AI's potential to increase the agility and responsiveness of project management, providing a strategic advantage in today's fast-paced project environments.

Please note that while we have delineated sections for waterfall and agile use cases, there is a notable overlap in their applicability. For instance, the use cases for creating a communication plan, managing stakeholders, resolving conflict, and maintaining a risk register, presented within the waterfall context, are equally relevant in agile environments. Conversely, the *sprint retrospective* use case, typically associated with agile, can also be effectively utilized in waterfall settings as a method for capturing lessons learned.

Concluding with final thoughts, *Chapter 16* synthesizes the AI applications across both waterfall and agile approaches, contemplating the future trajectory of AI in project management and offering best practices for its integration. This culminating discussion affirms the book's role as a comprehensive handbook for modern project managers looking to harness AI's capabilities, propelling their projects and leadership into the future.

As we conclude the introduction of this book, we stand at the threshold of a new era in project management, one that is being redefined by the innovative applications of Gen AI. The subsequent chapters will serve as a roadmap, guiding you through the intricacies of AI's current and potential impact on the profession. From the foundational AI concepts to their practical applications in both traditional and agile project management frameworks, this journey is designed to equip project professionals with the foresight and tools necessary for excellence in an AI-enhanced future. Our exploration is not just about understanding the *what* and *how* of Gen AI applications but also about sparking a transformation in how we approach, execute, and lead projects. As you navigate through the rich landscape of this book, we invite you to embrace the insights and strategies that will empower you to take the helm in this new frontier, forging pathways that leverage the full spectrum of AI's capabilities in project management.

# 2

# INTRODUCTION TO AI IN PROJECT MANAGEMENT

Integrating artificial intelligence (AI) into project management transforms how projects are conceived, planned, and executed. This chapter aims to provide a comprehensive overview of AI's role in project management, exploring its potential to revolutionize the field. By examining both the theoretical underpinnings and practical applications of AI, we will highlight how these advanced technologies are reshaping the project management landscape.

The journey begins with a fundamental understanding of AI, its origins, and its evolving definition over time. We'll briefly trace the history of AI from its early conceptualization by pioneers like John McCarthy to its current state, where it encompasses a wide array of technologies designed to mimic human intelligence (McCarthy, 1958). This historical context sets the stage for understanding how AI has progressively integrated into project management practices, offering tools that enhance efficiency, decision making, and strategic planning.

One of the most exciting developments in AI is the advent of generative AI (Gen AI), particularly with the launch of ChatGPT in November 2022. Gen AI represents a significant leap forward, moving beyond traditional AI applications that focus on pattern recognition and data analysis. Instead, Gen AI has the capability to create new content, including text, images, computer code, and even music, by learning from existing data. This transformative potential of Gen AI opens new avenues for innovation in project management, from automating routine tasks to generating sophisticated project reports and predictive analyses.

However, the integration of AI into project management is not without its challenges. As we explore the opportunities AI presents, we will also address the hurdles that project managers must overcome to effectively harness these technologies. Issues such as data quality, ethical considerations, model hallucinations, and the need for continuous learning and adaptation are critical to ensuring the successful implementation of AI-driven solutions.

As we conclude this chapter, we will outline a pragmatic roadmap for embedding AI within project management practices. This roadmap provides actionable insights and best practices for project managers looking to integrate AI into their workflows. It will cover essential steps such as identifying suitable AI applications, preparing and managing data, selecting the right AI tools, and fostering a culture of innovation and continuous improvement.

In essence, this chapter is designed to equip you with a foundational understanding of AI in project management. Whether you are a seasoned project manager or a newcomer to the field, our goal is to enable you to engage in informed dialogue about AI and apply its principles and tools effectively in your projects. By embracing AI, project managers can unlock new levels of efficiency, creativity, and strategic insight, ultimately leading to more successful and innovative project outcomes.

## ARTIFICIAL INTELLIGENCE

The term *artificial intelligence* was coined by John McCarthy in 1955 (McCarthy, et al., 1955). Before that, the field was often referred to by various terms that described aspects of machine intelligence or automated reasoning, such as *cybernetics* and *automata theory*. McCarthy proposed the term for the Dartmouth Conference in 1956, the first AI conference, aiming to explore the possibilities of machines using language, formulating abstractions, and solving problems reserved for humans (Nilsson, 2009). He envisioned AI as a distinct branch of computer science focusing on creating intelligent machines.

## DEFINITIONS OF AI

Every AI expert has their own definition of AI (see Table 2.1). A simple definition of AI for a layperson is machines that mimic human behavior. It is like giving a computer a brain that allows it to think, learn, and make decisions. Imagine a robot that can solve a math problem, a computer program that can predict the weather, or even a virtual assistant on your phone that understands what you are saying. At its core, AI is the technological magic that empowers machines to mimic human intelligence. Think of it as the brain behind the machine, enabling it to learn from data, make decisions, and even solve problems—much as we do. AI combines computer science and robust datasets to enable problem-solving. For project managers, AI acts as a powerful ally, automating repetitive tasks, predicting outcomes, and offering valuable insights to enhance decision making. We will review these capabilities in more detail in the upcoming chapters. Table 2.2 summarizes keywords or phrases in the AI field that are useful for those who are more interested in the applications of AI rather than the AI itself.

**Table 2.1** AI Definitions by popular authors

| Definition | Reference |
|---|---|
| The science and engineering of making intelligent machines. | McCarthy, 1958 |
| AI is a collection of practices for creating intelligent machines. | Brooks, 1991 |
| A branch of computer science synthesizing intelligence. | Simon, 1995 |
| AI makes machines intelligent and able to function appropriately in their environment. | Nilsson, 2009 |
| Intelligence that is not biological. | Tegmark, 2017 |
| Machines acting in ways that seem intelligent. | Malone, 2018 |
| Intelligence is solving problems or creating valued products within cultural settings. | Gardner, 1983; Goleman, 2020 |

**Table 2.2** Key terms in AI

| Term | Description |
|---|---|
| AGI (artificial general intelligence) | A type of AI designed to understand, learn, and apply intelligence across a wide range of tasks as well as or better than a human. It is AI with broad capabilities. |
| AI agent and agentic AI | An AI agent is an autonomous system that perceives its environment, processes information, and acts to achieve specific goals. While some are simple and rule-based, others use machine learning to adapt over time. Agentic AI takes this further by enabling agents to operate with greater autonomy and initiative—breaking down complex tasks, collaborating with other agents or tools, and making context-aware decisions with minimal human input. |
| AI bias | The tendency of AI systems to make unfair decisions or predictions based on skewed data or misaligned algorithms. It is a critical concern in AI ethics. |
| AI ethics | The field of study that scrutinizes the moral implications and societal impacts of AI, focusing on creating responsible AI. |
| Algorithms | Step-by-step procedures for calculations, data processing, and automated reasoning. They are like recipes that tell AI how to solve problems. |
| ANI (artificial narrow intelligence) | AI focused on a single task or group of tasks, exhibiting intelligence within a specific, limited context. It is highly specialized AI. |
| Artificial intelligence (AI) | A broad area of computer science aiming to create machines capable of performing tasks that typically require human intelligence. It is like giving computers a brain. |
| Chatbots | AI programs designed to simulate conversation with human users, especially over the internet. They help automate customer service or information gathering. |
| Data governance | The process of managing the availability, usability, integrity, and security of the data used in an organization, including AI applications. |
| Data mining | The process of analyzing large datasets to discover patterns and relationships. It is like digging through data to find hidden treasures of information. |
| Deep learning | An advanced type of machine learning using multilayered neural networks to learn from vast amounts of data, much like how the human brain operates. |
| Generative AI (Gen AI) | AI that can generate new content, such as text, images, or music, that resembles human-created content. It is creative AI. |
| LLMs (large language models) | Advanced AI models trained on vast amounts of text data, capable of understanding and generating human-like text. They power tools like chatbots and virtual assistants. |
| Machine learning (ML) | A method by which AI systems learn from data to make decisions and predictions, improving over time without being explicitly programmed. |
| Natural language processing (NLP) | AI's ability to understand and interact using human languages, enabling machines to read, decipher, understand, and make sense of human languages. |
| Neural networks (NNs) | Computing systems vaguely inspired by the biological NNs of animal brains, designed to recognize patterns and interpret data. |
| Predictive analytics | Using historical data, statistical algorithms, and ML techniques to predict future outcomes based on past data. |
| Reinforcement learning | A type of ML where AI learns to make decisions by taking actions in an environment to achieve some objectives. It learns through trial and error. |
| Supervised learning | An ML approach where models are trained on a labeled dataset, which means the data is already tagged with the correct answer. |
| Transfer learning | A technique where a model developed for a task is reused as the starting point for a model on a second task. It is like applying knowledge from one area to another. |
| Unsupervised learning | An ML approach where models learn from data that is not labeled, trying to identify patterns and relationships on their own. |

## STRONG AI AND WEAK AI

AI can be broadly categorized into two types: strong AI (or artificial general intelligence, AGI) and weak AI (or artificial narrow intelligence, ANI) (Bory, et al., 2024). AGI embodies systems with human-equivalent intelligence, not only capable of performing a wide array of tasks independently—such as managing a project from inception to completion and adapting to changes—but also equipped to handle aspects of emotional intelligence, such as leadership and team building. These systems can engage in decision-making processes akin to a seasoned project manager, displaying a capacity for empathy and ethical considerations, traits that are essential in navigating the complex social interactions inherent to managing diverse teams.

In contrast, ANI is designed to perform specific tasks within predefined parameters and lacks the general cognitive abilities of AGI. In the realm of project management, ANI excels at optimizing schedules, managing resources, and automating routine tasks with high efficiency and accuracy. These systems are programmed to follow explicit rules and are confined to their designated roles, which means they do not possess the broader understanding or adaptability that characterizes AGI. For instance, ANI can analyze historical data to forecast project timelines and budget requirements, and it can automate communication workflows and documentation processes. However, unlike AGI, ANI cannot engage in creative problem-solving or adapt to new, undefined situations without human intervention. This specialization makes ANI incredibly reliable and effective within its scope but limited when faced with tasks that require broader contextual judgment or cross-functional knowledge.

Currently, most AI applications in project management are examples of ANI, particularly classified as *limited memory machines.* These tools analyze historical project data to enhance future planning and execution but operate without the long-term learning and adaptation that AGI promises. As AI technology progresses, the anticipation grows for a shift toward AGI, thereby expanding the scope of AI's capabilities in project management.

This concise overview underscores AI's potential in project management, bridging the gap from narrowly focused tools to advanced systems poised to revolutionize how projects are managed and executed.

## SUPERVISED AND UNSUPERVISED LEARNING

Now, we will attempt to demystify how AI is constructed in layman's terms. At its foundation are algorithms—step-by-step instructions that guide the machine. These algorithms learn patterns and rules from data, becoming smarter over time. Imagine teaching a computer to recognize cats: it analyzes countless cat images, identifying common features like whiskers and ears. This process, known as supervised learning, forms the bedrock of machine learning (ML).

In simple terms, supervised learning is like learning with a teacher. The *teacher* is a dataset that already has the answers. Just as a student learns to associate questions with the correct answers, in supervised learning, the system learns to connect input data to known responses, which helps it predict answers for new, similar questions.

Let's extrapolate this example to project management and imagine we could feed thousands of project descriptions with a label: project successful or project failed. Of course, we would have to define success and failure beforehand (e.g., a failed project had a cost overrun of 50%+ or it failed to generate promised value), and for each project, we could add 20 or 30 variables such as duration, budget, industry, maturity of team, etc. With all that information, we could generate a supervised ML model that could predict, given the same variables, if a project would succeed or not.

Unsupervised learning is like self-study without a guide. The system tries to make sense of data without predefined answers, looking for patterns and structures on its own. It is akin to letting the computer explore independently, trying to find hidden connections within data. Think of unsupervised learning as a detective looking for clues without knowing exactly what crime has been committed. This type of AI can sift through tons of project work, spotting hidden patterns, like which tasks often take longer than planned or which team communications often precede a delay. It then groups these findings into clusters, sort of like gathering similar clues together. Project managers can use these clusters to identify potential issues before they occur, helping them to stay on track.

Now, picture this learning process with layers of complexity—enter deep learning. Inspired by the human brain's neural networks (NNs), deep learning structures the data through multiple layers, unraveling intricate patterns. This layered approach transforms raw data into intelligent actions, making AI an invaluable asset for project managers navigating the complexities of modern projects. Tangible applications of deep learning are natural language processing (NLP), speech recognition, image processing, and others.

## MACHINE LEARNING AND DEEP LEARNING

ML and deep learning serve as the foundational technologies behind both ANI and AGI. In the case of ANI, ML algorithms are optimized to perform specific tasks, such as image recognition or language translation, with high precision. Deep learning, leveraging its multilayered architecture, enables ANI systems to process large datasets efficiently, making it essential for applications like voice recognition in smartphones. For AGI, which remains a theoretical concept—with potential breakthroughs on the horizon—ML and deep learning would play a pivotal role in equipping systems with the ability to learn, adapt, and handle a broad spectrum of tasks intelligently, mirroring the way humans acquire knowledge and make decisions across varied contexts. ML uses algorithms that enhance their performance over time as they process increasing amounts of data, similar to how practicing homework improves one's understanding of a subject. Deep learning, a more advanced subset of ML, relies on large NNs and hierarchical models to analyze and learn from vast quantities of unstructured data, doing so autonomously without requiring human intervention.

## NEURAL NETWORKS

ML is a cornerstone of modern computer science, enabling systems to analyze data, identify patterns, and make predictions without being explicitly programmed for each specific task. Within this vast field, NNs serve as one of the most influential tools, modeled loosely after the structure and functioning of biological neurons in the human brain. An NN is composed of layers of interconnected nodes, or *neurons*, that process information by passing it through mathematical transformations. These networks are particularly effective in recognizing complex patterns in data—such as images, speech, or text—and have formed the basis for many advances in AI. Each layer in an NN progressively refines the input data, extracting higher-level features that make it possible to handle intricate problems with remarkable accuracy.

Deep learning takes NNs to the next level by incorporating many layers, often referred to as *deep* architectures, which enable the model to learn representations of data at increasing levels of abstraction. These deep NNs have revolutionized fields such as computer vision, NLP, and autonomous systems by achieving unprecedented performance in tasks previously thought to be out of reach for machines. The strength of deep learning lies in its ability to automatically discover features from raw data, minimizing the need for human intervention in feature engineering. As a subset of ML, deep learning exemplifies the power of NNs to tackle highly complex tasks, making them indispensable tools in the development of cutting-edge technologies.

## GENERATIVE AI

A recent development in AI that took the world by storm is Gen AI. It can create new content by learning from data. It is different from traditional AI, which typically focuses on recognizing patterns, analyzing data, or making decisions based on input data. Gen AI can create text, images, music, and other forms of media, as well as write computer code—activities that involve human-like creativity. It uses advanced ML models, such as NNs, to produce outputs that can be novel and not just replicative of existing examples (Goodfellow, et al., 2014; Vaswani, et al., 2017).

ML provides the tools and techniques that are foundational to Gen AI. It begins with systems that learn patterns and features from data. As these systems advance through ML processes, they can begin generating new content similar to what they have learned. For instance, by understanding language structures, they can create realistic text. This progression from analysis to creation, facilitated by complex algorithms and computational power, is what bridges ML to the generative capabilities of AI, enabling the generation of new, original outputs.

Gen AI represents a leap beyond traditional AI applications that simply interpret and act on data. It uses deep learning to not only understand data but also to create new, original outputs that didn't exist before using what are known as large language models (LLMs). Well-known examples of such LLMs are Open AI's *ChatGPT* and Google's *Gemini*. This evolution from reactive and limited memory AI toward Gen AI showcases a move from understanding and analyzing the world to adding to it creatively, hinting at strides toward more advanced AGI forms like *theory of mind* and *self-awareness*.

Project management professionals have welcomed Gen AI with enthusiasm, recognizing its transformative potential since its advent in the broader AI landscape (Mariani and Mancini, 2024). Gen AI enables the automation of tasks such as writing reports, creating project documentation, and generating realistic project simulations, all of which can save considerable time and effort for project professionals. By learning from vast datasets of past projects, it can produce comprehensive risk assessments and tailored management strategies. This capability not only streamlines workflow but also enhances decision making with predictive insights, offering a forward-looking tool that supports project managers in leading more successful, efficient projects. The introduction of Gen AI marks a significant shift from manual, time-intensive processes to more strategic and creative project management.

## EVOLUTION OF AI

The evolution of AI has been a remarkable journey from simple, rule-based systems to the complex architectures of today. Initially, AI began as reactive machines, similar to early NNs and expert systems, that could perform tasks without the ability to learn or remember past actions. Progressing from these foundations, the advent of ML introduced systems capable of learning from data, marking a significant leap in AI's development. This was further enhanced by deep learning, which utilizes sophisticated NNs to process and interpret vast amounts of information, akin to mimicking the human brain's operations.

Today, AI is on the brink of achieving theory of mind, where systems would understand and react to emotions, and ultimately, self-awareness, envisioning machines with full consciousness. These theoretical stages represent a shift toward AI that can understand, learn, and interact in ways that mirror human intelligence, leading to AGI.

This condensed history underscores the potential for AI to evolve from performing specific tasks to exhibiting complex cognitive abilities, including emotional understanding and consciousness, fundamentally altering how machines interact with the world and themselves. Figure 2.1 presents a timeline of the main milestones of the AI industry.

**1943–1956: First AI Concepts**
Pioneering work on neural networks, machine learning, and what would become AI was conducted by McCulloch, Pitts, Turing, Von Neumann, and others.

**1956: Dartmouth College**
The field of artificial intelligence was officially named and kicked off at this influential conference of scientists at Dartmouth College.

**1965: Expert Systems**
The first expert system, DENDRAL, was created by Edward Feigenbaum and others in the U.S. to identify molecular structures.

**1987: Neural Networks Breakthrough**
The development of efficient deep learning algorithms for neural networks led to revolutionary breakthroughs down the road.

**1997: Deep Blue**
IBM's Deep Blue defeated world chess champion Garry Kasparov in the U.S. using traditional AI methods like tree search algorithms and evaluating 200 million positions per second.

**2012: AlexNet**
Researchers at the University of Toronto in Canada created AlexNet, which classified 1.2 million images in the ImageNet competition. This demonstrated deep learning's effectiveness.

**2014: DeepMind Founded**
Researchers Demis Hassabis, Shane Legg, and others founded DeepMind in the UK, which would create breakthrough deep learning algorithms for games and other areas.

**2016: AlphaGo (UK)**
DeepMind's AlphaGo program beat the world champion in the game Go using deep neural networks, advancing AI capabilities.

**2022: Generative AI, ChatGPT**
In the U.S., OpenAI launched a conversational agent called ChatGPT, which can answer questions, explain concepts, summarize texts, and more at an advanced level.

**Figure 2.1** Key AI milestones

## NEXUS OF PROJECT MANAGEMENT AND AI

Project management and AI have been like parallel lanes on a highway, occasionally acknowledging each other but seldom merging. Over the last two decades, little collaboration has emerged from this union. It mainly involved crunching numbers and handling repetitive tasks, like sorting through vast amounts of data and making predictions, such as the probability of finishing on time and within budget. It was more of a backstage dynamic than a mainstream activity. However, Gen AI has changed this dynamic, shifting the potential of AI to a more primary role, generating tools that could lead to problem-solving and assistance in the project management scene with incredible efficiency. It is the responsibility of the project manager to leverage this potentially enormous leap of technology—or not.

As the world becomes increasingly interconnected and automated, project management stands at a pivotal crossroads with AI. The fusion of project management and AI, which we refer to as the nexus of project management and AI, is transforming how projects are planned, executed, and delivered. AI's profound analytical capabilities are empowering project managers to forecast project risks, optimize resource allocation, and streamline communication processes. At this nexus, traditional project practices are being reimagined, creating a symbiotic relationship where AI provides data-driven insights and project management offers the strategic framework to implement them effectively. This integration heralds a new era where the adaptability of AI and the strategic prowess of project management converge to elevate the efficiency and success rates of projects across industries.

## USES OF AI IN PROJECT MANAGEMENT

If we look back over the last 20 years, we will notice AI's footprints in project management. Some companies utilized statistical techniques to optimize intricate project schedules, ensuring everything aligned seamlessly, and combining a series of dependencies, resources, and work packages (Butt, 2018). In the business domain, forward-looking companies (e.g., IBM, Oracle) utilized mathematical techniques to predict project risks, foresee potential obstacles, and improve mitigation techniques before the project even started. They can be considered early pioneers of the AI reality the world is living in today. Their vision is highly appreciated, and now, more than ever, it makes sense. It is the responsibility of the project management practice to leverage AI's potential and transform this industry.

Before Gen AI made its mark, AI in project management focused on automating and enhancing decision-making processes. Tools like AI-powered analytics were used for predicting project outcomes, analyzing risks, and optimizing resource allocation. ML algorithms helped in task prioritization, identifying patterns in project performance data to recommend improvements. Chatbots and virtual assistants automated routine communications, freeing managers for more complex tasks. AI was also employed in scheduling, using historical data to predict project timelines more accurately. These applications significantly improved efficiency, accuracy, and productivity in project management, laying the groundwork for the more advanced capabilities brought by Gen AI (Mariani and Mancini, 2024; Taboada, et al., 2023).

Fast forward to the present, and AI has the potential to be center stage. It means real-time insights, predictive analytics, and even automation. Imagine an AI assistant analyzing project data on the fly, identifying bottlenecks, and suggesting optimizations. It is the difference between having a GPS that tells you about traffic ahead and having one that reroutes you before you hit the traffic jam.

Gen AI introduces new capabilities like automated content creation for project documents and reports, enhancing creativity in problem-solving by generating novel ideas and solutions. It also offers advanced predictive analytics for project outcomes, enabling more accurate forecasting and planning. Additionally, Gen AI can improve stakeholder communication with personalized updates and feedback and refine risk management strategies by simulating various project scenarios. These advancements represent a significant leap beyond traditional AI applications, offering more nuanced and intelligent support to project managers (Bainey, 2024; Kanabar and Wong, 2024).

The key benefit of AI for project managers is that it augments human capabilities, allowing the project team to focus their efforts on high-value, strategic tasks while significantly reducing the amount of time devoted to repetitive work.

## BENEFITS OF AI IN PROJECT MANAGEMENT

In project management, AI's benefits can be broadly categorized into three areas: efficiency enhancement, insightful analytics, and forward-looking predictions:

- *Efficiency enhancement*: AI automates routine tasks like scheduling, freeing up project managers to focus on more strategic activities. Tools like AI-powered chatbots streamline communication, ensuring that project stakeholders are kept in the loop without manual intervention. This automation significantly reduces the time spent on administrative tasks, enhancing overall project efficiency.
- *Insightful analytics*: Through the analysis of vast amounts of project data, AI offers deep insights into project performance, highlighting areas for improvement. It can identify patterns and trends that are not immediately apparent to human analysts, aiding in more informed decision making. This capability extends to evaluating team performance and resource utilization, ensuring optimal allocation and utilization.
- *Forward-looking predictions*: AI excels in forecasting project outcomes based on historical data and ongoing trends. Predictive models can anticipate potential project delays, budget overruns, and scope creep, allowing for preemptive corrective measures. This foresight is invaluable in maintaining project timelines and budgets.

The integration of AI into project management heralds a shift toward more proactive, data-driven approaches. By enhancing efficiency, providing analytical insights, and predicting future challenges, AI empowers project managers to deliver successful projects with greater consistency and accuracy.

## POTENTIAL USE CASES OF AI IN PROJECT MANAGEMENT

There are numerous potential use cases of AI in project management. They can be categorized into three areas: operational, tactical, and strategic:

- *Operational use cases*: Here, AI focuses on automating routine, day-to-day tasks to enhance efficiency and reduce manual workload. They include automated scheduling, task prioritization, and progress reporting, thereby streamlining the project's operational aspects and allowing project teams to focus on more complex tasks.
- *Tactical use cases*: These AI applications involve more sophisticated analyses and decision making to support short- to medium-term project objectives. They include risk assessment, quality control, and change management forecasting, enabling project managers to

make informed decisions and adjust project plans dynamically in response to emerging challenges or opportunities.

- *Strategic use cases*: This type of AI in project management examines the big picture, helping to align project goals with broader organizational strategies. This encompasses long-term planning, market trend analysis, and portfolio management optimization. AI in this context supports high-level decision making, ensuring projects contribute to long-term business success and adaptability in a changing market landscape. It can also enhance project governance by providing data-driven insights and automating compliance tracking. Furthermore, it can ensure alignment with key performance indicators to deliver successful outcomes.

Tables 2.3, 2.4, and 2.5 present lists of potential use cases of AI in project management—in both predictive waterfall and adaptive agile environments—in each of the three categories. These lists are by no means exhaustive. In the dynamic world of project management, the potential applications of AI are vast and varied, painting a landscape brimming with possibilities.

**Table 2.3** Potential operational use cases of AI in project management

| Potential Use Case | Description |
|---|---|
| Task automation | Handling routine tasks such as data entry and report generation |
| Schedule optimization | Using AI to optimize project schedules based on resource availability and constraints |
| Resource allocation | Efficiently allocating personnel and materials where they are needed most |
| Time tracking | AI tools to automatically track time spent on project tasks for productivity analysis |
| Communication coordination | Streamlining project-related communication through AI-powered chatbots and virtual assistants |
| Document management | Organizing and retrieving project documents using NLP |
| Procurement | AI-driven systems to automate the purchase of materials at optimal prices |
| Risk identification | Early detection of operational risks through pattern recognition in project data |
| Enhanced project monitoring | Utilizing AI for real-time tracking and status updates of project milestones |
| Stakeholder engagement analysis | Analyzing communication to gauge stakeholder satisfaction and engagement |
| Knowledge management | Organizing and providing access to accumulated project knowledge |
| Sprint planning optimization | Optimization of task assignments and timelines |
| Real-time team collaboration tools | Enhanced communication with AI-powered tools |
| Automated backlog grooming | Sorting and prioritizing backlog items |
| Agile metrics analysis | Evaluating agile performance metrics |
| Burndown chart generation | Generating predictive burndown charts |
| Retrospective insights analysis | Identifying key insights from sprint retrospectives |
| User story refinement | Assisting in refining user stories for clarity |
| Impediment detection | Detecting and alerting about potential roadblocks |
| Feedback loop automation | Automating collection and integration of feedback |

**Table 2.4** Potential tactical use cases of AI in project management

| Potential Use Case | Description |
|---|---|
| Brainstorming | Brainstorming for ideas for various purposes |
| Risk assessment and mitigation strategies | Identifying potential risks and planning preventive measures |
| Enhanced decision making through data analysis | Making informed choices using detailed data insights |
| Critical path analysis | Identifying key tasks for project timelines |
| Task prioritization | Sorting tasks by urgency and importance |
| Stakeholder analysis | Understanding stakeholder needs and influences |
| Vendor and supplier selection | Choosing the best vendors using AI |
| Communication optimization | Streamlining project communications effectively |
| Project health monitoring | Tracking project status and health indicators, including earned value management (EVM) metrics |
| Forecasting future budget needs and schedule performance | Forecasting future performance using EVM metrics |
| Dynamic risk modeling | Continuously updating risk assessments with new data |
| Agile retrospective insights | Gleaning lessons from past agile sprints |
| Customer feedback analysis | Using AI to interpret customer feedback comprehensively |
| Risk prediction for sprints | Forecasting risks for upcoming sprints |
| Capacity planning optimization | Enhancing team capacity planning accuracy |
| Dependency management | Identifying and managing task dependencies |
| Quality assurance automation | Automating testing, improving product quality |
| Stakeholder feedback analysis | Interpreting stakeholder feedback for improvements |

**Table 2.5** Potential strategic use cases of AI in project management

| Potential Use Case | Description |
|---|---|
| Long-term project portfolio optimization | Maximizing portfolio value over extended periods |
| Strategic resource allocation across projects | Allocating resources for optimal project synergy |
| Market trend analysis for project selection | Identifying market trends to inform project choices |
| Strategic risk management planning | Planning for risks at the strategic level |
| Aligning projects with organizational strategy | Aligning projects with overarching business goals |
| Sustainability and environmental impact analysis | Assessing projects' environmental and sustainability impacts |
| Strategic stakeholder engagement | Engaging stakeholders in strategic project discussions |
| Innovation management and ideation | Facilitating innovation within project management |
| Predictive analytics for strategic decision making | Informing strategic decisions with predictive insights |

*Continued*

**Table 2.5** *continued*

| Potential Use Case | Description |
|---|---|
| Competitive analysis and strategic positioning | Analyzing competitors for strategic project positioning |
| Agile transformation road mapping | Outlining steps for full agile adoption at scale |
| Strategic resource forecasting | Predicting long-term resource needs and allocations |
| Innovation life-cycle management | Identifying opportunities for innovation within projects |
| Agile maturity assessment | Evaluating and suggesting improvements for agile practices |
| Product roadmap prioritization | Prioritizing features on product roadmaps |
| Long-term impact analysis | Forecasting the long-term impact of project decisions |

Currently, we find ourselves at an exciting juncture where certain AI tools are already enhancing our project management capabilities, offering solutions for a select array of use cases. However, it is important to recognize that not all envisioned use cases have transitioned into reality—at least, not yet. This gap largely stems from the current state of AI tool development, which, while advanced, has not fully matured to cover the entire spectrum of potential applications.

As AI technology continues to evolve, the realm of feasible use cases expands, transforming what was once theoretical into practical, actionable tools. This evolution is not without its challenges; a significant hurdle is the availability—or lack thereof—of quality project data. For AI to truly revolutionize project management, it requires rich datasets to learn from—datasets that are not always readily available or sufficiently comprehensive.

In this book, our focus narrows to those AI applications that are not just theoretical possibilities but are actively being utilized by project management professionals today. We will explore the most common and impactful use cases, shedding light on how these applications are currently shaping the industry. As we look to the future, we anticipate not only the realization of existing use cases as AI tools mature but also the emergence of new applications, further enriching the project manager's toolkit.

## CHALLENGES WITH INTEGRATING AI INTO PROJECT MANAGEMENT

Integrating AI into project management, although promising, presents several challenges that stem from both technological limitations and the nuanced demands of leadership and interpersonal interactions. First, the effectiveness of AI relies heavily on the availability of high-quality, extensive datasets. Many project environments, however, may lack this comprehensive data, hindering AI's learning process. Furthermore, the complexity of AI tools poses a significant barrier to widespread adoption, particularly for those without a technical background. This complexity can lead to an overreliance on AI decisions, potentially causing project managers to blindly trust and overlook critical nuances that require human intuition and emotional intelligence.

At the core of project management lies the necessity for strong leadership skills and the ability to navigate interpersonal dynamics—capabilities that AI, in its current form, cannot replicate. Leadership in project management involves more than just strategic decision making; it requires an understanding of team dynamics, empathy, and the ability to motivate and inspire. These aspects of leadership are critical for resolving conflicts, managing stakeholder expectations, and guiding teams through challenges. AI, while valuable for optimizing certain operational and tactical tasks, falls short in areas that demand emotional intelligence, personal interaction, and nuanced judgment.

Another pressing concern is the ethical implications of AI, including issues related to privacy and the potential for algorithmic bias. These ethical challenges necessitate careful consideration and management to ensure the responsible use of AI in project settings. Moreover, the reliability of AI-generated answers remains an issue, as models still often produce inaccurate or inconsistent outputs, requiring human oversight. Additionally, the high costs associated with implementing and maintaining advanced AI solutions can be prohibitive, limiting their accessibility and integration into project management practices.

Another layer of complexity arises from the significant training and adaptation period required for both AI systems and the project teams that use them. Integrating new technologies often meets with resistance to change, a human factor that can complicate the adoption of AI tools within traditional project management frameworks. Moreover, dependency on AI can lead to vulnerability during system downtimes or failures, raising concerns about project continuity and the robustness of contingency planning. Equally critical is the aspect of data security and integrity; as project management increasingly relies on AI, the potential for data breaches and the corruption of sensitive project data escalates. This requires stringent security measures and robust data management protocols to ensure that data used by AI systems is not only accurate but also securely maintained, protecting against unauthorized access and ensuring the reliability of project outputs.

As project managers embrace AI, they must balance its advantages with an open and proactive approach to its challenges. Remember that the very fact that there is a chatbot answering questions about the project does not make the project magically happen and that even if you can generate a risk register in seconds, it still would not mitigate the risk, and a delay prediction would not magically avoid it. Leveraging AI on a project does not ensure the project will even finish, let alone finish successfully. The future of project management will undoubtedly see AI as a powerful tool augmenting human capabilities rather than replacing the essential human elements of leadership and interpersonal skills.

## STRATEGIC INTEGRATION OF AI IN PROJECT MANAGEMENT

The strategic integration of AI stands at the forefront of innovation. The following paragraphs outline a series of best practices and actionable tips that will guide project management professionals through the intricate process of embedding AI into their operational fabric. From the initial stages of assessing the fertile grounds within your existing processes ripe for AI's intervention to the meticulous nurturing of data quality and model development, this guide offers a scaffold to build AI competencies.

### Assessment and Planning

Embarking on AI integration in project management begins with a comprehensive assessment and planning stage. It is essential to scrutinize current processes to pinpoint where AI can make a meaningful impact. Defining clear objectives for AI adoption guides the path forward. Creating a phased implementation roadmap is crucial because it allows teams to adapt gradually to new AI tools, fostering a learning culture and minimizing disruption. By thoughtfully planning the AI integration, teams can align new technologies with project goals, ensuring a cohesive evolution from traditional practices to a more innovative, AI-enhanced approach. This foundational step is not just about laying the technical groundwork; it is about preparing the project ecosystem for a seamless transition into a future where AI becomes a key player in driving project success.

## Data Preparation and Quality

The success of AI in project management hinges on the bedrock of high-quality data. It is crucial to ensure the data is clean, relevant, and robust, laying the groundwork for AI models to function effectively. Engaging in meticulous data preparation and cleansing processes removes inaccuracies and biases, which could otherwise lead to flawed insights. Establishing stringent data governance protocols sustains the caliber of data over time. This is a continuous endeavor, often necessitating dedicated personnel to enrich and manage the data meticulously. Investing time in this stage is paramount, as the adage "garbage in, garbage out" holds particularly true in AI applications—the quality of input data directly determines the quality of the output. This best practice is not merely about data hygiene; it is an investment in the credibility and reliability of AI-driven decision making in project management.

## Model Development and Integration

Selecting the appropriate AI model is pivotal for project management applications. With a variety of LLMs available (e.g., OpenAI's ChatGPT, Google's Gemini, Microsoft's CoPilot), each offers unique strengths. The selection should align with specific project needs and data characteristics. Training these models with diverse datasets ensures they are well-equipped to handle a range of scenarios, becoming a reliable asset for project inputs. Collaboration with data scientists can elevate this process, enabling the fine-tuning of models for seamless integration into existing workflows. This step is about precision and alignment, ensuring the AI tools not only fit into the project management framework but enhance it, adapting intelligently to the nuances of each project.

## Monitoring and Continuous Improvement

Effective AI deployment in project management necessitates vigilant monitoring and an unwavering commitment to continuous improvement. Instituting a robust system to observe AI model performance in real scenarios enables teams to validate and refine AI decisions. Critical to this process is the gathering of feedback from project managers and team members, integrating their on-the-ground insights to improve model accuracy and functionality. Regular, iterative updates to AI models, informed by this feedback and evolving project requirements, are vital. Assigning a dedicated AI steward within the team ensures that the AI tools are not only kept up-to-date with the latest developments but also tailored continuously to serve the project's changing landscape. This iterative loop fosters an environment where AI becomes an ever-improving participant in project management, adapting to provide the most relevant and impactful support.

## Stakeholder Engagement

Integrating AI into project management requires the buy-in and active involvement of stakeholders. Early and transparent engagement helps to align the AI initiatives with stakeholder expectations and project goals. It involves educating them about AI's capabilities and potential impact on project outcomes, thereby fostering a collaborative environment that promotes a shared understanding. Stakeholder engagement is an ongoing dialogue that ensures their needs and concerns are addressed, resulting in tailored AI solutions that truly enhance project effectiveness. This proactive involvement can also facilitate smoother adoption by demystifying AI and involving stakeholders in the transformation journey.

## Ethical Considerations and Bias

The deployment of AI in project management must be underpinned by strong ethical guidelines to ensure fairness, privacy, and transparency. It is imperative to recognize and mitigate biases in AI algorithms that could skew decision making. Regular audits of AI models to check for biases, ensuring diverse datasets, and maintaining transparency in AI decision processes are crucial steps. By prioritizing these ethical considerations, project management can leverage AI not only to advance efficiency and accuracy but also to uphold the integrity and trustworthiness of project practices.

## Data Privacy and Security

As AI systems process large volumes of data to drive project decisions, the risk of data breaches and unauthorized access increases. It is crucial to implement robust security measures that comply with legal standards and industry best practices to safeguard all data involved in project management. This involves encryption, secure data storage and transmission, regular security audits, and access controls that limit data exposure to authorized personnel only. Additionally, project managers must ensure that AI systems are designed to comply with privacy laws relevant to the geographical locations and sectors in which the projects operate. By maintaining high standards of data privacy and security, organizations can prevent potential vulnerabilities that could compromise project integrity and stakeholder trust.

## Skill Development and Training

As AI technologies become integral to project management, skill development and training emerge as critical components. It is vital to equip the project team with the skills necessary to leverage AI tools effectively. Tailored training programs that cover AI functionalities, best practices, and usage guidelines can enhance team competence and confidence. Continuous learning opportunities should be provided to keep pace with AI advancements, ensuring that the project team remains agile and can maximize the potential of AI innovations.

## Intergenerational Challenges in AI Adoption

The integration of AI in project management also introduces intergenerational challenges within teams. Younger professionals, who often have a natural affinity for technology tools, may quickly adapt to AI and find innovative ways to improve efficiency. However, more experienced team members, who bring deep industry knowledge and traditional problem-solving approaches, may struggle with these changes or resist relying on AI-driven results. This generational divide can lead to friction, with *old hands* feeling skeptical of AI's value, while younger colleagues push for faster adoption. Addressing these differences requires thoughtful change management, fostering a culture of collaboration, and implementing mentorship programs where both groups can learn from each other—balancing technological proficiency with seasoned expertise to drive project success.

## Change Management

The introduction of AI in project management signifies a significant shift in operations and culture. A well-structured change management strategy is essential to facilitate this transition. It involves preparing the team for change, communicating the benefits, and providing support throughout the adoption process. Effective change management addresses resistance by involving team members in the development and implementation phases, ensuring that the change is not just top-down but is embraced across the organization. This approach minimizes disruption and paves the way for a collaborative, AI-enabled project management environment.

## Sustainability and Environmental Considerations

When integrating AI into project management, the sustainability and environmental impact of deploying these technologies must be considered. This includes assessing the energy efficiency of AI systems and their contributions to the carbon footprint, especially when large-scale computations are required (Nieto-Rodriguez and Vargas, 2023). Project managers should aim to implement environmentally sustainable practices, such as using energy-efficient algorithms and selecting hardware that meets energy conservation standards. Additionally, evaluating the life cycle of AI technologies and advocating for systems that offer greater longevity can minimize environmental impact and promote sustainability within project operations.

Through the aforementioned efforts, the strategic integration of AI into project management heralds a new era of efficiency and innovation. As we look forward, the fusion of AI with project management promises to unlock unprecedented potential, driving success in an ever-evolving project landscape.

# FUTURE TRENDS

Looking ahead, the merging of AI and project management holds promise for a brighter future. Expect AI to evolve into a strategic partner—not just a number cruncher, but actively participating in decision making. Think about AI predicting project outcomes, recommending courses of action, and even generating solutions. As AI continues to learn from data and adapt, it could become the trusted advisor every project manager needs, guiding the way through complexity and uncertainty. Expanding on the transformative impact of AI in project management, the future holds a blend of heightened efficiency, nuanced analytics, and strategic foresight.

Assurance of speed is guaranteed. AI-driven automation is set to redefine and accelerate task execution, minimizing manual efforts in scheduling and administrative tasks, thereby streamlining project workflows. AI could seamlessly integrate into every project from the inside, acting as a highly experienced team member rather than just an assistant. AI algorithms will certainly become more innovative and faster at understanding project dynamics, providing insights, and handling routine tasks. At that time, project managers would finally be able to focus on what they should focus on: strategic decision making, creative problem-solving, and leadership. Project management, as a practice, will evolve since trivial tasks will become less time-consuming, and operational project managers will be relegated to minor roles or even become obsolete.

The realm of analytics will witness a revolution with AI's capacity to digest vast datasets, offering unprecedented insights into project dynamics, team performance, and resource deployment. These analytics will enable a more agile response to changing project requirements, enhancing adaptability and resilience.

The predictive capabilities of AI stand to elevate project management to new levels of precision in risk identification and mitigation strategies. AI could foresee potential risks, opportunities, and resource needs. By analyzing historical data and current trends, AI models can forecast potential project hurdles, facilitating proactive measures to safeguard timelines and budgets. This predictive power will enrich the planning phase and improve the speed of reaction. It is now the responsibility of the project managers to listen and analyze these recommendations. They must ensure that decisions derived from AI models are not only data-driven but also practical and aligned with project goals, requiring them to critically assess and approve AI-generated insights before implementation.

The journey toward fully realizing AI's potential in project management will navigate through challenges, including ensuring data integrity, managing the complexity of AI tools, and addressing ethical considerations. Despite these hurdles, the integration of AI promises a future where project management is not only more efficient and informed but also more aligned with achieving strategic objectives. This evolution toward AI-enhanced project management will undoubtedly necessitate a balanced approach, blending AI's technological strengths with the irreplaceable value of human judgment and emotional intelligence—a dynamic that is essential for navigating AI's *jagged frontier* of capabilities while maintaining human oversight (Mollick, 2024). The future of project management with AI is not just about efficiency but also about empowerment. Project leaders should be aware that their skills need to be updated as soon as possible.

To stay ahead in the evolving landscape of AI in project management, both project and organizational leaders must enhance their competencies beyond traditional know-how. Key skills include data literacy to understand and leverage AI insights, as well as change management to navigate AI integration effectively. Additionally, a solid grasp of AI capabilities and limitations is crucial. As Gen AI evolves, its response to user queries should be regarded as an initial draft, requiring human expertise for refinement and validation. The quality of the data used to train or inform Gen AI tools significantly impacts the accuracy and relevance of the generated outputs.

Emotional intelligence remains vital, ensuring AI tools are used to complement human judgment. Embracing these skills prepares project managers for an AI-augmented future, balancing technology with the irreplaceable human element.

## IN CONCLUSION

This chapter introduced the fundamentals of AI, including its definitions, evolution, and applications in project management. It highlighted how AI supports project professionals across operational, tactical, and strategic domains. From predictive analytics to automation, AI empowers project managers with tools to optimize resources, manage risks, and drive improved project outcomes.

The next chapter, *Generative AI,* will focus on the transformative subset of AI that is reshaping creativity and problem-solving. It will explore key concepts, trace its historical development, and examine the evolution of Gen AI. It will also touch on the ethical considerations underpinning the use of Gen AI. This introduction to Gen AI will equip you to effectively integrate it into project management practices, unlocking its full potential for innovation and efficiency.

# 3

# GENERATIVE AI

Generative artificial intelligence (Gen AI) represents one of the most groundbreaking advancements in AI, merging computational prowess with creative capability. This chapter embarks on a comprehensive exploration of Gen AI, offering an in-depth understanding of its fundamentals and evolution. By unpacking the core principles and distinctive features of Gen AI, we aim to illuminate how this technology is transforming the boundaries of what machines can achieve.

The journey begins with a definition and overview of Gen AI, shedding light on its ability to autonomously generate diverse content, including text, images, music, and even software code. Unlike traditional AI, which primarily focuses on analyzing and interpreting existing data, Gen AI excels in creating novel outputs, pushing the envelope of machine creativity. This section will demystify how Gen AI operates, leveraging vast datasets and sophisticated learning models to produce outputs that often rival human ingenuity.

Tracing the historical context and evolution of Gen AI, we will explore the pivotal milestones that have propelled this technology from early theoretical models to its current state of sophistication. Key developments such as the introduction of generative adversarial networks (GANs) (Langr and Bok, 2019) and variational autoencoders (VAEs) (Kingma and Welling, 2019) have significantly enhanced Gen AI's capabilities, enabling the creation of highly realistic and complex content. This historical perspective not only highlights the rapid advancement of Gen AI but also underscores its growing importance in various domains.

As we delve deeper, we will differentiate Gen AI from other AI technologies, emphasizing its unique focus on content creation rather than mere data analysis. This distinction is crucial for understanding the transformative potential of Gen AI and how it stands apart in the broader AI landscape. The section on large language models (LLMs) will provide a closer look at the engines behind Gen AI, explaining how these models understand and generate human-like text, as well as their profound implications for industries that are reliant on textual data.

The role of data in Gen AI models cannot be overstated. Quality data is the lifeblood of these systems, driving their ability to learn and generate accurate, nuanced outputs. We will examine how data influences the performance of Gen AI and the importance of maintaining high standards of data quality to ensure the efficacy of these models. Additionally, we will compare *New Search* powered by Gen AI with traditional search methods, illustrating the paradigm shift in information retrieval and interaction facilitated by advanced AI technologies.

In addressing the ethical considerations surrounding Gen AI, this chapter will tackle the critical issues of intellectual property, authenticity, and bias. As Gen AI continues to advance, it is imperative to navigate these ethical landscapes responsibly, ensuring the technology is used for the greater good. We will also highlight the commercial players leading the charge in the Gen AI space, providing insights into the companies and innovations driving this exciting field forward.

Ultimately, this chapter aims to equip you with a general understanding of Gen AI, its capabilities, and its implications. By exploring the theoretical foundations and practical applications of Gen AI, we hope to inspire you to envision how this technology can be harnessed to drive innovation and creativity in your respective fields.

## DEFINITION AND OVERVIEW

Gen AI, within the expansive realm of AI, represents a class of technologies with the unique capability to generate content autonomously. This content ranges broadly in form, including but not limited to text, images, music, and computer code, crafted to a standard that often renders it indistinguishable from that produced by human intelligence. What sets Gen AI apart from more traditional AI systems is its focus not on the analysis, interpretation, or processing of existing information but rather on the creation of entirely new, original content. This innovative capacity is deeply rooted in the system's ability to digest and learn from vast and diverse datasets and its advanced semantic capability, which permits these models to *talk* like humans. Through this learning process, Gen AI discerns complex patterns, styles, or structures inherent in the data. These learned elements serve as a foundation upon which AI can construct new outputs that, while reflective of the original data's essence, are unique creations.

The term *generative* aptly captures the essence of these AI systems' capabilities. Unlike their traditional counterparts, which are typically engineered for tasks such as data analysis, prediction, or pattern recognition, Gen AI takes a proactive role in the creation process. It synthesizes new content from the ground up, based on the extensive knowledge it has acquired through its training. The adjective *generative* thus underscores the AI's function as a creator, imbuing it with the role of an inventor or artist who brings novel concepts, visuals, and ideas into existence. This distinction is crucial, highlighting the transition from AI as a tool for understanding the world to AI as a participant in the creative process.

The innovative prowess of Gen AI is underscored by its reliance on sophisticated learning models, such as LLMs, GANs, and VAEs. LLMs, in particular, are engineered to comprehend and generate human language, showcasing remarkable proficiency in text-based tasks. Prominent LLMs in the commercial realm include OpenAI's ChatGPT, Google's Gemini, and Microsoft's Co-Pilot. The landscape is vibrant with numerous existing models, and many more are under rapid development. (Throughout this book, the term LLM may refer to any of these models. Similarly, references to ChatGPT may denote any LLM, underscoring their interchangeable use in generative applications.)

GANs and VAEs help create highly realistic images or videos. These models enable the AI to produce outputs that not only emulate but occasionally surpass the complexity and nuance of human-generated content. By iterating through cycles of creation and evaluation, these systems refine their ability to generate outputs that are increasingly sophisticated and authentic.

The generative nature of these AIs heralds a new era of technology, where machines are not mere repositories of information or passive processors of data but active contributors to the creative endeavors of humanity. In doing so, Gen AI blurs the lines between human and machine creativity, offering a glimpse into a future where AI-enabled innovation becomes an integral part of artistic, technological, and intellectual pursuits.

Like any specialized field, Gen AI is filled with numerous technical terms, abbreviations, and acronyms. To help you navigate these, Table 3.1 offers a list of commonly used Gen AI terms, along

**Table 3.1** Common Gen AI terms

| Term | Description |
|---|---|
| Autoregressive models | AI models that predict future data points by learning from sequences of known data points; often used in generating sequential data like text or music |
| Big data | Large and complex datasets that are difficult to process using traditional data processing applications, but can be leveraged by AI for deeper insights and predictions |
| Clustering | A method of unsupervised learning used to group a set of objects in such a way that objects in the same group are more similar to each other than to those in other groups |
| Data mining | The process of analyzing large datasets to discover patterns and relationships; it is like digging through data to find hidden treasures of information |
| Fine-tuning | A process where a pre-trained model (like GPT) is further trained on a smaller, domain-specific dataset to tailor its outputs more closely to the desired context or application |
| GAN | A machine learning (ML) framework where two neural networks (NNs) contest with each other to generate new, synthetic instances of data that can pass for real data |
| Gen AI | AI that can generate new content, such as text, images, or music, that resembles human-created content; it is creative AI |
| Generative pre-trained transformer (GPT) | A type of LLM that is pre-trained on a diverse internet dataset to generate human-like text based on the input it receives |
| Overfitting | A modeling error in statistical analysis that occurs when a function is too closely fit to a limited set of data points |
| Parameters | Values that define the configuration of a model; in AI, these are learned from data during the training process |
| Retrieval-augmented generation (RAG) | A technique that integrates retrieval into generative models, allowing LLMs to access external datasets to generate more accurate, context-aware, and up-to-date responses, eliminating the need to retrain the underlying LLM |
| Semantic analysis | The process of understanding and deriving meaning from language inputs in AI systems; crucial for tasks that involve human-like understanding of text |
| Tokenization | The process of converting input data into a set of tokens, which are then processed by Gen AI models; it is crucial for text generation tasks |
| Tokens | The smallest units of data that AI models process, like those in natural language processing (NLP); typically, words or *sub-words* in text applications |
| Transformer models | Architectures designed for deep learning tasks that handle ordered data, like sequences of words or time series, which are essential for generating coherent and contextually relevant outputs in generative AI tasks |
| Validation | The process of evaluating an AI model during the training phase by using a separate portion of the dataset to check for accuracy, overfitting, and generalization |
| VAE | A type of NN used to generate complex data like images and sounds that are similar but not identical to the inputs in the training set |
| Visualization | The technique of creating visual representations of data or results within AI models to make the analysis accessible and understandable to humans |

with short explanations. You will find many of these terms used throughout this book, although there are also some that we do not cover beyond this table.

## EVOLUTION OF GEN AI

The evolution of Gen AI traces back to the foundational days of AI, where the initial goal was to create machines capable of performing tasks that typically require human intelligence. However, the concept of Gen AI began to crystallize with the development of neural networks (NNs) and the advent of machine learning (ML) techniques that enabled computers to learn from data. Early generative models were rudimentary, focusing on simple pattern recognition and basic content generation. It was not until the introduction of more complex models, such as the VAE in 2013 and the GAN in 2014, that the potential for high-fidelity content generation began to be fully realized. These models marked a pivotal moment, demonstrating that machines could not only learn from data but could also use this learning to generate new, original content that mirrors the complexity and variability of the data on which they were trained.

Over the years, the field of Gen AI has undergone exponential growth fueled by advancements in computing power, algorithmic innovation, and the availability of large datasets. This evolution has expanded the capabilities of generative systems, far surpassing the early days of simple text and image creation. Today, Gen AI encompasses a broad spectrum of applications, including the generation of photorealistic images, the composition of music, the creation of realistic synthetic voices, and the automatic generation of written content. Each leap forward has not only demonstrated the growing sophistication of these systems but has also highlighted the potential for Gen AI to transform industries, from entertainment and art to design and engineering. As we stand on the cusp of new breakthroughs, the historical journey of Gen AI serves as a testament to the relentless pursuit of mimicking and augmenting human creativity through technology, paving the way for a future where the boundaries between human and machine-generated content continue to blur.

## DISTINCTION BETWEEN GEN AI AND OTHER AI TECHNOLOGIES

Gen AI stands distinct within the realm of AI by its primary function: the ability to create new, original outputs. Traditional AI technologies are often developed for specific tasks, such as analyzing large datasets, optimizing processes, making predictions based on historical data, or recognizing and categorizing information—these are generally referred to as discriminative models. Discriminative models are adept at identifying features and making decisions based on the input data they are provided, such as classifying images or filtering spam. In contrast, Gen AI does not merely interpret or filter input data; it uses its understanding of this data to produce entirely new content that reflects learned patterns, relationships, and structures.

The distinction is akin to the difference between understanding a language and being able to compose a poem in that language. Gen AI, through models like GANs and VAEs, does not stop at comprehending the *grammar* (the data structures) it is trained on; it goes a step further to *speak* (generate) new *sentences* (outputs) that are coherent, contextually relevant, and often indistinguishable from those created by humans. This represents a significant shift from the typical AI applications in ML, which might predict the next word in a sentence but would not construct a novel story. The generative approach enables the creative and exploratory use of AI, initiating possibilities in design, art, and other creative fields where novelty and innovation are key. This creative ability to generate new data points, rather than just analyze existing ones, sets Gen AI apart and marks a new horizon in the potential applications of AI.

## GEN AI

LLMs are a cornerstone of Gen AI, providing the foundation for creating new content, from writing articles to coding. They are advanced AI systems trained on vast amounts of text data, enabling them to understand and generate human-like text. One prominent example of such systems is the generative pre-trained transformer (GPT), which has become synonymous with advanced language generation and forms the backbone of many Gen AI applications. LLMs can predict the next word in a sentence, making them incredibly effective for tasks requiring an understanding of language nuances. Their relationship to Gen AI lies in their ability to produce coherent, contextually relevant text based on the patterns they have learned, showcasing a significant leap in AI's capability to mimic human-like creativity.

LLMs are built upon the principles of ML and deep learning. Deep learning, with its complex NN architectures, enables LLMs to process and learn from vast amounts of text data. This process involves understanding the intricacies of language patterns, semantics, and grammar. ML contributes by allowing these models to improve over time as they are exposed to more data, enhancing their ability to generate coherent, contextually accurate text. Essentially, LLMs are a sophisticated application of deep learning technologies, representing a significant advancement in ML's capacity to mimic human language.

The role of LLMs in Gen AI is increasingly significant, providing the backbone for systems that require a deep understanding of language and the ability to produce it naturally, further expanding the horizon of what Gen AI can accomplish.

## ROLE OF DATA IN GEN AI MODELS

The lifeblood of Gen AI models is data; it serves as the foundation upon which these models are built and refined. In Gen AI, the quality, variety, and volume of the input data are crucial because the models learn to detect and replicate complex patterns within this data. For instance, a GAN trained to generate images of faces requires a diverse dataset of facial images to produce varied and realistic results. The data acts as a teacher, providing examples from which the AI learns what it means to create a face, understand its features, and how they vary among different people. Similarly, for a language-based model, the breadth and depth of text data determine its ability to comprehend and generate language with human-like fluency. In essence, the data fed into these models directly influences their creative potential, determining the richness and diversity of the outputs they can generate.

Beyond the scope of what data Gen AI models can generate lies the significance of how this data is utilized within the model. The training process for Gen AI involves an intricate understanding of data distribution, learning not only the superficial characteristics but also the underlying structures and complexities of the data. For instance, in image generation, understanding pixel distribution and how it correlates to form shapes and textures is vital. In the context of language, it is about understanding syntax, semantics, and context. This complexity is why large datasets are indispensable for training more sophisticated models; they need extensive information to accurately capture and recreate the intricacies of the data. Hence, the role of data in Gen AI is not only to provide the raw material for creation but also to teach the models the fundamental principles of the domains they are learning to mimic.

## *NEW SEARCH* VS. TRADITIONAL SEARCH

*New Search*, often epitomized by systems using LLMs, represents a significant shift from traditional search engine technologies. Traditional search engines are based on indexing and keyword matching; they rank information primarily by how well the content of a webpage matches the keywords in a user's query. This methodology requires users to carefully consider the keywords they choose, interpret the list of results, and find the information they need, which can be both time-consuming and imprecise.

In contrast, New Search refers to the next generation of search technologies that use advanced AI models to understand and process natural language in a way that is increasingly similar to human conversation. These systems are designed to understand the context and intent behind a user's query, not just the literal keywords. This means users can ask complex questions in full sentences, and the search system will interpret the query and generate a direct answer or a summary of information rather than a list of links. For example, instead of typing in *symptoms of dehydration*, a user could ask, "What are the signs that someone is dehydrated?" and receive a synthesized response.

This new paradigm, largely powered by LLMs, can sift through vast amounts of information to provide responses that feel intuitive and conversational. By leveraging these sophisticated AI models, New Search systems can offer a more natural and efficient way to find information, which can be especially useful for complex inquiries that would otherwise require multiple searches or sifting through several articles. This technology not only finds information; it also interprets it, creating an interactive experience that mimics asking a knowledgeable friend or a personal assistant, thereby marking a departure from traditional search methodologies.

With the advent of New Search, searching the internet has become akin to having a conversation with another person. This transformative approach allows users to engage in a natural, intuitive dialogue with the technology, receiving contextually rich and nuanced responses that mirror human-like understanding and interaction.

## GEN AI ENGAGEMENT

The key to unlocking the full potential of Gen AI lies in the nuanced interaction between humans and AI systems. It is not just about what AI can do but how we, as users, engage with these technologies to guide and refine their outputs. This interaction goes beyond mere command execution, evolving into a dialogue that requires understanding, intuition, and iterative refinement. In the next chapter, we introduce a new concept that we call Gen AI engagement, which is a framework that encapsulates the interactive process between users and Gen AI technologies. It emphasizes a dynamic, conversational approach to leveraging AI's capabilities, focusing on creating a symbiotic relationship where human intuition and AI's computational power work in concert.

## ETHICAL CONSIDERATIONS

Ethical considerations related to Gen AI are increasingly coming to the forefront as these technologies gain the ability to create content that is indistinguishable from that produced by humans. One of the primary concerns in this realm is the impact on intellectual property and copyright laws. Gen AI's ability to produce original artwork, music, written content, and even software code raises questions about the ownership of AI-generated creations. Who holds the copyright to a piece of music composed by an AI trained on thousands of songs from various artists? The potential for Gen AI to inadvertently infringe upon existing copyrights by producing a work that closely mimics protected content without clear attribution or licensing challenges existing legal frameworks and necessitates a reevaluation of intellectual property rights in the age of AI.

Another ethical concern is the authenticity and trustworthiness of content generated by Gen AI. With the advent of deepfakes and other forms of synthetic media, distinguishing between real and AI-generated content is becoming increasingly difficult. This capability poses significant risks in the context of misinformation, where convincingly real-looking images, videos, or audio files can be generated to spread false narratives, manipulate public opinion, or perpetrate fraud. The ethical use of Gen AI thus involves stringent measures to ensure transparency about the origins of AI-generated content and the implementation of technological solutions to verify authenticity. It also requires a societal dialogue about the responsibilities of creators, platforms, and regulators in preventing the malicious use of these technologies.

Furthermore, the democratization of Gen AI tools brings about concerns related to bias and societal impact. AI models reflect the data they are trained on, which can perpetuate and amplify existing biases if the data contains historical prejudices or lacks diversity. The uncritical use of Gen AI can thus reinforce stereotypes or exclude marginalized voices, leading to unequal representation in AI-generated content. Ethically deploying Gen AI necessitates a commitment to fairness, inclusivity, and the proactive mitigation of biases. This includes diverse and equitable training data, transparency in AI development processes, and continuous monitoring for unintended consequences. As Gen AI continues to evolve, ethical considerations must be an integral part of the conversation, guiding the responsible development and application of these powerful technologies.

## COMMERCIAL PLAYERS IN GEN AI

In the commercial landscape of Gen AI, several key players are making significant strides, with OpenAI's ChatGPT being one of the most prominent. ChatGPT, which is built upon the foundation of the GPT series, has gained widespread attention for its ability to generate human-like text. Its applications range from conversation and composition to coding assistance, showcasing the commercial viability of Gen AI in providing solutions that augment human capabilities in various fields. OpenAI's offering has been widely adopted by businesses seeking to enhance customer service with chatbots, assist content creators with writing tasks, and support software developers in coding endeavors. The sophistication of ChatGPT's language processing and generation is a testament to the potential for commercial AI systems to perform tasks traditionally reserved for humans, transforming how businesses operate and engage with their customers.

ChatGPT is a cutting-edge LLM designed to understand and generate text in a manner similar to that of humans. As a project manager, think of it as having a virtual team member who specializes in communication. It can assist in generating ideas, answering queries, and even offering language-based insights, making it a handy tool for enhancing collaboration and communication within your project team.

Now, let us take a closer look at the inner workings of ChatGPT. Imagine it as a diligent learner immersed in a vast sea of text—articles, books, and websites. During pre-training (the *P* in GPT), it absorbs the intricacies of language, recognizing patterns, grammar, and the diverse ways we humans express ourselves. This foundational understanding provides ChatGPT with broad linguistic knowledge, enabling it to comprehend and generate coherent text. The last element is the transformer (the *T* in GPT), a model that uses mechanisms to focus on the most relevant parts of input text, enabling it to provide coherent and contextually accurate responses.

The next step in the LLM is fine-tuning. This automatic stage involves trimming the model to align with specific requirements and objectives. It is comparable to coaching a team member and guiding the language nuances relevant to your project domain. Through this meticulous process, ChatGPT transforms from a general language model into a specialized assistant, finely tuned to contribute intelligently to your project management discussions. This fusion of extensive pre-training and targeted fine-tuning results in a versatile tool that is ready to assist you in navigating the nuances of communication within your project team.

ChatGPT and other players in the market include *versioning*, as with any software. Versioning is influenced by several factors: the number of training words utilized for the model (parameters), the ability to tailor your model to your specific domain, ensuring the removal of harmful or inappropriate content, and the general misuse of the LLM, as well as the likelihood of generating inaccurate or misleading responses. For example, ChatGPT 3.5 was trained using 175 billion parameters, while ChatGPT 4o used one trillion parameters—meaning, if you use ChatGPT 4o you have ten times more knowledge at your disposal.

Finally, all LLMs use *tokens* to determine the amount of data to be processed. Tokens are units coming from texts, and we can easily think about them as the number of words in a sentence. This is an oversimplification since there are other optimization techniques utilized to reduce the size, but it is a simple way to visualize them. All tokens are compiled into vocabularies, which are the ones an ML model could recognize. For example, the English vocabulary consists of approximately 170,000 words, which need to be *tokenized* to ensure efficiency.

## Other Players

It is worth noting that ChatGPT is not the only player in the market—dozens of players have emerged over the last year, competing for this space. Table 3.2 provides a list of major players in the Gen AI space at the time of writing this book. Numerous commercial players are entering the market almost every month.

**Table 3.2** Major commercial players in the AI arena

| Company Name | Orientation | Main Products | Description |
|---|---|---|---|
| Alibaba DAMO Academy | B2B, consumer | AliMe, City Brain | Focuses on AI for e-commerce, urban management, and cloud computing |
| Amazon Web Services (AWS) | B2B | AWS Rekognition, AWS SageMaker | Provides a suite of AI services that integrate with cloud computing for business applications |
| Anthropic | B2B, consumer | Claude | Focuses on safe and steerable AI models |
| Baidu | B2B, consumer | PaddlePaddle, Baidu Brain | Leads in AI in China with search engines, autonomous driving, and other AI services |
| ByteDance | Consumer | TikTok recommendation algorithms | Utilizes AI extensively in content distribution and interaction algorithms |
| CloudMinds | B2B | Cloud AI solutions, humanoid robots | Develops cloud AI solutions and robots for service industries |
| DataRobot | B2B | Automated ML platforms | Provides a platform for building and deploying ML models |
| DeepMind | Research | AlphaFold, AlphaGo | Focuses on AI research for solving complex problems, including protein folding |

*Continued*

**Table 3.2** *continued*

| Company Name | Orientation | Main Products | Description |
|---|---|---|---|
| Deepseek | Open-Source LLM | DeepSeek-VL, DeepSeek-Coder | Developer-focused AI models for language and code generation, emphasizing transparency and open research |
| Facebook AI (Meta AI) | Research, B2B | PyTorch, AI Habitat, Llama | Develops AI research projects and tools, focusing on virtual reality and more |
| Graphcore | B2B | Intelligence processing units | Manufactures processors specifically designed for AI and ML applications |
| Google AI | B2B, consumer | TensorFlow, Google Assistant, Veo 3 | Works on AI technologies across various Google products for consumer and business applications |
| H2O.ai | B2B | Driverless AI, H2O Wave | Develops open-source ML platforms for enterprises |
| HuggingFace | B2B, research | Transformers, Datasets | Specializes in NLP and open-source tools |
| IBM | B2B | Watson, IBM Cloud Pak for Data | Offers AI solutions for business, including healthcare, finance, and IoT |
| Lovable | Agentic AI Platform | AI Agents, Workflow automation | No-code platform for building and orchestrating AI agents that automate tasks across apps and systems with human-like reasoning |
| Mistral | Research | Generative AI models | Develops advanced Gen AI technologies |
| Microsoft AI | B2B, consumer | Azure AI, Microsoft Cognitive Services | Provides AI tools and cloud services to enhance productivity and business processes |
| Mobileye | Consumer | Autonomous driving systems | Develops vision-based advanced driver-assistance systems |
| NVIDIA | B2B | CUDA, DGX Systems, EGX | Specializes in AI computing, offering hardware and software for training AI models |
| OpenAI | B2B, consumer | ChatGPT, DALL-E, Codex | Develops advanced AI models and applications, known for NLP |
| Palantir Technologies | Defense, B2B | Gotham, Foundry | Specializes in big data analytics for defense and large-scale enterprise AI solutions |
| Perplexity | Consumer | Perplexity AI assistant | Provides an AI assistant for search and information retrieval |
| Project Management Institute | B2C, consumer | Infinity | AI solution designed to enhance project management efficiency through predictive insights and automation |
| SenseTime | B2B, consumer | Computer vision and deep learning technologies | Specializes in facial recognition technology for various applications |
| Tencent AI Lab | B2B, consumer | WeChat AI, Medical AI | Works on AI for gaming, social media, and healthcare applications |
| Tesla | Consumer | Autopilot, full self-driving | Integrates AI in electric vehicles for autonomous driving features |
| UiPath | B2B | Robotic process automation tools | Offers AI-powered automation tools for business processes |
| Waymo | Consumer | Autonomous vehicles | A subsidiary of Alphabet developing self-driving technology |
| x (Grok) | Consumer | Grok AI | Focuses on AI tools for real-time learning and automation |

Beyond text generation, companies like NVIDIA, the major manufacturer of chips specialized in AI, have pushed the boundaries of visual content generation with their work on GANs. NVIDIA's technology has been crucial in the development of graphics, gaming, and virtual simulations, enabling the creation of photorealistic images and environments that can be used in entertainment, architectural visualization, and training simulations. These capabilities have profound commercial implications, particularly in industries where visual content is paramount and the demand for scalable, high-quality content creation is high.

Other notable commercial players include DeepMind, which merged with Google's Brain division in 2023. DeepMind is known for its cutting-edge research in AI that has led to advancements in both generative models and reinforcement learning. While DeepMind's work spans a range of AI technologies, its contributions to the field of Gen AI through projects like WaveNet (van den Oord, et al., 2016), which generates natural-sounding human speech, demonstrate the commercial potential of AI in the realm of voice synthesis and beyond. Additionally, startups like Runway are democratizing access to Gen AI by providing tools that enable creators with limited technical expertise to generate novel visual content, from images to video sequences. This widespread access is catalyzing a new wave of creativity and innovation, highlighting the vast commercial possibilities that Gen AI holds across industries.

## IN CONCLUSION

As we close this chapter on Gen AI, we have navigated the contours of its evolution, its defining characteristics, and the pivotal role of data in shaping its outcomes. We have contemplated the ethical landscape and identified the key commercial entities propelling this technology forward. With these foundational insights, we stand on the precipice of practical application.

The forthcoming chapter, *Generative AI Engagement*, will transition from the theoretical underpinnings laid out here to the art of dialogue with LLMs. We will explore the nuanced craft of prompt engineering—how carefully constructed queries can harness the full potential of Gen AI, enabling a symbiosis of human intent and machine intelligence that can redefine the possibilities within project management.

# 4

# GENERATIVE AI ENGAGEMENT

In this chapter, we shift from exploring the vast landscape of generative artificial intelligence (Gen AI) to focusing on how we interact with it to optimize project management activities. At the heart of this interaction lies the Gen AI engagement (GAE) framework. Here, we will examine GAE in detail, revealing the structured approach that enables project professionals to communicate with AI effectively and ethically. We start by asking, "What is GAE?"—a question that calls for clarity on the nature and scope of our interactions with AI systems. Understanding this is crucial for harnessing the full capabilities of Gen AI while maintaining the human-centric vision that defines project management.

We will then articulate the *principles of GAE*, which serve as the foundational ethics and best practices guiding our use of these technologies. The heart of practical GAE is the *PRIME operating methodology for GAE*, a set of procedures that project managers can follow to ensure their engagement with AI is productive, responsible, insightful, meaningful, and ethical. *Prompt engineering* (Sahoo, et al., 2024) emerges as a key skill in this methodology, one that involves crafting queries and instructions that lead to the best possible outcomes from AI systems. However, not all that glitters in AI is gold; we must also address the phenomenon of *hallucinations* (Maleki, et al., 2024), where AI generates false or nonsensical responses, and understand how to mitigate this. Through examples of applying PRIME with GAE principles, we will illustrate the practical application of these principles and methodologies, demonstrating how proper engagement can lead to enhanced project management outcomes. This chapter aims to empower you with the knowledge to become adept at interacting with Gen AI, ensuring that these interactions are not only fruitful but also conducted with a high standard of professionalism and responsibility.

## WHAT IS GAE?

GAE refers to the interactive process between humans and advanced AI systems capable of producing original outputs. It is a dialogue where we, the users, provide the AI system with prompts—specific instructions or questions—and the AI responds with novel content, ideas, or solutions. Imagine it as a brainstorming session with a very creative partner who has read almost everything there is to read and can generate a multitude of ideas at a moment's notice. This type of AI can synthesize vast amounts of data to propose new designs, draft detailed reports, or develop comprehensive strategies, all tailored to the user's request.

To effectively collaborate with Gen AI, one must master the art of communication—posing questions and statements with precision to guide the AI model toward the desired outcome. Gen AI inherently produces slightly different responses when the same question is posed multiple times.

This variability is a natural aspect of how these models function and should be considered when setting expectations for consistency in their outputs, even with identical prompts.

It is an iterative dance, adjusting each prompt in response to the AI system's previous output, homing in on the target objective. This iterative nature can be both a strength and a challenge, allowing users to refine and broaden their exploration while requiring thoughtful prompts to extract consistent and actionable results. In this partnership, it is imperative that we maintain ethical stewardship, ensuring the AI contributions are free from bias and ethically sound. Ultimately, the human touch remains pivotal; we need to refine and adapt the AI proposals, infusing them with personal insight and context-specific nuances. This ensures that the final product not only benefits from the AI model's computational power but also reflects the depth and discernment of human expertise, embodying a symbiotic relationship that is the hallmark of GAE.

In essence, GAE is a dynamic conversation—a series of back-and-forth exchanges between the user and the AI system. It is a collaborative process aimed at crafting content, generating images, or producing various forms of creative output on topics specified by the user. The goal is to guide the AI system with clear prompts and refine the outcomes through continuous interaction, shaping the AI's raw generative capabilities into refined end products that meet the user's specific interests and needs. This conversational journey represents the core of GAE, harnessing its full creative potential to achieve targeted and meaningful results.

## PRINCIPLES OF GAE

The philosophy of GAE is built upon five guiding principles (Figure 4.1) that ensure meaningful, effective, and ethical interaction between humans and Gen AI technologies. These principles form the bedrock of GAE, ensuring that the application of Gen AI in any domain, including project management, is both productive and responsible.

Here, we delineate the core principles underpinning GAE:

1. *Clarity in communication*: The effectiveness of Gen AI begins with the precision of our prompts and queries. Clear communication ensures that the AI system understands and executes tasks accurately, minimizing irrelevant or erroneous outcomes.
2. *Critical evaluation*: This principle remains a cornerstone of Gen AI, where human oversight is paramount. It involves rigorously assessing the accuracy and relevance of AI-generated content, ensuring it aligns with the intended objectives and ethical standards.
3. *Iterative personalization*: For this principle, we combined iterative interaction with personalization and refinement, thus advocating for a cyclical engagement process. Here, prompts are continually refined based on AI feedback, and outputs are customized to fit the unique context and goals of the project, embodying the iterative nature of project management and the personal touch of the user.
4. *Ethical transparency and accountability*: This principle emphasizes the integration of ethical integrity with transparency and accountability in AI engagements. It requires openly communicating the AI system's capabilities, limitations, and decision-making processes to ensure responsible use. Accountability means taking ownership of how AI outputs are utilized, including addressing any unintended consequences or ethical concerns. By adhering to this principle, organizations can build trust, foster responsible AI use, and mitigate risks associated with AI-driven decisions.
5. *Collaborative synergy*: Viewing AI as a partner that augments human expertise, this principle emphasizes the synergy between human intuition and the AI system's analytical

**Figure 4.1** Guiding principles of GAE

prowess. It values the distinctive strengths of both collaborators, driving toward shared objectives in project management.

With these five principles, GAE becomes a more streamlined yet robust framework, emphasizing clarity, critical human oversight, adaptable personalization, ethical responsibility, and collaborative strength. These guiding principles help ensure that AI is leveraged effectively and responsibly in project management contexts.

## PRIME

To operationalize the GAE concept, we introduce the PRIME process—prepare, relay, inspect, modify, execute. PRIME is a practical methodology that outlines the sequential steps for effective interaction with Gen AI, ensuring that each phase of engagement is purposeful and leads toward optimized outcomes (Figure 4.2). In essence, PRIME serves as an actionable guide within the broader vision of GAE, providing a structured pathway for harnessing the generative capabilities of AI in an iterative, reflective, and adaptive manner. Through PRIME, the ideals of GAE are realized, enabling users to navigate the complexities of AI engagement with clarity and strategic insight.

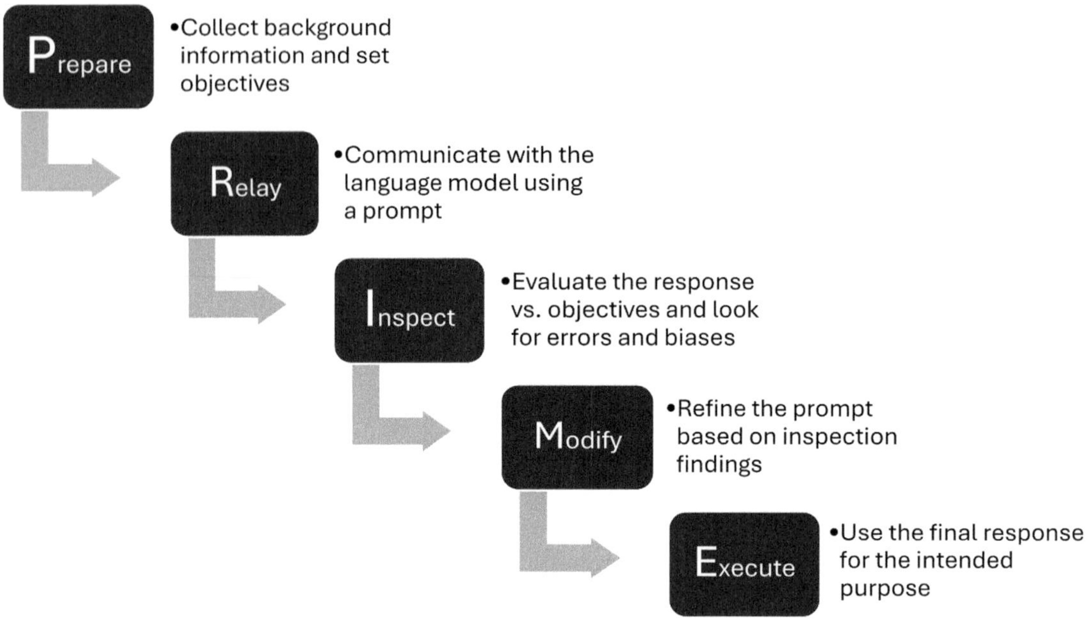


**Figure 4.2** PRIME methodology

PRIME is a manifestation of the GAE philosophy, distilled into actionable steps that guide users from the inception of an idea to the realization of AI-generated content. By adopting it, users embark on a structured journey, ensuring that every interaction with the AI system is purposeful and aligned with their objectives. This methodology not only streamlines the engagement process but also enhances the creative synergy between human intuition and AI capabilities. As a bridge between the abstract principles of GAE and practical application, PRIME offers a clear and methodical approach to unlocking the transformative potential of Gen AI technologies.

## Prepare

The *prepare* phase is foundational, where you delineate the objectives and collect the necessary data for the Gen AI task at hand. This step requires you to crystallize your intentions into a clear and concise directive. For instance, if the goal is to generate marketing copy, you must collate product details, target audience demographics, and determine the desired tone of voice. The more relevant information you provide with your query, the better the quality of Gen AI's results. Accurate and detailed preparation ensures that the AI has all the relevant information to generate content that aligns with your needs. During preparation, you should also consider the limitations and biases of your data sources, aiming to provide a balanced and comprehensive dataset that will inform the AI system's output.

## Relay

In the *relay* step, you communicate with the AI by transmitting the prepared query with detailed instructions called prompts. This is where your ability to effectively employ what has come to be known as *prompt engineering* comes into play (more on prompt engineering later). The aim is to construct prompts that are unambiguous and guide the AI system toward the desired outcome.

You should be aware of the nuances of language that might affect the AI's performance, including context, specificity, and the potential need for creative interpretation. For example, rather than a vague prompt like: "Create an ad," a more effective relay would be: "Generate a catchy, upbeat 30-word ad for our new herbal tea targeting health-conscious consumers aged 20 to 30."

### Inspect

During the *inspect* phase, you evaluate the AI-generated content against the original objectives set in the *prepare* phase. It is critical to assess not only for factual accuracy but also for tone, style, and alignment with goals. This might involve cross-referencing with source data or checking against brand guidelines in the case of a marketing copy. You should scrutinize the output for any unintentional biases or errors that could have been introduced by the language model. It is also a time to identify areas that may require further development or refinement of your prompt.

### Modify

The *modify* stage is iterative, where you refine the AI system's output based on the inspection findings. If the generated content does not meet the set objectives or requires improvements, you adjust the input data, fine-tune the prompt, or directly edit the generated content. The key is to pinpoint where the output diverged from expectations and to craft modifications that will steer the AI closer to the desired result. This step may be repeated several times, with each iteration bringing the output more in line with your goals.

### Execute

Finally, the *execute* phase is when you decide on the final form of the AI-generated content and put it to use. This decision is informed by the thorough preparation, relaying, inspection, and modification that preceded it. It is the culmination of the generative process, where you approve the AI-created content for its intended application, whether that be publishing the marketing copy, deploying the chatbot, or using the AI-generated design. For instance, if the AI system has produced satisfactory ad copy, you would then proceed to incorporate it into the marketing campaign.

### Example

In a simple example, let us say you want to generate a poem about a sunset. In *prepare*, you would gather descriptive words and phrases about sunsets. For *relay*, you might input, "Write a four-stanza poem about a sunset over the ocean, conveying a sense of peace and awe." After receiving the AI-generated poem, you *inspect* it for vivid imagery and emotional impact. If the poem lacks emotion, you *modify* the prompt to add, "Emphasize the warm colors and the tranquil atmosphere." Finally, once satisfied, you *execute* by sharing the poem on your blog or social media.

## HALLUCINATIONS

In the nuanced art of GAE, it is crucial to address a phenomenon inherently tied to the interactions with Gen AI: hallucinations. As we refine our prompts to achieve clearer, more relevant responses from the AI system, understanding and mitigating hallucinations becomes paramount.

Hallucinations in the context of Gen AI refer to instances where the AI generates false or misleading information that is not supported by its training data or reality. These are not simply errors or inaccuracies but are more akin to the AI fabricating details or outcomes that have no basis in the information provided or in factual accuracy. This can occur due to various factors, including *overfitting*, where the model too closely adheres to its training data and fails to generalize properly, or *underfitting*, where the model hasn't learned enough from its training data to make accurate predictions. Additionally, the complexity and opacity of the AI system's decision-making processes can sometimes lead to unpredictable or nonsensical outputs. It may be also because you are not specific enough about what you want.

Recognizing and addressing hallucinations is particularly critical during the *inspect* and *modify* steps of the PRIME model. During the inspection step, project managers must vigilantly review AI-generated outputs, applying a critical eye to distinguish between genuine insights and potential hallucinations. This requires not only a deep understanding of the project's context and objectives but also an awareness of the AI model's limitations and biases. It is a process that emphasizes the need for human oversight in interpreting AI-generated content, ensuring that decisions are based on reliable and accurate information.

To reduce the risk of hallucinations, it is essential to refine how prompts are crafted and interactions with the AI system are structured. First, project managers can explicitly instruct the AI not to fabricate information and to admit when it does not have the answer. By asking the AI to focus only on credible sources or references provided—such as published project documentation or industry standards—the reliability of outputs can be significantly improved. This approach encourages the AI to base its responses on validated and relevant data.

Additionally, leveraging meta-prompts, where the AI system is first asked to generate or reframe the question itself before answering, can help clarify its understanding of the task and minimize ambiguity. Project managers can also adopt chain-of-thought prompting, which involves breaking down complex questions into smaller, logical steps, enabling the AI to reason systematically and reduce errors. Asking the AI to double-check its outputs is another effective technique, encouraging the model to reassess its own responses for inconsistencies or inaccuracies.

In the *modify* step, iterative prompting becomes crucial. This involves refining the prompts and inputs based on the AI system's initial outputs, whether by adjusting the level of detail, providing additional context, or explicitly stating underlying assumptions. By engaging in a dynamic dialogue with the AI, project managers can guide it toward generating more precise and relevant responses. Iterative refinement not only reduces hallucinations but also improves the clarity and alignment of outputs with the project's unique requirements.

By combining these strategies—careful inspection, focused and explicit prompting, meta-prompting, chain-of-thought reasoning, and iterative dialogue—the PRIME model provides a robust framework for navigating the challenges posed by AI hallucinations. These techniques help ensure that project management decisions are built on trustworthy and relevant AI-generated insights, enhancing the overall reliability of AI-assisted workflows.

## EXAMPLE OF APPLYING PRIME WITH GAE PRINCIPLES

In this section, we introduce a practical example from project management that exemplifies the PRIME framework, aligning with the principles of GAE. It showcases AI-assisted decision making for event planning. Subsequent chapters will expand upon this initial case, providing a spectrum of use cases that highlight the versatility and effectiveness of PRIME in real-world project management applications.

## Example: Event Planning

Let us explore how the PRIME model seamlessly integrates into the broader concept of GAE through a straightforward project management scenario: organizing a small corporate event. This example will integrate GAE principles explicitly at each step, offering a clear illustration of their practical application. An initial prompt for this example could be: "I am planning a corporate event for my company with 50 attendees to celebrate the end-of-year holidays and recognize our achievement of securing the top market share after five challenging years of price wars and cost-cutting measures. Could you please provide a detailed event agenda and suggest ideas for celebration awards to honor the team's efforts? Thank you!"

### *Prepare*

Adhering to *clarity in communication*, the project manager compiles relevant data impacting the event's scheduling, such as company-wide calendars, holidays, and historical attendance rates, into a comprehensive file. This file can be in the form of a Word document, a PDF file, or a spreadsheet. The file is attached to the prompt to enrich the context that the large language models (LLMs) will consider in generating the answer to your query. This step ensures a thorough, well-informed basis for engaging with AI, providing all necessary context for accurate and relevant output generation.

### *Relay*

In the *relay* step of this example, the principle of *clarity in communication* is central, ensuring the prompt sent to the AI system is explicit and detailed, guiding the technology to produce a date selection aligned with the project's requirements. Simultaneously, the *iterative personalization* principle is at play, as the project manager preemptively refines the prompt to streamline the AI system's focus, setting the stage for a productive exchange that may involve further prompt adjustments based on the AI's responses. Your prompt may include: "Identify the best three dates for the corporate event to ensure high attendance, considering the company-wide calendars, holidays, and historical attendance data provided."

### *Inspect*

Upon receiving the AI system's date suggestions, the project manager critically evaluates the output, applying the *critical evaluation* principle. This involves assessing the feasibility and appropriateness of the suggested dates against the project's unique context and any new developments, ensuring decisions are informed and reliable.

### *Modify*

If the initial suggestions do not fully align with the project's requirements or if new constraints emerge, the project manager refines the prompt as: "Considering the newly scheduled company-wide training session from December 10th to December 12th, identify the three best alternative dates for the corporate event to ensure high attendance. Exclude the second week of December and reevaluate, with a preference for Thursdays or Fridays." This revised prompt incorporates specific new constraints (the training session dates) and preferences (Thursdays or Fridays) based on additional context, which was not part of the initial analysis. It exemplifies the *iterative personalization* and *critical evaluation* principles of GAE, demonstrating a tailored, dynamic approach to refining AI-generated recommendations to better meet the project's evolving needs.

### *Execute*

In the final *execute* step, the project manager embodies the GAE principles of *ethical transparency and accountability* and *collaborative synergy.* Upon settling on a date that fulfills all the refined criteria, they initiate a collaborative, two-tiered process. First, they fine-tune the details, confirming the availability of key stakeholders and synchronizing with preferred vendors, embodying the meticulous nature of project management. This ensures that the chosen date is not only decided upon but also honed with a keen eye, adhering to the project's quality benchmarks and objectives. Then, they take decisive action, firmly integrating this polished, AI-informed selection into the project's framework. This dual-phase execution—refinement followed by decisive action—reinforces the active role of the project manager in the successful application of AI insights, driving the project forward with informed confidence. Incorporating final touches under the *execute* phase highlights the user's proactive role in ensuring the output's quality and effectiveness.

This approach to selecting a corporate event date through the PRIME model, grounded in GAE principles, showcases a methodical, principled way to leverage Gen AI in project management. By emphasizing clarity, critical evaluation, iterative dialogue, ethical considerations, and transparency, project managers can navigate the complexities of AI engagement, ensuring outcomes are both impactful and aligned with project objectives.

## PROMPT ENGINEERING

Within the structured journey of the PRIME process, which is integral to GAE, lies the pivotal practice of an emerging skill set known as prompt engineering. This crucial component is especially prominent in the *relay* and *modify* stages, where the art of crafting and refining prompts determines the direction and quality of the AI system's output. As we delve deeper into the intricacies of PRIME, it becomes clear that mastering prompt engineering is not just a skill but a necessary dialogue with AI, shaping the path from initial query to final execution.

In a nutshell, prompt engineering is a technique that involves crafting precise input instructions to elicit desired outputs from LLMs. Prompting an LLM is not the same as prompting a search engine. For more than 20 years, we have been prompting web searches with simple and sometimes not-so-simple phrases that occupied one or at most two lines. But an elaborate prompt for Gen AI could easily take 10 to 15 lines. Think of it as the key that unlocks the potential of these sophisticated language models, enabling you to tailor their responses to meet your project's specific needs.

As users engage with these advanced AI systems through natural language interfaces, the effectiveness of their interactions often hinges on how they frame their questions or prompts. Prompt engineering is the art and science of crafting queries that elicit the most informative, accurate, and relevant responses from AI models. It involves an understanding of the AI's underlying mechanisms and the ability to formulate prompts that guide the AI to comprehend and generate the desired output. As such, the transition from traditional search to *New Search* is not only about the technology itself but also about how users interact with it, making prompt engineering an essential component of the user experience.

In the realm of LLMs, prompt engineering is particularly crucial due to the models' sensitivity to input. A well-engineered prompt can leverage the AI system's vast knowledge base and contextual understanding, resulting in an output that seems almost intuitively aligned with the user's intent. This process may include specifying the tone, style, or format of the desired answer, which can be as critical as the content of the query itself. For instance, when interacting with a model like ChatGPT 4o, the difference between asking, "What is the recipe for a chocolate cake?" and instructing, "Write a detailed recipe for a chocolate cake including preparation steps," can lead to substantially different levels of detail and structure in the response. The development of prompt engineering strategies thus becomes pivotal in optimizing the performance of Gen AI in various applications, from creative writing to technical troubleshooting.

Prompt engineering transcends simple command input; it is an iterative dialogue that refines the AI system's understanding and direction with each interaction. At its core, it involves the strategic formulation of prompts to guide Gen AI toward desired outcomes, balancing specificity and creativity to elicit responses that align with user intentions. This requires not only a deep understanding of the AI's capabilities and limitations but also an insight into how different phrasings can influence the generated content. Effective prompt engineering can dramatically enhance the relevance, accuracy, and creativity of AI outputs, turning generic responses into tailored, contextually appropriate content.

## Strategies for Crafting Effective Prompts

Having explored the foundations of prompt engineering, we now turn to refining your ability to craft prompts that will elicit the most effective responses from Gen AI. This section offers a suite of strategic tips, each serving as a beacon to guide you through the nuanced process of advanced prompt crafting. These strategies are the keystones for deepening your interaction with AI systems, tailored to elevate the sophistication of your queries and the quality of the AI's output.

The tips provided as part of a repeatable process for crafting effective prompts include: (1) assigning a role, (2) providing context, (3) defining the objective of the prompt, (4) framing the desired output, (5) setting boundaries, (6) determining the tone of the response, (7) being specific, and (8) outlining the sequence for the process. While this list might appear comprehensive, it should be considered a dynamic resource that evolves alongside advancements in LLMs. These tips are not intended to be applied in a rigid order but rather used in a logical and flexible manner. Think of them as interconnected pieces of a puzzle that, when combined effectively, will enhance the precision, relevance, and quality of the AI system's responses. When you apply these tips, you are not just communicating with AI; you are engaging in a collaborative process that enhances project management outcomes, ensuring that every piece of AI-generated content is as actionable and aligned with your project goals as possible. The following list elaborates on those eight tips:

1. *Assign role*: Defining the role of the AI system is crucial for aligning its outputs with specific project management tasks. For instance, you might set the AI system's role as a *risk management consultant* to focus on identifying and mitigating project risks using standard practices. Alternatively, you could specify the role based on a specific framework or thought leader, such as *project management expert following the PMBOK® Guide* or *strategist using Michael Porter's frameworks*. This approach helps tailor the AI's responses to fit the specific needs and strategic goals of your project, whether you are seeking broad guidance or detailed, framework-aligned insights.
2. *Provide context*: Contextualizing your prompt is possibly the most impactful tip for eliciting effective responses from Gen AI. It enriches the AI system's understanding and aligns its outputs closely with your project's specific requirements. By providing detailed background information, such as the project's industry, goals, and the unique challenges you face, you significantly enhance the relevance and precision of the AI's output. This can be the difference between asking for a generic work breakdown structure (WBS) and receiving a customized one that considers specific details of your project. For example, rather than simply requesting a WBS for building a house, providing detailed project documents,

PDFs, or Excel sheets about your specific house project—including architectural plans and client requirements—will transform a broad question into a tailored inquiry. This depth of detail enables the AI to generate outputs that are not only accurate but also perfectly suited for your particular project scenario.

3. *Define objective*: Clearly defining your objective is essential to guide the AI system toward the results you need. If your goal is to generate a risk analysis, then state that objective explicitly in your prompt. This instructs the AI to focus its vast knowledge on identifying potential risks related to your project's unique parameters, ensuring the output is directly applicable to your needs.
4. *Frame output*: Dictating the format is essential for presenting your information in a usable way. If the situation calls for a quick project update that can be easily read by team members, request the AI system to format the information as bullet points. This instruction helps the AI present its vast data analysis in a concise format suitable for quick digestion and immediate application.
5. *Set boundaries*: Imposing limits on the output helps to maintain focus and relevance. In project management, this could mean setting a word or character limit for project updates to ensure they are concise. For example, if the AI system is generating a project status report, you might limit the output to 200 words to encourage brevity and clarity.
6. *Determine tone*: Specifying the tone sets the mood of the communication. In a project management context, this could range from formal for boardroom presentations to inspirational for team meetings. For instance, if you are addressing your project team to motivate them about the upcoming project phase, you would prompt the AI to adopt an inspirational tone, infusing enthusiasm and confidence into the communication.
7. *Be specific*: Clarity is key when defining tasks for Gen AI. By providing precise details and instructions, you help the AI system understand exactly what is expected, leading to more accurate and useful outputs. For instance, when asking for a budget analysis, specify not only to analyze costs but to break down the costs according to different project phases or departments. This level of detail helps the AI to focus its analysis and provide insights that are directly applicable and actionable. An example could be, "Analyze the allocated budget versus actual spending by department for the Q3 project cycle, highlighting variances and potential overruns."
8. *Describe sequencing*: Finally, specifying the order of tasks or steps in a process is crucial, as the sequence of actions can impact the outcome. When interacting with Gen AI, detailing the sequence in which project tasks should be analyzed or reported can ensure that the output aligns with project timelines and workflow dependencies. For example, you might prompt the AI system to, "Outline the project initiation steps sequentially, starting with stakeholder analysis, followed by resource allocation, and ending with risk assessment." This guides the AI to structure its output in a way that mirrors the project's operational flow, providing a logical and practical roadmap for project execution.

Continuous advancements in LLMs like ChatGPT are reducing the need for highly detailed prompts, thanks to their training on extensive and diverse datasets. These models can infer context and generate coherent responses from less specific prompts. However, the accuracy and relevance of the outputs still benefit from well-crafted prompts, especially for complex or critical applications in project management. While everyday interactions may not require meticulous prompt engineering, for professional tasks, a more detailed approach can significantly enhance the model's effectiveness and the utility of its outputs.

## Benefits of Well-Crafted Prompts

A well-crafted prompt can significantly enhance the quality and relevance of the AI system's output. Here are several benefits of using well-crafted prompts:

- *Improved accuracy*: Tailored prompts lead to more accurate responses, ensuring that the AI system's output is closely aligned with the specific needs of your project.
- *Efficiency in results*: When prompts are clear and well-structured, the AI system can provide the needed information faster, reducing the time spent on back-and-forth clarifications.
- *Reduction of misinterpretation*: A perfectly crafted prompt minimizes the chance of misinterpretations by the AI system, leading to outputs that require less revision.
- *Enhanced relevance*: Specific prompts result in more relevant responses, providing insights and content that are directly applicable to the project at hand.
- *Cost-effectiveness*: Time is money, and by reducing the need for multiple iterations, well-crafted prompts save resources.
- *Better decision making*: Quality prompts can yield comprehensive and nuanced outputs that can inform and improve project-related decision making.
- *Customized solutions*: A well-crafted prompt allows the AI system to generate solutions that are not just generic but customized to the unique aspects of your project.
- *Increased productivity*: By obtaining useful responses on the first try, project teams can progress without unnecessary delays.
- *Ethical alignment*: Clear prompts can guide the AI to produce content that is ethically sound and free from unintended biases.
- *User empowerment*: Users feel more in control of the AI tool, knowing that they can direct its vast knowledge toward productive ends.

As Gen AI technologies evolve, the role of prompt engineering grows in complexity and significance. It becomes a dynamic process of experimentation, learning, and adaptation, where each prompt is an opportunity to refine the AI system's performance. Through this lens, prompt engineering is seen as a critical lever for unlocking the full potential of AI, enabling users to navigate the vast possibilities of generative technologies. Whether crafting a piece of writing, generating new images, or developing complex code, the quality of interaction through prompt engineering directly impacts the effectiveness and innovation of the AI's creations.

As Gen AI continues to infiltrate commercial and creative sectors, prompt engineering is becoming a valued skill in the job market. Companies are seeking individuals who can effectively communicate with AI to produce desired outcomes, whether it is generating marketing copy, coding, or providing customer support. The role of prompt engineers is not just to interact with AI but to do so in a way that maximizes the utility and efficiency of these powerful tools. This skill set is rapidly evolving, with best practices and methodologies emerging as businesses and individuals gain more experience with the nuances of *New Search* platforms and LLMs. The result is a symbiotic relationship where human expertise in prompt engineering helps unlock the full potential of generative AI technologies.

## Project Input Folder: A Cornerstone of Prompt Engineering

Effective use of AI tools in project management begins with providing accurate, comprehensive, and project-specific input data. This is where the concept of the project input folder (PIF) becomes essential—a structured and strategic repository for all project-related data, designed to enhance the relevance and effectiveness of AI-generated outputs. LLMs like ChatGPT are trained on vast amounts of publicly accessible data. While this training equips them to provide generic and often insightful responses, it inherently lacks the unique context and nuances of your organization, such as its mission, values, culture, and strategic priorities. This gap can lead to AI-generated answers that are helpful but not entirely accurate or aligned with your specific project or organizational needs. A thoughtfully prepared PIF serves to bridge this gap, offering the AI system the necessary context to generate outputs that are both tailored and actionable. It builds on the *provide context* strategy discussed earlier, emphasizing how a thoughtfully constructed PIF can optimize AI applications across various project management tasks.

For organizations seeking higher-quality results, building a private LLM trained on historical organizational and project data is a viable option. Such an LLM can produce outputs that better align with your organization's context. However, even with a private LLM, the need for project-specific data remains critical. This is where the PIF concept truly shines. By compiling and organizing all relevant project documents—ranging from initial charters and business cases to ongoing reports and communication records—the PIF equips the AI with the essential context to refine its outputs further. Importantly, the PIF is not a one-time effort but a living repository that evolves as the project progresses through its life cycle. As new documents are generated during the project, they are added to the PIF to ensure the AI system remains informed with the most current data.

Even for those who use commercial LLMs rather than custom-built ones, a well-maintained PIF can still deliver significant value. To address concerns about privacy, specific project and organizational details can be anonymized before uploading. Additionally, commercial LLMs often have settings to ensure that uploaded data is not retained beyond the session, preserving confidentiality. Once uploaded in an ongoing chat session, documents typically do not need to be re-uploaded for subsequent queries related to the same context, streamlining the process. For example, if you want the LLM to generate lessons learned at the end of the project, previously uploaded documents such as charters, risk registers, and meeting minutes can be utilized without needing to be uploaded again.

By strategically leveraging the PIF, project managers can ensure that LLMs provide outputs that are not only aligned with the unique context of their projects but also reduce the iterative effort required to refine generic AI outputs. Whether creating initial project documentation or generating insights at later stages, the PIF is a cornerstone for integrating AI into effective project management workflows.

In addition to utilizing the PIF, tools like NotebookLM and Copilot Studio play a pivotal role in managing private and personalized project information securely. These platforms are specifically designed to handle sensitive organizational data while offering tailored, AI-driven insights. By integrating these tools, project managers can centralize and customize knowledge bases, streamlining access to relevant project documents for AI-assisted tasks. Copilot Studio further enhances collaboration by enabling teams to engage with project-specific data through a secure and intuitive interface. These tools prioritize data privacy with strong safeguards against unauthorized access, ensuring that no information is retained beyond the intended session. Together, NotebookLM, Copilot Studio, and similar platforms complement the PIF framework by creating trusted environments where rich project-specific data can be securely integrated with AI capabilities, generating accurate and actionable insights for effective project management.

### *What Goes into a PIF?*

A PIF contains all the critical documentation needed to define and describe your project. Please refer to Table 4.1 for a summary of broad project areas and high-level project data required to enhance AI tool effectiveness. This table does not cover every single area of project management

**Table 4.1** PIF data needs for LLMs

| General Project Areas | Specific Project Data |
|---|---|
| **Project Overview:** | |
| Project name and description | Provides a clear understanding of what the project is about and its goals |
| Project objectives | Specific, measurable goals the project aims to achieve, giving the LLM context on desired outcomes |
| Business needs and strategic alignment | Explains the business needs that the project addresses and how it aligns with organizational strategies, ensuring the AI's recommendations support strategic objectives |
| **Stakeholder Information:** | |
| Stakeholder list | Names and roles of all stakeholders involved in the project to identify key players and their responsibilities |
| Contact information | Email addresses, phone numbers, and other contact details for effective communication strategies |
| Stakeholder interests and influence | Describes each stakeholder's interest in the project and their influence level to prioritize engagement strategies |
| **Project Scope and Requirements:** | |
| Scope statement | Detailed description of the project's deliverables and the boundaries of the project, helping the LLM define the project's limits |
| High-level requirements | Key functional and nonfunctional requirements that the project must meet to ensure completeness |
| Out-of-scope items | Specific items or activities that are not included in the project, preventing scope creep |
| Work breakdown structure (WBS) | Hierarchical decomposition of the total scope of work to provide a clear framework for task allocation |
| **Schedule and Timeline:** | |
| Project timeline | Major milestones and key deadlines to help the LLM create accurate schedules |
| Detailed schedule | Start and end dates for all tasks and activities, ensuring precise timeline generation |
| Dependencies | Identification of task dependencies and sequences for logical workflow planning |
| Milestones | Key project milestones and their target dates to track progress and achievements |
| **Cost and Budget Information:** | |
| Budget estimate | Initial financial estimate for the project to guide cost management |
| Detailed cost breakdown | Costs associated with resources, materials, labor, and other expenditures for accurate budgeting |
| Funding source | Information on where the project funding will come from to ensure financial feasibility |
| Cost baseline | Approved budget for the project against which performance will be measured, aiding in financial control |

*Continued*

**Table 4.1** *continued*

| General Project Areas | Specific Project Data |
|---|---|
| **Risk Management and Quality Assurance:** | |
| Risk register | List of identified risks, including their potential impact and likelihood to prepare mitigation plans |
| Risk mitigation strategies | Plans for managing and mitigating identified risks to enhance project resilience |
| Quality requirements | Standards and criteria that the project's deliverables must meet to ensure quality |
| Quality assurance plan | Processes for ensuring that the project meets the required quality standards, guiding the LLM in maintaining high-quality outputs |
| **Communication and Reporting:** | |
| Communication plan | Detailed plan for how project information will be communicated to stakeholders, ensuring effective information dissemination |
| Status reporting frequency | Schedule for when and how status updates will be provided to keep stakeholders informed |
| Key metrics for reporting | Specific metrics that will be used to measure project progress and performance, ensuring relevant and timely reports |
| Reporting formats | Templates or formats for status reports, progress dashboards, and other communications for consistency and clarity |
| **Project Progress Data:** | |
| Current status of tasks | Real-time data on the progress of various tasks and activities |
| Performance metrics | Measurements such as earned value, planned value, and actual cost to assess project health |
| Issue log | Record of current issues, their impact, and resolutions |
| Change requests | Documentation of changes requested, their status, and approvals |
| Lessons learned | Insights gained from project activities that can inform future project phases and initiatives |

or show the data needs in every single domain or knowledge area. Project management is a broad discipline with many different aspects, and it is not feasible to list all possible areas and their respective data requirements within the scope of this table. Instead, we have focused on the most important areas to provide a foundational understanding. This should give you a general idea of the types of data you should consider gathering and organizing for your own specific project needs.

When preparing a PIF, it is also important to consider data privacy and security. If you are not using your own organization's private LLM, ensure that any confidential or sensitive information belonging to your organization is either removed or anonymized before saving it in the folder. This practice helps protect your organization's proprietary information while still enabling the LLM to deliver valuable insights and support based on the provided project data. By maintaining a well-organized and sanitized project input folder, you can maximize the effectiveness of LLM tools in managing and executing your projects successfully.

### *How to Build a PIF*

1. *Collection*: Gather all relevant project documents and data that define the project's goals, challenges, and operational environment

2. *Digitization*: Ensure all materials are in accessible digital formats (e.g., PDFs, CSVs, Excel files)
3. *Organization*: Categorize and clearly label documents to facilitate quick retrieval and easy integration with AI tools

The PIF can evolve throughout the project life cycle, with outputs generated by the AI system (e.g., refined plans, updated reports) being added back into the folder. This iterative approach creates a living archive of project progress and AI interactions.

### *Key Benefits of a PIF*

- *Contextual relevance*: Provides the AI with comprehensive background information, enabling it to generate outputs that align closely with project needs
- *Continuity and memory*: Using the same chat session for ongoing queries allows the AI system to build on previous outputs, reducing the need for repetitive input and improving response coherence
- *Privacy and security*: Ensure sensitive or proprietary data is anonymized or removed if not using a private, organization-specific LLM

By tailoring input data to the project's specific requirements, the PIF serves as the foundation for AI tools to function not merely as assistants but as integral, informed collaborators in the project management process. It ensures the AI system can provide actionable insights and recommendations that are both technically competent and contextually adapted.

# CHALLENGES AND THE STRATEGIES FOR OVERCOMING THEM IN APPLYING GEN AI TO PROJECT MANAGEMENT

As exciting as the possibilities of Gen AI may be in project portfolio management, waterfall, and agile environments, implementing these technologies comes with its own set of challenges. Recognizing these obstacles and adopting strategies to overcome them is essential for maximizing the potential of Gen AI while ensuring its responsible and effective use. Next, we will highlight some of the primary challenges and provide actionable strategies for addressing them.

## Challenges in Applying Gen AI to Project Management

1. *Data quality and context*: One of the most significant challenges lies in the quality and relevance of the data provided to the Gen AI system. LLMs like ChatGPT rely heavily on the context provided to generate outputs. Inadequate or incomplete input data can lead to generic or irrelevant outputs, undermining their usefulness.
2. *Lack of customization*: Publicly available LLMs are trained on general data, making it difficult for them to account for the unique nuances of an organization or project. They may miss the subtle, project-specific details necessary for actionable outputs.
3. *Overreliance on AI*: Teams may fall into the trap of depending too heavily on AI-generated outputs, leading to a lack of engagement, critical thinking, or collaboration among team members. This overreliance can diminish the quality of decision making.
4. *Ethical and privacy concerns*: Sharing sensitive project data with public LLMs can raise concerns about confidentiality and compliance, especially in industries with stringent regulations like healthcare or finance.

5. *AI interpretability and validation*: Understanding how the AI system arrives at its recommendations can be challenging. This *black-box* nature of AI can make it difficult for teams to validate its suggestions or explain them to stakeholders.
6. *Resistance to change*: Introducing AI tools into established project management practices may face resistance from team members unfamiliar with or skeptical of these technologies.

## Strategies for Overcoming These Challenges

1. *Build a comprehensive PIF*: Create a PIF that consolidates all relevant project data, such as scope documents, risk registers, resource availability, and historical performance data. This provides the AI system with a richer context for generating accurate and actionable outputs.
2. *Invest in custom LLMs*: Where possible, organizations should invest in training custom LLMs on their historical project data. This ensures that the AI understands the organization's specific context, leading to more relevant and reliable outputs.
3. *Encourage human oversight and collaboration*: Use Gen AI outputs as a starting point rather than a definitive answer. Teams should review, refine, and validate AI-generated results to ensure they align with the project's unique needs and foster team engagement and collaboration.
4. *Implement strong data governance*: Anonymize sensitive data when using public LLMs and configure appropriate privacy settings to ensure compliance with confidentiality requirements. For industries with high regulatory requirements, explore private cloud-based AI solutions.
5. *Provide training and support*: Offer training to team members on how to use Gen AI effectively. This includes educating them on the limitations of the technology and how to interpret and validate its outputs.
6. *Foster a culture of experimentation*: Encourage teams to view Gen AI adoption as an iterative process. Pilot the tools on smaller projects, collect feedback, and refine the implementation strategy over time.

By addressing these challenges and implementing the outlined strategies (summarized in Table 4.2), organizations can fully leverage the transformative potential of Gen AI while mitigating risks and fostering team confidence in its adoption.

**Table 4.2** Challenges and strategies for overcoming them in Gen AI applications

| Challenges | Strategies |
|---|---|
| Data quality and context | Build a comprehensive PIF to provide AI with rich, relevant context |
| Lack of customization | Invest in training custom LLMs on organizational data for tailored and specific outputs |
| Overreliance on AI | Use AI-generated outputs as drafts and encourage team validation, collaboration, and critical thinking |
| Ethical and privacy concerns | Anonymize data, configure privacy settings, and consider private AI solutions for sensitive projects |
| AI interpretability and validation | Train teams to interpret and validate AI outputs, integrating them with project-specific insights |
| Resistance to change | Provide training, demonstrate value through pilots, and foster a culture of experimentation |

## IN CONCLUSION

As we conclude our exploration of GAE, this chapter has provided a comprehensive introduction to this transformative concept. We outlined the PRIME methodology as a structured approach for interacting with AI systems effectively and emphasized the critical role of prompt engineering in achieving meaningful outputs. These foundational elements serve as the bedrock for integrating Gen AI into project management, enabling a deeper understanding of how to leverage AI's capabilities to enhance project efficiency and decision making. While there are exciting possibilities of Gen AI in project management, there are limitations as well that you should keep in mind in applying the tools.

In the next chapter, we take the Gen AI principles into action, showcasing real-world AI use cases tailored for day-to-day project management tasks. From composing professional emails to generating impactful presentations and summarizing complex reports, we will illustrate how these methodologies can be applied to streamline workflows and boost productivity. This practical dive will equip you with actionable techniques to harness Gen AI for immediate value in managing projects effectively.

# 5

# AI USE CASES FOR EVERYDAY PROJECT TASKS

Building on the foundation laid out in the previous chapter on generative AI engagement (GAE), we now turn our attention to practical applications of artificial intelligence (AI) for routine tasks that are central to project management. While these tasks may seem mundane, they often demand a significant portion of time from project management professionals. Optimizing them through AI will not only streamline workflows but also allow project managers to focus on higher-value activities like strategic planning and decision making. By integrating generative AI (Gen AI) tools into these day-to-day processes, teams can achieve greater efficiency and productivity while maintaining the quality and consistency of their outputs.

This chapter explores five operational use cases that project management professionals encounter daily:

1. *Writing professional emails*: Gen AI can assist in crafting polished and contextually appropriate emails, ensuring clarity, professionalism, and alignment with the intended audience. From responding to stakeholders to providing updates, AI tools can quickly generate drafts that save time and reduce the risk of miscommunication.
2. *Creating presentations*: Gen AI can automate the creation of visually engaging and data-driven presentations, complete with tailored content and design elements. By inputting key details, project managers can produce professional decks that effectively communicate project goals, updates, or outcomes.
3. *Summarizing reports*: AI tools excel at distilling lengthy reports into concise summaries, highlighting key points and actionable insights. This enables project professionals to absorb critical information quickly and share it with stakeholders in a digestible format.
4. *Generating templates*: AI can create reusable templates for standard project documents, such as risk registers, meeting agendas, and status reports. These templates ensure consistency, reduce manual effort, and maintain alignment with organizational standards.
5. *Analyzing data*: Advanced AI capabilities can process large datasets, uncover patterns, and generate actionable insights to support decision making. Whether tracking project performance or identifying risks, AI-driven data analysis enhances a manager's ability to respond proactively.

While Gen AI can significantly enhance these tasks, it is important to note that these are just a few examples of the myriad day-to-day activities that can benefit from Gen AI. The potential applications are vast, from scheduling meetings to generating progress reports and prioritizing tasks. By providing illustrative examples, this chapter aims to equip you with the skills to craft effective prompts for these and other everyday project tasks, enabling you to explore the broad utility of AI in project management. Here, we demonstrate how mundane tasks can be streamlined and also enhanced, elevating routine project management tasks beyond the ordinary. This showcases the substantial yet practical impact of AI, emphasizing its role in enhancing standard project management activities.

## 1. WRITING PROFESSIONAL EMAILS

According to different prominent authors, project managers dedicate an astonishing 75–90% of their time communicating with stakeholders (Haus, 2013), and a significant portion of this communication unfolds through email. This statistic underscores the importance of mastering email correspondence; it is not just about conveying information but about doing so with clarity, professionalism, and precision. As we navigate through the art of drafting emails, we utilize the principles of GAE and the PRIME (prepare, relay, inspect, modify, execute) methodology discussed in the previous chapter to ensure our messages resonate effectively with our audience. It is about striking the right balance between detail and brevity, formality and approachability, precision and accessibility. The perfect orchestration of these elements is particularly crucial in delicate situations such as addressing project delays.

Table 5.1 shows a prompt for ChatGPT to draft an email addressing a sensitive issue: a project delay due to a vendor's late shipment of supplies. This table also includes the results from the large language model (LLM), demonstrating how the application of our outlined principles can yield an email that precisely encapsulates our needs. The response, also presented in Table 5.1 is clear, well-mannered, and considerately crafted, showcasing the effectiveness of our prompt in achieving the objective, which was to communicate the delay while maintaining trust and confidence on the one hand and gently warning of possible legal action on the other. Depending upon your need, you may tweak our prompt or use a totally different prompt altogether. For example, while our prompt indicates a relatively gentle tone for the email, you may request the LLM to use a more confrontational one.

Gen AI offers a valuable tool for crafting emails in project management, providing a quick and efficient way to generate professional, coherent correspondence. This technology excels in structuring content that adheres to standard communication practices, which can significantly streamline daily email tasks, allowing project managers to focus more on strategic decisions rather than administrative details. AI's ability to tailor emails to specific project contexts and recipient needs enhances communication effectiveness, ensuring messages are both relevant and appropriately formatted.

However, users must be aware of the limitations of Gen AI, including its potential to miss subtle project nuances or convey unintended tones, especially in sensitive or complex interactions. To best utilize AI for email generation, it is crucial to provide detailed, clear prompts and to thoroughly review AI-generated emails before dispatch. Regular feedback to AI systems helps refine their performance, reduce errors, and ensure outputs remain aligned with project-specific requirements. By maintaining a cautious approach to AI's use in crafting emails, project professionals can ensure it acts as an aid in improving workplace efficiency and communication accuracy rather than as a replacement for human judgment.

**Table 5.1** Use case for crafting a professional email

| **Prompt** |
|---|
| You are an experienced purchasing manager. Your vendor, ACME, Corp., is three months behind schedule in delivering the electrical components required for an infrastructure project called *Riverside Defense*. You are getting pushback from the project manager because of this delay. The first month of delay was not a big issue, since there is some slack time. But further delay will soon create a new critical path potentially delaying the project. Please write a 200-word email asking ACME to think outside the box, find alternative solutions, and ship the electrical components as quickly as next week, since the project cannot wait any longer. Be strong and decisive. Mention that we have legal recourse, but do not want to trigger it, as this could harm our long-term relationship. |
| **Response** |
| **Subject:** Urgent: Immediate action required to expedite deliveries for Riverside Defense project<br><br>Dear ACME Team,<br>I hope this email finds you well. I am writing to express my deep concern regarding the substantial delays we have experienced in the delivery of electrical components for the Riverside Defense project. As you are aware, the project is currently facing a critical timeline, and the prolonged delay in your deliveries is jeopardizing our ability to meet key milestones.<br>While I understand that unforeseen challenges can arise in the production and supply chain, the current situation requires immediate attention and innovative solutions. We cannot afford any further setbacks, and I urge you to think outside the box to expedite the delivery of the required components. Our critical path elements are at risk of delay within the next two weeks, posing a significant threat to the overall success of the Riverside Defense project.<br>I want to emphasize the importance of finding alternative solutions that would allow you to deliver the required electrical components by next week. I believe that, as a reputable vendor, ACME has the capability to address this challenge promptly. It is crucial to avoid triggering legal measures that could harm our long-term relationship; however, we must prioritize the success of the Riverside Defense project.<br>I trust that you will give this matter the urgency and attention it deserves. Your cooperation in resolving this issue promptly is essential for the successful completion of the project and the maintenance of our positive working relationship.<br>Thank you for your immediate attention to this matter. |

## 2. CREATING PRESENTATIONS

Transitioning from the written word to visual storytelling, we approach the essential project management skill of creating impactful PowerPoint presentations (PPTs). In this section, we explore an example that showcases the versatility and sophistication of Gen AI in crafting presentation materials. We leverage the capabilities of Gen AI and its *agents* to create a common business application: a slide deck. Here we use the premium features of ChatGPT, augmented with a SlidesGPT plug-in, to produce a detailed and context-specific slide presentation. Slide generation is not a standard feature of ChatGPT. To produce such results, you would need a paid version with access to various specialized *GPTs* (generative pre-trained transformers) or agents capable of generating these outputs. This advanced approach tailors the content to the unique details of the project, offering a depth of customization that genuinely demonstrates the prowess of the latest AI tools in project management. The prompt for this example is included in Table 5.2, along with a ChatGPT-generated response and a comprehensive slide presentation that can be seen directly after the user enters the prompt or accessed via a downloadable link. A selection of the slides that were crafted by AI is displayed for illustrative purposes at the end of the table.

**Table 5.2** Use case for creating a PPT presentation

**Prompt[1]**

You are an experienced project manager. Please develop a high-level executive quarterly summary for stakeholders highlighting project achievements, future milestones, and strategic implications. Tailor the summary for a diverse audience, incorporating key performance indicators and visual elements for clarity. Please translate this summary into 4 slides. Every slide should have a title, bullet points, and 1 or 2 graphics depending on the information to be shown. Main points to be communicated:

1. We have a 15% overrun in machinery costs because of exchange rate differences that were not anticipated on time.
2. There is a risk of resource shortages due to the holidays.
3. We need to make two payments to our bank during the next month. These are all in the budget, but they account for 10% of the project's total and need CFO approval.
4. As for time, we are not doing too bad. We are showing a 3.5% delay (2 weeks) on the project and the main risks that could happen didn't occur, which is a relief.

Provide a forward-looking perspective on the project's strategic alignment with organizational goals.

**Response**

Here is the proposed structure for your 4-slide executive summary presentation:

**Slide 1[2]:** *Project Achievements*

**Title:** Quarterly Project Achievements and Performance

**Key Points:**

- **On-Time Progress:** Minimal 3.5% delay (2 weeks), well within buffer limits.
  *(Icon: fa-clock)*
- **Risk Management Success:** No materialization of major risks, ensuring operational stability.
  *(Icon: fa-shield-alt)*
- **Milestone Completion:** All core deliverables for the quarter achieved.
  *(Icon: fa-check-circle)*

**Graphics:**

1. A timeline showcasing achieved milestones against planned dates.
2. A risk matrix highlighting avoided critical risks.

Should I proceed with creating the slides, researching visual elements, and generating the final design?

Yes[3]

*Continued*

**Table 5.2** *continued*

## Financial Insights and Challenges

- **Cost Overrun:** 15% increase in machinery costs due to unforeseen exchange rate fluctuations.
- **Upcoming Payments:** Two major bank payments (10% of project budget) due next month, requiring CFO review.
- **Budget Contingencies:** All overruns remain manageable within the approved financial framework.

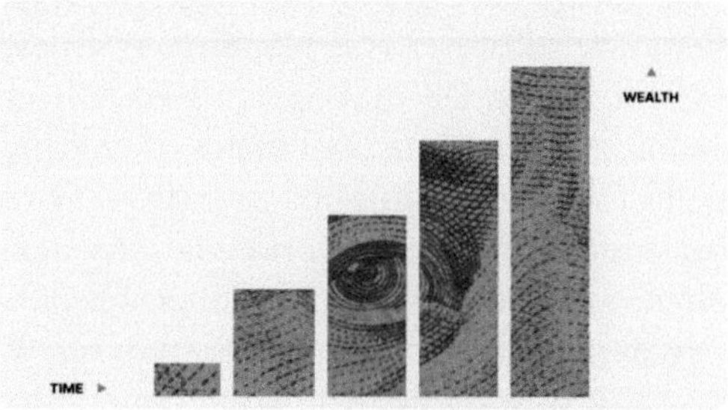


Photo by Morgan Housel on Unsplash

## Identified Risks and Mitigation Plans

**Resource Availability**
Potential staff shortages during holidays identified.

**Mitigation Plan**
Proactive scheduling adjustments and cross-training underway.

**Strategic Monitoring**
Enhanced tracking of vendor deliveries and staffing needs.

## Forward Momentum and Organizational Goals

- **Organizational Goals:** Project remains aligned with strategic initiatives of operational efficiency and market positioning.
- **Upcoming Milestones:** Next quarter focuses on finalizing production setup and operational testing.
- **Long-Term Benefits:** Expected ROI remains on track, with high stakeholder value predicted post-completion.

Photo by engin akyurt on Unsplash

[1] The interaction involved using ChatGPT to send the user's prompt to SlidesGPT, a plug-in that generates PowerPoint slides directly based on the provided input.
[2] The LLM generated the structure for three additional slides, but they are not included in the table to maintain brevity and conserve space.
[3] This is our response to the question asked by the LLM.

When leveraging Gen AI for presentations, it is essential to remember that creating a compelling presentation requires clear objectives, a well-thought-out slide structure, and careful consideration of visual design elements. While premium solutions that integrate ChatGPT with image generators like DALL-E or FLUX can offer the convenience of generating complete slides dynamically, those using the free versions of AI tools can still achieve professional results. The AI will provide a structured outline and the creative task of incorporating visual flair using your preferred presentation software. This blend of AI efficiency with human creativity ensures that each slide conveys the intended message and visually captures the audience's attention. Whether you are fine-tuning AI-generated templates or crafting slides from scratch, the end goal is a presentation that effectively communicates your project's vision and data with clarity and impact.

For crafting compelling presentations, several specialized AI tools exist that go beyond the capabilities of general-purpose models like ChatGPT. One notable example is Gamma, a tool explicitly designed for creating presentations. Unlike ChatGPT, which can assist with generating content that requires further manual assembly into slides, tools like Gamma are built with specific algorithms to handle the aesthetics and layout of presentations directly. These specialized tools can automatically arrange text, integrate visuals coherently, and optimize slide transitions based on the context of the contents. They can even generate abbreviated text for slides as well as images related to the text based on your specific prompt requests. This automation streamlines content development as well as the design process. Moreover, these AI-driven presentation tools often come with advanced features such as theme customization, intelligent suggestions for graphical data representation, and real-time collaboration capabilities, making them powerful allies in crafting professional and visually engaging presentations.

Gen AI tools can efficiently organize information into engaging layouts, select relevant images, and suggest content enhancements based on the project's scope and requirements. However, it remains essential for users to guide the AI with precise, context-rich prompts and review the generated slides critically to ensure accuracy and appropriateness. Regular interaction and refinement help in tuning the AI system's output, making it a valuable assistant in crafting presentations that convey the intended message clearly and effectively.

## 3. SUMMARIZING REPORTS

In managing projects, synthesizing dense reports into digestible summaries is not just beneficial—it is essential for efficiency. With Gen AI, this task has become more streamlined than ever. However, it is crucial to note that while free versions of tools like ChatGPT can offer basic summarization capabilities, accessing and summarizing content from PDFs may require the more advanced features of their premium paid versions. (Free versions of Perplexity or Claude can access a limited number of PDF files. You can also paste a limited amount of text to be analyzed and summarized directly in the prompt itself.) Please remember that to make the most of these features for summarizing reports, it is important to apply the PRIME methodology and GAE principles to guide the AI in producing clear, concise, and insightful summaries.

Let us consider the task of summarizing a series of insightful blogs by one of us (Prasad Kodukula), focusing on the "Secrets to Success of Organizational Transformation," available at https://kodukula.com/kodukula-blog/. By inputting a PDF compilation of these blogs into a premium Gen AI model, we can generate comprehensive summaries that encapsulate the core messages and insights. This saves time and ensures that stakeholders can quickly grasp the essence of these detailed materials. The prompt that guides the LLM, along with the results, is shown in Table 5.3, demonstrating the ease of integrating Gen AI to enhance project management workflow.

**Table 5.3** Use case for summarizing reports

| Prompt |
|---|
| Please summarize the contents of the attached file.[1] Generate a concise two-paragraph report about the blogs in the file. Use simple phrases and make it easy to understand. Think of it as an invitational article to read the actual blogs. Also, generate a 1–2 sentence description of each blog.[2] |
| **Response** |
| The file contains a series of enlightening blogs focused on the essential strategies for organizational transformation. Here is a concise summary and a brief description of each blog to invite readers to explore them further:<br><br>**Summary:**<br>The blogs delve into the nuanced secrets of organizational transformation through practical insights and real-world examples. The author discusses various critical aspects such as purpose, leadership, empowerment, alignment, speed, and execution. Each blog is crafted to not only provide theoretical knowledge but also actionable steps that organizations can implement to achieve successful transformation. The guidance provided is rooted in decades of experience and interactions with Fortune 100 companies, making it invaluable for leaders looking to drive change within their organizations.<br><br>**Blog Descriptions:**<br>1. **Purpose:** This blog emphasizes the foundational role of purpose in organizational transformation. It uses compelling narratives to illustrate how a clear and inspiring purpose can significantly influence employee motivation and overall project success.<br>2. **Leadership:** Leadership is portrayed as a pivotal element in transformation. The blog highlights how authentic leadership can foster change by shaping a culture that aligns with the organization's goals.<br>3. **Empowerment:** Focusing on empowerment, this entry discusses how giving teams autonomy and confidence can lead to remarkable outcomes, enhancing innovation and efficiency.<br>4. **Alignment:** The importance of alignment with the organization's mission and vision is explored. The blog explains how strategic alignment ensures that every effort contributes positively to the overarching objectives.<br>5. **Speed:** Here, the focus is on the necessity of speed in today's fast-paced business environment. The blog argues that the ability to act quickly is a critical competitive advantage that can determine the success or failure of transformation efforts.<br>6. **Execution:** The final blog in the series addresses execution, stressing that even the best-laid plans require effective implementation to achieve desired results. It discusses strategies to ensure that execution is as flawless as the vision itself.<br><br>These blogs serve as a masterclass in organizational transformation, offering wisdom that is both profound and practical. They are a must-read for any business leader or manager involved in guiding their organization through change. |

[1] The attached file contained PDFs of the blog posts by Prasad Kodukula available at: https://kodukula.com/kodukula-blog/.

[2] We have not assigned a role (e.g., you are an experienced project manager) in the prompt because this is part of an ongoing chat where the role was already assigned in a previous prompt. (We have taken the same approach for many of the prompts of the other use cases presented in this book.)

Gen AI streamlines summarizing extensive reports, allowing project managers to quickly distill large volumes of information. This capability is crucial for rapid decision making based on complex data. By inputting reports, users obtain tailored summaries highlighting key points, ensuring stakeholders stay informed without navigating dense documentation. As with many other use cases, effectiveness depends on the clarity of prompts and document quality, requiring well-structured inputs and clear definitions of needed insights for precise outputs.

## 4. GENERATING TEMPLATES

The utility of Gen AI extends significantly to the creation of standardized templates. With repetitive tasks marking a considerable portion of a project manager's workload, the ability to swiftly generate templates for essential documents is invaluable. Templates for project charters, risk registers, communication plans, procurement strategies, and more can be easily produced. This automation saves time and ensures consistency and adherence to best practices across projects.

Table 5.4 exemplifies this capability, showcasing how a simple prompt to an LLM can result in a well-structured project plan template. With a simple prompt, project managers can obtain a foundational document that can be customized and filled in for specific projects. This process streamlines document preparation and encourages standardization and quality control. It is a testament to how Gen AI can transform administrative tasks, freeing project managers to focus on strategic decision making and leadership. The efficiency gained here is not merely in terms of time but also in the elevation of project documentation quality, contributing to the overall success of project management endeavors. It is important to mention that every time you run the prompt, the results will be slightly different; therefore, applying PRIME to the prompt is necessary if you want more repeatable results.

**Table 5.4** Use case for generating templates: project plan

| Prompt |
|---|
| You are an experienced project manager. I need you to develop a generic project plan template so I can use it for my future project plans. It should contain blank fields so I can fill them with proper information. Please provide instructions on what to include in each section. Present the template in a compact fashion as a table. |
| **Response** |
| Here is a compact and structured project plan template that you can adapt and use for your future projects. It includes blank fields and instructions to guide you in filling out each section. Tables are used to organize information efficiently. |

**1. Project Overview**

| Field | Description |
|---|---|
| Project Title | [Enter the title of the project] |
| Project Manager | [Your name and contact information] |
| Start Date | [Projected start date of the project] |
| End Date | [Projected end date of the project] |
| Objectives | [Briefly outline the key objectives of the project] |
| Scope | [Define the scope: what is included and excluded in the project] |

*Continued*

**Table 5.4** *continued*

**2. Project Team**

| Role | Name | Responsibilities | Contact Information |
|---|---|---|---|
| [e.g., Developer] | [Fill in] | [Detail the responsibilities] | [Fill in] |
| [e.g., Designer] | [Fill in] | [Detail the responsibilities] | [Fill in] |

**3. Stakeholders Analysis**

| Stakeholder | Interest | Influence | Communication Plan |
|---|---|---|---|
| [Name/Group] | [High/Medium/Low] | [High/Medium/Low] | [How will they be kept informed?] |

**4. Project Schedule**

| Task ID | Task Description | Start Date | End Date | Dependencies | Assigned To |
|---|---|---|---|---|---|
| 1 | [Task description] | [Date] | [Date] | [Task ID/s] | [Team member] |
| 2 | [Task description] | [Date] | [Date] | [Task ID/s] | [Team member] |

**5. Budget**

| Item | Estimated Cost | Actual Cost | Variance |
|---|---|---|---|
| [e.g., Software] | [$ Amount] | [$ Amount] | [$ Difference] |
| [e.g., Hardware] | [$ Amount] | [$ Amount] | [$ Difference] |

**6. Risk Management**

| Risk ID | Risk Description | Probability | Impact | Mitigation Strategies |
|---|---|---|---|---|
| 1 | [Describe risk] | [High/Medium/Low] | [High/Medium/Low] | [Describe mitigation strategies] |
| 2 | [Describe risk] | [High/Medium/Low] | [High/Medium/Low] | [Describe mitigation strategies] |

**7. Communication Plan**

| Audience | Frequency | Method | Purpose |
|---|---|---|---|
| [e.g., Team] | [e.g., Weekly] | [e.g., Meeting] | [Primary reasons] |
| [e.g., Stakeholders] | [e.g., Monthly] | [e.g., Email] | [Primary reasons] |

**8. Approval**

| Approval Authority | Signature | Date |
|---|---|---|
| [Name] | [Sign here] | [Date] |

*Continued*

**Table 5.4** *continued*

**Instructions for Use:**

- **Project Overview:** Clearly define what the project will achieve and outline the boundaries of what will be done.
- **Project Team:** List all key participants in the project along with their roles, responsibilities, and contact information.
- **Stakeholders Analysis:** Identify all stakeholders, their interest, influence, and how they will be communicated with throughout the project.
- **Project Schedule:** Detail all major tasks, their start and end dates, dependencies, and assignments.
- **Budget:** Prepare an itemized list of all costs anticipated and track actual expenses to monitor any variances.
- **Risk Management:** Identify potential risks, their likelihood, potential impact, and strategies for mitigation.
- **Communication Plan:** Specify how often you will communicate with the project team and other stakeholders, what methods will be used, and the main purpose of communication.
- **Approval:** Document approvals needed for the project to proceed.

Feel free to modify this template to better fit your specific project needs and the methodologies you follow.

## 5. ANALYZING DATA

Let us now turn our attention to the capabilities of LLMs like ChatGPT for data analysis tasks. While the use of LLMs for parsing spreadsheets and datasets is an exciting frontier, it is important to approach this tool with a clear understanding of its current limitations. To engage LLMs for data analysis, you must often have a subscription to access advanced features, which might include the handling of file attachments. Yet, even with these advanced features, LLMs may not excel at analyzing extensive datasets.

You may encounter issues such as *network* errors or receive outputs with inaccuracies since these models are still evolving their competency in complex data interpretation. We have often observed errors even with simple calculations involving summating a set of numbers. For more reliable outcomes, specificity and validation of results using another approach (e.g., Excel calculation) are key when engaging an LLM to analyze data. General prompts like "Analyze this dataset" are less likely to yield valuable insights. Instead of giving broad instructions, you need to be specific with your queries. For instance, request the LLM to "Calculate the variance between baseline and actual costs of project tasks completed to date" or "Compare the net present value of the projects in the portfolio and rank them accordingly." These targeted questions help the LLM to home in on the specific data points that are most relevant to your queries.

Here are a few additional recommendations for crafting prompts for data analysis in alignment with the PRIME model and the strategies for crafting effective prompts discussed in Chapter 4:

1. *Preprocess the data*: Ensure your data is clean, well-organized, and clearly labeled before input since this can significantly impact the LLM's ability to interpret and analyze the information.
2. *Segment the analysis*: Break down complex data into smaller segments. Analyze parts of the data in separate queries to avoid overwhelming the model and improve the accuracy of each step of the analysis.

3. *Validate results*: Cross-verify the AI's conclusions with known benchmarks or through manual checks. Given the possibility of errors, independent validation is crucial. In addition, validate the AI's interpretation by following up with a prompt: "Explain the rationale for reaching this particular value."
4. *Utilize visualizations*: Request the LLM to generate or suggest graphical representations of data, such as charts or graphs. For example: "Create a bar chart showing monthly expenses for each project."
5. *Iterate*: Use the responses from the LLM to refine your queries further. If the results are unsatisfactory, adjust the prompt iteratively based on the output until the desired clarity is achieved.
6. *Document assumptions*: Have the LLM list any assumptions it made during the analysis. Understanding these assumptions is key to interpreting the results correctly.
7. *Leverage descriptive analytics*: Start with prompts that ask the LLM to describe the dataset, providing summaries and basic statistical descriptions, which can form a solid base for more in-depth analysis.
8. *Specify the technique of analysis*: Direct the AI to employ statistical methods that are appropriate for your data. For example, instruct the LLM to "Utilize regression analysis to identify factors influencing project timelines based on historical data." This ensures that the AI applies the correct analytical approach to your query.
9. *Request actionable insights*: Instead of seeking broad observations, ask the AI to "identify the top three most common reasons for project delays" to provide actionable information.

To illustrate the Gen AI application for data analysis, we prepared a simple spreadsheet, as shown in Table 5.5. This table presents a distilled overview of a kitchen renovation project, charting tasks against their baseline schedules and associated costs, and captures a snapshot of the project's progress a few days after it started. To keep the schedule simple, we made the predecessor/successor relationships of the tasks as *finish-to-start*. Furthermore, the tasks are scheduled in a *serial* order without *parallel* tasks. Table 5.6 shows the specific prompt deployed to engage the LLM for data analysis, along with the outcomes it generated. In addition, Figures 5.1 and 5.2 present the bar charts ChatGPT produced, showing a comparison of baseline vs. actual task costs and durations, respectively.

While leveraging Gen AI for data analysis presents groundbreaking potential, our experiences revealed some issues that are essential to consider. We encountered several challenges, even with the simple project used here for illustrative purposes, where we employed simple *finish-to-start* task relationships and avoided parallel tasks and multiple *paths* of tasks. Achieving precise and meaningful outputs from AI, particularly in more complex data scenarios, requires a strategic and methodical approach to prompt engineering.

The initial attempts to extract the bottom-line results from AI using simplistic, broad queries often resulted in inaccurate and, at times, meaningless responses. This inefficacy prompted a more detailed strategy where queries were broken down into simpler, sequential steps. This approach not only improved the clarity of the queries but also enhanced the accuracy of the AI's responses, helping us navigate toward the final desired outcomes with greater precision.

One notable issue encountered was the AI system's inability to interpret the input data with high accuracy. This challenge was partly overcome by meticulously formatting the input data—ensuring rows, columns, and data points were clearly labeled and organized. Such structuring was crucial for the AI to process the information correctly and produce reliable outputs.

Even with well-structured inputs, the verification of AI-generated results against manual calculations was indispensable. Surprisingly, the AI struggled with basic arithmetic operations, such as

**Table 5.5** Kitchen renovation project data

| Task No. | Task | Predecessor Task | Baseline Duration (days) | Actual Duration (days) | Delay in Starting the Task (days) | Baseline Cost ($) | Actual Cost ($) | Task Started | % Complete |
|---|---|---|---|---|---|---|---|---|---|
| 1 | Initiate project | — | 2 | 2 | 0 | $500 | $500 | Yes | 100% |
| 2 | Design layout | 1 | 3 | 3 | 0 | $2,000 | $1,500 | Yes | 100% |
| 3 | Demolish structure | 2 | 5 | 6 | 2 | $1,000 | $1,200 | Yes | 100% |
| 4 | Repair structure | 3 | 5 | 5 | 0 | $1,500 | $1,800 | Yes | 100% |
| 5 | Update wiring | 4 | 3 | 2 | 0 | $1,500 | $1,500 | Yes | 100% |
| 6 | Install flooring | 5 | 5 | 5 | 0 | $3,500 | $4,000 | Yes | 100% |
| 7 | Mount cabinets | 6 | 4 | | | $4,000 | | No | 0% |
| 8 | Place appliances | 7 | 3 | | | $6,000 | | No | 0% |
| 9 | Apply finishes | 8 | 2 | | | $2,000 | | No | 0% |
| 10 | Close project | 9 | 1 | | | $500 | | No | 0% |

**Table 5.6** Use case for summarizing data: kitchen renovation project

| Prompt |
|---|
| From the attached file,[1] please calculate the following metrics. No need to be longwinded in describing all the steps; only the results are needed.<br>A. What is the baseline duration (workdays) for the project?<br>B. What is the baseline duration for the tasks completed to date (earned time)? Use the % Complete column as a reference.<br>C. What is the baseline cost for the project?<br>D. What is the baseline cost for the tasks completed to date (earned value)?<br>E. What is the actual time? (How many workdays have passed since the start of the project, including any delay in starting a task?)<br>F. What is the actual cost?<br>G. What is the schedule variance? B – E<br>H. What is the schedule efficiency? B/E<br>I. What is the cost variance? D – F<br>J. What is the cost efficiency? D/F<br>K. Cost comparison graph: A bar chart with 2 series—baseline cost and actual cost, with the task names as the X-axis. Use a multi-series graphic, not a stacked one. Data series should be black and gray. The graphic should not include a title or grid lines. Include the Y-axis line and the label "Cost, $."<br>L. Schedule comparison graph: A bar chart with 2 series—baseline duration and actual duration, with the task names as the X-axis. Use a multi-series graphic, not a stacked one. Data series should be black and gray. The graphic should not include a title or grid lines. Include the Y-axis line and the label "Duration, days." |
| **Response** |
| Here are the calculated metrics for the project:<br>A. Baseline duration for the project: 33 workdays<br>B. Baseline duration for tasks completed to date (earned time): 23 workdays<br>C. Baseline cost for the project: $22,500<br>D. Baseline cost for tasks completed to date (earned value): $10,000<br>E. Actual time (total workdays passed considering the delay): 25 days<br>F. Actual cost: $10,500<br>G. Schedule Variance (B – E): –2 days (behind schedule)<br>H. Schedule Efficiency (B/E): 0.92 (92% efficient)<br>I. Cost Variance (D – F): –$500 (over budget)<br>J. Cost Efficiency (D/F): 0.952 (95.2% efficient)<br><br>These values provide insights into the project's performance relative to the planned timeline and budget. Here are the two graphs:<br>1. Cost comparison graph:[2] This bar chart compares the baseline cost to the actual cost for each task in the project. The x-axis shows the task names, while the y-axis represents the costs.<br>2. Schedule comparison graph:[3] This bar chart compares the baseline duration to the actual duration for each task. The x-axis lists the task names and the y-axis shows the duration in days. |

[1] Please see Table 5.5.
[2] Please see Figure 5.1.
[3] Please see Figure 5.2.

summing the baseline costs in a project. These discrepancies highlighted the limitations of AI in handling numerical data effectively. To counteract this, we had to provide explicit formulas within the prompts to guide the AI, ensuring it applied the correct computational methods.

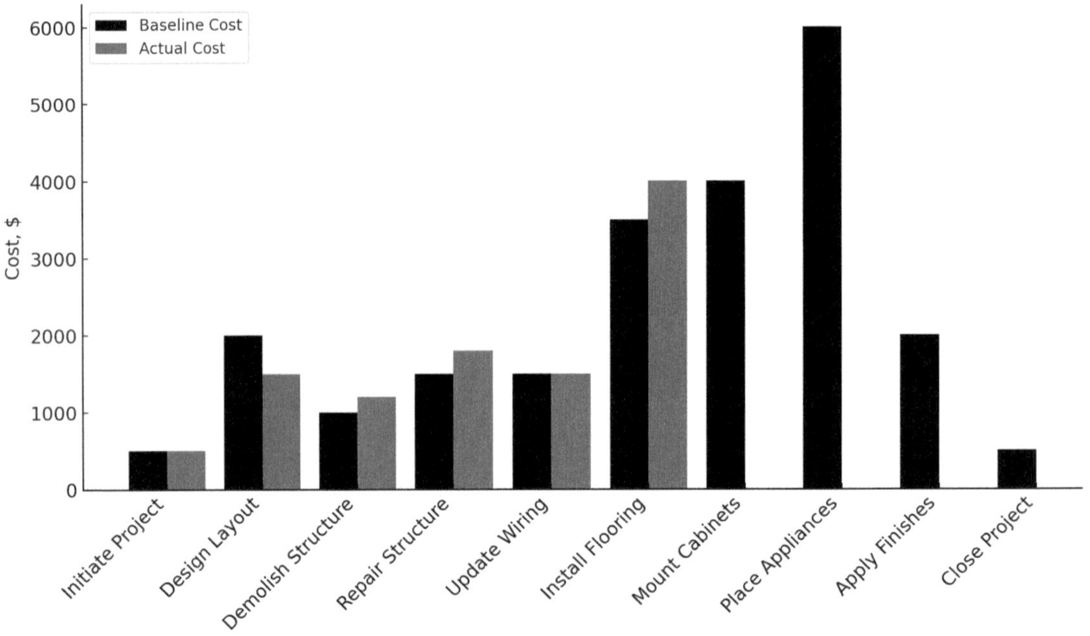


**Figure 5.1** Comparison of baseline vs. actual task costs

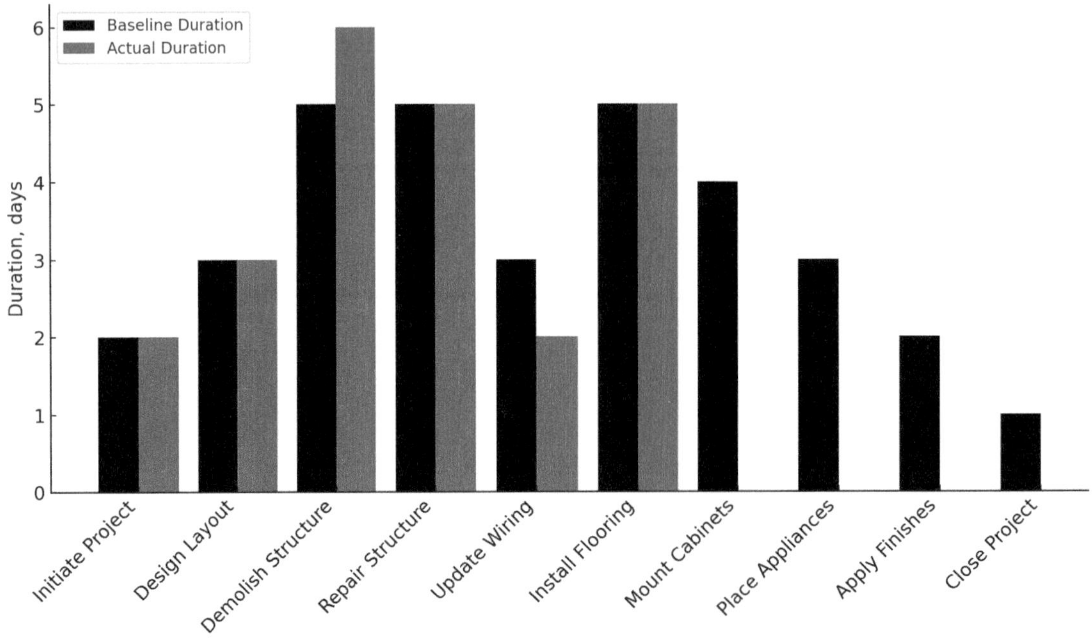


**Figure 5.2** Comparison of baseline vs. actual task durations

Our experience also underscored the differential capabilities of various LLMs. While ChatGPT excelled in textual interpretation and analysis, its proficiency in numeric data processing was limited. Other LLMs, like Claude, showed slightly better performance in numerical analysis but still fell short of delivering consistently accurate results.

This practical insight leads to a broader recommendation for AI users: the need for meticulous prompt engineering. As outlined in our PRIME methodology, it is crucial to prepare your prompts with detailed context, relay them in a structured and straightforward manner, inspect the responses for accuracy, modify the prompts or inputs as necessary, and execute the analysis while being prepared for iterative refinement.

In sum, while AI offers transformative potential for data analysis in project management, its current limitations necessitate a proactive and detailed approach in crafting prompts and interpreting outputs. Keeping these experiences in mind, users are better positioned to harness AI effectively, adapting their strategies to align with the evolving capabilities of AI technologies.

## IN CONCLUSION

Throughout this chapter, we have showcased a selection of use cases demonstrating how LLMs can streamline the daily repetitive tasks that project managers and their teams frequently handle. By detailing specific examples, we have illuminated the practical ways in which LLMs can enhance efficiency and productivity in project management. The provided examples are but a glimpse into the myriad possibilities; countless other applications await those who seek to leverage this technology further. While the scope of this book allows us to present only a handful of scenarios, we invite you to explore additional examples and extend your learning through our book's website, which can be found at www.pmaihandbook.com.

Section 2 of this book, AI in Portfolio Management, consists of Chapters 6 and 7. There we will explore the application of Gen AI tools for managing project portfolios.

SECTION 2

*AI in Portfolio Management*

# 6

# PROJECT PORTFOLIO MANAGEMENT ESSENTIALS

In the dynamic landscape of modern business, the effective management of project portfolios stands as a cornerstone for organizational success. Project portfolio management (PPM) serves as the strategic compass guiding businesses through the complexities of project selection, prioritization, and execution. In this chapter, we introduce the basics of portfolio management before delving into the application of artificial intelligence (AI) tools.

Defined as the centralized management of a collection of projects to achieve strategic objectives, PPM encapsulates a multifaceted approach to project governance. It encompasses a range of processes, methodologies, and tools used to select the right projects for investment, optimizing resource allocation, mitigating risks, and maximizing returns on investment. As we probe into the intricacies of PPM, we begin by providing a comprehensive overview of its definition and fundamental principles.

Central to our exploration is an examination of the pivotal functions of PPM, each serving as a vital cog in the machinery of project governance. From project selection and prioritization to resource allocation and performance monitoring, these functions collectively drive the strategic direction of an organization's project portfolio.

As we navigate through the landscape of PPM, we unveil the potential of AI in revolutionizing traditional portfolio management practices. AI, with its capacity for data analysis, pattern recognition, and predictive modeling, emerges as a powerful ally in the quest for portfolio management. We explore generative AI (Gen AI) tools tailored to enhance decision making, streamline processes, and unlock actionable insights within the realm of PPM.

Furthermore, we delve into the critical role of input data in fueling AI applications within PPM. From organizational strategic frameworks to project descriptions and financial benchmarks, the quality and quantity of input data play a pivotal role in shaping the efficacy of AI-driven solutions. We dissect the key components of input data and their implications for AI-driven decision-making processes.

## DEFINITION AND OVERVIEW

At its core, PPM is the strategic management process that enables organizations to prioritize, govern, and execute a portfolio of projects in alignment with their strategic objectives. It encompasses the systematic evaluation, selection, and optimization of projects to achieve desired outcomes while effectively managing resources, risks, and constraints.

PPM transcends the traditional approach of managing individual projects in isolation, offering a holistic framework that enables organizations to visualize, prioritize, and optimize their project portfolios to maximize value creation and drive sustainable growth. By providing a structured methodology for decision making and resource allocation, PPM empowers organizations to navigate complexities, seize opportunities, and mitigate risks in an ever-evolving business landscape.

## IMPORTANCE OF PPM IN ORGANIZATIONAL SUCCESS

The significance of PPM in organizational success cannot be overstated. PPM serves as the linchpin that aligns projects with overarching business objectives, ensuring that every endeavor contributes to the realization of strategic goals. Here is why PPM is indispensable (Kodukula, 2014):

1. *Change management*: PPM facilitates effective change management by providing a structured approach to initiate, plan, and execute strategic initiatives, fostering organizational agility and adaptability in response to market dynamics.
2. *Strategic alignment*: By aligning projects with strategic objectives, PPM ensures that resources are invested in initiatives that create tangible value and drive sustainable growth, fostering a culture of strategic focus and alignment across the organization.
3. *Value creation*: PPM enables organizations to optimize resource allocation and prioritize projects based on their potential to generate value, thereby maximizing return on investment and enhancing shareholder value.
4. *Value balancing*: PPM facilitates the balancing of short-term goals with long-term objectives, ensuring that the portfolio reflects a judicious mix of projects that deliver immediate benefits while laying the foundation for future growth and innovation.
5. *Long-term risk management*: PPM enables proactive identification and mitigation of risks across the project portfolio, safeguarding against potential threats and ensuring resilience in the face of uncertainty.
6. *Efficient resource allocation*: PPM enables organizations to allocate resources strategically, ensuring that talent, capital, and other critical resources are deployed to projects that deliver the greatest value and impact, thereby maximizing efficiency and productivity.

## KEY FUNCTIONS OF PPM

PPM serves as a bridge between the organizational strategy and the projects in the portfolio. It encompasses a set of key functions that collectively enable organizations to prioritize, manage, and monitor projects effectively. From strategic alignment to project prioritization and resource management to risk mitigation, each function plays a critical role in ensuring that projects contribute to the achievement of organizational goals. By executing these functions systematically and strategically, organizations can enhance decision-making processes, optimize resource utilization, and drive sustainable growth and success in an increasingly complex and dynamic business environment. A list of key functions follows:

1. *Strategic alignment*: Strategic alignment ensures that projects within the portfolio align with organizational strategy, goals, and priorities. By aligning projects with strategic goals, organizations can ensure that resources are invested in initiatives that contribute effectively to achieving those goals.
2. *Project prioritization*: Project prioritization involves evaluating and ranking potential projects based on their alignment with strategic objectives, potential value, and resource requirements. By prioritizing projects strategically, organizations can optimize resource allocation, mitigate risks, and maximize the overall value of the project portfolio.
3. *Resource management*: Resource management entails effectively allocating and managing resources, including capital, personnel, and equipment, across various projects within the portfolio. By optimizing resource utilization, organizations can ensure that projects have the necessary resources to succeed while avoiding resource shortages or overallocation.
4. *Risk management*: Risk management involves identifying, assessing, and mitigating risks associated with individual projects and the overall project portfolio. By proactively managing risks, organizations can minimize the likelihood of project failures, mitigate potential impacts, and enhance overall portfolio resilience.
5. *Performance monitoring*: Performance monitoring involves tracking and evaluating the progress, performance, and outcomes of projects within the portfolio. By monitoring project performance metrics, organizations can identify deviations from planned targets, address issues promptly, and make informed decisions to optimize project outcomes.
6. *Decision support*: Decision support provides stakeholders with the information, insights, and tools needed to make informed decisions about project selection, prioritization, and resource allocation. By providing decision makers with timely and accurate data, organizations can enhance decision-making processes and optimize the overall performance of the project portfolio.

## AI TOOLS IN PPM

The integration of AI tools in PPM has emerged as a transformative force, empowering organizations to maximize value creation. AI tools, encompassing a diverse array of technologies, offer innovative solutions to complex challenges faced in PPM. By leveraging AI, organizations can analyze vast amounts of project data, identify patterns and trends, and make informed decisions to drive strategic success and competitiveness. In this dynamic environment, the strategic adoption of AI tools in PPM represents a paradigm shift, enabling organizations to enhance decision-making processes, improve portfolio performance, and achieve sustainable growth and success. The following list describes some of the AI tools commonly used in PPM:

- *Machine learning algorithms*: Machine learning (ML) algorithms, such as regression, classification, clustering, and neural networks, play a crucial role in PPM by analyzing project data, identifying patterns, and making predictions. These algorithms can predict project outcomes and success, assess risks, and optimize resource allocation. By learning from historical project data, ML algorithms can provide valuable insights into project performance, enabling organizations to make data-driven decisions and enhance portfolio management processes. Moreover, ML algorithms can automate repetitive tasks, such as project scoring and prioritization, freeing up valuable time for portfolio managers and stakeholders to focus on strategic decision making.

- *Natural language processing*: Natural language processing (NLP) techniques enable AI systems to analyze and interpret unstructured text data, such as project descriptions, reports, and stakeholder feedback. In PPM, NLP can extract key insights from project documents, identify project risks and opportunities, and facilitate stakeholder engagement. By analyzing project-related text data, NLP algorithms can identify trends, sentiments, and themes, enabling organizations to gain a deeper understanding of project dynamics and stakeholder perspectives. Additionally, NLP can enhance communication and collaboration among project teams by facilitating the exchange of information and ideas in a structured and efficient manner.
- *Semantic analysis*: AI can perform semantic analysis to understand the context and meaning of project descriptions in relation to strategic objectives. By analyzing the semantics of words and phrases, AI can discern subtle nuances and implications that may impact strategic fit assessment.
- *Predictive analytics*: Predictive analytics leverages statistical algorithms and ML techniques to forecast future project outcomes, identify potential risks, and optimize resource allocation. In PPM, predictive analytics can be used to anticipate project delays, budget overruns, and resource shortages, allowing organizations to take proactive measures to mitigate risks and ensure project success. By analyzing historical project data and identifying patterns and correlations, predictive analytics algorithms can provide valuable insights into project performance and help organizations make informed decisions about project selection, prioritization, and resource allocation. Additionally, predictive analytics can enable organizations to optimize project schedules, budgets, and resource allocations to maximize value creation and minimize risk.
- *Optimization models*: Optimization models, such as linear programming, integer programming, and genetic algorithms, play a critical role in PPM by identifying the most efficient allocation of resources across projects to maximize portfolio value. These models can consider various constraints and objectives, such as project dependencies, resource availability, and strategic priorities, to recommend optimal portfolio configurations. By leveraging optimization techniques, organizations can optimize resource utilization, minimize costs, and maximize returns on investment. Additionally, optimization models can help organizations evaluate alternative scenarios and make informed decisions about project selection, prioritization, and resource allocation, enabling them to achieve their strategic objectives more effectively.
- *Visualization and dashboards*: AI-powered visualization tools can generate interactive dashboards and visual representations of portfolio analysis. This allows stakeholders to gain insights at a glance, explore relationships between projects and strategic objectives, and make data-driven decisions more effectively.
- *Decision support systems*: Decision support systems (DSS) integrate AI technologies, such as ML, NLP, and predictive analytics, to provide stakeholders with the information, insights, and tools needed to make informed decisions about PPM. These systems can analyze project data, identify trends and patterns, and recommend optimal courses of action to stakeholders. By providing decision makers with timely and accurate information, DSS

enable organizations to optimize resource allocation, mitigate risks, and maximize portfolio value. Additionally, DSS can facilitate collaboration and communication among project teams, stakeholders, and decision makers, enhancing decision-making processes and improving overall portfolio performance.

## PPM INPUT DATA FOR AI APPLICATIONS

Preparing input information for AI models in PPM is crucial for ensuring the effectiveness and accuracy of the AI outputs. The value of AI outputs is directly dependent on the quantity and quality of the input data provided to the models. While large language models (LLMs), like ChatGPT, are trained on publicly available information, they lack access to an organization's specific data and context. Therefore, organizations must proactively prepare and provide relevant input information to enable AI tools to make informed decisions and recommendations.

In the context of the PRIME (prepare, relay, inspect, modify, execute) model introduced in Chapter 4, the *prepare* step is foundational in setting the stage for successful AI-driven PPM. During this stage, organizations must gather and organize a wide range of input data, including the organizational strategic framework, project descriptions, benefit/cost estimates, resource constraints, and so on. This comprehensive input information serves as the building blocks for LLMs to effectively analyze and evaluate projects within the portfolio.

Failure to provide sufficient and accurate input information can lead to suboptimal outcomes and unreliable recommendations from AI tools. Without access to key data, AI models may struggle to assess project viability, prioritize initiatives, and optimize resource allocation properly. Consequently, decision makers may make ill-informed decisions, leading to project failures, resource wastage, and missed opportunities for value creation.

Therefore, organizations must prioritize the *prepare* step of the PRIME model by dedicating resources and efforts to collect, validate, and organize input data for AI-driven PPM. By investing in data preparation and ensuring the availability of high-quality input information, organizations can unlock the full potential of AI tools to drive strategic decision making, optimize portfolio performance, and achieve organizational objectives in PPM.

In the following sections, we will probe into each key function of PPM and highlight the critical importance of preparing input data for optimal AI-driven decision making. We will demonstrate why it is essential to gather and provide key input information for each PPM function, explaining the significance of various data points and their role in informing AI tools. By understanding what input data is needed, why it is necessary, and how it is utilized by AI tools, you will gain insights into the underlying mechanisms that drive the generation of actionable insights and recommendations in PPM.

### Strategic Framework

To effectively evaluate the strategic fit of a project, AI tools require a comprehensive understanding of the organization's strategic framework (in other words, the *big picture*), including its mission, vision, values, and strategy. This information serves as the foundation for assessing how well a project aligns with the overarching goals and objectives of the organization. The mission defines the purpose of the organization by answering the question of *why* it exists and the *impact* it seeks to make. The vision outlines what the organization aspires to achieve in the future, providing a clear picture of its desired outcomes. Values represent the principles and beliefs that guide the organization's actions and decisions, shaping its culture and identity. Finally, the strategy delineates how the organization plans to achieve its mission and vision, outlining the steps and approaches it will take to realize its goals. It should be noted here that AI tools can also assist you in articulating that strategic framework.

AI tools need to be informed of any changes in the organizational strategy and goals on a continuous basis. It is common for executives to adjust strategies and objectives in response to external market demands, economic conditions, and leadership transitions. By staying abreast of these changes, AI models can dynamically evaluate the strategic fit of projects within the portfolio and provide timely recommendations. As the organizational strategic framework evolves, AI tools can alert stakeholders to projects that no longer align with the updated objectives, enabling them to make informed decisions about project continuation or termination based on strategic alignment.

## Project Descriptions

In evaluating the strategic alignment of a project, it is imperative for LLMs to possess comprehensive knowledge about the project itself. Without a deep understanding of the project's objectives, scope, and specifics, LLMs would be unable to assess its alignment with organizational strategy and goals effectively. Key information about the project, such as its purpose, objectives, deliverables, stakeholders, and potential risks, is essential for LLMs to gauge its strategic fit within the broader organizational context. Additionally, LLMs require insights into the project's timeline, budget, and resource requirements to evaluate its feasibility and alignment with strategic priorities.

Furthermore, LLMs need access to project descriptions that provide detailed information about the project's scope, anticipated benefits, and potential challenges. By analyzing project descriptions, LLMs can identify how the project contributes to the achievement of organizational objectives and determine whether it aligns with the overarching strategic direction of the organization. Moreover, understanding the context and rationale behind the project, including the drivers for its initiation and the anticipated outcomes, allows LLMs to assess its strategic relevance and potential impact on the organization's long-term goals.

## Benefit/Cost Data

In evaluating project viability and informing strategic decision making, one crucial aspect is conducting a comprehensive benefit/cost analysis. As part of this analysis, you must provide data on the projected benefits and costs associated with each project. This includes estimates of expected annual cash flows, which are essential inputs for calculating key financial metrics such as benefit-cost ratio, internal rate of return, net present value, and payback period. By incorporating these financial metrics, LLMs can assist in assessing the feasibility and attractiveness of investment opportunities, guiding decision makers in determining the optimal allocation of resources across the project portfolio.

Furthermore, organizations must provide investment benchmarks, such as the minimum acceptable rate of return or hurdle rates, maximum acceptable payback period, and any other relevant benchmarks. These benchmarks serve as criteria for evaluating the financial attractiveness and feasibility of investment opportunities, guiding decision makers in assessing whether projects meet the organization's investment criteria and strategic objectives. By incorporating these benchmarks into the analysis, LLMs can provide more accurate and relevant insights to stakeholders, facilitating more informed decision making in PPM.

Additionally, ongoing updates to benefit forecasts and cost performance data are vital inputs for LLMs in providing real-time insights into project performance and financial viability. As organizations adjust benefit forecasts or encounter deviations in cost performance from initial estimates,

LLMs can dynamically incorporate these changes and update financial metrics accordingly. This continuous monitoring and updating process enables stakeholders to make timely and informed decisions regarding project continuation or termination, ensuring that resources are allocated efficiently and projects align with strategic objectives.

## Resources

In preparing input data for LLMs to accomplish portfolio management tasks, it is essential to provide information about organizational resources and their constraints. Resources include investment capital, talent, personnel, equipment, facilities, and more. It is common for project demands to exceed the available resources within an organization. In such scenarios, AI tools play a critical role in balancing project needs with resource constraints by optimizing resource allocation across the project portfolio.

Given the limited availability of capital and human resources, organizations must prioritize projects based on their expected returns and alignment with strategic objectives. Optimization models and algorithms enable AI-driven tools to identify the most effective combination of projects that yield the highest return on investment while adhering to resource constraints. For instance, in a portfolio with numerous projects, the number of possible combinations can quickly become overwhelming. With AI-driven optimization models, organizations can efficiently evaluate and recommend project combinations that maximize value creation.

Consider a scenario where an organization has 20 projects in its portfolio. The number of potential combinations of projects, or portfolios, exceeds one million (2 to the power of 20), showcasing the complexity of portfolio optimization. If the organization increases the number of projects to 30, the possible combinations grow to over one billion (2 to the power of 30). AI-driven optimization models are indispensable in selecting the optimal combination.

Moreover, while optimization models are typically applied to projects generating financial returns, AI tools can also assist in prioritizing projects that yield nonfinancial value, such as process improvements or quality enhancements. Scoring models can rank these projects based on predefined criteria, allowing organizations to create portfolios that align with strategic objectives and maximize overall value. By leveraging AI-driven approaches, organizations can make data-driven decisions, optimize resource utilization, and achieve better outcomes in PPM.

## Evaluation Criteria

Defining evaluation criteria is pivotal for effectively assessing the merits of projects within the portfolio. While AI can autonomously select criteria for project evaluation, organizations often benefit from specifying the project characteristics they prioritize. These criteria may include strategic fit, profitability, risk mitigation, resource allocation, and alignment with organizational objectives. Additionally, AI-powered tools can leverage visual capabilities to generate intuitive visuals, such as heatmaps, bubble charts, or matching diagrams, that help stakeholders interpret project evaluations more effectively. By outlining preferred evaluation criteria as part of input data, organizations ensure that AI-driven tools align with their strategic priorities and decision-making frameworks.

Furthermore, organizations may employ weighted scoring models to provide a structured approach to project evaluation. Weighted scoring assigns importance to each evaluation criterion by specifying percentage weightage factors. These factors sum up to 100%, reflecting the relative significance of each criterion in the decision-making process. AI tools utilize these weightage factors to calculate scores for individual projects, considering their performance across various evaluation criteria. Subsequently, projects are ranked based on their scores, enabling stakeholders to prioritize projects that best align with organizational goals and objectives.

By incorporating evaluation criteria and weighted scoring models into the input data provided to AI tools, organizations streamline the project evaluation process and ensure consistency and transparency in decision making. This approach empowers stakeholders to make informed choices regarding project selection and resource allocation, ultimately enhancing the strategic alignment and performance of the project portfolio.

## IN CONCLUSION

This chapter underscored the pivotal role of PPM in steering organizations toward strategic success. As we prepare to explore the impact of AI in PPM in Chapter 7, it is evident that the integration of AI, coupled with robust input data, will be instrumental in revolutionizing traditional practices and unlocking new realms of efficiency and strategic alignment.

In Chapter 7, we unveil many of the previously mentioned AI applications showcasing project evaluation, categorization, prioritization, optimization, and selection, among others. These use cases are presented to offer valuable insights into the transformative potential of AI in driving portfolio success. Through real-world examples and practical illustrations, we illuminate the path toward harnessing AI for optimal PPM.

# 7

# AI USE CASES IN PORTFOLIO MANAGEMENT

The integration of artificial intelligence (AI) into project portfolio management (PPM) has opened transformative opportunities for improving efficiency, strategic alignment, and decision making. By leveraging generative AI (Gen AI) tools like ChatGPT, organizations can optimize their project portfolios, ensuring effective resource allocation, risk mitigation, and alignment with strategic goals. This chapter explores key AI use cases in PPM, showcasing how these tools can address critical functions and enhance portfolio management practices.

We begin with the strategic framework, which serves as the foundation for PPM by providing the organizational context necessary for evaluating projects. AI synthesizes complex strategic data, presenting it in a simplified format to support informed decision making. Next, project evaluation comes into focus, where individual projects are assessed for their strategic alignment, benefits vs. costs, and resource requirements. AI tools ensure thorough and unbiased evaluations during this step. AI also supports project categorization, automating the classification of projects into diverse categories—such as revenue generation, customer satisfaction, and operational efficiency improvement—enabling organizations to build balanced and risk-aware portfolios. The chapter then moves to project prioritization, demonstrating three techniques: ranking by metrics, simple scoring models, and weighted scoring models. These approaches help rank projects effectively based on different evaluation criteria. Once projects are ranked, project selection uses AI-powered optimization models to identify the ideal mix of projects that maximize return on investment while accounting for resource constraints. Finally, we explore the efficient frontier, a concept that AI tools use to visualize trade-offs between investment levels and portfolio performance, offering insights into achieving an optimal balance.

Among the many major AI use cases available for PPM (see Table 7.1), in this chapter, we explore seven key applications:

1. *Strategic framework*: AI synthesizes complex strategic data to articulate an organization's strategy and *big picture*
2. *Project evaluation*: AI tools analyze potential benefits, alignment, and resources for individual projects and evaluate their merit for investment
3. *Strategic alignment*: Gen AI tools can assess the strength of the strategic fit for every project in the portfolio
4. *Project categorization*: AI automates the classification of projects into categories for balanced risk management
5. *Project prioritization*: Techniques like straightforward ranking by numbers (metrics), simple scoring models, and weighted scoring models streamline project prioritization

6. *Project selection and optimization*: Optimization models recommend the best project mix within resource constraints
7. *Efficient frontier*: AI visualizes trade-offs between investment levels and expected returns for portfolio optimization

Each use case is illustrated through a case study of GeneMatrix, Corp. (GMX), a fictional biotechnology company. The case study, titled GMX, highlights how Gen AI tools like ChatGPT can streamline complex PPM processes, optimize resource allocation, and enable strategic decision making. By the end of this chapter, you will have gained a detailed understanding of how AI can transform traditional PPM practices and enhance portfolio management capabilities.

**Table 7.1** Major AI use cases for PPM

| Use Case | Description |
|---|---|
| Strategy formulation | Assist in formulating the organizational mission, vision, strategy, and goals |
| Strategic alignment | Analyze organizational goals and objectives and project data to ensure alignment with strategic objectives |
| Project evaluation and prioritization | Evaluate project feasibility, assess risks, and prioritize projects based on their potential value and impact |
| Project categorization | Categorize projects into different groups to create a balanced portfolio across the categories |
| Resource optimization | Optimize resource allocation by analyzing project requirements, team capabilities, and resource availability |
| Risk management | Identify, assess, and mitigate project risks by analyzing historical data, market trends, and risk factors |
| Forecasting | Forecast project outcomes, estimate costs, and predict potential risks and opportunities through AI-powered predictive analytics |
| Portfolio balancing | Balance the project portfolio by considering factors such as project size, complexity, and strategic importance |
| Portfolio optimization | Optimize the portfolio with the right mix of projects, considering various resource constraints and project dependencies using optimization algorithms |
| Project selection | Identify the right mix of projects in different categories to create the optimal portfolio that would yield the highest return |
| Stakeholder engagement | Facilitate stakeholder engagement by analyzing stakeholder feedback, preferences, and priorities |
| Decision support | Provide recommendations and insights to stakeholders to facilitate decision making |
| Performance monitoring | Monitor project performance in real time, identify deviations from planned targets, and suggest corrective actions |
| Continuous improvement | Support continuous improvement efforts by analyzing project outcomes, identifying lessons learned, and recommending process enhancements |
| Success prediction | Predict the success of projects in the portfolio based on project characteristics |

## GENEMATRIX CASE STUDY

The case study of GMX was originally developed by one of the coauthors of this book (Prasad Kodukula), and was described in detail in his previous book on PPM (Kodukula, 2014). He has successfully used this fictional case in several PPM workshops that he conducted in various parts of the world. We have made minor revisions to the case to adapt it to the needs of *this* book. The case centers around a project portfolio that is undergoing the process of streamlining 27 projects within its purview. While the case is fictitious, it draws from the author's experience working in the biotechnology field, ensuring that the scenarios presented are rooted in real-world challenges and considerations. Despite the specific industry focus of the case, the principles underlying the application of AI tools remain universal across various sectors.

Table 7.2 presents a short profile of GMX with a brief description of its products and underlying technology. It is important to note that while certain aspects of the case material may appear highly technical, they reflect the intricate nature of PPM in today's business landscape. Through this case study, we demonstrate how Gen AI tools can be leveraged to navigate complex project portfolios and drive strategic decision making, irrespective of industry vertical.

**Table 7.2** GeneMatrix case study: company profile

| |
|---|
| GeneMatrix, Corp. (GMX) is a San Diego, California-based biotechnology company founded by two MIT molecular biology PhDs, who met at Stanford while doing their executive MBAs. The founders' mission is to save lives and improve quality of life through human genomics, a relatively new science, sparked by the *human genome* project and the exponential growth of computing power. They envision GMX to become the most innovative company in this space. The guiding principles of the company are product innovation, technology excellence, and customer focus. GMX was started in 2020 with seed capital from angel investors and received a series of investments from venture capitalists in the last few years. This year (2024), it is expected to make operating revenues of about $15 million. The company is contemplating an initial public offering in the next few years. |
| **DNA Technology** |
| DNA technology has revolutionized the fields of biology and medicine by providing powerful tools to study and understand genetic information. Two key components of DNA technology are DNA microarrays and DNA sequencers. These tools serve different purposes but can also work together to give a comprehensive understanding of genetic material. |
| **DNA Microarrays** |
| DNA microarrays, also known as DNA chips, are used to study the expression levels of many genes simultaneously. A microarray consists of a small glass slide or silicon chip with thousands of DNA probes arranged in a grid. These probes are specific DNA sequences that can bind to the sample DNA or RNA. During an experiment, labeled samples are added to the microarray, and the binding to probes produces a signal. By measuring these signals, scientists can determine which genes are active and how much they are expressed. This technique is valuable for understanding gene function, detecting genetic variations, and studying how genes respond to different conditions. |
| **DNA Sequencers** |
| DNA sequencers are machines used to determine the exact order of nucleotides (A, T, C, G) in a DNA molecule. This process is called sequencing. By reading the sequence, scientists can understand the genetic instructions that are encoded in an organism's DNA. Sequencers are essential for discovering new genes, identifying genetic mutations, and studying the genetic basis of diseases. They provide detailed and precise genetic information, which is crucial for research, diagnostics, and developing personalized medicine. |

*Continued*

**Table 7.2** *(continued)*

| **DNA Technology *continued*** |
|---|
| **Working in Tandem**<br>DNA sequencers and microarrays can work together to provide a complete picture of genetic information. Sequencers can be used first to discover the exact genetic sequence of an organism. This detailed sequence data can identify specific genes and genetic variations. Once these genes are known, DNA microarrays can be used to study how these genes are expressed in different conditions or stages of development. For example, after sequencing the DNA of a cancer cell to identify mutations, microarrays can analyze how these mutations affect gene expression. This combined approach helps researchers understand both the genetic blueprint and how it functions in real life, leading to better insights into biology and potential treatments for diseases. |
| **GMX's Product Lines** |
| GMX's core competence is in the development of DNA microarrays. It has developed a robust portfolio organized into three main divisions:<br>• *Arrays division*: This division specializes in the design and production of microarrays or gene chips. GMX's flagship product, the AcuChip 1K, is a low-density array with a significant market share. GMX is considering the development of mid-density (AcuChip 10K) and high-density (AcuChip 100K) arrays that promise faster processing of samples and greater throughput, aimed at supporting advanced genetic research and clinical diagnostics.<br>• *Reagents division*: This division supplies essential reagents needed for the preparation of test samples such as blood, oral swabs, or hair. These reagents are critical for extracting and preparing DNA, ensuring samples are ready for detailed genetic analysis.<br>• *Software division*: Creates sophisticated software solutions, such as AcuTrack, to process and analyze the vast amounts of data generated from DNA sequencing. AcuTrack enables extensive data management capabilities, accommodating the complex needs of GMX's diverse clientele. Although the AcuTrack application was created specifically for GMX's arrays, it has been so successful that customers have recently requested its use with products from other array producers. |
| **Customer Base** |
| GMX primarily serves medical testing laboratories, which form the core of its customer base. These labs purchase GMX's arrays and reagents to prepare and analyze genetic samples. Additionally, they utilize GMX's software solutions to manage the large volumes of data generated from the sequencing process. However, these laboratories acquire DNA sequencers separately from other providers. Recognizing this, GMX has established strategic partnerships with various manufacturers of gene sequencers to ensure that their products are compatible with GMX's arrays, reagents, and software, thereby providing a seamless experience for customers. This strategic alignment allows GMX to cater effectively to the needs of medical testing labs, ensuring they receive comprehensive support throughout the genetic testing process. |
| **Strategic Focus and Future Directions** |
| GMX's leadership remains committed to pushing the boundaries of microarray technology and enhancing its partnerships with sequencer manufacturers. The recent strategic planning session identified major goals for the near future: expansion of revenue streams through new product development and entry into emerging markets, increasing customer satisfaction, improving current business processes, and enhancing the skills of project and product managers. |
| **Challenges and Opportunities** |
| Despite its innovative edge, GMX faces challenges such as stiff competition, particularly from cost-effective solutions emerging from China and India, and the fast pace of technological advancement. However, the expanding global market for genomics presents significant opportunities for GMX to leverage its technological leadership to capture new business and continue its path of growth and innovation. |

# 1. STRATEGIC FRAMEWORK

Understanding an organization's strategic framework is paramount for effective PPM. Without this knowledge, portfolio managers cannot accurately assess the strategic fit of project candidates. Similarly, large language models (LLMs) like ChatGPT rely on this strategic context to provide meaningful insights. In this section, we illustrate the use case where ChatGPT synthesizes the strategic framework of GMX and presents it in simplified terms based on the input data provided.

Table 7.2, containing a brief profile of GMX, serves as the foundation for the strategic framework synthesis exercise. Attaching this table to the prompt shown in Table 7.3, we tasked ChatGPT to articulate the organization's strategic framework. Also included in Table 7.3 is the output from the LLM. In line with our request, ChatGPT succinctly summarized the strategic framework in straightforward terms, ensuring ease of understanding for portfolio managers, team members, and other stakeholders. It identified the SMART (specific, measurable, agreed to, realistic, and time-bound) objectives and explained how each objective meets the SMART format. This synthesized strategic framework is a crucial reference point for evaluating how well a project candidate aligns with the organization's overarching strategy and objectives.

**Table 7.3** Use case for delineation of strategic framework

| **Prompt** |
|---|
| The attached file* contains a profile of GeneMatrix, Corp. (GMX). As an experienced strategy consultant, please describe GMX's strategic framework by articulating the company's mission, vision, values, and strategic goals. Also, for each goal, identify two objectives. Make sure the objectives are specific, measurable, agreed-to, realistic, and time-bound. |
| **Response** |
| Based on the detailed profile provided for GeneMatrix, Corp. (GMX), here is a comprehensive description of the company's strategic framework, which includes its mission, vision, values, strategic goals, and specific objectives.<br><br>**Mission**<br>To save lives and enhance the quality of life through groundbreaking advancements in human genomics.<br><br>**Vision**<br>To be recognized as the most innovative biotechnology and DNA sequencing technology leader.<br><br>**Core Values**<br>• *Innovation*: Commitment to pioneering new technologies and improving existing solutions<br>• *Technological excellence*: Upholding the highest standards of quality and effectiveness in all products and services<br>• *Customer focus*: Dedication to understanding and fulfilling the needs of our customers, ensuring their satisfaction and success |

*Continued*

**Table 7.3** *continued*

**Strategic Goals and Objectives**

- **GOAL 1:** Expand revenue streams
  - **Objective 1:** Develop and launch mid-density and high-density DNA microarrays by Q2 2025 to increase product offerings and capture a broader market segment
    - *Specific*: Launch new mid-density and high-density DNA microarrays
    - *Measurable*: Aim to capture an additional 15% of the market share in the high-throughput sequencing market within two years of launch
    - *Agreed to*: Collaboratively set with the R&D and marketing departments
    - *Realistic*: Build on existing technologies with incremental innovations
    - *Time-bound*: Target set for Q2 2025
  - **Objective 2:** Enter at least three new emerging markets by 2026 with tailored marketing strategies for each region
    - *Specific*: Target emerging markets with customized entry strategies
    - *Measurable*: Establish presence and achieve $2 million in sales from these markets by 2026
    - *Agreed to*: Developed in consultation with the international sales and marketing teams
    - *Realistic*: Supported by market research and feasibility studies
    - *Time-bound*: Deadline of 2026
- **GOAL 2:** Enhance customer satisfaction
  - **Objective 1:** Implement a customer feedback and resolution system by Q1 2024 to improve service response times and satisfaction rates
    - *Specific*: Develop and launch a feedback system to track and respond to customer service interactions
    - *Measurable*: Reduce response times by 30% and achieve a customer satisfaction rate of over 90%
    - *Agreed to*: Agreed upon by the customer service and IT departments
    - *Realistic*: Achievable with the planned improvements in IT infrastructure
    - *Time-bound*: Set for implementation by Q1 2024
  - **Objective 2:** Increase customer engagement through quarterly webinars and workshops starting in Q2 2024
    - *Specific*: Host quarterly educational webinars and workshops for customers
    - *Measurable*: Aim to increase customer participation in these events by 50% year over year
    - *Agreed to*: Supported by the marketing and customer support teams
    - *Realistic*: Resources and expertise are available to host these sessions
    - *Time-bound*: Starting from Q2 2024

*Continued*

**Table 7.3** *continued*

- **GOAL 3:** Improve operational efficiency
    - **Objective 1:** Automate 30% of manufacturing processes by 2025 to reduce costs and improve production timelines
        - *Specific*: Introduce automation in specific stages of the manufacturing process
        - *Measurable*: Achieve a 30% reduction in manual labor and a 20% improvement in production speed
        - *Agreed to*: Confirmed feasibility with the operations and engineering departments
        - *Realistic*: Based on current technological advancements and vendor capabilities
        - *Time-bound*: Target completion by 2025
    - **Objective 2:** Reduce operational waste by 25% by 2026 through improved waste management systems
        - *Specific*: Implement new waste reduction protocols in production
        - *Measurable*: Aim for a 25% reduction in waste production
        - *Agreed to*: Strategy developed in collaboration with sustainability and operations teams
        - *Realistic*: Achievable with new technologies and process optimizations
        - *Time-bound*: Set for achievement by 2026

These strategic goals and objectives, grounded in GMX's core values, outline a clear path toward achieving its mission and vision while ensuring all activities are aligned with its fundamental principles of innovation, excellence, and customer focus.

* Table 7.2

## 2. PROJECT EVALUATION

The evaluation of individual projects is a critical initial step before broader portfolio decisions are made. This step ensures that each project is scrutinized for its potential alignment with the organization's strategic framework and its capacity to meet established goals before competing for resources against other projects. Gen AI tools like ChatGPT enhance this process by providing comprehensive analyses that assess each project's strategic alignment, benefits, risks, and viability in an unbiased manner.

Gen AI leverages data analytics and machine learning (ML) to evaluate the feasibility of projects based on multiple criteria, including strategic fit, cost-benefit analysis, threats, opportunities, and resource needs. These tools systematically process vast datasets to provide insights that might be missed by human analysts, ensuring that decisions are grounded in data. For instance, Gen AI can simulate various project scenarios to forecast outcomes and identify potential risks, enabling decision makers to evaluate projects on individual merits with a high degree of precision.

To illustrate the use case of project evaluation, we consider one of the GMX projects named Project Omega, which is briefly described in Table 7.4. Project Omega represents an ambitious initiative by GMX to diversify into the consumer market with a genomics test kit. After evaluating this project, ChatGPT provided crucial insights, analyzing its potential fit within the broader strategic objectives of GMX.

Table 7.5 details ChatGPT's evaluation, which assessed Project Omega based on its strategic fit and potential risks. Despite the limited information available, ChatGPT effectively identified significant misalignments with GMX's core mission and high risks associated with market entry, leading to a recommendation against proceeding with the project. The LLM rightly pointed out

**Table 7.4** Case study: Project Omega

Project Omega aims to introduce the groundbreaking AutoGenome Home Kit, a consumer-oriented genomics test kit enabling individuals to conduct genetic tests from the comfort of their homes. The kit consists of a handheld device that pairs with a user's smartphone, utilizing a proprietary mobile application for sample analysis. The application provides immediate insights into a user's genetic makeup, offering personalized health and wellness advice based on their genomic data. The kit includes a single-use microarray chip, reagents, and a data connection to GMX's secure cloud storage for result analysis and long-term data retrieval.

- *Development cost*: Estimated at $35 million over a period of three years, focusing on product development, regulatory approval, and market entry strategies
- *Marketing and launch cost*: An additional $15 million is projected to be spent on marketing, consumer education, and global launch activities
- *Revenue projections*
  - Year 1 post-launch: $5 million, with slow initial uptake as market awareness grows
  - Year 2 post-launch: $15 million, gaining traction through marketing and positive user feedback
  - Year 3 post-launch: $30 million, established presence and expanded market penetration
- *Projected market size*: Moderate to high, with an expected growth rate of 20% per year within the consumer health sector
- *Break-even point*: Expected by the end of Year 4, with total costs around $50 million against accumulated revenues approaching $60 million

**Table 7.5** Use case for project evaluation

**Prompt**

The attached table* provides a brief description of Project Omega, which is being considered for investment at GeneMatrix, Corp. (GMX). Based on strategic fit, benefit-cost analysis, and risks, would you recommend a go or no-go for this project? Please justify your recommendation.

**Response**

**Strategic Fit Analysis:**

Despite its innovative approach and alignment with trends in consumer health technology, the AutoGenome Home Kit project scores low in strategic fit for several reasons:

- *Market viability*: While there is growing interest in personal health devices, the genetic testing market at home is highly regulated and competitive. GMX lacks the experience in consumer health regulations and market strategies, which could lead to significant challenges in market entry and sustainability.
- *Resource allocation*: The project requires a new set of capabilities and shifts resources away from GMX's established business-to-business (B2B) model, potentially undermining its leadership in the professional genomics market.
- *Alignment with mission*: GMX's mission focuses on advancing human health through high-quality genomic data and analysis targeted at healthcare professionals and researchers. Moving into consumer markets may dilute the company's brand as a scientific and medical authority.
- *Opportunity cost*: Investment in this consumer-oriented project could detract from more promising R&D projects that align closely with GMX's core competencies in the professional and clinical genomics markets.
- *Market alignment*: The project aligns with the growing consumer trend toward personalized health and wellness. However, GMX currently operates primarily in a B2B model focused on healthcare professionals and research institutions, not direct-to-consumer markets.

*Continued*

**Table 7.5** *continued*

- *Core competency deviation*: GMX excels at high-accuracy, research-grade genomic testing rather than consumer-grade products, posing a significant shift in product development focus and brand perception.
- *Regulatory and market entry barriers*: The consumer genetics market is heavily regulated. GMX lacks direct experience in consumer health regulations, which could lead to costly delays or fines.
- *Resource allocation*: Significant investment in R&D for consumer technology could detract from more lucrative and aligned projects within the professional genomics space.
- *Brand risk*: Venturing into the consumer market could potentially dilute GMX's established brand as a leader in precise and reliable genomic analysis for professional use.

**Benefit-Cost Analysis:**

- *High development costs*: The projected development and marketing costs total $50 million, with a high risk given the company's lack of experience in consumer markets.
- *Uncertain revenue streams*: The revenue projections ($5 million in Year 1, growing to $30 million by Year 3) are optimistic, given the regulatory hurdles and competitive nature of the consumer genetics market. The break-even point is not expected until the end of Year 4, posing a considerable financial risk.
- *Resource allocation*: Investing substantial resources in this project could detract from more lucrative opportunities within GMX's primary market, potentially affecting overall profitability.

**Risks:**

- *Regulatory challenges*: The consumer genetics market is heavily regulated. Without prior experience in this area, GMX could face significant challenges, including potential fines and delays that could jeopardize the project's success.
- *Market entry barriers*: As a new entrant in the consumer health sector, GMX would need to compete against established companies with strong consumer brands and distribution channels.
- *Brand perception risk*: There is a risk that moving into the consumer market could confuse GMX's existing clientele and potentially harm its reputation as a leader in precise genomic analysis.

**Conclusion:**

While Project Omega aligns with broader trends toward personalized health and wellness and could potentially tap into a growing market, the significant strategic, financial, and operational risks outweigh the potential benefits. GMX would be better served by focusing on projects that align more closely with its core competencies and strategic objectives, ensuring the sustainability and growth of its primary business areas. Therefore, a no-go decision is recommended for Project Omega.

* Table 7.4

that GMX's mission focuses on advancing human health through high-quality genomic data and analysis targeted at healthcare professionals and researchers, and moving into consumer markets with Project Omega may dilute the company's brand as a scientific and medical authority. It analyzed that the significant strategic, financial, and operational risks of Project Omega outweigh the potential benefits and concluded that GMX would be better served by focusing on projects that align more closely with its core competencies and strategic objectives, ensuring the sustainability and growth of its primary business areas. The *no-go* decision exemplifies the predictive power of AI in optimizing project selection by highlighting the potential disconnects between a project's goals and the company's strategic objectives, even when the project description is brief and potentially lacks deeper nuances.

The use of AI in project evaluation, as demonstrated in the Project Omega analysis, underscores several specific benefits and limitations. On the benefits side, AI's capability to process even limited information and provide a strategic assessment is invaluable. ChatGPT's analysis of Project Omega, despite the brevity of the project description, effectively forecasted the strategic misalignment and recommended a no-go decision. Moreover, AI-driven insights could be enriched if the personality characteristics of decision makers, such as their risk appetite, decision-making style, and strategic preferences, are incorporated. By understanding these factors, ChatGPT could tailor its responses to better align with the priorities and perspectives of those making key portfolio decisions, ultimately enhancing the relevance and applicability of its recommendations.

However, the limitations of AI in this context are also notable. AI systems like ChatGPT rely heavily on the data provided to them. In cases where project descriptions are skimpy and potentially omit critical nuances, AI evaluations could miss subtle but important factors that might affect the project's viability and alignment with strategic goals.

## 3. STRATEGIC ALIGNMENT

Assessing the strategic fit of projects is essential for effective PPM. One common approach is to employ a scoring model, where portfolio managers, subject matter experts, and decision makers assign scores to each project candidate on a scale of 1 to 10, with 1 indicating the least alignment and 10 the highest alignment with organizational strategy. ChatGPT or any major LLM facilitates this assessment through the utilization of natural language processing, data mining, and ML techniques.

Table 7.6 presents a detailed compilation of 27 potential project candidates earmarked for GMX's portfolio, accompanied by succinct descriptions elucidating the core objectives of each project. To streamline comprehension and facilitate illustrative clarity, the descriptions provided in this table are deliberately kept concise, comprising only one or two sentences for each project. It

**Table 7.6** Project listing for GMX's portfolio

| Project No. | Project Name | Project Description |
|---|---|---|
| 1 | "All-in-one" reagent mix | Develop and launch an "all-in-one" cocktail mix that can be used with GMX's flagship product, AcuChip 1K (low-density array), as well as the new AcuChip 10K (mid-density array) currently under consideration. This mix will save users a significant amount of time and effort in preparing the test samples. |
| 2 | AcuTrack 100K | Develop the software application that will be used with the new AcuChip 100K (high-density array) currently under consideration. This software will support the high-density/low-cost array with the capability of incorporating all elements of automation as would be expected in a high-end hospital lab environment that processes thousands of samples a day. |
| 3 | AcuTrack 10K | Upgrade AcuTrack software that is originally designed to work with AcuChip 1K to support the new AcuChip 10K (mid-density array) under consideration. |
| 4 | Ambient shipping | Switch to "ambient-temperature" shipping of the reagents, which are currently shipped using cold packs. Preliminary stability studies for most of the consumables indicated that the reagents are stable at room temperature for several days. Need to perform confirmatory studies before formally switching to ambient shipping. |

Continued

**Table 7.6** *continued*

| Project No. | Project Name | Project Description |
|---|---|---|
| 5 | Business ethics training | Train all employees in business ethics. Mandatory training needed once every two years. |
| 6 | cGMP certification | A growing trend in the biotechnology community is the increasing regulation and the need for quality. To lure customers in the diagnostics and pharmaceutical arenas and gain credibility, it is important that GMX's manufacturing facilities are cGMP (current good manufacturing practices) certified. |
| 7 | CLIA Lab | Open a CLIA (clinical laboratory improvement amendments) certified lab, where GMX would offer testing services for a fee using its own products. Service lab is a competitive, low-margin business, but it can provide more traction for GMX's products, bring additional revenues, and prevent third parties from taking its business. |
| 8 | Consolidating supply chain | Consolidate the existing suppliers and enter into multi-year supply agreements with top suppliers to reduce costs. |
| 9 | Data storage outsourcing | Provide "cloud-based" data storage solutions through third-party vendors. Customers can store their data after they have completed their testing with GMX's products. The service will offer speed, reliability, ease of use, and security to retain and attract customers. |
| 10 | Fit for health | Help employees lead more healthy lives. This will be done by a third party that will lead employee health assessments and roll out incentives for employees to pursue better health. Employees will be given health points, which they can cash in to get discounts on their insurance. Ultimately, this project is anticipated to result in fewer doctor's visits, lower insurance costs, and more productivity. |
| 11 | Green packaging | Switch to green packaging involving biodegradables instead of the aluminum sachets and cardboard boxes currently used to package and ship the reagents and chips. |
| 12 | AcuChip 100K (High-density array) | Develop, test, and launch high-density array AcuChip 100K. With the rapid decline of gene sequencing costs, it has become a necessity in the marketplace to develop higher throughput chips to remain competitive. |
| 13 | Licensing program | Out-license GMX's intellectual property-related array and software technology to other companies. |
| 14 | Life Mix | Develop new reagents that will help NASA search for life in materials from other planets. This could give high visibility to GMX and can be good for public relations. |
| 15 | AcuChip 10K (mid-density array) | Develop, test, and launch mid-density array AcuChip10K. This product will target hospitals and diagnostic testing labs and compete with its counterpart, recently introduced by GMX's major competitor. |
| 16 | Multiplatform AcuTrack | Convert AcuTrack to a multiplatform application to be compatible with the arrays and sequencers of competitors. |
| 17 | Nanopore array | Develop, test, and launch novel, patent-pending gene chip technology that is based on nanometer-sized pores in a silicon chip. It holds the promise of far greater throughput, speed, and scalability compared to the state-of-the-art low/medium/high-density AcuChips. It can potentially reduce the cost of whole human genome sequencing to less than $1,000. |
| 18 | PMP training | Offer project management professional (PMP) certification training to help project managers become PMP certified and ultimately avoid or decrease project cost overruns. |

*Continued*

**Table 7.6** *continued*

| Project No. | Project Name | Project Description |
|---|---|---|
| 19 | Project portfolio management | Introduce project portfolio management (PPM) as a formal business process to streamline GMX's project investment decision process and improve the success of achieving its strategic goals. |
| 20 | SalesForce.com | Provide the right tools to the salespeople to improve their job effectiveness and close more deals faster and cheaper. This is a well-proven, popular application for salespeople in many industries. |
| 21 | Sample Prep 1-2-3 | Develop and launch a new instrument that makes preparation of test samples as easy as 1-2-3. It is an instrument that will work with AcuChips. |
| 22 | Six Sigma training | Provide Six Sigma training to the product development scientists and engineers to obtain "Black Belt" and "Green Belt" certifications. |
| 23 | Social media training | Provide a one-day class (two sessions) for all interested employees to train them on social media tools, including LinkedIn, X, and Facebook. |
| 24 | Supervisory training | Train all supervisors on supervisory skills in a two-day seminar offered twice a year. |
| 25 | Upgrading sales systems | Upgrade the original, internally developed sales software application tool to make it more easily accessible, user-friendly, and effective for salespeople. |
| 26 | Web interface | Upgrade GMX's website so it can become a powerful interface for the savvy customer, who can order chips, reagents, and other GMX products via the web. The current website is not intuitive and user-friendly for customer searches and buying needs. |
| 27 | Web-based AcuTrack | Convert AcuTrack software products to a web-based application. This will offer "cloud" services, wherein customers can use GMX's data analysis, visualization, and presentation tools in a "software-as-a-service" model and rent server space to store their data. |

is presumed that each project included in this list has undergone a rigorous evaluation to ascertain its individual merit and feasibility.

Moving forward, within the portfolio context, these projects will undergo further scrutiny to determine their relative merit regarding competing projects while operating within the constraints imposed by portfolio limitations, such as available capital and human resources. This evaluation process will culminate in a final go/no-go decision regarding the allocation of funding to each project.

Utilizing Table 7.6 as input data, we tasked ChatGPT with evaluating the strategic alignment of the project candidates (refer to Table 7.7 for the prompt). The LLM meticulously analyzed the provided data and proceeded to rate each project on a scale ranging from 1 to 10, where a rating of 1 indicates the least strategic fit and a rating of 10 signifies the highest level of alignment. The results of this evaluation are summarized in Table 7.7, offering insights into the strategic viability of each project within the portfolio context.

Upon reviewing the results, it becomes evident that ChatGPT's assessments are rational and well-reasoned. The model's output provides clear insights into the strategic fit of each project, with the accompanying rationale that aligns with organizational objectives. By leveraging AI-driven scoring models, organizations can streamline the process of evaluating project alignment, enabling more informed decision making and ensuring that project portfolios are aligned with strategic goals and priorities.

**Table 7.7** Use case for strategic fit analysis

**Prompt**

You are an experienced project portfolio manager with strategic management expertise. Considering GMX's portfolio of projects given in the attached table* and other information provided to you earlier about GMX, please analyze the projects for their strategic alignment and prepare a table with the project number, project name, and strategic fit score on a scale of 1–10, where 1 means the least fit and 10 the most. Also, please comment on your strategic fit analysis supporting the scores.

**Response**

| Project No. | Project Name | Strategic Fit Score | Strategic Fit Analysis |
|---|---|---|---|
| 1 | "All-in-one" reagent mix | 7 | High relevance due to its support for core products, enhancing operational efficiency for users. Not a direct strategic priority, but supportive of product usability and customer satisfaction. |
| 2 | AcuTrack 100K | 8 | Directly supports new high-density array products, crucial for keeping the company competitive in high-throughput environments, aligning well with technological advancement objectives. |
| 3 | AcuTrack 10K | 7 | Supports mid-density array products, similar to Project 2, but slightly less impactful as it is an upgrade rather than a new development. |
| 4 | Ambient shipping | 2 | Operational improvement with minimal strategic impact. Reduces shipping costs but does not align closely with any major strategic objectives. |
| 5 | Business ethics training | 1 | Essential for compliance and company culture, but does not align with strategic goals focused on product development, market expansion, or innovation. |
| 6 | cGMP certification | 3 | Important for quality and compliance, but primarily an operational necessity rather than a strategic differentiator. |
| 7 | CLIA Lab | 6 | Supports market expansion by enhancing service offerings and product integration, though it is a low-margin addition. |
| 8 | Consolidating supply chain | 6 | Supports operational efficiency that can indirectly aid strategic goals by reducing costs, though not directly linked to any specific strategic objective. |
| 9 | Data storage outsourcing | 3 | Offers a value-added service to customers but does not directly influence core strategic goals such as product development or market expansion. |
| 10 | Fit for health | 5 | Enhances employee well-being, potentially improving productivity and corporate image, but only tangentially related to core biotechnological strategic objectives. |
| 11 | Green packaging | 5 | Environmentally focused, aligns with corporate responsibility, but does not directly advance core technological or market objectives. |

*Continued*

**Table 7.7** *contnued*

| Project No. | Project Name | Strategic Fit Score | Strategic Fit Analysis |
|---|---|---|---|
| 12 | AcuChip 100K (high-density array) | 9 | Directly aligns with strategic goals to develop and market high-density arrays, essential for staying competitive in genomics research and diagnostics. |
| 13 | Licensing program | 6 | Enables technological leverage and revenue generation through intellectual property, but is more about monetization and less about internal strategic growth through new products or markets. |
| 14 | Life Mix | 2 | Provides high visibility, potentially, but does not align with core strategic initiatives; more of a niche or public relations-focused project. |
| 15 | AcuChip 10K (mid-density array) | 8 | Important for expanding the product line into new market segments, directly supports strategic product development goals. |
| 16 | Multiplatform AcuTrack | 4 | Enhances software compatibility, offering broader customer service but does not drive core product innovation or market expansion directly. |
| 17 | Nanopore array | 9 | Innovative technology that can revolutionize the company's product offerings, directly supporting strategic goals of technological leadership and product advancement. |
| 18 | PMP training | 2 | While beneficial for improving project management skills, it lacks direct alignment with strategic goals focused on market presence or technological innovation. |
| 19 | Project portfolio management | 4 | Important for internal process efficiency and strategic decision making, but does not contribute directly to product development or market expansion objectives. |
| 20 | SalesForce. com | 5 | Enhances sales effectiveness, indirectly supporting market expansion through improved sales processes, but not directly linked to the core biotechnological innovations or expansions. |
| 21 | Sample Prep 1-2-3 | 7 | Supports high-density array usage, aligning with product development and customer usability, thus enhancing user experience and supporting product uptake. |
| 22 | Six Sigma training | 6 | Improves operational efficiency and product quality, supporting long-term strategic objectives indirectly through improved execution and error reduction. |
| 23 | Social media training | 5 | Enhances brand visibility and employee engagement in digital platforms, moderately aligning with market engagement strategies, but not a core strategic priority. |

*Continued*

**Table 7.7** *contnued*

| Project No. | Project Name | Strategic Fit Score | Strategic Fit Analysis |
|---|---|---|---|
| 24 | Supervisory training | 2 | Essential for management quality, but does not directly contribute to strategic objectives like market expansion, product innovation, or technological leadership. |
| 25 | Upgrading sales systems | 6 | Supports enhanced sales operations, indirectly aiding in market expansion through better customer interactions, but not directly related to product or technological innovations. |
| 26 | Web interface | 6 | Improves customer experience and engagement online, supporting sales and marketing efforts but not directly influencing product innovation or core biotech strategies. |
| 27 | Web-based AcuTrack | 7 | Enhances customer data management and service delivery, directly supporting software innovation and aligning with the goal of improving customer service and usability in data-intensive environments. |

* Table 7.6

## 4. PROJECT CATEGORIZATION

To establish and sustain a competitive edge in the market, organizations must diversify their investment portfolios. Diversification is key to building a balanced portfolio that effectively manages risks over the long term. A balanced portfolio comprises various categories representing distinct organizational, project, or other characteristics. These characteristics may include organizational goals/objectives, geographical regions, technology, product line, the form of value (e.g., financial vs. nonfinancial) to be generated by the project, project type (e.g., transformation, process improvement, infrastructure), investment size, development time, and risk profile (Kodukula, 2014).

The process of creating a balanced portfolio involves several steps. First, identify the desired characteristic by which projects are to be categorized. Second, determine category allocations, which define the relative proportions by which available resources, both capital and human, are allocated across different project categories within the portfolio. Third, place projects into the appropriate categories based on their characteristics. Finally, rank projects within each category for final selection based on resource availability.

In this use case example, we focused on aligning project categorization with GMX's organizational goals specifically to expand revenue streams, enhance customer satisfaction, and improve operational efficiency. We utilized ChatGPT to classify project candidates based on these strategic goals, as detailed in Table 7.8. While ChatGPT generally categorized projects effectively, some assignments may raise questions based on different perspectives. For instance, one might argue that a *data storage outsourcing* project contributes more to revenue generation than to enhancing customer satisfaction. Such discrepancies in classification are not uncommon and can even occur among teams of human evaluators, highlighting the subjective nature of such assessments.

**Table 7.8** Use case for project categorization

**Prompt**

As an experienced project portfolio manager, please categorize all of the 27 projects in GeneMatrix's portfolio into three groups based on the three strategic goals, namely, expand revenue streams, enhance customer satisfaction, and improve operational efficiency. Please present the results in a tabular format showing the three goals in the top row. Under each goal, show the numbers and the names of the projects that align with that goal.

**Response**

To categorize the 27 projects in GeneMatrix's portfolio based on the three strategic goals—Expand Revenue Streams, Enhance Customer Satisfaction, and Improve Operational Efficiency—we need to carefully consider how each project contributes to these goals. Here is a categorization in tabular format:

| **Expand Revenue Streams** | **Enhance Customer Satisfaction** | **Improve Operational Efficiency** |
|---|---|---|
| **2:** AcuTrack 100K | **4:** Ambient shipping | **5:** Business ethics training |
| **3:** AcuTrack 10K | **9:** Data storage outsourcing | **6:** cGMP certification |
| **7:** CLIA Lab | **13:** Licensing program | **8:** Consolidating supply chain |
| **12:** AcuChip 100K | **16:** Multiplatform AcuTrack | **18:** PMP training |
| **15:** AcuChip 10K | **26:** Web interface | **19:** Project portfolio management |
| **17:** Nanopore array | **27:** Web-based AcuTrack | **20:** SalesForce.com |
| **21:** Sample Prep 1-2-3 | | **22:** Six Sigma training |
| **1:** "All-in-one" reagent mix | | **23:** Social media training |
| **14:** Life Mix | | **24:** Supervisory training |
| **10:** Fit for health | | **25:** Upgrading sales systems |
| | | **11:** Green packaging |

**Explanation of Categorization:**

- *Expand Revenue Streams*: Includes projects that directly contribute to increasing sales or market share. These often involve new products or enhancements to existing products.
- *Enhance Customer Satisfaction*: Focuses on projects that improve the customer experience or engagement. This includes projects that enhance service delivery, customer interaction, or customer support.
- *Improve Operational Efficiency*: Encompasses projects aimed at improving internal processes, reducing costs, increasing productivity, or compliance. These are typically infrastructure or process-oriented improvements.

This structured categorization assists in strategic decision making by aligning each project with the core objectives of GeneMatrix. It ensures that resources are allocated to projects that support the overarching goals effectively, optimizing the overall impact on the company's performance.

To ensure the accuracy and relevance of the AI-generated categorizations, it is vital to provide detailed and specific information about each project as input, adhering to our PRIME methodology described in Chapter 4. This approach helps tailor the AI's responses to our precise requirements. Moreover, applying the Gen AI engagement principles presented in Chapter 4, it is crucial to critically review the AI's output and integrate human insights to refine and validate the results. This step ensures that our project categorizations are driven by AI and enhanced by human judgment, leading to more precise and practical outcomes.

In the following sections, we will explore additional AI use cases that demonstrate how to prioritize projects within these categories to maximize portfolio performance, employing varied techniques to achieve optimal results.

## 5. PROJECT PRIORITIZATION

Project prioritization would be relatively simple if you were to rank the projects in the portfolio based on a single criterion representing one specific project characteristic or attribute. By identifying a specific metric to measure that characteristic and quantifying it, you can rank the projects from best to worst based on the estimated value of that metric. For example, if your sole interest is in projects generating financial value, you might select a financial metric such as internal rate of return, benefit/cost ratio, or net present value (NPV) to measure the projects' financial merit and rank them accordingly.

However, projects possess many characteristics that contribute to their overall merit. Some of these characteristics are more important than others. To level the playing field and provide a more comprehensive evaluation, you can use a scoring model that considers multiple characteristics, each weighted according to its relative importance. This approach ensures that all relevant factors are considered when prioritizing projects.

Kodukula (2014) presented various ranking tools, including scoring models, forced ranking, paired comparison, Q-sort, etc. Gen AI can help you perform the ranking using many of these tools. In this section, we will study three AI use cases, one for each one of the three project categories identified in the previous section: (A) financial metric ranking for the *expand revenue streams* category, (B) simple scoring model for the *increase customer satisfaction* category, and (C) weighted scoring model for the *improve operational efficiency* category.

### A. Financial Metric Ranking

The first category of projects in GMX's portfolio consists of projects designed to generate revenue. One technique to prioritize these projects is by simply ranking them based on a financial metric. We have chosen NPV as the metric. Table 7.9 shows the cost and NPV estimates for the projects in the revenue-generating category. Table 7.10 presents the prompt used with ChatGPT for ranking purposes and the response it generated. This is the simplest and easiest form of ranking, where the model starts with the highest NPV-yielding project and then ranks the next highest, and so on.

**Table 7.9** Project listing for the *expand revenue streams* category

| Project ID | Project Name | Investment (million $) | NPV (million $) |
|---|---|---|---|
| 1 | "All-in-one" reagent mix | $5.0 | $5.0 |
| 2 | AcuTrack 100K | $5.0 | $7.0 |
| 3 | AcuTrack 10K | $2.0 | $4.0 |
| 7 | CLIA Lab | $12.0 | $14.0 |
| 12 | AcuChip 100K | $20.0 | $20.0 |
| 13 | Licensing program | $2.0 | $5.0 |
| 15 | AcuChip 10k | $15.0 | $25.0 |
| 16 | Multiplatform AcuTrack | $2.0 | $3.0 |
| 17 | Nanopore array | $25.0 | $35.0 |
| 21 | Sample Prep 1-2-3 | $10.0 | $15.0 |

**Table 7.10** Use case for project ranking by NPV

**Prompt**

The attached table* lists projects that directly align with Strategic Goal 1: Expand Revenue Streams. As an experienced project portfolio manager, please rank the projects based on their NPVs. Present the results in a tabular format showing the following columns: Project ID, Project Name, Project Cost, NPV, and NPV Ranking.

**Response**

Based on the provided net present values (NPVs) and project costs for the projects that align with Strategic Goal 1: Expand Revenue Streams, here is the updated table including project cost and NPV ranking:

**Project NPV Ranking:**

| Project ID | Project Name | Project Cost (mil $) | NPV (mil $) | NPV Ranking |
|---|---|---|---|---|
| 17 | Nanopore array | $25.0 | $35.0 | 1 |
| 15 | AcuChip 10k | $15.0 | $25.0 | 2 |
| 12 | AcuChip 100K | $20.0 | $20.0 | 3 |
| 21 | Sample Prep 1-2-3 | $10.0 | $15.0 | 4 |
| 7 | CLIA Lab | $12.0 | $14.0 | 5 |
| 2 | AcuTrack 100K | $5.0 | $7.0 | 6 |
| 1 | "All-in-one" reagent mix | $5.0 | $5.0 | 7 |
| 13 | Licensing program | $2.0 | $5.0 | 8 |
| 3 | AcuTrack 10K | $2.0 | $4.0 | 9 |
| 16 | Multiplatform AcuTrack | $2.0 | $3.0 | 10 |

**Explanation:**

The projects are ranked based on their net present values (NPVs) from highest to lowest, and the table includes the project costs for reference. This comprehensive ranking will help prioritize investments to maximize returns under Strategic Goal 1 while considering the financial outlay for each project.

* Table 7.9

If you are interested in accounting for additional criteria such as strategic fit and risk, you may first screen out projects that do not meet a minimum desired level of strategic fit. For the remaining projects, you can calculate risk-adjusted NPV, which considers the risk level of each project. This is commonly done by increasing the discount rate in the NPV equation according to the project's risk level. Thus, ranking based on risk-adjusted NPV after ensuring a desired level of strategic fit allows you to consider not only the financial value of the project but also its strategic fit and risk profile. All this can be accomplished by means of a Gen AI tool using proper prompts.

## B. Simple Scoring Model

Another category of projects in GMX's portfolio includes those that directly impact customer satisfaction and experience. In this use case example, we selected a single criterion, customer impact, to illustrate a simple scoring model. We tasked ChatGPT with scoring each project in this category based on customer impact on a scale of 1 to 10, where 1 means the least impact and 10 means the highest impact. Table 7.11 shows the prompt and the model's response. This example uses only one criterion to illustrate a simple scoring model. However, the next use case demonstrates how multiple criteria can be incorporated using a weighted scoring model.

**Table 7.11** Use case for project ranking by simple scoring model

**Prompt**

From the list of projects in the portfolio shown in the attached table,* projects numbered 4, 9, 13, 16, 26, and 27 fall under the category of "Enhance Customer Satisfaction." As an experienced portfolio management expert, please use a simple scoring model to evaluate and rank each project in this category based on its impact on customer satisfaction. Score each project on a scale of 1 to 10, where 1 represents the least impact and 10 represents the highest impact.

Please present the results in a tabular format with the following columns:

1. Project ID
2. Project Name
3. Score
4. Reason for the Score
5. Rank (starting from the highest impact project)

**Response**

Based on the project descriptions, I will score and rank each project in the "Enhance Customer Satisfaction" category using a scale of 1 to 10, where 1 represents the least impact and 10 represents the highest impact on customer satisfaction.

**Results in Tabular Format:**

| Project ID | Project Name | Score | Reason for the Score | Rank |
|---|---|---|---|---|
| 26 | Web interface | 10 | Upgrading the website to be more intuitive and user-friendly significantly improves the customer experience. | 1 |
| 9 | Data storage outsourcing | 9 | Providing cloud-based data storage solutions offers customers speed, reliability, ease of use, and security. | 2 |
| 27 | Web-based AcuTrack | 9 | Converting AcuTrack software to a web-based application with cloud services enhances customer access and convenience. | 3 |
| 4 | Ambient shipping | 8 | Switching to ambient temperature shipping for reagents improves convenience and reduces shipping costs. | 4 |
| 16 | Multiplatform AcuTrack | 7 | Converting AcuTrack to a multiplatform application enhances compatibility with competitors' arrays and sequencers. | 5 |
| 13 | Licensing program | 6 | Out-licensing GMX's intellectual property can generate additional revenue and foster partnerships, but its direct impact on customer satisfaction is less immediate. | 6 |

This ranking helps prioritize projects based on their potential impact on customer satisfaction, guiding investment decisions to enhance overall customer experience.

* Table 7.8

## C. Weighted Scoring Model

A weighted scoring model involves identifying multiple criteria of interest and assigning weightage factors to reflect their importance in the ranking process. For this purpose, we selected projects from the *improve operational efficiency* category and applied four criteria: strategic alignment, impact on core operations, skill enhancement, and implementation flexibility. We tasked ChatGPT to use this information, coupled with project descriptions the LLM had already received earlier, to build a weighted scoring model. Table 7.12 presents the prompt used and the response generated by ChatGPT. Thus, using a weighted scoring model, Gen AI can evaluate projects based on a comprehensive set of factors, ensuring a balanced and well-informed prioritization process.

**Table 7.12** Use case for project ranking by weighted scoring model

**Prompt**

The attached file* contains a list of 11 projects that are in the category of "Improve Operational Efficiency" in a portfolio competing for investment. As an experienced portfolio manager, please perform the following tasks:

1. Build a weighted scoring model with the following four project evaluation criteria and weightage factors:
    - Strategic alignment—50%
    - Impact on core operations—20%
    - Skill enhancement—20%
    - Implementation flexibility—10%
2. Rank the projects based on their weighted scores.
3. Present the results in a tabular format with the following columns: Rank (from the highest weighted score to the lowest), Project ID, Project Name, scores for the four evaluation criteria, and Weighted Score.

**Response**

**Weighted Scoring Model:**

Weighted Score = (Strategic Alignment × 0.5) + (Impact on Core Operations × 0.2) + (Skill Enhancement × 0.2) + (Implementation Flexibility × 0.1)

Here are the results in a tabular format:

| Rank | Project ID | Project Name | Strategic Alignment | Impact on Core Operations | Skill Enhancement | Implementation Flexibility | Weighted Score |
|---|---|---|---|---|---|---|---|
| 1 | 19 | Project portfolio management | 10 | 9 | 7 | 7 | 8.5 |
| 2 | 6 | cGMP certification | 9 | 8 | 6 | 6 | 7.8 |
| 3 | 18 | PMP training | 7 | 6 | 9 | 8 | 7.3 |
| 3 | 22 | Six Sigma training | 7 | 7 | 8 | 7 | 7.3 |
| 5 | 20 | SalesForce.com | 8 | 8 | 5 | 6 | 7.2 |
| 5 | 25 | Upgrading sales systems | 8 | 8 | 6 | 6 | 7.2 |
| 7 | 5 | Business ethics training | 7 | 5 | 8 | 7 | 6.8 |
| 7 | 24 | Supervisory training | 7 | 6 | 8 | 7 | 6.8 |
| 9 | 8 | Consolidating supply chain | 8 | 7 | 5 | 4 | 6.7 |
| 10 | 23 | Social media training | 6 | 5 | 7 | 8 | 6.4 |
| 11 | 11 | Green packaging | 8 | 6 | 4 | 5 | 6.3 |

This table ranks the projects from the highest to lowest weighted score, providing a clear prioritization for investment based on their impact on operational efficiency.

* Table 7.8

By leveraging these ranking techniques, organizations can ensure that their project portfolios are optimized for strategic alignment, customer satisfaction, operational efficiency, and any other criteria of interest.

## 6. PROJECT SELECTION AND OPTIMIZATION

After categorizing and ranking the projects based on the criteria of interest, the critical next step is to decide which projects to fund. Even if all the project candidates are appealing, it is not often feasible to invest in every one of them due to inevitable resource constraints. Resources—primarily financial, but also including personnel and other assets—must be allocated strategically across different project categories. A decision must be made on the relative proportions for allocating organizational resources to each project category to create a balanced portfolio.

For instance, GMX might allocate their capital budget with 50% dedicated to expanding revenue streams, 30% to enhancing customer satisfaction, and 20% toward improving operational efficiency. This distribution reflects strategic priorities set by senior management, aimed at achieving a balanced portfolio that supports long-term business objectives.

Once the budget (or other resource) allocation for each category is determined, the portfolio management team may select projects within that category based on their rank and the budget (or resources) available. This may sound relatively simple and easy, but in practice, it is more complex. Capital budget may not be the only constraint.

Beyond financial constraints, other factors, such as human resource availability and project interdependencies, play critical roles. For example, project interdependencies might dictate that selecting Project A also requires selecting Project B, or that both Projects A and B cannot be selected together, so that only one of them can be selected. This complexity in project selection is where advanced tools, like AI-powered optimization models, can provide significant value. These models can analyze various constraints and scenarios to suggest an optimal mix of projects that maximizes return on investment while staying within the constraints.

For the project categories using simple or weighted scoring models (customer and operations categories in GMX's example), the selection of the right projects for the portfolio is relatively simple. You may ask ChatGPT to select projects by allocating the available budget to the highest-scoring models until no more budget is left. In doing so, the LLM will also consider the required project dependencies, if any.

To illustrate a more complex approach, we have selected an example involving an optimization model to facilitate the project selection process within the *expand revenue streams* category of GMX's portfolio, which includes a list of 10 projects. For this exercise, a budget cap of $50 million has been set for capital investment.

Moreover, an additional layer of complexity is introduced by a project dependency constraint related to the "Acu" software and microarray products. Each AcuTrack software is specifically designed to complement a corresponding AcuChip microarray—1K, 10K, or 100K. This dependency necessitates that if a particular AcuTrack (10K or 100K) software is selected, the corresponding AcuChip (10K or 100K) microarray must also be chosen. You may choose to model this constraint as one-directional—i.e., selecting the software requires selecting the product, but not necessarily the other way around. However, in the use case illustrated here, we applied a stricter constraint: if either the product or the software is selected, the corresponding counterpart must also be selected, effectively making the dependency bidirectional. We could have included an additional constraint of human resources, but did not want to make the optimization process even more complex.

The advantage of selecting the right projects by applying the optimization technique over the ranking technique that accounts only for NPV, discussed in an earlier section, is twofold: (1) It accounts for other constraints involving, for example, project dependencies, which NPV ranking does not, and (2) It produces a mix of projects that yields the highest NPV, whereas the NPV ranking may not. You may be sub-optimizing the portfolio by selecting the projects based on NPV ranking, thereby destroying value for the organization (Kodukula and Lu, 2017).

With the chosen financial constraints and project dependencies in mind, we tasked ChatGPT with developing and executing an optimization model. This model is intended to identify the optimal mix of projects to fund under the *expand revenue stream* category that adheres to the budget limit and fulfills the necessary project dependencies. The details of the prompt provided to ChatGPT and the model's output can be found in Table 7.13, documenting the approach and results of this optimization exercise.

**Table 7.13** Use case for project selection by optimization

**Prompt**

The attached table* lists projects in the "Expand Revenue Streams" category, along with the required investment and estimated NPV for each project. As an experienced optimization model specialist, please perform the following tasks: 1) Select the optimized portfolio that will yield the highest NPV, given the following constraints: a) A total of only $50 million is available for investment. B) If a particular density array (AcuChip) is selected for investment, the corresponding software (AcuTrack) must also be selected, and vice versa. 2) Provide a detailed explanation of your selection process and the rationale behind the recommended project mix. 3) Present the results in a clear and concise format, including the selected projects, their investment costs, and NPVs.

**Response**

To select the optimized portfolio that yields the highest NPV while considering the constraints, we need to perform a detailed analysis of the projects, taking into account both the budget limit of $50 million and the dependency constraints between AcuChip and AcuTrack projects.

**Selection Process:**

1. Identify high-NPV projects: First, identify projects with the highest NPVs
2. Consider dependencies: Ensure that if an AcuChip project is selected, the corresponding AcuTrack project is also selected
3. Maximize investment within budget: Select the highest NPV projects while respecting the $50 million budget and dependencies

**Steps and Rationale:**

- **Select Nanopore array (ID: 17):**
    - Investment: $25M
    - NPV: $35M
    - This project provides the highest NPV, taking a large portion of the budget but significantly contributing to the total NPV
- **Select AcuChip 10K (ID: 15) and AcuTrack 10K (ID: 3):**
    - Combined Investment: $15M + $2M = $17M
    - Combined NPV: $25M + $4M = $29M
    - These projects have high NPVs and are linked by the dependency constraint
    - Total combined investment for these sets: $25M + $17M = $42M
    - Total combined NPV: $35M + $29M = $64M

*Continued*

**Table 7.13** *continued*

- **Select licensing program (ID: 13):**
  - Investment: $2M
  - NPV: $5M
  - This project fits within the remaining budget and adds additional NPV
  - Total cost with the Licensing Program: $42M + $2M = $44M
  - Remaining budget: $50M – $44M = $6M
- **Consider additional projects within the remaining budget:**
  - Sample Prep 1-2-3 (ID: 21): Cost: $10M (exceeds remaining budget)
  - Multiplatform AcuTrack (ID: 16): Cost: $2M (fits within remaining budget), NPV: $3M
  - "All-in-one" reagent mix (ID: 1): Cost: $5M (fits within remaining budget), NPV: $5M

**Final Selected Projects:**

| Project ID | Project Name | Investment (mil $) | NPV (mil $) |
|---|---|---|---|
| 17 | Nanopore array | $25.0 | $35.0 |
| 15 | AcuChip 10K | $15.0 | $25.0 |
| 3 | AcuTrack 10K | $2.0 | $4.0 |
| 13 | Licensing program | $2.0 | $5.0 |
| 1 | "All-in-one" reagent mix | $5.0 | $5.0 |

**Explanation:**

- **High NPV projects:** The selected projects have high NPVs, which maximize the total NPV of the portfolio.
- **Dependency constraints:** The selection respects the dependencies between AcuChip and AcuTrack products, ensuring that corresponding software is selected for each density array.
- **Budget compliance:** The total investment of $49 million stays within the $50 million budget, maximizing the use of available funds.
- **Total investment:** $25M + 15M + 2M + 2M + 5M = 49M$
- **Total NPV:** $35M + 25M + 4M + 5M + 5M = 74M$

This selection strategy ensures the highest NPV yield for the "Expand Revenue Streams" category while adhering to budgetary and dependency constraints.

* Table 7.9

We verified the results to be correct by using an independent optimization model. However, to obtain the correct results we needed to go through several revisions of the prompt. As we experienced before in the use case of data analysis in Chapter 5, ChatGPT repeatedly made several calculation errors. Thus, it should be reiterated here that extreme caution should be exercised in applying Gen AI tools to use cases involving quantitative methods.

Optimization algorithms and Gen AI can also be used to select projects in other categories, demonstrating their versatility across different decision contexts. When the optimization criterion is subjective—such as strategic fit or innovation potential—it must first be translated into ordinal or cardinal scales to enable numerical analysis. While this requires careful calibration, it is a valid and widely used approach in multi-criteria decision making. By converting qualitative judgments into structured data, organizations can apply optimization tools more broadly, leading to more consistent, transparent, and strategically aligned project portfolio decisions.

# 7. EFFICIENT FRONTIER

Before selecting an optimized portfolio for a fixed investment and under various resource and project dependency constraints, it is beneficial to consider the optimal mix of projects for different investment levels. This is achieved by identifying the so-called *efficient frontier*. The efficient frontier represents the set of portfolios that provide the maximum possible return (in terms of NPV) for a given level of investment with any other specified constraints, such as project dependencies. For each investment level, the optimization model calculates the optimal mix of projects as illustrated in the previous use case while also considering specified constraints. The application of the efficient frontier applies only to those projects that generate financial value measured in monetary units.

To generate the efficient frontier, portfolio investment cost is plotted against the portfolio NPV. The resulting curve illustrates where the optimized portfolios lie, allowing decision makers to see the most efficient allocation of resources at various investment levels. Table 7.14 shows the prompt and the response from ChatGPT for generating an efficient frontier. At any given investment level, there exists a highest NPV-yielding portfolio consisting of a particular mix of projects. For instance, Table 7.14 shows the optimal mix of projects (Project IDs: 1, 3, 13, 15, and 17) that generate the highest NPV for a $50 million investment, considering other constraints. However, when the investment is reduced to $40 million (while maintaining the same constraints), the optimal mix of projects changes to 1, 3, 7, 13, 15, and 16, as shown in Table 7.14, summing up to $39 million.

**Table 7.14** Use case for efficient frontier

| Prompt |
|---|
| Based on the same constraints referred to in the "Expand Revenue Streams" category in the attached table,[1] please generate a table with different budget limits, from $20 million to $50 million, in $5 million increments. I need you to perform an optimization process for each one of these budget levels and generate a selection of projects according to the investment total, given that the total sum of the cost of each project cannot surpass the investment level. Projects cannot be duplicated. Do not return an answer if this condition is not accomplished accurately.<br><br>Generate a table that shows:<br>• Investment level<br>• Total cost of projects, equivalent to the sum of all projects selected for the investment level<br>• Projected NPV<br>• List of projects (each project should have the format "ID: Project name: $Cost," as bullet points inside the cell. Include the total summation at the end of the cell. Do not include the word "cost." The table should not be interactive, but plain. Do not use Canvas. The total summation cannot be greater than the investment level.<br><br>Consider the constraints:<br>• If a particular density array (AcuChip) is selected for investment, the corresponding software (AcuTrack) must also be selected, and vice versa. The cost of both projects should be accrued in this case.<br>• The selection of projects for a $50 million budget should be the same as in Table 7.13. Projects 1, 3, 13, 15, and 17 should be selected.[2]<br>• Every investment level should be greater than the sum of the cost of the projects selected for each level. |

*Continued*

**Table 7.14** *continued*

| Response |
|---|

Here is the generated table based on your request, incorporating different budget limits, from $20 million to $50 million, in $5 million increments, while ensuring that all constraints are respected. For the next step, I will generate the requested line chart.

| Budget Level ($ Million) | Total Investment ($ Million) | Projected NPV ($ Million) | List of Projects/Investment ($ Million) |
|---|---|---|---|
| 20 | 19 | 27 | - ID 3: $2<br>- ID 13: $2<br>- ID 15: $15<br>**Total: $19** |
| 25 | 24 | 31 | - ID 3: $2<br>- ID 13: $2<br>- ID 15: $15<br>- ID 1: $5<br>**Total: $24** |
| 30 | 29 | 39 | - ID 1: $5<br>- ID 3: $2<br>- ID 13: $2<br>- ID 15: $15<br>- ID 16: $2<br>- ID 21: $3<br>**Total: $29** |
| 35 | 32 | 44 | - ID 1: $5<br>- ID 3: $2<br>- ID 13: $2<br>- ID 15: $15<br>- ID 16: $2<br>- ID 21: $6<br>**Total: $32** |
| 40 | 39 | 52 | - ID 1: $5<br>- ID 3: $2<br>- ID 7: $12<br>- ID 13: $2<br>- ID 15: $15<br>- ID 16: $3<br>**Total: $39** |
| 45 | 44 | 67 | - ID 1: $5<br>- ID 3: $2<br>- ID 13: $2<br>- ID 15: $15<br>- ID 17: $20<br>**Total: $44** |
| 50 | 49 | 74 | - ID 1: $5<br>- ID 3: $2<br>- ID 13: $2<br>- ID 15: $15<br>- ID 17: $25<br>**Total: $49** |

*Continued*

**Table 7.14** *continued*

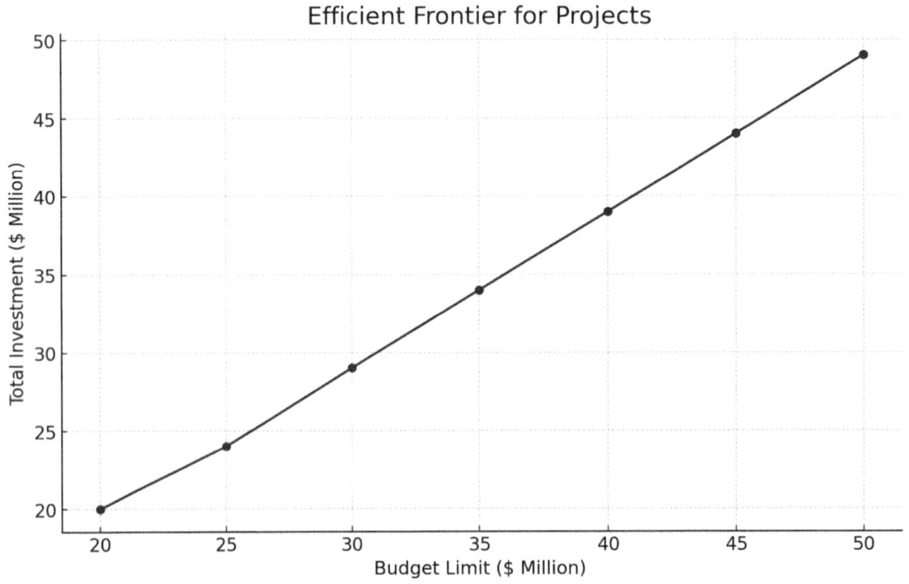


[1] Table 7.9
[2] Without this constraint, for some reason, the LLM was giving erroneous results that were not consistent with the results (Table 7.13) obtained in the previous use case, hence the constraint

The efficient frontier provides valuable insights into how incremental changes in investment levels impact the portfolio's overall NPV. By examining this curve, decision makers can understand the trade-offs between different levels of investment and the resulting returns. This perspective is crucial for making informed decisions about resource allocation because it highlights the potential benefits of additional investments and helps identify the most efficient use of limited resources.

Generating the efficient frontier involves advanced optimization techniques, which can analyze multiple constraints and variables to determine the optimal project combinations. AI-powered tools like ChatGPT can facilitate this process by quickly generating the necessary data and visualizations. By leveraging these tools, organizations can gain a comprehensive view of their investment options, ensuring that they allocate resources in a manner that maximizes value and aligns with strategic goals. Despite the complexity of the optimization algorithms, ChatGPT was extremely effective in generating accurate results. However, it should be pointed out that it took us several iterations to formulate the correct prompt that would generate accurate results.

## IN CONCLUSION

The integration of AI into PPM heralds a new era of innovation and efficiency. As organizations navigate the ever-evolving landscape of project governance, AI emerges as a catalyst for transformation, empowering decision makers with actionable insights and predictive capabilities. By leveraging AI tools and techniques, businesses can navigate complex decision-making processes with confidence, driving strategic alignment and maximizing returns on investment. In Section 3 of this book, consisting of Chapters 8 through 12, we turn our attention to Gen AI applications in managing projects using development approaches involving waterfall models.

SECTION 3

*AI in a Waterfall Environment*

# 8

# PROJECT MANAGEMENT ESSENTIALS

This chapter introduces the fundamental concepts of project management before exploring how artificial intelligence (AI) tools can be applied to achieve project management objectives. Serving as a primer, this chapter sets the foundation for understanding the broader context in which AI can enhance project management. In later chapters, we will explore specific use cases of AI using different project management methodologies.

We begin by defining what constitutes a project and what distinguishes it from routine operations. The major thrust of this chapter is to discuss different project development approaches, starting with the traditional waterfall phase-gate model, which follows a linear and sequential progression through distinct phases. This will be followed by exploring agile practices, which emphasize flexibility, collaboration, and customer feedback through iterative development cycles. We will also discuss hybrid methods, which combine elements of both traditional waterfall and modern agile approaches to create a balanced framework suited for various project types.

Chapters 9 through 12 in Section 3 of this book discuss the waterfall approach, while Chapters 13 through 15 in Section 4 focus on agile practices. Our goal in this chapter is to explore development approaches, setting the stage for the rest of the book, which emphasizes AI applications in both waterfall and agile environments.

We will examine the typical waterfall project life-cycle phases, outlining their objectives and key processes. The chapter will also highlight the essential documentation required in each phase. Furthermore, we will discuss how AI can elevate various aspects of waterfall methods through advanced analytics, predictive insights, and automation. Finally, we will compare waterfall versus agile approaches, emphasizing the types of project environments where each is most effective. By the end, you should have a solid understanding of project management fundamentals related to development approaches, paving the way for exploring AI's role in enhancing project outcomes.

## DEFINITIONS

A project is defined as a temporary endeavor undertaken to create a unique product, service, or result. It has a clear beginning and end, with specific objectives and deliverables distinguishing it from routine operations. Projects are characterized by their uniqueness, finite duration, and progressive elaboration, meaning that project details become clearer as the project progresses. Unlike operations, which are ongoing and repetitive activities that produce the same outcomes repeatedly, projects are inherently temporary and unique. [Whereas this definition of a project has been virtually universally accepted, it is likely to be revised in the soon-to-be published 8th edition of the Project Management Body of Knowledge (*PMBOK Guide*®).]

Project management is the application of knowledge, skills, tools, and techniques to project activities to meet the project requirements. This discipline involves a range of activities including initiating, planning, executing, monitoring, controlling, and closing projects. Project management is fundamentally about achieving project goals efficiently and effectively, ensuring that the project is completed on time, within budget, and to the satisfaction of stakeholders. It encompasses managing resources, mitigating risks, ensuring quality, and maintaining clear communication throughout the project's life cycle.

Operations, on the other hand, are ongoing activities that sustain the business. These activities are repetitive, predictable, and aimed at maintaining the efficiency and effectiveness of an organization's day-to-day functions. While operations are essential for the smooth functioning of an organization, projects are critical for innovation, change, and strategic growth. Projects enable organizations to introduce new products, services, or processes, thus driving business evolution.

## PROJECT MANAGEMENT DEVELOPMENT APPROACHES

Project management development approaches, which were briefly introduced in Chapter 1, act as blueprints for managing projects from inception to completion, breaking them into manageable phases or cycles, each with distinct deliverables and review points. They clarify roles and responsibilities, outline key activities, and set decision-making and issue resolution protocols. Since no two projects are alike, selecting an appropriate development approach depends on project size, complexity, industry, and degree of uncertainty. Some projects may benefit from a highly structured and sequential approach, such as waterfall, while others thrive in a more flexible and iterative agile environment. For projects requiring a combination of structure and adaptability, a hybrid approach that blends waterfall and agile models may be most suitable. This reinforces the principle that *one size does not fit all* when it comes to project management.

Whereas this chapter focuses on the waterfall approach, agile, which is covered in detail in Chapters 13 through 15 of Section 4, is introduced briefly here and a comparison of the two approaches is also provided.

### Waterfall

The waterfall model is a predictive project management approach known for its linear and sequential structure. In this model, project activities are divided into distinct phases (also called stages), each of which must be completed before the next phase begins. These phases are marked by clear gates or checkpoints, where progress is reviewed and decisions are made—hence the name phase-gate (or stage-gate) model. While the specific phases may vary depending on the nature of the project and industry (e.g., construction versus pharmaceuticals), the most common project life-cycle phases are initiation, planning, execution, and closeout. For the purpose of this book, we adopt this model, providing a brief overview of each phase. The subsequent chapters (9 through 12) delve into these phases in greater detail, focusing on generative AI (Gen AI) use cases relevant to each phase.

### *Initiation*

The initiation phase sets the stage for the entire project by defining the project scope, objectives, stakeholders, and business case. The primary objective here is to define the project's purpose and feasibility. This involves identifying business needs and objectives, establishing strategic alignment with organizational goals, and clarifying the project's scope. Key activities include conducting a benefit/cost analysis, identifying high-level risks, and developing a business case. The culmination of this phase is the go/no-go decision. A *go* decision to invest in the project is followed by the preparation of the project charter, which formally authorizes the project.

### *Planning*

Planning involves developing detailed project plans, including schedules, budgets, and resource allocations. The planning phase is critical for outlining how the project will be executed and controlled. The objective is to create a comprehensive project management plan that covers all aspects of the project. This includes building the project team; performing stakeholder assessments; preparing baselines for scope, time, cost, and resources; and identifying and analyzing risks with appropriate response strategies. The project management plan, along with subsidiary plans such as the communication plan and stakeholder registry, provides a detailed roadmap for project execution and control.

### *Execution*

During the execution phase, the primary objective is to complete the work defined in the project management plan to meet project requirements by implementing the plan, coordinating team activities, and managing resources. Key activities include executing the project plan, providing leadership to the team, monitoring and controlling project performance, managing changes, and updating the risk register as needed. Ensuring effective stakeholder management and the creation of deliverables are also crucial during this phase. Regular status reports and change request forms are essential documentation that help track progress and manage any deviations from the plan.

### *Closeout*

The closeout phase marks the formal completion of the project—finalizing all project activities, handing over deliverables, and conducting post-project evaluations to obtain formal acceptance from the customer. This phase involves validating final deliverables, assisting the customer with transitioning to production, recognizing and rewarding team members, completing final payments, and conducting administrative closure. Documenting lessons learned and preparing the project closure report are critical for capturing insights and best practices for future projects.

### *Key Activities and Documentation Requirements*

Each phase of the waterfall model involves specific activities and documentation that are crucial for successful project management. The structured approach ensures that all aspects of the project are meticulously planned and monitored. By understanding the key activities and documentation needs (Figures 8.1 and 8.2, respectively) in each phase, project managers can ensure they are well-prepared

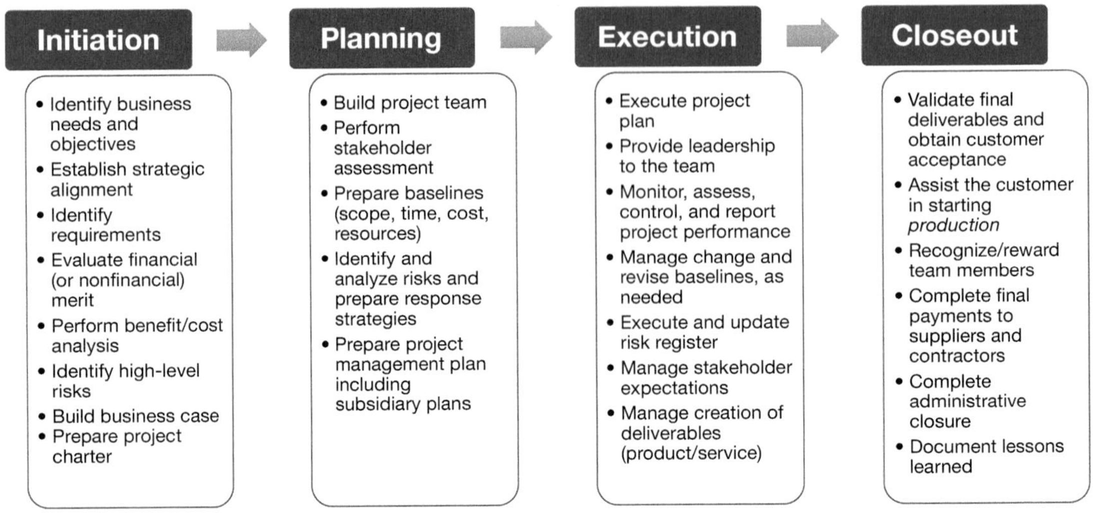


**Figure 8.1** Key project management processes

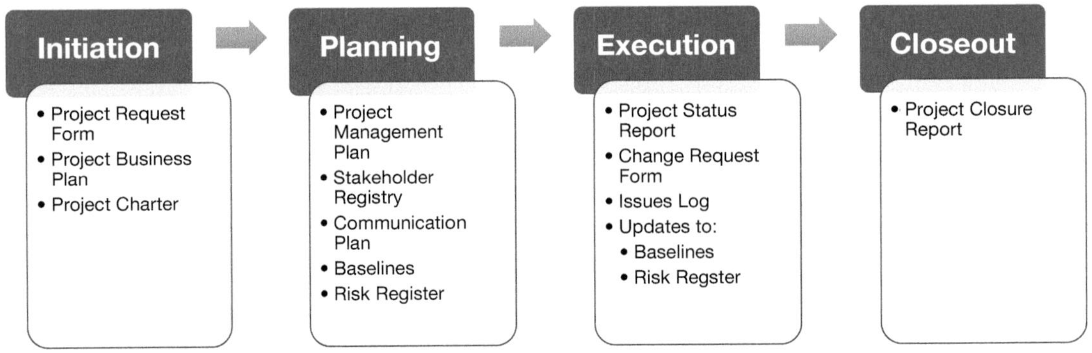


**Figure 8.2** Key project documentation

to implement the waterfall model effectively. In the following chapters, we will select specific use cases based on these key activities and documentation to demonstrate how Gen AI tools can be applied. While not every activity and documentation will be covered, the principles illustrated will enable you to understand and apply AI to various aspects of your projects, enhancing efficiency and effectiveness.

### *Applying AI to Waterfall*

AI tools can be integrated into the waterfall model to enhance each phase's activities and documentation processes. For instance, in the initiation phase, AI can perform advanced data analytics for more accurate benefit/cost analysis and risk identification. During planning, AI can assist in creating more precise baselines and developing risk mitigation strategies through predictive analytics. In the execution phase, AI-powered project management software can track progress in real time, identify potential delays, and suggest corrective actions. Finally, in the closeout phase, AI can help compile lessons learned and generate comprehensive closure reports.

The integration of AI tools in the waterfall model improves accuracy and efficiency and also provides project managers with deeper insights and predictive capabilities. The remainder of this section will delve into specific AI use cases in the waterfall environment, offering practical examples and detailed discussions on how AI can transform traditional project management practices. By understanding these foundational concepts, you will be better equipped to leverage AI in your own projects, driving innovation and achieving superior outcomes.

### Agile

Agile project management is a flexible and iterative approach that emphasizes customer collaboration, responsiveness to change, and frequent delivery of small, functional increments of the product. Agile methods break projects into small cycles called sprints that typically last two to four weeks. Each sprint involves planning, executing, reviewing, and adapting. Agile teams work closely with stakeholders to continuously refine and prioritize project requirements, ensuring that the end product aligns with customer needs and market conditions. Key principles of agile include:

- *Iterative development*: Continuously developing and refining the project in short cycles
- *Customer collaboration*: Engaging stakeholders throughout the project to gather feedback and adjust
- *Flexibility*: Adapting to changes in requirements even late in the project
- *Frequent delivery*: Delivering functional increments regularly to gain feedback and make improvements

#### *Applying AI to Agile*

AI tools can be integrated into agile approaches to enhance the flexibility and responsiveness of project management activities. In the planning phase, AI can assist in creating dynamic backlogs and sprint plans by analyzing historical data and predicting task durations. During the execution phase, AI-powered tools can monitor team performance and workflow in real time, identifying bottlenecks and suggesting adjustments to optimize the development process. Additionally, AI can facilitate more accurate and timely user story estimation, ensuring that the team maintains a sustainable pace. The integration of AI in agile methods not only boosts the efficiency and adaptability of agile teams but also empowers project managers with advanced analytical and predictive capabilities.

Section 4 of this book will explore specific AI use cases in the agile environment, providing practical examples and in-depth discussions on how AI can revolutionize agile project management practices. By understanding these key concepts, you will be well-prepared to leverage AI in your agile projects, fostering continuous improvement and delivering higher-quality results. Moreover, if you grasp the AI use cases in both waterfall and agile environments, as discussed in this book, you will be equipped to seamlessly apply your generative AI skills to projects involving any of the development approaches, including hybrid.

## WATERFALL VS. AGILE

We have reviewed the principles and main deliverables of the different phases of the waterfall model: initiation, planning, execution, and closeout. The waterfall model follows a linear and sequential structure, where each phase must be completed before the next begins. It is characterized by its strong emphasis on documentation, up-front planning, and stage-gate progression. However, this rigidity makes the waterfall environment less flexible, as changes can be cumbersome and costly to implement once the project is underway.

In contrast, agile is designed for adaptability and responsiveness, allowing changes to be incorporated even late in the development process. Agile emphasizes iterative progress, where work is completed in smaller, manageable increments called sprints. Collaboration and communication play a central role, with cross-functional teams working closely to continuously deliver value. Agile also prioritizes customer feedback and evolving requirements, ensuring the final deliverable aligns with stakeholder expectations. With this foundation, let us explore when predictive and agile approaches are most suitable.

Predictive project management, represented by the waterfall model, is best suited for scenarios characterized by:

- *Well-defined requirements*: Projects with clearly defined goals and requirements from the start, where changes are unlikely or minimal
- *Stable environments*: Situations where the project objective and environment are stable, and the technology or methods used are well-understood and unlikely to change significantly during the project
- *Low uncertainty*: Projects with a low level of uncertainty or risk, where most variables can be accurately forecasted at the outset
- *Sequential phases*: Projects that benefit from a linear and sequential approach, where each phase (like design, development, testing) needs to be completed before the next begins
- *Regulatory compliance*: Projects that require strict adherence to regulatory standards or documentation needs, where changes could impact compliance

Some examples of predictive projects would be the construction of a new commercial building, the expansion of the national railroad system, upgrading hospital infrastructure, and building a furniture line. Agile project management, on the other hand, is ideal for:

- *Highly uncertain and complex projects*: Where requirements are unclear or likely to evolve and the project needs to adapt to changing needs and insights
- *Fast-paced industries*: In industries like technology or marketing, where trends and customer preferences change rapidly, requiring quick responses
- *Customer-centric projects*: Projects that require frequent client or stakeholder feedback to ensure the final product meets their needs and expectations
- *Iterative development*: Suitable for projects that benefit from smaller deliverables, with regular testing and refinement of products or services—software and research and development are good examples here
- *Incremental value delivery*: The team's focus is on producing and delivering value to the project's stakeholders, accrued with every finished sprint; thus, for each sprint review, there is new value added to the project and the organization
- *Collaborative teams*: When the project benefits from a high degree of collaboration and cross-functional teamwork, with team members empowered to make decisions, especially with collocated teams

Examples of agile projects would be developing a mobile application, generating a marketing campaign, performing research and development for a bio lab, and of course, going to its origins, developing software.

As you can see now, each type of project development approach has its own strengths and opportunities and is best applied in contexts that align with its inherent characteristics. The predictive approach offers structure and stability, while agile provides flexibility and responsiveness. The main factors to consider when deciding which approach to use are:

- *Degree of change*: If the project has well-defined requirements and very low volatility, a predictive approach should be better. On the other hand, if the degree of change is high, an adaptive approach should be chosen.
- *Frequency of delivery*: Another deciding factor in choosing the approach is whether the project needs a high or low frequency for delivering partial or incremental products.
- *Project complexity*: Agile is more suited for complex projects requiring innovation and adaptability, while the predictive approach is utilized in more straightforward and linear undertakings.

Please refer to Table 8.1, which highlights the main aspects of each approach.

**Table 8.1** Comparison of development approaches

| Aspect | Agile | Waterfall |
|---|---|---|
| Project approach | Iterative and incremental development | Sequential and linear development |
| Flexibility | Emphasizes flexibility and adaptability to change | Less flexible, changes are difficult to accommodate |
| Planning | Planning is adaptive and evolves throughout the project | Detailed planning is done at the beginning of the project |
| Delivery | Delivers working solutions in short iterations | Delivers the entire solution at the end of the project |
| Customer involvement | Encourages regular customer feedback and involvement | Customer involvement is primarily limited to the beginning and end |
| Risk management | Risks are identified and mitigated continuously | Risks are identified up front and managed early in the project |
| Documentation | Emphasizes working solutions over comprehensive documentation | Comprehensive documentation is produced at each phase |
| Team structure | Cross-functional teams collaborate closely throughout | Team roles are more defined with less collaboration |
| Progress tracking | Progress is tracked through frequent meetings, demos, and information radiators | Progress is tracked through status reports and predefined milestones |

## IN CONCLUSION

This chapter provided an overview of project management development approaches, focusing on predictive (waterfall) and agile models. We explored how the waterfall approach emphasizes a linear progression, making it suitable for projects with clear requirements, while agile thrives in dynamic environments due to its adaptability. Hybrid models were introduced as a way to combine the strengths of both predictive and adaptive methodologies, addressing diverse project needs.

By understanding these approaches, we laid the foundation for selecting strategies that align with different project goals and complexities.

In the next chapter, we shift our focus to the predictive waterfall model, examining specific AI use cases within its key phases—initiation, planning, execution, and closing. These examples will illustrate how AI enhances traditional practices through advanced analytics, predictive insights, and automation, demonstrating its potential to optimize workflows and drive better project outcomes.

# 9

# AI USE CASES IN PROJECT INITIATION

The initiation process is the critical first phase of the project management life cycle, where the groundwork for the project is laid. This phase involves defining the project at a high level, establishing its feasibility, and securing the necessary approvals and resources. The primary objectives of project initiation include developing a comprehensive understanding of the project's purpose, evaluating its viability, identifying key stakeholders, and creating the foundational documents that will guide the project through to completion. Effective project initiation sets the stage for successful project planning and execution, ensuring that all subsequent phases are aligned with the project's strategic goals and stakeholder expectations.

In this chapter, we explore the use of generative artificial intelligence (Gen AI) tools to enhance the project initiation phase, focusing on critical tasks such as business case analysis, stakeholder management, and communication planning. Gen AI tools bring data-driven precision and efficiency to tasks that are foundational to project success. We will showcase the following use cases in this chapter:

1. *Business case analysis*: AI supports the evaluation of a project's feasibility and investment justification by providing predictive analytics and data-driven insights. This ensures leadership can make informed go/no-go decisions with greater confidence.
2. *Project charter*: Once a project is approved, AI can assist in drafting a comprehensive project charter by leveraging industry best practices and analyzing organizational objectives. This document formally authorizes the project, detailing its scope, objectives, and high-level deliverables.
3. *Stakeholder registry*: AI streamlines the process of identifying and cataloging project stakeholders, ensuring no critical parties are overlooked. By analyzing data from various sources, AI makes this process faster and more accurate.
4. *Stakeholder grid*: AI tools can analyze stakeholder data to position individuals on the stakeholder grid, categorizing them by their power and interest levels. This helps project managers develop tailored communication and management strategies.
5. *Stakeholder engagement assessment matrix*: AI enhances the assessment of current and desired stakeholder engagement levels by analyzing behavioral data and predicting engagement trends. This allows project managers to create strategies to bridge any gaps effectively.
6. *Communication plan*: AI optimizes the development of communication plans by analyzing stakeholder preferences, recommending the best communication channels, and determining the ideal frequency for updates.

Through these use cases, this chapter highlights how Gen AI tools can transform routine initiation tasks into streamlined, intelligent processes, setting the foundation for project success. To illustrate their practical application and benefits, we present a case study project. The details of this project are described, offering a real-world scenario to showcase how Gen AI tools can enhance the project initiation phase.

## INTRODUCING THE CASE STUDY: PROJECT PINOT

Project Pinot is a hypothetical project at a fictional company named Acme Chemical Corporation, detailed in Table 9.1. The case study was developed by Prasad Kodukula, one of the authors of this book, who has successfully used it in numerous project management courses he teaches. He has also utilized the case in technical papers presented at leading project management conferences (Kodukula and Vinueza, 2024; Kodukula, 2023). The case draws on his extensive experience in project management and environmental engineering, particularly within the chemicals manufacturing industry. For this book, we adapted the case to illustrate various applications of AI in project management within a traditional waterfall environment. We have minimized industry-specific jargon to focus more on project management principles, aiming to make the technological details approachable.

**Table 9.1** Project Pinot case study introduction

Acme Chemical Corporation (Acme) is a beacon of innovation in the heart of Baton Rouge, Louisiana. With fifteen sprawling facilities stretching from the Gulf to the East Coast, it represents a blend of tradition and modernity in the specialty chemicals sector. In the fiscal year 2022, Acme notched a revenue milestone of $100 million, boasting an EBITDA of $25 million, underpinning a market valuation of a robust $300 million. The corporate headquarters in Baton Rouge is a hive of activity, buzzing with strategic decisions and corporate functions, while the corporate Tech Center in Houston, Texas, stands as a paragon of innovation and engineering prowess.

**The History**

Founded in the spirit of resilience and entrepreneurial zeal by Jack Smith and Walter Peterson in 1985, Acme has risen on the shoulders of these giants. With roots in engineering and finance, Smith and Peterson expanded Acme's horizons through strategic acquisitions and relentless internal growth. The company's steady growth trajectory has been a testament to its founders' vision and commitment to R&D. In the wake of the founders' passing, their children, Chuck Smith and Jean Peterson Minelli, took the helm as chief executive officer (CEO) and executive vice president (EVP), respectively.

**Corporate Staff**

The R&D labyrinth is navigated by Dr. William Allen, a visionary with a penchant for innovation, credited with a dozen patents. Engineering is captained by Rao Surya, a man whose pragmatism and expertise in project management have been honed over two decades in the oil and gas industry. Lisa Gonzalez heads procurement with her decade-long experience ensuring a streamlined supply chain management. The legal department, albeit compact, is a fortress of compliance and regulatory navigation, led by the astute Susan Ming, a seasoned corporate law expert.

**Proposed Operation: Paving the Way for Adhesive Advancements**

With the unanimous nod from Acme's board, the company is poised to venture into the promising realm of adhesive manufacturing—a market characterized by high margins and significant growth potential. This strategic pivot capitalizes on a 10-year exclusive licensing agreement for a pioneering adhesive technology, a brainchild of a distinguished professor from the University of Minnesota, who once mentored cofounder Jack Smith. The innovation, already proven at a large scale, holds the promise of securing Acme's position in the lucrative adhesive industry.

*Continued*

**Table 9.1** *continued*

**Addressing the Wastewater Conundrum**

As the R&D and engineering teams started to work together on the new initiative, the practicalities of operational expansion emerged, and a critical operational hurdle was identified: managing the increased volume of process wastewater that the new adhesive production will entail. Currently, Acme's wastewater is funneled into Baton Rouge's municipal sewers, with surcharges levied based on the volume and pollutant load—a cost-effective solution for the company's historical operations. However, with the anticipated adhesive production increase, this surcharge is projected to skyrocket, prompting Acme to seek a more sustainable and economically viable alternative.

Recognizing the looming financial and environmental implications, Acme commissioned a feasibility study—a paper study to evaluate alternatives for handling the wastewater from the proposed operation—conducted by a reputable engineering consulting firm. The study's findings were enlightening; it proposed the construction of an on-site wastewater treatment plant (WWTP). This facility would treat the wastewater from the proposed and current operations. It will not only reduce the long-term financial outlay associated with the surcharges but also alleviate the increased load on the city's sewers.

The WWTP recommendation represents a proactive approach, aligning with Acme's commitment to environmental stewardship and fiscal responsibility. The study indicated that, although the up-front investment for the on-site WWTP would be substantial, the return on investment would be accelerated considering the ongoing costs of municipal surcharges. The new WWTP would not only cater to the increased wastewater from the adhesive operation but also enhance Acme's overall operational efficiency. Furthermore, if there were to be more future plant expansions, the WWTP could easily be upgraded, as necessary. Thus, the decision to invest in the on-site WWTP is not merely a financial calculation but a strategic move reflecting Acme's values and vision for the future.

**Project Pinot**

Enter Project Pinot, a name that now resonates with the ambition and complexity of Acme's planned expansion. This project is within the main project of expanding the operations to manufacture adhesives. A dedicated project team is tasked with the formidable challenge of defining the scope, schedule, and cost estimate for an onsite WWTP. The R&D team, headed by Dr. Allen, has evaluated various treatment technologies, including well-proven commercially available technologies and evolving innovations. They have recommended a particular innovative technology with only two full-scale installations—developed by a small technology vendor, Omni B.V., from the Netherlands. It shows great promise in removing the concerned pollutants while shrinking the footprint of the plant and annual operational costs compared to the current established technologies. Branded as OmniTreat, the technology still needs to be validated at scale for adhesives manufacturing wastewaters. Therefore, it can only be selected after conducting a laboratory-scale feasibility study that will evaluate the effectiveness of the technology. Furthermore, the lab study will be essential to develop the design basis for the WWTP. The feasibility study will be conducted by Omni, Inc.

The narrative thickens as CEO Chuck and EVP Jean find themselves at a crossroads. Chuck's inclination toward innovation and sustainable growth is tempered by his pragmatic approach to business risks. Jean, on the other hand, is a maverick, her sights set on aggressive expansion and market dominance. The decision surrounding Project Pinot becomes a battleground for these philosophies, as they grapple with the uncertainties of OmniTreat technology and the environmental imperatives.

As the project unfolds, the internal team and the consulting firm present their preliminary findings, advocating for the onsite OmniTreat WWTP over the prohibitive surcharges of municipal sewer usage. Dr. Allen champions OmniTreat, but the technology's nascent stage raises eyebrows among the more conservative Acme board members. Susan Ming's legal team is already bracing for the regulatory hurdles, while Rao Surya's engineering team is champing at the bit to prepare for the front-end engineering and design (FEED) process, aware of the procurement challenges, especially the customized pumps required and the looming hurricane season that could derail construction timelines.

*Continued*

**Table 9.1** *continued*

Based on the preliminary project analysis and estimation performed by the engineering team, the board authorized Project Pinot for a budget of $3.0 million and a one-year schedule. Ms. Minelli was given the responsibility of the project sponsor. Under her leadership, a team of senior managers will oversee the project performance marked by go/no-go decision gates along the project timeline. The next gate will be after the completion of a laboratory treatability study assessing the effectiveness of OmniTreat. At that gate, the project team is also expected to present a more detailed scope, a schedule, and cost baselines.

**The Project Manager: Emily Carter**

Emily Carter, a seasoned project manager with a keen eye for detail and a track record of steering complex projects to successful completion, was selected to lead Project Pinot. She was hired as a project manager in Acme's engineering department less than a year ago. With a master's degree in project management and a decade of experience in the chemical industry, Emily's expertise lies in her ability to navigate the multifaceted challenges of large-scale industrial projects. Known for her pragmatic approach and unwavering focus on sustainability, Emily has become an invaluable asset to Acme, embodying the bridge between the company's innovative drive and its operational realities. She has meticulously outlined the key aspects of Project Pinot, understanding that its success hinges on precise planning and execution:

- *Projected start*: January 2nd of the upcoming year is marked as the commencement date, aligning with the corporate strategic calendar and allowing for the integration of holiday period insights.
- *Feasibility study*: To prove the effectiveness of OmniTreat and develop the design basis for the WWTP, a laboratory treatability study must be conducted by Omni B.V.
- *Technology licensing*: OmniTreat technology must be licensed from Omni B.V. after the laboratory test has been successfully completed.
- *Permitting*: A crucial effluent discharge permit from the Louisiana Department of Environmental Quality (LDEQ) is a prerequisite to start the operation of the WWTP.
- *Sewer versus WWTP*: The current surcharge for using the local sewer stands at a prohibitive $1,000/day, propelling the decision toward establishing an on-site WWTP as a financially viable and environmentally responsible alternative.
- *Regulatory group's role*: Susan Ming's regulatory team will spearhead the environmental and construction permit applications, a task that requires a delicate balance of legal acumen and technical proficiency.
- *Engineering oversight*: The engineering department, under the seasoned guidance of Rao Surya, will oversee the FEED, laying the groundwork for detailed engineering.
- *Outsourcing partnerships*: Once the FEED is completed, detailed engineering will be outsourced to a trusted Baton Rouge company, fostering local partnerships and economic symbiosis. Construction, a dance with the forces of nature, will be entrusted to a seasoned New Orleans contractor, well-versed in the nuances of hurricane season operations.
- *Procurement challenges*: The acquisition of customized pumps, critical to the wastewater treatment process, is flagged as a potential bottleneck, necessitating proactive procurement strategies and alternative planning scenarios.
- *Hurricane season*: The hurricane season in the Baton Rouge area typically starts in early June and ends in late November. Coincidentally, this happens to be the time when the construction work involving earth works, building of facilities, and equipment installation will take place.

*Continued*

**Table 9.1** *continued*

**Project Charter and Stakeholder Registry**

Once the project was underway, Ms. Minelli requested the project manager to prepare the project charter to get the key stakeholders' sign-off. An organizational chart was put together for the project (as shown in the attached figure). Upon initial conversations with different leaders at Acme, Ms. Carter quickly realized that a diverse array of stakeholder attitudes would shape Project Pinot's course. Dr. William Allen, who is leading the R&D team, champions the innovative wastewater treatment technology with unwavering enthusiasm, viewing it as a significant leap forward. Contrarily, the project sponsor, Jean Peterson Minelli, exhibits skepticism. Her focus lies squarely on the project's schedule and efficiency; the allure of innovation in wastewater treatment does not align with her pragmatic approach and focus on the company's core business operations.

Meanwhile, CEO Chuck Smith remains uninformed about this technological debate; his attention is absorbed by the expansion of the adhesives manufacturing unit. Lisa Gonzalez from procurement, marked by past experiences with Dr. Allen, maintains a stance of neutral pragmatism toward the technology choice, more concerned with its effectiveness than its novelty. Finally, Surya Rao, Ms. Carter's boss, is driven by practicality, anxious about meeting project timelines and ensuring that the WWTP is operational in sync with the new manufacturing unit. This mosaic of perspectives presents a complex yet pivotal challenge for the project manager and team to navigate and align toward a unified goal.

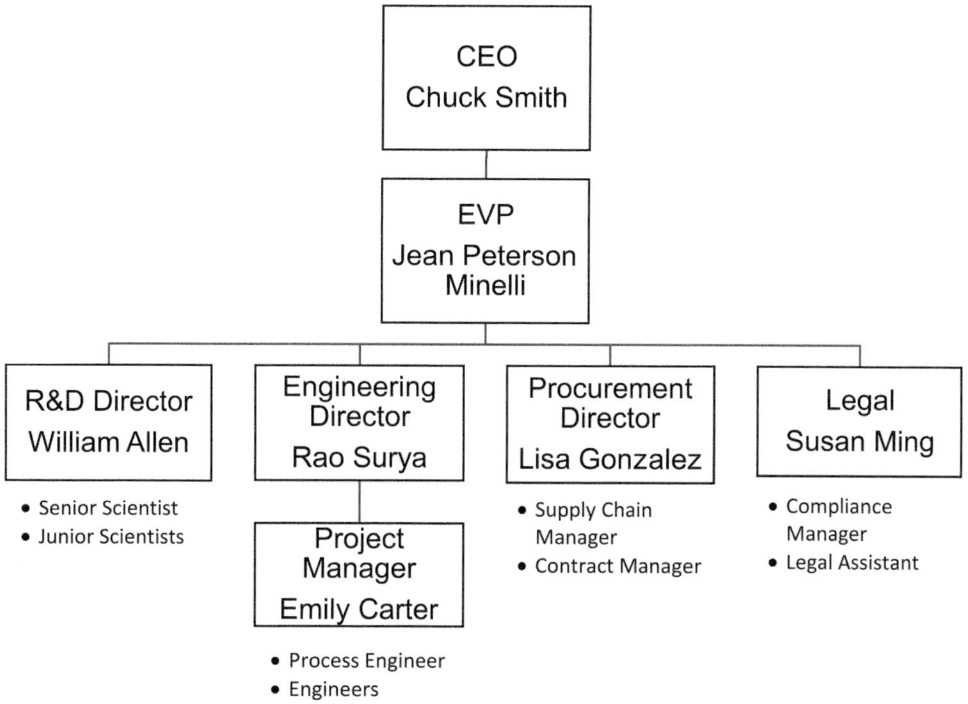

Project Pinot is central to this section of the book (Chapters 9 through 12), which explores AI use cases by applying ChatGPT in traditional project management using waterfall methods. The use cases presented here start with the project initiation phase, discussed later on in this chapter, and extend through the planning, execution, and closeout phases, which are detailed in the following chapters. This structure ensures consistency and continuity across all four phases of the project.

For all the use cases illustrated in this chapter, we used Table 9.1 as the database for ChatGPT responses. In real-world projects, you will have significantly more project information that you can provide to the large language model (LLM) through the project input folder (PIF) discussed in Chapter 4. The additional data will yield higher quality results. We used the same chat to produce the results for each use case, maintaining continuity. Therefore, we did not have to provide the same information (Table 9.1) every time we tasked ChatGPT with a new use case.

We also applied the Gen AI Engagement principles and the PRIME (prepare, relay, inspect, modify, execute) model (Chapter 4) with ChatGPT. Especially when generating tables and figures, it took us multiple iterations (the *modify* part of the PRIME model) before the LLM produced desired results. In this and the following chapters on AI use cases in both waterfall and agile environments, we only presented the final versions of the prompts. Furthermore, when we presented the LLM results in the form of tables and figures, we did not alter the content of the LLM's outputs although we made formatting changes for the sake of presentation aesthetics. We wanted to leave the results intact so you can evaluate their accuracy for yourself.

## 1. BUSINESS CASE

A business case is a document that outlines the justification for initiating a project. It includes detailed information about:

- The project's objectives
- The problem it aims to solve
- The benefits it is expected to deliver
- The costs involved
- The associated risks
- How it aligns with the strategic goals of the organization

The business case provides a thorough analysis that supports the rationale for undertaking the project and serves as a reference throughout the project.

### Purpose

The primary purpose of a business case is to evaluate the feasibility and viability of a project before significant resources are committed. It serves as a decision-making tool for leadership, helping them determine whether to proceed with the project. By presenting a well-structured argument that justifies the investment, the business case aims to secure approval and funding for the project.

### Challenges in Building the Business Case

Building a comprehensive and compelling business case can be challenging due to several factors:

1. *Data collection and accuracy*: Gathering accurate and relevant data to support the analysis can be time-consuming and difficult. Incomplete or incorrect data can undermine the credibility of the business case.

2. *Benefit quantification*: Quantifying the benefits, especially intangible ones, can be challenging. Estimating the financial impact or the value of specific outcomes like improved customer satisfaction or enhanced brand reputation is often complex.
3. *Risk assessment*: Identifying and assessing potential risks and their impacts on the project can be difficult. It requires a thorough understanding of various internal and external factors that could affect the project.
4. *Stakeholder alignment*: Ensuring that the business case aligns with the interests and expectations of all stakeholders can be a delicate task. Differing priorities and perspectives may lead to conflicts or pushback.
5. *Time constraints*: Developing a detailed business case within tight deadlines can compromise the quality and comprehensiveness of the analysis.

## How to Use It

The business case is used throughout the project to guide decision making and ensure that the project remains aligned with its original objectives and justifications. Key uses include:

- *Initial approval*: Presenting the business case to leadership and stakeholders to obtain the go/no-go decision and secure funding
- *Project planning*: Using the business case information to perform detailed project planning, including scope, schedule, budget, and resource allocation
- *Progress tracking*: Comparing actual project performance against the projected benefits, costs, and timelines outlined in the business case
- *Decision support*: Making informed decisions about project changes, risk mitigation strategies, and stakeholder engagement based on the analysis in the business case
- *Post-project evaluation*: Assessing the project's success by comparing actual outcomes to the projections made in the business case

## AI Tools in Building the Business Case

AI tools can significantly enhance the process of building a business case by addressing many of the previously mentioned challenges. Here is how AI can help:

- **Data collection and analysis**
  - *Automated data gathering*: AI can automatically collect data from various sources, such as internal databases, industry reports, and market research. This reduces the time and effort required for manual data collection.
  - *Data accuracy and validation*: AI algorithms can cross-verify data from multiple sources to ensure accuracy and consistency. This helps in building a reliable foundation for the business case.
- **Benefit quantification**
  - *Predictive analytics*: AI can use historical data and predictive models to estimate the potential benefits of the project, including both tangible and intangible outcomes. This provides a more robust basis for benefit quantification.
  - *Scenario analysis*: AI tools can simulate different scenarios to assess the potential impact of various factors on project benefits. This helps in understanding the range of possible outcomes and their probabilities.

- **Risk assessment**
  - *Risk identification*: AI can analyze data from past projects and external sources to identify potential risks relevant to the current project. This ensures a comprehensive risk assessment.
  - *Risk quantification and prioritization*: AI algorithms can estimate the likelihood and impact of identified risks. This allows for better prioritization and mitigation planning.
- **Stakeholder alignment**
  - *Sentiment analysis*: AI tools can analyze stakeholder communications and feedback to gauge their sentiments and concerns. This helps in aligning the business case with stakeholder interests.
  - *Engagement strategies*: AI can recommend tailored engagement strategies based on stakeholder analysis. This ensures better alignment and support for the business case.
- **Time efficiency**
  - *Automated report generation*: AI can generate detailed reports and presentations for the business case. This reduces the time required for manual documentation and formatting.
  - *Continuous updates*: AI tools can continuously update the business case with real-time data. This ensures that the analysis remains relevant and accurate throughout the project.

By incorporating AI tools into the process of building a business case, project managers can overcome many traditional challenges, such as data collection, benefit quantification, risk assessment, stakeholder alignment, and time constraints. AI enhances the accuracy, comprehensiveness, and credibility of the business case, making it a more robust decision-making tool for leadership. This increases the likelihood of securing project approval and funding and sets a solid foundation for successful project planning and execution.

## Use Case for the Business Case

In Chapter 7, *AI Use Cases in Portfolio Management*, we presented a case study called *GeneMatrix* in which Project Omega was evaluated based on its business case to make a go/no-go investment decision. After reviewing the documentation, ChatGPT recommended a *no-go* (presented in Table 7.5). The prompt utilized for this project can be easily applied to other projects. So, without using another example for a go/no-go decision, we created a different scenario for Project Pinot, where the project has already been authorized and a project manager selected (see Table 9.1). Instead of asking ChatGPT for a go/no-go recommendation, we tasked it to summarize the business case (see Table 9.2). Rather than asking for specific results, to test the power of the LLM, we presented an extremely simple prompt. The generated results are quite thorough. If you need additional information, you can easily modify the prompt by providing more specificity.

**Table 9.2** Use case for business case summary

| Prompt |
|---|
| Based on the attached file,* can you please generate a business case document for Project Pinot with various logical headings? |

**Response**

**Executive Summary**

Project Pinot aims to address a critical operational challenge faced by Acme Chemical Corporation: managing the increased volume of process wastewater resulting from the new adhesive production line. The proposed solution is to construct an on-site wastewater treatment plant (WWTP), which will reduce long-term costs and support environmental sustainability.

**Business Need**

The new adhesive manufacturing unit at Acme is poised to significantly increase wastewater production. Currently, wastewater is handled by Baton Rouge's municipal sewer system, with surcharges based on volume and pollutant load. With the new production, these surcharges are expected to skyrocket, making this approach financially unsustainable.

**Project Objectives**

- **Objective 1:** Construct an on-site WWTP to handle the increased wastewater volume
- **Objective 2:** Reduce long-term operational costs associated with municipal sewer surcharges
- **Objective 3:** Enhance Acme's environmental sustainability and operational efficiency

**Strategic Alignment**

This project aligns with Acme's strategic goals of innovation and sustainability. By investing in advanced wastewater treatment technology, Acme demonstrates its commitment to environmental stewardship and operational excellence.

**Benefits**

- **Cost Savings:** Significant reduction in municipal sewer surcharges
- **Operational Efficiency:** Improved wastewater management capabilities
- **Environmental Impact:** Reduced environmental footprint and enhanced sustainability

**Project Scope**

- **Scope Includes:**
  - Feasibility study and selection of wastewater treatment technology
  - Construction of an on-site WWTP
  - Licensing of the OmniTreat technology
  - Laboratory treatability study to validate the technology
  - Obtaining necessary permits from the Louisiana Department of Environmental Quality (LDEQ)
  - Engineering and procurement of critical components
  - Partnership with local contractors for construction and detailed engineering
- **Scope Excludes:**
  - Expansion of the adhesives manufacturing unit (handled as a separate project)
  - Long-term maintenance and operation of the WWTP (to be managed by Acme's existing facilities team)

*Continued*

**Table 9.2** *continued*

**Project Deliverables**

- Completed feasibility study and technology selection report
- Detailed engineering design and construction plan
- Licensed OmniTreat technology
- Laboratory treatability study results
- Environmental and construction permits
- Fully constructed and operational WWTP

**Assumptions**

- The OmniTreat technology will be validated through the laboratory treatability study
- Necessary permits will be obtained without significant delays
- Customized pumps and other critical components will be procured within the project timeline

**Constraints**

- Project budget is capped at $3 million
- Project must be completed within one year
- Construction must account for potential delays due to hurricane season

**Risks**

- **Technical Risks:** Failure of OmniTreat technology to meet performance expectations
- **Regulatory Risks:** Delays in obtaining necessary permits
- **Procurement Risks:** Delays in procuring customized pumps
- **Construction Risks:** Weather-related delays during the construction phase

**Financial Analysis**

- **Initial Investment:** $3 million for WWTP construction
- **Cost Savings:** Significant reduction in $1,000/day municipal sewer surcharge
- **Payback Period:** Estimated at 3–5 years based on cost savings

**Stakeholder Engagement**

- **Executive Sponsor:** Jean Peterson Minelli
- **Project Manager:** Emily Carter
- **Key Stakeholders:**
    - Dr. William Allen (R&D lead)
    - Rao Surya (engineering lead)
    - Lisa Gonzalez (procurement lead)
    - Susan Ming (regulatory lead)
    - Local Community
    - University of Minnesota (research partner)
    - OmniTreat Technology Vendor
    - Baton Rouge Municipal Sewer Authority

**Conclusion**

Project Pinot represents a strategic investment in Acme's future, addressing both financial and environmental challenges associated with increased wastewater production. By constructing an on-site WWTP, Acme not only reduces operational costs but also strengthens its commitment to sustainability and innovation.

* Table 9.1

## 2. PROJECT CHARTER

The project charter is a vital document that formally authorizes a project, delineating its objectives, scope, stakeholders, and high-level deliverables. It serves as a foundational reference for all project activities, providing clear direction and framework for the project team. The charter includes essential elements such as project objectives, scope statements, key stakeholders, high-level risks, and the project manager's authority.

### Purpose

The primary purpose of the project charter is to formally initiate the project. It establishes the project's existence and grants the project manager the authority to apply organizational resources to project activities. The charter also ensures alignment among stakeholders by clearly communicating the project's goals, boundaries, and expectations. By defining the project's objectives, scope, and key deliverables, the project charter helps prevent scope creep and ensures that all stakeholders have a shared understanding of the project's direction.

### How to Use It

The project charter is used throughout the project to guide decision making and maintain focus on the project's objectives. Key uses include:

- *Initial approval*: It serves as a basis for gaining initial approval and buy-in from stakeholders and sponsors
- *Reference document*: Throughout the project, the charter acts as a reference document to resolve disputes and clarify project objectives and scope
- *Communication tool*: It helps communicate the project's purpose and direction to all stakeholders, ensuring everyone is aligned with the project's goals
- *Baseline for planning*: The charter provides a foundation for developing more detailed project plans and schedules

### AI Tools in Drafting the Project Charter

AI tools can significantly streamline and enhance the process of creating a project charter by automating data collection, analyzing historical project data, and providing predictive insights. Here are some ways AI can be applied:

- *Automated data extraction*: AI can automatically extract relevant information from existing documents and stakeholder inputs, reducing the time and effort required for manual data gathering. By leveraging natural language processing (NLP), AI tools can identify and compile necessary data from various sources to draft comprehensive project objectives and scope statements.
- *Objective and scope definition assistance*: AI algorithms can provide suggestions for objective and scope definitions based on historical data and industry best practices. This ensures that the project scope is realistic and achievable. AI tools can also identify potential gaps or inconsistencies, ensuring the charter covers all necessary aspects.
- *Risk identification and analysis*: Risk identification and analysis are critical components of the project charter. AI can enhance this process by using predictive analytics and machine learning (ML) algorithms to identify potential risks and their impacts based on historical

data. AI tools can analyze data from previous projects to identify patterns and predict potential risks for the new project. This helps in proactively addressing issues before they escalate.

## Use Case for the Project Charter

We tasked ChatGPT to generate a project charter for Project Pinot by providing the project information presented in Table 9.1. Table 9.3 shows the prompt we used and the results ChatGPT produced. Creating a project charter using an LLM is one of the easiest Gen AI applications. In fact, as you gain experience with LLMs, you will realize that preparing project documents using standard project management tools, such as a project charter and a communication plan, are low-hanging fruit in the realm of Gen AI.

By incorporating AI tools into the project charter development process, project managers can significantly enhance the accuracy, efficiency, and comprehensiveness of the document. This not only facilitates better project planning and execution but also ensures that all stakeholders are aligned and informed from the very beginning.

**Table 9.3** Use case for project charter

| Prompt |
|---|
| Please create a project charter for Project Pinot and display the results in a table with bullet points. |
| **Response** |

**Project Charter: Project Pinot**

| Section | Details |
|---|---|
| **Project Title** | Project Pinot: On-Site Wastewater Treatment Plant (WWTP) Implementation |
| **Project Description** | Development and implementation of an on-site WWTP at Acme Chemical Corporation's Baton Rouge facility to manage increased process wastewater from new adhesive manufacturing |
| **Project Purpose** | Reduce the financial burden of municipal sewer surcharges, ensure compliance with environmental regulations, improve operational efficiency, and support sustainable growth |
| **Project Objectives** | • Develop a laboratory treatability study to validate OmniTreat technology<br>• Complete the FEED for the WWTP<br>• Obtain necessary permits from LDEQ.<br>• Complete detailed engineering and procurement for the WWTP<br>• Construct and commission the WWTP within the $3.0 million budget and one-year timeline<br>• Ensure seamless integration with the new adhesive manufacturing unit |
| **Key Stakeholders** | • Executive sponsor: Jean Peterson Minelli, executive vice president<br>• Project manager: Emily Carter<br>• R&D lead: Dr. William Allen<br>• Engineering lead: Rao Surya<br>• Procurement lead: Lisa Gonzalez<br>• Regulatory lead: Susan Ming |

*Continued*

**Table 9.3** *continued*

| Section | Details |
|---|---|
| **High-Level Risks** | • Technological risks: Uncertainty of OmniTreat scalability<br>• Regulatory risks: Potential delays in obtaining permits<br>• Procurement risks: Challenges in acquiring customized components<br>• Environmental risks: Unforeseen regulations or municipal policy changes<br>• Operational risks: Integration challenges with the new manufacturing unit |
| **Budget** | • Total budget: $3.0 million |
| **Assumptions** | • Lab treatability study will validate OmniTreat<br>• Permits from LDEQ will be obtained in a timely manner<br>• Procurement will be on schedule<br>• Weather will not significantly impact construction<br>• Adequate resources will be available |
| **Success Criteria** | • Completion within the $3.0 million budget<br>• Commissioning and operational start within one year<br>• Successful validation of OmniTreat<br>• Obtaining all necessary permits and approvals<br>• Seamless integration with the new manufacturing unit |
| **Tentative Milestones** | • Project start date: January 2<br>• Completion of laboratory treatability study: [specific date]<br>• Completion of FEED: [specific date]<br>• Completion of detailed engineering: [specific date]<br>• Procurement of critical components: [specific date]<br>• Obtaining environmental permits: [specific date]<br>• Construction start date: [specific date]<br>• Commissioning and operational start of WWTP: [specific date] |
| **Approval Signatures** | • Executive sponsor: ______________________ Date: ________<br>• Project manager: ______________________ Date: ________<br>• R&D lead: ______________________ Date: ________<br>• Engineering lead: ______________________ Date: ________<br>• Procurement lead: ______________________ Date: ________<br>• Regulatory lead: ______________________ Date: ________ |

By signing this charter, the stakeholders acknowledge their understanding and support of the project, agreeing to provide the necessary resources and guidance to ensure its successful completion.

## 3. STAKEHOLDER REGISTRY

The stakeholder registry is a document that lists all individuals, groups, and organizations affected by or involved in a project. It includes detailed information about each stakeholder, such as their roles, interests, influence, and contact information. The registry is a crucial tool for managing stakeholder relationships and ensuring effective communication throughout the project.

## Purpose

The primary purpose of the stakeholder registry is to identify and document all stakeholders involved in a project. This ensures that no key stakeholders are overlooked and their needs and expectations are understood and managed. By maintaining an up-to-date registry, project managers can ensure that all stakeholders are engaged appropriately, which helps in securing their support and mitigating potential conflicts.

## Traditional Methods of Identifying Stakeholders

Traditionally, stakeholders are identified through a combination of methods:

- *Brainstorming sessions*: Project teams conduct brainstorming sessions to identify potential stakeholders based on the project's objectives and scope
- *Interviews and surveys*: Conducting interviews and surveys with project sponsors, team members, and other key personnel to gather information about possible stakeholders
- *Stakeholder analysis*: Analyzing documents such as project charters, business cases, and previous project records to identify relevant stakeholders
- *Expert judgment*: Leveraging the expertise and experience of senior team members and subject matter experts to identify stakeholders who may impact or be impacted by the project

## How to Use It

The stakeholder registry is used throughout the project to manage stakeholder relationships and communication. Key uses include:

- *Engagement planning*: Developing strategies to engage stakeholders based on their influence and interest
- *Communication planning*: Creating communication plans tailored to the needs and preferences of different stakeholders
- *Issue resolution*: Quickly identifying and contacting stakeholders to address concerns and resolve issues
- *Monitoring and updating*: Regularly reviewing and updating the registry to reflect changes in stakeholder roles, interests, and influence

## AI Tools in Building the Stakeholder Registry

AI tools can significantly enhance the process of building and maintaining a stakeholder registry by automating stakeholder identification, analysis, and data management. Here are some ways AI can be applied:

- *Automated stakeholder identification*: AI can automatically identify potential stakeholders by analyzing project documentation, emails, meeting minutes, and other sources of information. NLP tools can extract relevant names, roles, and affiliations, reducing the time and effort required for manual identification.
- *Stakeholder data collection*: AI-driven tools can gather and compile stakeholder information from various databases and communication platforms. This ensures that the registry is comprehensive and up-to-date. AI can also cross-reference data to verify accuracy and fill in missing details.

- *Stakeholder analysis*: AI algorithms can analyze stakeholder data to determine their influence, interest, and potential impact on the project. This analysis helps categorize stakeholders and develop appropriate engagement strategies. ML models can predict stakeholder behavior and preferences, enabling more effective communication and relationship management.
- *Predictive insights*: AI tools can provide predictive insights into stakeholder dynamics, such as identifying potential conflicts or predicting changes in stakeholder influence over time. These insights enable proactive management and help mitigate risks associated with stakeholder relationships.

## Use Case for the Stakeholder Register

Table 9.4 shows the prompt we used requesting ChatGPT to build a stakeholder register and the output it produced. As in the case of a project charter, the stakeholder register is a relatively easy application of an LLM.

**Table 9.4** Use case for stakeholder registry

**Prompt**

Attached file* describes Project Pinot. As an experienced project manager specializing in the chemicals manufacturing industry, please build a comprehensive stakeholder registry for Project Pinot by following these steps:

1. Identify the key stakeholders for the project. In addition to identifying obvious stakeholders, think beyond to include stakeholders who may have indirect but significant impacts or interest.
2. Determine whether each stakeholder is internal or external to the organization.
3. Analyze and rate their power and interest on a scale of 1 to 5.
4. Present this information in a clear and detailed table format.
5. Provide critical comments on each stakeholder's role, power, and interest in the project.
6. List the stakeholders in descending order of their combined power and interest levels.

**Response**

Based on the information provided, here is the stakeholder registry for Project Pinot:

| Stakeholder | Role | Internal/ External | Power | Interest | Comments |
|---|---|---|---|---|---|
| Jean Peterson Minelli | Executive sponsor | Internal | 5 | 5 | Critical decision maker focused on project schedule and efficiency |
| Emily Carter | Project manager | Internal | 5 | 5 | Responsible for overall project execution and success |
| Dr. William Allen | R&D lead | Internal | 4 | 5 | Strong advocate for the OmniTreat technology |
| Rao Surya | Engineering lead | Internal | 4 | 5 | Oversees the FEED and ensures project alignment with manufacturing schedules |

*Continued*

**Table 9.4** *continued*

| Stakeholder | Role | Internal/ External | Power | Interest | Comments |
|---|---|---|---|---|---|
| ACME Board Members | Governing body | Internal | 5 | 4 | Provide oversight and approval for major project decisions and budgets |
| Chuck Smith | CEO | Internal | 5 | 3 | Focused on the expansion of the adhesives manufacturing unit |
| Louisiana Department of Environmental Quality (LDEQ) | Regulatory body | External | 5 | 3 | Grants necessary environmental permits for the WWTP |
| Lisa Gonzalez | Procurement lead | Internal | 3 | 4 | Focused on effective procurement of critical components |
| Susan Ming | Regulatory lead | Internal | 3 | 4 | Manages environmental and construction permit applications |
| New Orleans Construction Contractor | Construction partner | External | 3 | 4 | Responsible for the construction phase, especially experienced with hurricane season operations |
| Baton Rouge Engineering Firm | Detailed engineering partner | External | 3 | 4 | Conducts detailed engineering work post-FEED phase |
| University of Minnesota | Research partner | External | 3 | 4 | Provides research support and validation for OmniTreat technology |
| OmniTreat Technology Vendor | Technology provider | External | 2 | 4 | Provides the innovative wastewater treatment technology |
| Baton Rouge Municipal Sewer Authority | Local authority | External | 4 | 2 | Manages the municipal sewer system and imposes surcharges on wastewater discharge |
| Supply Chain Vendors | Suppliers | External | 3 | 3 | Provide critical components and materials required for the WWTP construction and operation |
| Local Community | Community stakeholders | External | 2 | 3 | Interested in the environmental impact and benefits of the project |

This stakeholder registry identifies the key stakeholders for Project Pinot, categorizes them as internal or external, and assesses their power and interest levels.

*Table 9.1

By incorporating AI tools into the process of building and maintaining a stakeholder registry, project managers can enhance the efficiency and comprehensiveness of stakeholder management. This helps the project manager to ensure that all stakeholders are effectively engaged and that their needs and expectations are addressed throughout the project.

## 4. STAKEHOLDER GRID

The stakeholder grid is a visual tool used to categorize project stakeholders typically based on their power level and interest in the project. It helps project managers understand the relative importance of each stakeholder and develop tailored strategies to engage them effectively. The grid consists of a two-dimensional matrix with power on one axis and interest on the other, dividing stakeholders into four quadrants.

### Purpose

The primary purpose of the stakeholder grid is to provide a clear and concise representation of stakeholder dynamics, helping project managers prioritize their engagement efforts. By categorizing stakeholders according to their influence and interest, the grid allows for the development of targeted communication and management strategies that address the specific needs and expectations of each stakeholder group. This ensures that key stakeholders are appropriately managed and their support is secured, ultimately contributing to the project's success.

### Traditional Stakeholder Categorization Techniques

Traditionally, stakeholders are categorized using a variety of techniques:

- *Power/interest grid*: Stakeholders are plotted on a grid based on their level of power (influence) and interest in the project. This helps identify key players and minimal-effort stakeholders while keeping them informed and satisfied.
- *Influence/impact grid*: Similar to the power/interest grid but focuses on the stakeholders' ability to influence the project, along with the impact the project has on them.
- *Salience model*: This model categorizes stakeholders based on their power, legitimacy, and urgency. It helps identify which stakeholders deserve the most attention.
- *Stakeholder analysis matrix*: Lists stakeholders and assesses their influence, interest, impact, and other relevant factors in a tabular format.

### How to Use It

The stakeholder grid is used throughout the project to guide stakeholder engagement and communication strategies. Key uses include:

- *Identifying key stakeholders*: Determining which stakeholders have the most influence and interest and, therefore, require the most attention
- *Developing engagement strategies*: Creating tailored engagement plans based on the stakeholder's position on the grid
- *Prioritizing communication*: Ensuring that high-priority stakeholders receive the most timely and detailed information
- *Monitoring stakeholder dynamics*: Regularly updating the grid to reflect changes in stakeholder influence and interest over time

## AI Tools for the Stakeholder Grid

AI tools can significantly enhance the process of mapping stakeholders on the stakeholder grid by automating data collection, analysis, and visualization. Here are some ways AI can be applied:

- **Automated data collection:** AI can gather stakeholder information from various sources such as project documents, communication records, and social media. NLP tools can extract relevant data points, such as stakeholder roles, interests, and influence, reducing the manual effort involved.
    - *Influence and interest analysis*: AI algorithms can analyze stakeholder data to assess their level of influence and interest in the project. ML models can predict stakeholder behavior and preferences, helping project managers understand how stakeholders might react to different project decisions and changes.
    - *Dynamic visualization*: AI tools can create dynamic and interactive stakeholder grids that update in real time as new data becomes available. This allows project managers to monitor stakeholder dynamics continuously and adjust their engagement strategies accordingly.
    - *Predictive insights*: AI can provide predictive insights into how stakeholder influence and interest might change over the course of the project. This enables proactive management of stakeholder relationships and helps mitigate potential risks associated with stakeholder dynamics.

## Use Case for the Stakeholder Grid

Table 9.5 presents the prompt we used to generate the stakeholder grid for Project Pinot, along with the results grid that ChatGPT produced. Crafting the prompt for this purpose took us several iterations because of the complexity involved in creating the figure with our specific requirements regarding the format and notation. As mentioned in Chapter 4, being specific with your requirements is key to obtaining the desired results.

By incorporating AI tools into the process of creating and maintaining a stakeholder grid, project managers can enhance the accuracy, efficiency, and effectiveness of stakeholder mapping. This ensures that all stakeholders are appropriately categorized and engaged, ultimately contributing to

**Table 9.5** Use case for stakeholder grid

| Prompt |
| --- |
| Please create a graphic showing a 2D map of the stakeholders for Project Pinot by following these instructions:<br>• Prepare the 2D graphic showing each of the stakeholders. The X-axis shows interest, and the Y-axis shows power. The title should be "Stakeholder Grid." Show the grids in light gray.<br>• Prepare the legends. If you find stakeholders with the same score, e.g. (3,3), please combine the strings with the different names and new lines between them as follows: "(3,3) Name 1 Name 2 Name 3."<br>• For the legend, show to the right of each point: the score, e.g., (4, 5), and the initial of the person and last name, e.g., C. Smith, Dr. W. Allen, etc.<br>• Show each one of the stakeholders in a different color. Be careful so the image for each stakeholder does not overlap with the legend. Make the legend a little to the right.<br>• Make the size and fonts medium so it is easy to read. |

*Continued*

**Table 9.2** *(continued)*

| Response |
|---|

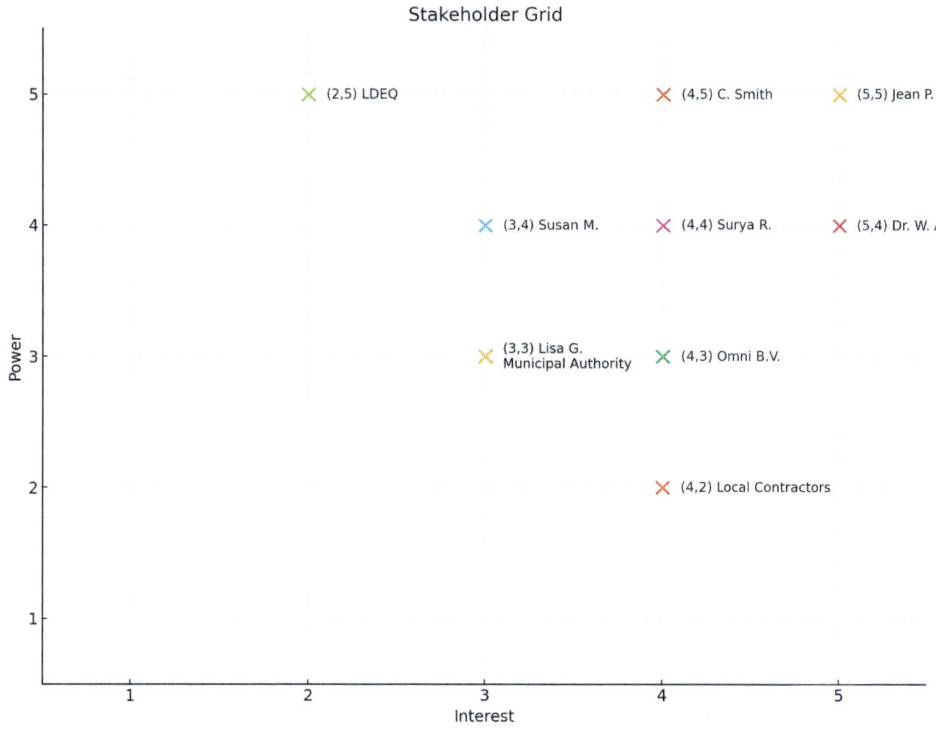


the project's success. The following sections will explore additional AI applications in stakeholder management, including the stakeholder engagement assessment matrix.

## 5. STAKEHOLDER ENGAGEMENT ASSESSMENT MATRIX

The stakeholder engagement assessment matrix is a tool used to evaluate and manage the engagement levels of project stakeholders. It helps project managers assess the current and desired levels of engagement for each stakeholder, providing a structured approach to developing engagement strategies. The matrix typically includes columns for identifying stakeholders, assessing their current level of engagement, determining the desired level of engagement, and outlining actions needed to bridge the gap.

### Purpose

The primary purpose of the stakeholder engagement assessment matrix is to ensure that all stakeholders are appropriately engaged throughout the project. By identifying discrepancies between the current and desired levels of engagement, project managers can develop targeted strategies to increase stakeholder involvement and support. This proactive approach helps in building strong relationships with stakeholders, addressing their concerns, and securing their commitment to the project's success.

## Traditional Methods of Engagement Assessment

Traditionally, engagement assessment involves several steps:

- *Stakeholder interviews and surveys*: Collecting qualitative data from stakeholders about their current level of involvement, interests, and concerns
- *Observation and interaction analysis*: Monitoring stakeholder behavior and interactions during meetings, communications, and project activities
- *Engagement scales*: Using predefined scales to rate the level of stakeholder engagement (e.g., unaware, resistant, neutral, supportive, leading)
- *Expert judgment*: Leveraging the knowledge and experience of project managers and team members to assess stakeholder engagement

## How to Use It

The stakeholder engagement assessment matrix is used throughout the project to guide and improve stakeholder engagement strategies. Key uses include:

- *Identifying engagement gaps*: Comparing current and desired engagement levels to identify areas that need improvement
- *Developing action plans*: Creating specific actions to move stakeholders from their current level of engagement to the desired level
- *Tracking progress*: Monitoring the effectiveness of engagement strategies and adjusting them as needed to ensure stakeholders remain appropriately engaged
- *Enhancing communication*: Tailoring communication plans to address the specific needs and preferences of different stakeholders based on their engagement levels

## AI Tools in Stakeholder Engagement Assessment

AI tools can significantly enhance the process of assessing and managing stakeholder engagement by automating data collection, analysis, and strategy development. Here are some ways AI can be applied:

- *Automated data collection*: AI can gather and analyze data from various sources, such as emails, meeting minutes, social media, and project management systems. NLP tools can extract insights about stakeholder sentiment, behavior, and engagement levels, reducing the need for manual data collection.
- *Engagement analysis*: AI algorithms can analyze stakeholder data to assess their current level of engagement and predict their future behavior. ML models can identify patterns and trends in stakeholder interactions, providing deeper insights into their engagement levels.
- *Customized engagement strategies*: AI tools can suggest tailored engagement strategies based on the analysis of stakeholder data. By understanding the specific needs and preferences of each stakeholder, AI can recommend actions that are more likely to increase their engagement and support.
- *Real-time monitoring and updates*: AI can provide real-time updates and alerts about changes in stakeholder engagement levels. This allows project managers to quickly respond to emerging issues and adjust their engagement strategies accordingly.
- *Predictive analytics*: AI tools can offer predictive insights into how stakeholder engagement levels might change over the course of the project. This enables proactive management of stakeholder relationships and helps mitigate potential risks associated with low engagement.

## Use Case for the Stakeholder Engagement Assessment Matrix

Table 9.6 presents the prompt applied to produce the stakeholder engagement assessment matrix, along with the results ChatGPT generated. The matrix can be generated in the form of a figure (Project Management Institute, 2021) or a table. For the sake of more clarity, we opted for the tabular format. ChatGPT was quite effective in sensing the attitude of different stakeholders by going through the brief description of the project provided as input. However, if email and other communications among the stakeholders are digitized and incorporated into the PIF, the LLM would detect the nuances of stakeholder behaviors and attitudes and perform an even better job in assessing their engagement and support.

**Table 9.6** Use case for stakeholder engagement assessment matrix

| Prompt |
|---|
| Please create a stakeholder engagement assessment matrix for Project Pinot. |
| **Response** |
| The stakeholder engagement assessment matrix assesses the current and desired levels of stakeholder engagement. This matrix helps to identify gaps and plan strategies to achieve the desired engagement levels. Based on the provided Project Pinot case study, here is the stakeholder engagement assessment matrix: |

| Stakeholder | Current Engagement Level | Desired Engagement Level | Comments |
|---|---|---|---|
| Jean Peterson Minelli | Resistant | Supportive | Jean is focused on project efficiency and schedule. Needs to be convinced of the technology's benefits. |
| Emily Carter | Leading | Leading | Emily is the project manager and is already leading the project. |
| Dr. William Allen | Supportive | Leading | Strong advocate for OmniTreat technology. Needs to lead the technical validation and promotion of the technology. |
| Rao Surya | Neutral | Supportive | Practical and focused on timelines. Needs to understand the technology's feasibility to support it. |
| ACME Board Members | Neutral | Supportive | Need detailed information on project benefits and financials to become supportive. |
| Chuck Smith | Neutral | Supportive | CEO focused on adhesives unit expansion. Needs to be informed about the project's strategic importance. |
| LDEQ (Louisiana Department of Environmental Quality) | Neutral | Supportive | Needs to be kept informed about environmental benefits and compliance aspects. |

*Continued*

**Table 9.6** *continued*

| Stakeholder | Current Engagement Level | Desired Engagement Level | Comments |
|---|---|---|---|
| Lisa Gonzalez | Neutral | Supportive | Pragmatic about technology. Needs evidence of effectiveness and procurement strategy. |
| Susan Ming | Neutral | Supportive | Focused on compliance and permits. Needs clear communication about regulatory requirements and project benefits. |
| New Orleans Construction Contractor | Neutral | Supportive | Needs clear timelines and expectations to support the construction phase. |
| Baton Rouge Engineering Firm | Neutral | Supportive | Needs detailed engineering plans and project timelines to support the detailed design phase. |
| University of Minnesota | Neutral | Supportive | Needs to be involved in the technology validation process. |
| OmniTreat Technology Vendor | Neutral | Supportive | Needs to be involved in the technology validation and implementation process. |
| Baton Rouge Municipal Sewer Authority | Neutral | Supportive | Needs to understand the benefits of reducing the municipal sewer load. |
| Supply Chain Vendors | Neutral | Supportive | Needs clear procurement plans and timelines. |
| Local Community | Neutral | Supportive | Needs to be informed about environmental benefits and community impact. |

By incorporating AI tools into the process of stakeholder engagement assessment, project managers can enhance the efficiency and effectiveness of their engagement strategies. This ensures that all stakeholders are appropriately engaged and their needs and expectations are addressed throughout the project.

## 6. COMMUNICATION PLAN

The communication plan is a strategic document that outlines how project information will be disseminated to stakeholders throughout the project. It details the communication objectives, methods, frequency, and responsible parties, ensuring all stakeholders are informed and engaged. The plan includes specifics on what information will be communicated, who will receive it, how it will be delivered, and when it will be shared.

## Purpose

The primary purpose of the communication plan is to facilitate effective information flow between the project team and stakeholders. It ensures that all parties are informed about project progress, changes, and issues, thereby promoting transparency and trust. An effective communication plan helps manage stakeholder expectations, minimize misunderstandings, and enhance collaboration. By clearly defining communication processes and responsibilities, the plan ensures that critical information reaches the right people at the right time.

## Traditional Communication Planning Challenges

Traditional communication planning faces several challenges:

- *Stakeholder diversity*: Managing the diverse communication needs and preferences of different stakeholders can be complex and time-consuming
- *Information overload*: Ensuring that stakeholders receive relevant information without overwhelming them with unnecessary details
- *Timeliness*: Delivering timely updates and responses to stakeholders, especially in dynamic project environments
- *Consistency*: Maintaining consistency in messaging to avoid conflicting or misleading information
- *Engagement*: Ensuring that communication efforts effectively engage stakeholders and encourage their active participation in the project

## How to Use It

The communication plan is used throughout the project to guide and manage stakeholder communications. Key uses include:

- *Defining communication objectives*: Establishing clear goals for what the communication efforts aim to achieve
- *Identifying stakeholders*: Determining who needs to be informed and engaged at various stages of the project
- *Selecting communication methods*: Choosing the appropriate channels and formats for delivering information (e.g., emails, meetings, reports)
- *Establishing communication frequency:* Setting a schedule for regular updates and meetings to keep stakeholders informed
- *Assigning responsibilities*: Designating individuals responsible for delivering communications and ensuring follow-through
- *Monitoring and adjusting*: Regularly reviewing the effectiveness of the communication plan and adjusting as needed to improve stakeholder engagement

## AI Tools in Developing Communication Plans

AI tools can significantly enhance the development and execution of communication plans by automating data collection, analysis, and strategy formulation. Here are some ways AI can be applied:

- *Stakeholder communication analysis*: AI can analyze past communications and stakeholder interactions to identify preferences, behaviors, and engagement levels. NLP tools can extract insights from emails, meeting notes, and feedback forms to inform communication strategies.

- *Tailored communication strategies*: AI algorithms can develop customized communication plans based on stakeholder profiles and preferences. By understanding each stakeholder's specific needs and interests, AI can recommend the most effective channels, content, and frequency for communication.
- *Automated updates and alerts*: AI tools can automate the delivery of project updates and alerts, ensuring that stakeholders receive timely and relevant information. Automated systems can be set up to send notifications about project milestones, changes, and issues, reducing the manual effort involved.
- *Sentiment analysis*: AI-powered sentiment analysis can assess stakeholder feedback and communications to gauge their attitudes and concerns. This allows project managers to proactively address issues and adjust communication strategies to improve stakeholder satisfaction.
- *Real-time monitoring and adjustments*: AI can provide real-time monitoring of communication effectiveness, offering insights into which strategies are working and which need adjustment. This enables project managers to continuously refine their communication efforts to ensure maximum engagement and impact.

## Use Case for the Communication Plan

Table 9.7 displays the prompt for Project Pinot's communication plan and the plan ChatGPT generated. As mentioned before, crafting a prompt for generating a communication plan is a relatively easy exercise that can be easily adapted by project professionals.

**Table 9.7** Use case for communication plan

**Prompt**

Please put together a comprehensive communication plan for Project Pinot and provide the information in a table.

**Response**

A comprehensive communication plan ensures that all stakeholders are kept informed and engaged throughout the life cycle of Project Pinot. The following table outlines the communication plan for Project Pinot, detailing the type of communication, frequency, audience, purpose, and responsible party.

| Communication Type | Frequency | Audience | Purpose | Responsible Party |
|---|---|---|---|---|
| **Kickoff Meeting** | Once | Project team, key stakeholders | Introduce the project; outline objectives, roles, and responsibilities | Project manager (Emily Carter) |
| **Project Status Reports** | Weekly | Project team, executive sponsor, key stakeholders | Provide updates on project progress, milestones, and any issues | Project manager (Emily Carter) |
| **Steering Committee Meetings** | Bi-weekly | Executive sponsor, project manager, key stakeholders | Review project status, address high-level issues, and make strategic decisions | Executive sponsor (Jean Peterson Minelli) |

*Continued*

**Table 9.7** *(continued)*

| Communication Type | Frequency | Audience | Purpose | Responsible Party |
|---|---|---|---|---|
| **Team Meetings** | Weekly | Project team | Discuss detailed project activities, progress, and immediate next steps | Project manager (Emily Carter) |
| **Stakeholder Updates** | Monthly | All stakeholders | Inform all stakeholders of major milestones, changes, and achievements | Project manager (Emily Carter) |
| **Risk Review Meetings** | Monthly | Project team, risk management team | Identify, assess, and mitigate project risks | Risk management lead (Susan Ming) |
| **Technical Review Meetings** | As needed | R&D team, engineering team, external consultants | Discuss technical issues, progress, and solutions | R&D lead (Dr. William Allen) |
| **Change Control Meetings** | As needed | Project team, change control board | Review and approve/reject changes to the project scope, schedule, or budget | Change control board chair (Jean Peterson Minelli) |
| **Regulatory Updates** | As needed | Regulatory authorities (LDEQ), legal team | Ensure compliance with regulations, update on permit status | Regulatory lead (Susan Ming) |
| **Construction Progress Reports** | Bi-weekly | Project team, construction contractor | Track construction progress, address any site issues | Construction manager (New Orleans contractor) |
| **Procurement Status Reports** | Monthly | Project team, procurement lead | Update on procurement status, address any supply chain issues | Procurement lead (Lisa Gonzalez) |
| **Community Briefings** | Quarterly | Local community, public relations team | Inform the local community about project progress and address concerns | Public relations manager (TBD) |
| **Project Closure Meeting** | Once (end of project) | Project team, key stakeholders | Review project outcomes, lessons learned, and formally close the project | Project manager (Emily Carter) |

By incorporating AI tools into the development and execution of communication plans, project managers can enhance the efficiency and effectiveness of their stakeholder communications. This ensures that all stakeholders are kept informed, engaged, and aligned with the project's goals and progress.

## IN CONCLUSION

As we conclude the chapter on AI use cases in the project initiation phase, it is clear that the integration of AI can significantly enhance the efficiency and accuracy of early project stages. The use of AI in stakeholder analysis and in developing key initiation documents, such as the project charter, has demonstrated the potential for reducing time and increasing the precision of project scope definition and stakeholder engagement. These advancements allow project managers to set a solid foundation for the projects, ensuring all necessary parameters are well understood and appropriately documented.

Moving forward, the next chapter will shift our focus to the planning phase, where AI's capabilities will be leveraged to streamline and optimize more complex aspects of project management. From scheduling to resource allocation and risk assessment, AI tools offer promising solutions that can adapt to the dynamic needs of project management. This transition from initiation to planning marks a critical step in exploring the depth of AI's utility in managing projects efficiently and effectively within a waterfall framework.

# 10

# AI USE CASES IN PROJECT PLANNING

Effective project planning is the cornerstone of successful project management. It is the process that guides project teams in defining objectives, allocating resources, and outlining the necessary steps to achieve the project's goals. Proper planning ensures that all aspects of the project are well-coordinated and that potential issues are identified and addressed early on. In this chapter, we will explore how artificial intelligence (AI) can revolutionize project planning by enhancing the development of the three most critical baselines: scope, schedule, and cost. The baselines define the work to be performed, how much it costs, and how long it will take. They comprise your plans, against which you compare the actual project progress to determine whether or not the project is on track.

The three baselines form the foundation upon which project planning is built. They provide a comprehensive framework for managing project performance and ensuring that project objectives are met efficiently and effectively. Each baseline serves a specific purpose:

1. *Scope baseline*: Defines the totality of work to be performed and sets the boundaries for what will be delivered
2. *Schedule baseline*: Establishes the project timeline, including start and finish dates for project activities
3. *Cost baseline*: Outlines the budget and financial requirements for the project

These baselines are crucial because they offer a structured approach to planning and controlling project activities, ensuring that the project remains aligned with its objectives and constraints.

In this chapter, we will demonstrate specific AI use cases that support the development and management of these baselines. Furthermore, we will also present use cases related to project resources and risk management that impact the three baselines. By integrating AI into project planning, we can leverage data-driven insights, enhance decision making, and improve overall project efficiency. Here is an overview of the use cases we will cover:

1. *Work breakdown structure (WBS)*: We will examine how AI can assist in creating a detailed WBS, which breaks down the project scope into manageable sections
2. *Project scheduling*: We will explore how AI tools can identify the critical path using the critical path method (CPM) and automate the generation of Gantt charts, aiding in schedule management
3. *Cost estimation*: We will discuss how AI can enhance the accuracy of bottom-up cost estimates by analyzing historical data and predicting future expenses

4. *RACI chart*: We will cover how AI can streamline the development of RACI (responsible, accountable, consulted, and informed) charts and resources, ensuring a clear definition of roles and responsibilities
5. *Integrated performance measurement baseline (IPMB)*: We will investigate how AI can facilitate the integration of scope, schedule, and cost baselines using a cumulative cost curve
6. *Risk register*: We will illustrate how AI can help you create a risk register to identify, analyze, and rank risks and opportunities
7. *Risk response planning*: Finally, we will show how AI can identify and plan risk response or treatment actions that align with each of the five common response strategies applied for threats and opportunities

While there are many other planning areas, including procurement and quality, we wanted to focus on these seven areas because of their critical importance to every project. As in the previous chapter, we first provide a primer for the tool or technique (e.g., WBS and CPM) behind the use case before illustrating how AI is applied. Two good references for project planning are the Project Management Body of Knowledge Guide by the Project Management Institute (2017) and a comprehensive textbook by Kerzner (2022).

To illustrate the various use cases, we will continue using the Project Pinot case study introduced in the previous chapter on project initiation. This ongoing example will maintain continuity and provide a cohesive narrative, making it easier to understand the practical application of AI in project planning. By following Project Pinot through each stage of planning, from scope definition to integrated performance baseline and risk planning, we aim to provide clear and relatable insights into how AI can enhance each aspect of the project planning process.

By the end of this chapter, you should have a comprehensive understanding of how AI can be applied to key aspects of project planning, ultimately leading to more successful and well-managed projects.

## 1. WORK BREAKDOWN STRUCTURE

One of the most fundamental tools in project scope management is the WBS. It is a hierarchical decomposition of the total scope of work to be carried out by the project team to accomplish the project objectives and create the required deliverables. It serves as a bridge between the project's high-level goals and the detailed tasks that need to be performed. By breaking down the project into smaller, more manageable components, the WBS helps in organizing and defining the total scope of the project. It facilitates easier assignment of responsibilities, resource allocation, and tracking of progress. Additionally, the WBS can be a powerful tool for identifying potential scope creep by clearly delineating what is included in the project and what falls outside its boundaries.

### Definition of a WBS

A WBS is a foundational tool used in project management. It represents a hierarchical decomposition of a project into smaller, more manageable components. The WBS organizes and defines the total scope of the project, breaking it down into discrete work elements that can be scheduled, estimated, and controlled.

## Use of a WBS in Project Planning, Monitoring, and Control

In project planning, the WBS serves as a roadmap, outlining the project's key deliverables and guiding the planning of activities, resources, and timelines. It helps in identifying all necessary tasks and provides a structured view of what needs to be accomplished.

During project execution, the WBS is vital in monitoring and control. It allows project managers to track progress at various levels, ensuring that each component of the project is progressing as planned. It also facilitates effective control by highlighting areas that may require additional attention or resources, thereby enabling timely interventions.

## Different Formats of a WBS

1. *Tree structure*: This is the most common format, resembling an organizational chart. The top level represents the project, and the subsequent levels represent major deliverables or phases broken down into smaller tasks in a hierarchical fashion. This format is suitable for relatively small projects.
2. *Outline view*: Similar to a bullet list, this format follows an outline structure and is simple and easy to create. It lists all elements of the WBS in a hierarchical manner. This format is common for large projects with numerous tasks.
3. *Tabular format*: This format presents the WBS in a table, with each level of breakdown represented as a new column. It is not as common as the first two formats, but is useful for projects with a clear, linear structure.

## Hierarchy and Levels in a WBS

A fundamental aspect of creating an effective WBS is understanding the optimal number of hierarchical levels. For most projects, maintaining four to five levels is adequate. This ensures enough detail for effective management without becoming unwieldy. Each level serves a specific purpose in breaking down the project's scope:

1. *First level—project title*: This is the top level, which represents the project as a whole.
2. *Second level—major phases or deliverables*: Typically, this level is reserved for major project phases or key deliverables. For instance, in a typical project, you might see phases such as initiation, planning, execution, and closeout. These phases align with the waterfall project life cycle, providing a structured approach to project management.
3. *Third level—sub-phases or sub-deliverables*: This level breaks down the major phases or deliverables into more specific segments. For example, in the planning phase, you could have requirements gathering, budgeting, and scheduling.
4. *Fourth level—work packages*: Here, the focus shifts to detailed work packages, which are the smallest units of work in a WBS. (A work package includes activities that are closely related and often completed together or in sequence.) Typically, this is the level where the resource, schedule, and cost estimates are made and work is allocated, monitored, and controlled.
5. *Fifth level (if applicable)—activities:* Some projects may require a further breakdown of work packages into specific activities. This level is more granular, detailing the individual actions needed to complete each work package.

This breakdown is just an example. There are no hard and fast rules on the criteria for a breakdown. It depends on myriad number of factors including the nature of your project, your organizational structure, project management information systems, etc.

## Benefits of a WBS

1. *Clear project scope definition*: WBS provides a detailed and clear outline of the work involved in a project, reducing ambiguities about project scope.
2. *Improved task management*: By breaking down the project into smaller tasks, WBS makes it easier to manage and assign responsibilities.
3. *Enhanced planning and scheduling*: WBS facilitates better estimation of time, cost, and resources, aiding in efficient project scheduling.
4. *Effective progress monitoring*: It provides a framework for tracking project progress and performance against established baselines and helps you manage change.
5. *Risk identification*: WBS helps in identifying risks at different levels of project work, allowing for proactive risk management.

## Guidelines for Creating a WBS

1. *Clear objectives*: Define each work package with a specific objective and measurable outcome, ensuring alignment with the project's overall goals.
2. *Stakeholder and team involvement*: Engage team members and stakeholders in the development process to ensure accuracy and comprehensive input.
3. *Use the 100% rule*: Ensure the WBS captures 100% of the project scope without omissions or unnecessary additions.
4. *Balanced detail*: Break work into manageable packages—neither too broad nor overly detailed—maintaining clarity and avoiding micromanagement.
5. *Action-oriented descriptions*: Begin each work package description with an action verb, such as *develop, conduct*, or *design*, to clarify the work that needs to be done.
6. *Defined accountability*: Assign responsibility for each work package to ensure accountability and facilitate progress tracking.
7. *Regular review and updates*: Periodically review and update the WBS to reflect changes, using tools like a WBS dictionary for detailed documentation.

By following these streamlined guidelines, project managers can create a structured, practical WBS that supports the efficient planning, execution, and control of project tasks.

## Use Case for a WBS

After working on WBSs for numerous projects, we observed that when you ask any generative AI (Gen AI) large language model (LLM) like ChatGPT to create a WBS by giving it some project background, it generates a meaningful structure but without enough detail. However, for a more detailed and comprehensive WBS, a better approach is to build it step by step, one level at a time. This hierarchical approach allows the AI to provide more detailed and thorough results.

As shown in Table 10.1, in our first step we prompted ChatGPT to create a WBS for the initiation phase of the project. (Although this phase was already covered in the previous chapter, we included it here for the sake of illustration.) After receiving the results, using the second prompt we asked for the WBS of the planning, execution, and close-out phases sequentially. To capture more detail, we divided the execution phase into implementation and monitoring & controlling.

**Table 10.1** Use case for a WBS

**Prompt**

**Prompt 1**

You are a project management expert specializing in work breakdown structures with more than 15 years of experience. I need you to create a WBS for Project Pinot described in the attached PDF.* Please use only four levels. Make the first level project title, the second level the generic project life-cycle phases (Initiation, Planning, Execution, Monitoring and Control, and Closeout), the third level functional groups (e.g., engineering, procurement, regulatory), and the fourth level the work packages. You will build the WBS one phase at a time. Start with the initiation phase. Make sure that the total number of work packages for each phase does not exceed 20. Start each work package with an action verb. Present the WBS in an outline format.

(After receiving the results for the above prompt, we tasked ChatGPT with the prompt below.)

**Prompt 2**

Please create the WBS for the next phase.

(We repeated this prompt for the remaining phases of the project.)

**Prompt 3**

Please combine the work breakdown structures for all the phases—Initiation, Planning, Execution, Monitoring and Control, and Closeout—with their respective work packages and present the comprehensive WBS for the entire project.

(The results from Prompt 3 for the execution phase only are presented below due to space limitations.)

**Response**

**Project Pinot WBS**

**1. Project Pinot**

**1.3 Execution**

**1.3.1 Pre-FEED (Front-End Engineering Design)**

1.3.1.1 Conduct Preliminary Analysis

1.3.1.2 Develop Pre-FEED Documentation

1.3.1.3 Review Pre-FEED Requirements

**1.3.2 FEED**

1.3.2.1 Develop FEED Plans

1.3.2.2 Conduct FEED Studies

1.3.2.3 Review and Approve FEED Deliverables

**1.3.3 Detailed Engineering**

1.3.3.1 Finalize Engineering Designs

1.3.3.2 Develop Detailed Specifications

1.3.3.3 Coordinate with Engineering Teams

**1.3.4 Procurement**

1.3.4.1 Develop Procurement Schedule

1.3.4.2 Identify and Select Vendors

1.3.4.3 Issue Purchase Orders

*Continued*

**Table 10.1** *continued*

| |
|---|
| **1.3.5 Regulatory** |
| 1.3.5.1 Obtain Necessary Permits |
| 1.3.5.2 Ensure Compliance with Regulations |
| 1.3.5.3 Coordinate with Regulatory Bodies |
| **1.3.6 Construction** |
| 1.3.6.1 Develop Construction Schedule |
| 1.3.6.2 Mobilize Construction Teams |
| 1.3.6.3 Monitor Construction Progress |
| **1.3.7 Commissioning** |
| 1.3.7.1 Develop Commissioning Plan |
| 1.3.7.2 Conduct Commissioning Tests |
| 1.3.7.3 Review and Approve Commissioning Results |

* Table 9.1

After the LLM generated the breakdown for all the phases, we asked it to combine all the results to produce the complete project WBS. The sequential prompts used and a section (execution phase) of the WBS produced by ChatGPT are shown in Table 10.1. We opted to show only a portion of the WBS due to space limitations in the book. For a complete breakdown of the WBS, you may visit the website: www.pmaihandbook.com.

The results demonstrate the effectiveness of an iterative approach when utilizing Gen AI for building a WBS, particularly for a relatively large project like Project Pinot. By breaking down the WBS creation process into smaller, manageable steps and providing specific prompts, we achieved a more comprehensive WBS. The final WBS generated for Project Pinot reflects a well-organized breakdown, showcasing the ability of AI to support complex project planning activities when guided with incremental inputs. We restricted the number of work packages for each phase to a maximum of 20 for the sake of simplicity. For a more comprehensive WBS, you may use a far higher number. Furthermore, for even more detail, you can ask the LLM to add another level to the WBS by breaking down the current work packages to the next level.

## ESTIMATION

With the WBS defining the project's scope in detail, the next crucial step in planning is to develop reliable estimates for schedule, cost, and resources. LLMs like ChatGPT bring notable strengths and limitations to project estimation. While they offer speed, flexibility, and automation, challenges arise due to their reliance on generalized data, a lack of project-specific context, and the absence of real-time updates. ChatGPT can quickly provide rough estimates using industry benchmarks, but they are often broad and require refinement to suit unique project needs. Without access to real-time data or organizational specifics, the model may produce generic schedules, inaccurate cost estimates, and impractical resource allocations.

Despite these limitations, ChatGPT excels at providing a starting point, leveraging historical benchmarks, and exploring scenario-based estimates. To address its gaps, project managers can provide detailed prompts, attach relevant project data, and iteratively refine outputs. Training the AI with organizational data and supplementing its estimates with expert input ensures a tailored and practical approach. Regular review and transparent communication of AI-generated results are essential for aligning estimates with actual project conditions, enhancing reliability.

By integrating ChatGPT into the estimation process with these strategies, teams can harness its efficiency while maintaining accuracy and relevance. The PRIME model—prepare, relay, inspect, modify, and execute—offers a structured framework for optimizing AI's role in project estimation.

The following sections will describe specific project management tools used for scheduling, cost estimation, and resource allocation. As before, we provide a primer for each tool before going through the use case example.

## 2. PROJECT SCHEDULING

Project scheduling is a vital aspect of project management, providing a framework for organizing tasks to ensure the timely completion of projects. It involves listing project activities, their dependencies and sequences (generally referred to as predecessor and successor relationships), and milestones with intended start and finish dates. Among various scheduling techniques, CPM stands out as a powerful tool for planning, monitoring, and controlling project timelines.

Developed in the late 1950s, CPM is a project modeling technique that identifies the longest sequence of dependent tasks necessary to complete a project. This sequence, known as the critical path, determines the shortest possible project duration. Delays in any critical path tasks directly impact the project's completion time. In applying CPM, it is implicitly assumed that all resources will be available to complete the tasks within their estimated time durations. If the durations change because of resource changes, the CPM calculations must be redone.

Instead of us describing the CPM, we asked ChatGPT to illustrate it using a simple example without giving any specific list of tasks and their durations and dependencies. The purpose of this exercise is to simply demonstrate the CPM calculations. (We will illustrate the use case of CPM calculations for Project Pinot later in this section.) Table 10.2 shows our prompt and the results the LLM produced. As requested, the LLM produced a simple example for illustration purposes and explained the calculations.

**Table 10.2** Illustration of the CPM

**Prompt**

Can you please explain the CPM with forward and backward pass calculations using a list of five tasks, where four of them are critical and one noncritical. 1) Build a table showing task number, duration (days), and predecessor(s) task number(s). 2) Show the calculations. 3) Prepare a Gantt chart showing the critical tasks in a dark shade and the noncritical in a light shade.

**Response***

**Project Summary Table:**

| Task No. | Duration (days) | ES | EF | LS | LF | Total Float | Critical Path |
|---|---|---|---|---|---|---|---|
| 1 | 3 | 0 | 3 | 0 | 3 | 0 | Yes |
| 2 | 5 | 3 | 8 | 3 | 8 | 0 | Yes |
| 3 | 2 | 3 | 5 | 6 | 8 | 3 | No |
| 4 | 4 | 8 | 12 | 8 | 12 | 0 | Yes |
| 5 | 3 | 12 | 15 | 12 | 15 | 0 | Yes |

*Continued*

**Table 10.2** *continued*

**Calculations:**

- Step 1: Forward Pass Calculations—Calculating ES and EF:

Task 1:

ES = 0 (start of the project)

EF = ES + Duration = 0 + 3 = 3

Task 2:

ES = EF of Task 1 = 3

EF = ES + Duration = 3 + 5 = 8

Task 3:

ES = EF of Task 1 = 3

EF = ES + Duration = 3 + 2 = 5

Task 4:

ES = max (EF of Task 2, EF of Task 3) = max (8, 5) = 8

EF = ES + Duration = 8 + 4 = 12

Task 5:

ES = EF of Task 4 = 12

EF = ES + Duration = 12 + 3 = 15

- Step 2: Backward Pass Calculations—Calculating LS and LF:

Task 5:

LF = EF = 15 (end of the project)

LS = LF − Duration = 15 − 3 = 12

Task 4:

LF = LS of Task 5 = 12

LS = LF − Duration = 12 − 4 = 8

Task 3:

LF = LS of Task 4 = 8

LS = LF − Duration = 8 − 2 = 6

Task 2:

LF = LS of Task 4 = 8

LS = LF − Duration = 8 − 5 = 3

Task 1:

LF = min (LS of Task 2, LS of Task 3) = min (3, 6) = 3

LS = LF − Duration = 3 − 3 = 0

- Step 3: Calculate Total Float and Identify Critical Path

Total Float Calculation:

Task 1: LS − ES = 0 − 0 = 0

Task 2: LS − ES = 3 − 3 = 0

Task 3: LS − ES = 6 − 3 = 3

Task 4: LS − ES = 8 − 8 = 0

Task 5: LS − ES = 12 − 12 = 0

*Continued*

**Table 10.2** *continued*

- Critical Path Identification:

Tasks with zero total float are on the critical path.

Critical Path Tasks: Task 1, Task 2, Task 4, Task 5

**Summary Table:**

| Task No. | Duration (days) | Predecessor Task No. | ES | EF | LS | LF | Total Float | Critical Path |
|---|---|---|---|---|---|---|---|---|
| 1 | 3 | | 0 | 3 | 0 | 3 | 0 | Yes |
| 2 | 5 | 1 | 3 | 8 | 3 | 8 | 0 | Yes |
| 3 | 2 | 1 | 3 | 5 | 6 | 8 | 3 | No |
| 4 | 4 | 2, 3 | 8 | 12 | 8 | 12 | 0 | Yes |
| 5 | 3 | 4 | 12 | 15 | 12 | 15 | 0 | Yes |

**Explanation:**

- The critical path is the sequence of tasks that cannot be delayed without delaying the project.
- Tasks on the critical path are Task 1, Task 2, Task 4, and Task 5.
- Noncritical tasks have float time, meaning they can be delayed without affecting the project's end date. Task 3 is noncritical with a total float of 3 days.

By identifying the critical path, project managers can focus on monitoring and managing these tasks closely to ensure the project stays on schedule.

**Gantt Chart:**

| Task No. | Days | | | | | | | | | | | | | | |
|---|---|---|---|---|---|---|---|---|---|---|---|---|---|---|---|
| | 1 | 2 | 3 | 4 | 5 | 6 | 7 | 8 | 9 | 10 | 11 | 12 | 13 | 14 | 15 |
| 1 | ■ | ■ | ■ | | | | | | | | | | | | |
| 2 | | | | ■ | ■ | ■ | ■ | ■ | | | | | | | |
| 3 | | | | ░ | ░ | | | | | | | | | | |
| 4 | | | | | | | | | ■ | ■ | ■ | ■ | | | |
| 5 | | | | | | | | | | | | | ■ | ■ | ■ |

■ Represents a day of work for a critical task (solid black).

░ Represents a day of work for a noncritical task (light gray).

*In CPM scheduling, ES and EF represent the earliest times an activity can start and finish, respectively, while LS and LF indicate the latest times it can start and finish, respectively, without delaying the overall project.

## Benefits of the CPM

1. *Project schedule determination*: Using the CPM, you can determine how long the project will take.
2. *Enhanced planning accuracy*: By identifying the critical path, project managers can focus on key tasks that influence the project's completion date, leading to more accurate and realistic schedules.
3. *Improved resource allocation*: CPM helps in allocating resources efficiently by highlighting tasks that require immediate attention.

4. *Risk management*: Identifying critical and noncritical tasks enables better risk management, allowing managers to allocate buffers for potential delays.
5. *Better decision making*: CPM provides a clear picture of project timelines, facilitating informed decision making regarding schedule adjustments and resource reallocation.
6. *Increased accountability*: Clear identification of critical tasks enhances accountability among team members, ensuring timely task completion.

## Guidelines in Applying a CPM

1. Ensure all tasks required for project completion are identified and listed
2. Ensure all task dependencies are clearly identified to avoid incorrect sequence assumptions
3. Use reliable data and expert judgment to estimate task durations accurately
4. Keep the project schedule updated with actual progress to reflect the current project status
5. Regularly analyze the critical path to identify any changes and take corrective actions promptly
6. Maintain clear communication with stakeholders about the project schedule, critical path activities, and any potential risks

## Network Diagrams and Gantt Charts

Underpinning the CPM is the network diagram, commonly shown as an activity-on-node diagram, where nodes represent tasks and arrows show dependencies. It helps visualize the project workflow and determine the earliest and latest start and finish times for each task to identify the critical path. Understanding how to apply CPM, translate it into network diagrams and Gantt charts, and leverage its benefits can significantly enhance project management practices, leading to more successful project outcomes.

The Gantt chart is a type of bar chart that represents the project schedule, showing task durations, start and finish dates, and dependencies. Typically, it uses a distinct color or style to highlight the critical path tasks. The advantages of network diagrams and Gantt charts include:

- *Visual clarity*: Both tools provide a clear visual representation of the project schedule, making it easier to understand and communicate
- *Tracking progress*: Gantt charts are particularly useful for tracking progress against the planned schedule
- *Identifying bottlenecks*: Network diagrams help identify potential bottlenecks and areas that may require additional attention

ChatGPT created a simple Gantt chart for the example project it created, while illustrating the CPM calculations. The results are included in Table 10.2.

## Use Case for Project Scheduling

ChatGPT can be employed in various ways for project scheduling, leveraging its capabilities to streamline and optimize project management tasks. One approach is to provide a list of project tasks and request ChatGPT to estimate their durations. While ChatGPT can generate duration estimates based on its extensive training data, as mentioned before, these estimates may not fully capture the unique conditions and constraints of your specific project. Therefore, it is crucial to complement these estimates with input from experienced project managers and historical data from similar projects in your organization, if possible, to ensure accuracy.

Another potential use of ChatGPT is to identify task dependencies. By analyzing the tasks provided, ChatGPT can suggest logical sequences and relationships between them. While these suggestions can be insightful and meaningful, they might not be perfectly tailored to the nuances of your project. It is essential to validate these dependencies through expert judgment and thorough project analysis to ensure they align with your project's specific requirements and constraints.

The application of CPM is a practical and valuable use case for ChatGPT in project scheduling. By supplying ChatGPT with a list of tasks along with their estimated durations and dependencies, it can effectively perform CPM calculations. This involves determining the earliest and latest start and finish times for each task, identifying the critical path, and calculating the total float.

It is important to note that while ChatGPT can handle CPM calculations for projects with a manageable number of tasks, it may struggle with schedules that include dozens of tasks due to processing limitations. Therefore, we recommend using ChatGPT to build your project schedule, utilizing higher-level WBS components. This approach allows ChatGPT to provide valuable insights and calculations without being overwhelmed by the complexity of extensive task lists.

Therefore, instead of using a detailed WBS of Project Pinot (see Table 10.1), we created a simplified list of high-level tasks and defined their durations and dependencies, as shown in Table 10.3. When attaching this table, we tasked ChatGPT to perform CPM calculations. The prompt we used and the results received are displayed in Table 10.4. For this exercise, ChatGPT performed the CPM calculations accurately without us going through too many iterations. This exercise demonstrates how ChatGPT can assist in identifying the critical path, calculating task durations, and providing a structured approach to project scheduling.

Using the high-level listing of tasks in Table 10.3, we also asked ChatGPT to create a Gantt chart. The prompt for this use case and ChatGPT's response are presented in Table 10.5. It took several iterations to refine the prompt and achieve the desired chart format. While ChatGPT was able to produce the simpler Gantt chart shown in Table 10.2 relatively easily with minimal instructions, generating the Gantt chart for Project Pinot proved to be significantly more challenging. This difficulty likely stemmed from the increased complexity of Project Pinot, which includes a larger number of tasks and multiple parallel paths. These factors add layers of intricacy to the

**Table 10.3** Project Pinot high-level tasks and schedule

| Task | | | |
|---|---|---|---|
| ID | Name | Baseline Duration, Weeks | Predecessor Task ID(s) |
| 1 | Start | 0 | None |
| 2 | Feasibility study | 12 | 1 |
| 3 | Project definition | 2 | 2 |
| 4 | Project sanction | 1 | 3 |
| 5 | Environmental permit | 50 | 4 |
| 6 | Construction permits | 14 | 4 |
| 7 | FEED | 3 | 4 |
| 8 | Procurement | 30 | 7 |
| 9 | Detailed engineering | 10 | 7 |
| 10 | Construction | 18 | 6, 9 |
| 11 | Equipment installation | 8 | 8, 10 |
| 12 | Commissioning & closeout | 4 | 11 |
| 13 | Finish | 0 | 5,12 |

scheduling and sequencing of tasks, requiring more explicit guidance in the prompt to ensure accuracy. Furthermore, the dependencies and overlap between tasks in Project Pinot demanded precise definitions, making it essential to provide additional context and structure in the input to guide ChatGPT effectively. This highlights the importance of tailoring prompts to the complexity of the project when leveraging AI for such tasks.

**Table 10.4** Use case for CPM calculations

**Prompt**

The attached table* shows a high-level list of tasks, durations, and predecessor relationships for Project Pinot. As an experienced project scheduler, please apply the critical path method and build a table with the following columns: Task ID, Task Name, Early Start (ES), Early Finish (EF), Late Start (LS), Late Finish (LF), and Total Float. Highlight the tasks that are on the critical path. No need to show the calculations.

**Response**

Here is the critical path method (CPM) analysis for Project Pinot, including the Early Start (ES), Early Finish (EF), Late Start (LS), Late Finish (LF), and Total Float for each task. Tasks on the critical path are highlighted.

| ID | Name | Duration (weeks) | Predecessor Task ID(s) | ES | EF | LS | LF | Total Float | Critical Path |
|---|---|---|---|---|---|---|---|---|---|
| 1 | Start | 0 | | 0 | 0 | 0 | 0 | 0 | Yes |
| 2 | Feasibility study | 12 | 1 | 0 | 12 | 0 | 12 | 0 | Yes |
| 3 | Project definition | 2 | 2 | 12 | 14 | 12 | 14 | 0 | Yes |
| 4 | Project sanction | 1 | 3 | 14 | 15 | 14 | 15 | 0 | Yes |
| 5 | Environmental permit | 50 | 4 | 15 | 65 | 15 | 65 | 0 | Yes |
| 6 | Construction permits | 14 | 4 | 15 | 29 | 21 | 35 | 6 | No |
| 7 | FEED | 3 | 4 | 15 | 18 | 22 | 25 | 7 | No |
| 8 | Procurement | 30 | 7 | 18 | 48 | 23 | 53 | 5 | No |
| 9 | Detailed engineering | 10 | 7 | 18 | 28 | 25 | 35 | 7 | No |
| 10 | Construction | 18 | 6, 9 | 29 | 47 | 35 | 53 | 6 | No |
| 11 | Equipment installation | 8 | 8, 10 | 48 | 56 | 53 | 61 | 5 | No |
| 12 | Commissioning & closeout | 4 | 11 | 56 | 60 | 61 | 65 | 5 | No |
| 13 | Finish | 0 | 5, 12 | 65 | 65 | 65 | 65 | 0 | Yes |

**Project Duration:**

The project duration, based on the critical path, is 65 weeks.

* Table 10.3

**Table 10.5** Use case for a Gantt chart

**Prompt**

Please generate a Gantt chart for Project Pinot using the high-level tasks shown in one of the attached files.* Use the name in the file as the task name. The task duration should be the baseline duration. The predecessor logic should use the predecessor task ID. Please follow these instructions:

- The title of the chart should be "Project Pinot High Level Gantt Chart."
- The "Start" task should be the first one on the Gantt chart, in line 1, and the rest of the tasks should go after that, in top-down order on the Y-axis. This is a hard constraint. Line 1 should be the superior one.
- The "Start" task should be shown with a diamond icon.
- All task names should be included following the format "Task Number: Task Name"
- X-axis should be in weeks, showing the week number only, not the date. Weeks will be shown in steps of 5, in ascending order.
- All taskbars should be colored according to their criticality. Critical tasks = Black, Noncritical tasks = Gray. Use the second attached file** for this selection.
- No need to identify each bar of the chart with its name.
- Draw each bar considering the predecessor order.
- Draw lines from the end of the predecessor's bar to the start of the line of the successor using black arrows.

**Response**

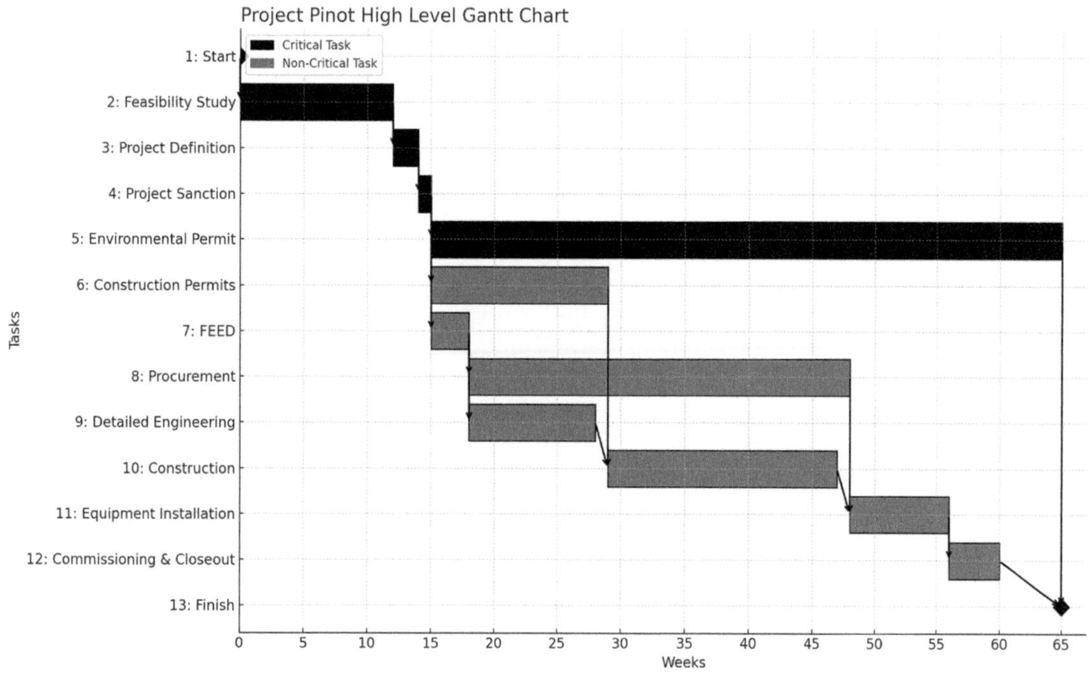


* Table 10.3

** Table 10.4

# 3. COST ESTIMATION

Cost estimation is a cornerstone of project management, with its accuracy and level of detail evolving as the project progresses through its life cycle. In the early stages, such as the feasibility or initiation phase, high-level estimates—often called rough order of magnitude estimates—provide a general understanding of potential costs. As more detailed project information becomes available, these initial estimates are refined. Detailed cost estimation becomes critical during the planning phase, enabling precise budgeting and resource allocation. This section focuses on bottom-up cost estimation, an approach that derives the total project cost by aggregating the costs of individual work packages, the smallest components of the WBS. This method is particularly effective in waterfall-managed projects, where a structured breakdown of tasks is integral to the planning process.

Bottom-up estimation involves calculating the costs of individual work packages and rolling them up through the WBS hierarchy to arrive at a comprehensive project cost. For even greater precision, work packages can be further broken down into smaller activities, with their costs rolled up in the same manner. This approach ensures a high degree of accuracy since it accounts for the unique requirements, resources, and complexities associated with each component of the project.

One of the primary advantages of bottom-up estimation is its ability to provide a comprehensive cost projection. By estimating costs at the granular level, project managers can account for all necessary resources, including labor, materials, and equipment. This level of detail helps in identifying potential cost overruns and areas where cost-saving measures can be implemented. Additionally, bottom-up estimates can be easily adjusted as project details become clearer, allowing for more accurate forecasting and budgeting throughout the project life cycle.

This method facilitates performance measurement and cost control by providing a clear baseline against which actual costs can be compared. Project managers can create an IPMB that encompasses scope, schedule, and cost baselines, ensuring a holistic approach to project planning and control by combining bottom-up cost estimation with the CPM for scheduling (as shown in a later section in this chapter).

Furthermore, bottom-up cost estimation enables better stakeholder communication and buy-in. Detailed cost breakdowns can be presented to stakeholders to justify budget requests and demonstrate that every aspect of the project has been thoroughly considered. This transparency helps build trust and ensures that stakeholders are well-informed about where and how project funds will be allocated.

The bottom-up estimate becomes the project cost baseline, serving as a benchmark for all future cost tracking and control activities. This baseline is crucial in the earned value management (EVM) method, which is proven to be effective for cost tracking and control. EVM integrates the project scope, schedule, and cost variables to assess project performance and progress. By comparing the planned cost baseline with actual costs and the value of work performed, project managers can gain insights into project health and make informed decisions to keep the project on track.

## Use Case for Cost Estimation

When using ChatGPT for project cost estimation, it is essential to recognize its strengths and limitations to achieve the best possible results. Simply providing ChatGPT with a list of tasks that comprise your project and asking it to come up with cost estimates will likely yield results that may not be highly relevant to your specific project context. This is primarily because ChatGPT generates responses based on a wide array of external data it was trained on, but without a deep understanding of the unique nuances and context of your project within your organization.

For our illustration purpose here, to keep it simple, we employed a *high-level* approach. Instead of using the detailed WBS of Project Pinot (see Table 10.1), we used the list of major project tasks (as shown in Table 10.3) that comprise the entire scope of work. We allocated a total budget of $3.0 million and provided specific instructions to ChatGPT, as shown in the prompt in Table 10.6.

In response to our prompt, ChatGPT calculated the costs for each task based on industry benchmarks. These costs may not be accurate but can be a good starting point. The project team needs to tweak these estimates from a high-level approach to make them specific and realistic for their project. As the next step for detail, they may break down these costs to a lower level of the WBS, providing more organizational and project context. While ChatGPT cannot give you the *final answer* per se, it can assist you to get there. Cost estimation/budgeting is an iterative process, and Gen AI can be an effective tool to help the project team in defining the final project budget.

For this use case, we needed to go through several iterations before we decided on the final prompt. We found that providing the exact formulas in the prompt was extremely helpful in generating correct answers. It should be noted that even when we used the same final prompt several times, the LLM gave inaccurate results in some of the trials. We had a similar experience with performing calculations for analyzing the project schedule and performance data for the kitchen renovation project in Chapter 5. Therefore, extreme caution should be exercised when using ChatGPT or any LLM for applications involving calculations.

We did not revise the final estimates ChatGPT generated and used them as such for illustrating the use cases for the next planning steps. While the cost estimates generated using our simplified approach may not reflect *real* costs, we aimed to demonstrate this use case for two key reasons. First, it provides a clear illustration of how ChatGPT can be leveraged to generate cost estimates. This example helps to showcase the potential applications, benefits, and limitations of using AI for initial project cost planning. Second, the information gathered from this exercise will be crucial for the IPMB use case discussed later in this chapter.

**Table 10.6** Use case for cost estimation

| Prompt |
|---|
| The attached table* shows a task listing of Project Pinot. The costs for the feasibility study, environmental permit, and construction permits are already estimated (say, as fixed costs, FC) at $100,000, $50,000, and $20,000, respectively. The total authorized project budget is $3 million. As an expert cost estimator, estimate the costs for the remaining tasks (CRT), project management (PM), and contingency reserve (CR). Please present the costs in a table. No need to show calculation details. Keep in mind:<br>• Total budget = FC + CRT + PM + CR<br>• Total cost of tasks (TCT) = FC + CRT<br>• Cost of each remaining task = X% of TCT, based on industry standards<br>• PM = 10% of TCT<br>• CR = 15% of (TCT + PM) |

*Continued*

**Table 10.6** *continued*

| Response |
|---|

**Cost Distribution Based on Industry Benchmarks**

Assume the following industry standard percentages for the remaining tasks (excluding fixed costs, project management, and contingency reserve):

- Project definition: 5%
- Project sanction: 2%
- FEED: 8%
- Procurement: 15%
- Detailed engineering: 10%
- Construction: 35%
- Equipment installation: 10%
- Commissioning & closeout: 5%

**Summary of Estimated Costs****

1. Feasibility study: $100,000
2. Environmental permit: $50,000
3. Construction permits: $20,000
4. Project definition: $118,636
5. Project sanction: $47,454
6. FEED: $189,818
7. Procurement: $355,909
8. Detailed engineering: $237,272
9. Construction: $830,454
10. Equipment installation: $237,272
11. Commissioning & closeout: $118,636

**Total Cost of Tasks (TCT):**

Feasibility study + environmental permit + construction permits + project definition + project sanction + FEED + procurement + detailed engineering + construction + equipment installation + commissioning & closeout = $2,305,451.

**Project Management Cost (10% of TCT):**

10% * $2,305,451 = $230,545

**Contingency Reserve (15% of (TCT + Project Management)):**

15% * ($2,305,451 + $230,545) = $380,399

**Total Project Cost:**

TCT + project management + contingency reserve = $2,305,451 + $230,545 + $380,399 = $2,916,395

**Adjusting the Contingency Reserve:**

CR = total budget – (FC + CRT + PM)

= $3,000,000 – ($170,000 + $2,135,451 + $230,545.10)

≈ $464,003.90

* Contains a list of high-level tasks shown in Table 10.4.

** The details of this calculation are omitted here for the sake of brevity.

## 4. RESOURCE ALLOCATION AND RESOURCE LEVELING

Efficient resource allocation and leveling are critical for project success, and tools like ChatGPT and other AI tools can provide significant support in these areas. Resource allocation involves assigning available resources—such as personnel, equipment, or facilities—to tasks based on project requirements and constraints. LLMs can assist by generating initial resource plans based on project inputs, identifying potential conflicts, and offering alternatives. While their outputs are not definitive, they serve as a strong starting point, saving time and encouraging thoughtful discussion. However, challenges arise in accounting for real-time availability, skill matching, and organizational nuances, which require supplementary inputs and oversight.

Resource leveling, aimed at minimizing peaks and troughs in resource utilization, is another area where LLMs can be leveraged effectively. The models can propose adjustments to task schedules to ensure that resources are deployed more evenly over time. For instance, by analyzing task dependencies, available task floats, deadlines, etc., LLMs can suggest redistributing workloads to reduce over-allocation and prevent burnout while at the same time minimizing under-allocation to prevent resource wastage.

While LLM's recommendations on resource allocation and leveling are helpful, the challenge lies in providing the models with proper data on resource skill sets, project resource requirements, needs of other projects for the shared resources, and so many other factors. Providing real-time resource and schedule data for adjusting the resource allocations on an ongoing basis for the models is even more challenging. Furthermore, LLMs currently lack the dynamic feedback loop of real-world project management tools and cannot account for spontaneous changes in resource availability or project priorities without continuous updated input from the user.

To maximize the value of the models in resource allocation and leveling, project managers should integrate LLMs with real-time data and expert judgment. Detailed prompts outlining project goals, constraints, and current resource status would enable the model to generate more precise recommendations. Combining ChatGPT with specialized resource management tools and regular team reviews allows for a balanced approach that aligns theoretical efficiency with the complexities of dynamic project environments.

We are not presenting use case examples for resource allocation or leveling because of the complexity of data that is needed as input to the LLM. As we mentioned before, the required data could include a list of resources available for Project Pinot, their requirements for the project, their availability for this project versus other shared projects, and many other factors.

## 5. RACI CHART

The RACI chart, also known as the responsibility assignment matrix, is a powerful project management tool that clarifies roles and responsibilities within a project. It enhances communication, streamlines workflows, and ensures accountability. RACI stands for responsible, accountable, consulted, and informed—four key roles that team members can play in relation to specific tasks or deliverables. The following paragraphs will discuss the structure, benefits, and implementation of RACI charts.

### Structure of a RACI Chart

A RACI chart is typically organized as a matrix. The rows represent the tasks or deliverables, while the columns represent the team members or roles involved in the project. Each cell in the matrix is populated with one of the RACI letters, indicating the specific role a team member plays in relation to a particular task:

1. *Responsible (R)*: The person or people responsible for completing the task. They are directly involved in executing the work and ensuring it is done correctly.
2. *Accountable (A)*: The person ultimately answerable for the task's completion. This person delegates the work to those responsible and ensures the task meets quality standards. To avoid confusion, there is usually only one accountable person per task.
3. *Consulted (C)*: Individuals or groups whose input is sought before a decision or action is taken. These are typically subject matter experts who provide valuable insights and feedback.
4. *Informed (I)*: Individuals or groups who need to be kept updated on the progress and outcomes of the task. They are not directly involved in the task's execution but need to be aware of its status.

## Benefits of a RACI Chart

1. *Clarifies roles and responsibilities*: A RACI chart provides a clear picture of who is responsible, accountable, consulted, and informed for each task. This clarity helps prevent overlap and confusion, ensuring that everyone knows their specific roles and duties.
2. *Enhances communication*: By defining who needs to be consulted and informed, a RACI chart facilitates better communication within the team. It ensures that relevant stakeholders are kept in the loop and their inputs are considered.
3. *Improves decision making*: With clearly defined roles, decision-making processes become more efficient. The accountable person has the authority to make decisions, while the responsible and consulted parties provide the necessary input and execution.
4. *Increases accountability*: By explicitly assigning accountability for each task, a RACI chart helps hold team members accountable for their work. This accountability can drive higher performance and ensure that tasks are completed on time and to the required standard.
5. *Streamlines project management*: A RACI chart simplifies project management by providing a structured approach to assigning and tracking responsibilities. This structure helps project managers ensure that all aspects of the project are covered and that responsibilities are evenly distributed.

## Implementing a RACI Chart

1. *Identify tasks and deliverables*: Begin by listing all the tasks and deliverables required for the project. This list will form the rows of the RACI matrix.
2. *Define roles and team members*: Identify all the roles and team members involved in the project. These will form the columns of the matrix.
3. *Assign RACI codes*: For each task, assign the appropriate RACI code to each team member. Ensure that each task has at least one responsible and one accountable person. Avoid assigning multiple accountable persons to a single task to prevent confusion.
4. *Review, validate, and monitor*: Review the RACI chart with the project team to ensure that all roles and responsibilities are accurately assigned. Validate the chart with stakeholders to confirm their understanding and agreement. Use the chart as a reference throughout the project to monitor progress, resolve conflicts, and ensure that responsibilities are being met.

## Use Case for a RACI Chart

The creation of a RACI chart requires detailed and accurate project input data to ensure the chart reflects the project's requirements effectively. The essential data includes the roles and positions of different team members assigned to the project. Additionally, it is crucial to provide specific instructions on how the chart should be structured and presented.

To enable ChatGPT to generate an accurate and useful RACI chart, we assembled three critical documents:

1. *Project description*: This document outlines the project's scope, objectives, and overall context, providing a clear understanding of what the project entails.
2. *List of work packages*: This includes a breakdown of the work packages or major tasks that need to be completed as part of the project. Each task is detailed to ensure clarity on what needs to be done. (To keep it simple for the sake of illustration, we used the work packages for the execution phase of the project only.)
3. *Project organizational chart*: This chart shows the roles of key team members involved in the project. It highlights the hierarchy and structure of the project team.

With these documents, we crafted a comprehensive prompt for ChatGPT, detailing the information and the desired format for the RACI chart. This prompt included descriptions of the tasks, the team members, and their roles in the context of the project's work packages. The result was a well-structured RACI chart that clearly delineated the responsibilities and accountabilities of each team member for the various project tasks. Table 10.7A shows the prompt we used with ChatGPT, and Table 10.7B presents the RACI chart it produced, demonstrating the effectiveness and efficiency of using Gen AI in this aspect of project management.

**Table 10.7A** Use case for a RACI chart: prompt

Attached* are several documents describing Project Pinot, including its organizational context, project team structure, and scope of work presented as a work breakdown structure (WBS). Please create a RACI chart based on the following instructions:

1. Rows:
    - Use the fourth level of the WBS, specifically focusing on the work packages under the execution phase (second level of the WBS) (Table 10.1).
    - Structure the rows hierarchically: list the execution phase, followed by its functions (third level), and then the corresponding work packages (fourth level) below each function.
    - Make sure the three levels are distinguishable.
2. Columns:
    - Use the project team members' titles as described in the provided organizational chart (Table 9.1) for Project Pinot as well as the key stakeholders (Table 9.4). For the work to be performed by outside contractors, refer to Table 9.1.
3. RACI role assignment:
    - Assign roles only for the work packages but not functions or the phase.
    - Each work package must include at least one accountable (A) and one or more responsible (R) roles.
    - Only one person should be designated as accountable for each work package.
    - The accountable person may also take on a responsible role, but this is not mandatory.
    - Multiple individuals may be assigned the responsible role for a single work package.
    - Assign consulted (C) and informed (I) roles as appropriate for each work package. Note that not every work package may require these roles.

*Continued*

**Table 10.7A** *continued*

4. Clarity and completeness:
    - Ensure the roles are clearly defined and aligned with the responsibilities and authority of the team members.
    - If there are ambiguities or overlaps in the scope or team roles, make logical assumptions and note them.

The goal is to produce a comprehensive and practical RACI chart that reflects the structure and dynamics of Project Pinot, optimizing clarity and accountability across the work packages.

* Tables 9.1, 9.4, and 10.1

LLMs present several challenges in creating RACI charts, many of which became evident during our exploration of this use case. One primary issue is that LLMs lack intrinsic knowledge of the skill levels, roles, and responsibilities of individual team members, which often results in oversimplified or inaccurate role assignments. The quality of the generated RACI chart heavily depends on the specificity and clarity of the input provided. When roles, responsibilities, or project-specific details are vague or incomplete, the output is likely to be flawed. Moreover, LLMs generate generalized responses based on their training data, which may not align with the nuanced requirements of your project or industry.

Complex projects with overlapping responsibilities, matrixed teams, or ambiguous accountabilities further complicate the use of LLMs, potentially leading to conflicting assignments or gaps in coverage. Additionally, LLM-generated outputs are inherently static, whereas RACI charts often require dynamic updates as project roles and circumstances evolve. LLMs may struggle to handle iterative refinements effectively. To overcome these limitations, it is essential to provide well-structured and detailed input. By building a comprehensive project input folder that includes detailed descriptions of the project scope, team members' qualifications, and specific responsibilities, the accuracy and relevance of LLM-generated RACI charts can be significantly improved. This structured approach allows the LLM to produce outputs that are better aligned with your project's needs.

Despite the absence of detailed input data, the quality of the RACI chart generated by the LLM (see Table 10.7B) is impressively high. Many role assignments appear relevant and realistic, demonstrating the LLM's ability to interpret broad contextual information and generate a structured output. However, some allocations may be subject to debate, as they lack the nuanced understanding of project-specific dynamics, such as individual team member capabilities, organizational constraints, or real-time project requirements. This underscores the importance of treating the AI-generated chart as an initial draft rather than a final product. It is critical for the project manager and team to carefully review and refine the suggested allocations based on their unique project data, organizational priorities, and stakeholder inputs.

## 6. INTEGRATED PERFORMANCE MEASUREMENT BASELINE

An IPMB, also known as a cumulative cost curve, is a crucial tool in project management that provides a visual representation of a project's planned budget over time. This baseline is called *integrated* because it combines the scope baseline (a WBS), schedule baseline (a Gantt chart), and cost baseline (bottom-up cost estimate) into a single, cohesive framework. It helps project

**Table 10.7B** Use case for a RACI chart: ChatGPT response

| Function | Work Package | Project Manager | Technical Lead | Engineering Team | Procurement Specialist | QA Specialist | Vendor/Contractor | Construction Manager | Deployment Team | Training Specialist | Stakeholder Rep. | Finance Manager | Legal Advisor | Regulatory Officer |
|---|---|---|---|---|---|---|---|---|---|---|---|---|---|---|
| Engineering | Conduct design reviews | R | A | R | | C | R | | | | I | | | C |
| | Prepare engineering drawings | I | A | R | | C | R | | | | | | | I |
| | Validate design with stakeholders | C | R | | | I | A | | | | R | | | |
| Procurement | Identify long-lead items | C | | | A, R | | | | | | I | | | |
| | Solicit vendor proposals | I | | | A, R | | R | | | | | | | |
| | Evaluate vendor proposals | C | | | A | | R | | | | I | | | |
| | Negotiate contracts | I | | | A | | R | | | | | | A | |
| Construction | Oversee site preparation | A | R | | | I | R | R | | | | | | |
| | Manage equipment installation | A, R | | | | C | R | R | | | | | | |
| | Conduct safety inspections | R | | | | A | | R | | | I | | | |
| Testing | Develop test plan | R | A | | | C | | | | | | | | |
| | Perform functional testing | C | | | | A, R | R | | | | | | | |
| | Review test results | C | R | | | A | | | | | | | | |
| Deployment | Prepare training materials | I | | | | | | | R | A | | | | |
| | Conduct user training | I | | | | | | | R | A | | | | |
| | Deploy final system | I | | | | | | R | | A | | | | |

managers and stakeholders monitor and control project costs effectively, offering a clear picture of budget allocation and spending patterns throughout the project life cycle.

The IPMB typically appears as an S-curve on a graph, where the X-axis represents time (such as weeks or months) and the Y-axis represents cumulative cost. The S-shape reflects the typical nature of project expenditures, which start slowly during the initial planning phases, accelerate during execution, and taper off as the project nears completion.

## Building the IPMB

Building an IPMB involves three major steps:

1. Establish the project baselines
2. Integrate the baselines
3. Plot the curve

### *Establish the Project Baselines*

As discussed in the earlier sections in this chapter, the three key baselines—scope, schedule, and cost—should be developed first. The WBS, the foundational framework, ensures that all aspects of the project are covered and serves as the backbone for planning and tracking. The schedule baseline, typically depicted in a Gantt chart, outlines the planned timeline for the project. The cost baseline is derived from a detailed bottom-up cost estimate.

### *Integrate the Baselines*

The cumulative cost curve is obtained by integrating the three baselines. This integration ensures that the financial plan reflects both the detailed scope of work and the scheduled timeline for task completion. First, you align the costs of each task with the timeline specified in the schedule baseline. This means distributing the planned expenditures over the project timeline according to when each task is scheduled to occur. For instance, if a task is planned to start in month three and end in month five, the cost for that task will be allocated across those months.

Next, the cumulative cost for each time period (e.g., each month) is calculated by summing the planned costs up to that point in time. Starting from the beginning of the project, the costs are added incrementally to reflect the total planned expenditure at each stage. This step-by-step addition creates the cumulative cost data points.

### *Plot the Curve*

The X-axis of the cumulative cost curve represents time. This can be divided into days, weeks, or months, depending on the project's duration and the level of detail required. The Y-axis represents the cumulative cost. It starts at zero and increases as the project progresses and costs accumulate. For each time period, you plot the cumulative cost data points on the graph.

## Importance of the IPMB

1. *Tracking performance*: The IPMB allows project managers to track and compare the planned budget against the actual progress of the project. This comparison is vital for identifying variances and determining whether the project is on track financially. This curve is one

of the building blocks of EVM, a method that has been proven effective for tracking cost performance as well as forecasting future budget needs.

2. *Early detection of issues*: By monitoring the IPMB, project managers can detect cost overruns or schedule delays early. This early detection enables timely corrective actions, preventing minor issues from escalating into major problems.
3. *Informed decision making*: The visual representation of project costs over time helps stakeholders make informed decisions regarding resource allocation, budgeting, and project priorities. It provides a clear snapshot of project health and progress, enabling proactive management.
4. *Forecasting*: The IPMB can be used to forecast future project performance and costs. By analyzing trends and patterns in the S-curve, project managers can predict potential future variances and take corrective actions in advance.

The IPMB is an indispensable tool for effective project cost management. It provides a comprehensive framework for tracking project performance and ensuring financial control. Monitoring it regularly and updating it as needed helps project managers maintain control over project finances and steer the project toward successful completion.

## Use Case for the IPMB

To leverage Gen AI in creating this curve, it is essential to provide comprehensive and accurate project data. In creating the IPMB with ChatGPT, we supplied the model with detailed information encompassing the project's high-level task listing, task schedules, and bottom-up cost estimates. By integrating these key elements into a prompt for ChatGPT, we instructed the LLM to generate a cumulative cost curve that reflects the project's planned expenditures over its timeline.

Table 10.8 illustrates the specific prompt used to guide ChatGPT and the IPMB it produced, showcasing the practical application and benefits of using Gen AI in project cost management.

**Table 10.8** Use case for the IPMB

| Prompt |
|---|
| You are an expert project manager. Please build a cost matrix table using the details of the project tasks (task ID, start and finish week, duration, and estimated cost) provided in the attached documents.*<br>• Calculate quarterly costs: Determine the number of weeks each task spans within each quarter. Allocate the task's total cost based on the number of weeks it spans within each quarter. If a task spans multiple quarters, divide its cost proportionally based on the duration within each quarter.<br>• Calculate total quarterly costs: Add up the costs for each quarter.<br>• Calculate cumulative costs: Sum the total quarterly costs from quarter to quarter cumulatively across the quarters.<br>• Ensure the total cumulative cost aligns with the project's total budget.<br>• Populate the table: Columns: Task ID, Task Name, Total Task Cost, Q1, Q2, Q3, Q4, Q5, Q6. Add a row for each task and fill in the cost for each quarter based on its duration. Include rows for project management and contingency reserve, total quarter costs, and cumulative costs.<br>• Generate a graphic plotting time in quarters vs. cumulative cost. |

*Continued*

**Table 10.8** *continued*

**Response**

**Project Pinot Cost Matrix**

| ID | Task Name | Q1 Cost | Q2 Cost | Q3 Cost | Q4 Cost | Q5 Cost | Q6 Cost | Total Cost |
|---|---|---|---|---|---|---|---|---|
| 1 | Start | $0 | $0 | $0 | $0 | $0 | $0 | $0 |
| 2 | Feasibility study | $100,000 | $0 | $0 | $0 | $0 | $0 | $100,000 |
| 3 | Project definition | $39,545 | $79,091 | $0 | $0 | $0 | $0 | $118,636 |
| 4 | Project sanction | $0 | $47,454 | $0 | $0 | $0 | $0 | $47,454 |
| 5 | Environmental permit | $0 | $10,784 | $12,745 | $12,745 | $12,745 | $980 | $50,000 |
| 6 | Construction permits | $0 | $14,667 | $5,333 | $0 | $0 | $0 | $20,000 |
| 7 | FEED | $0 | $189,818 | $0 | $0 | $0 | $0 | $189,818 |
| 8 | Procurement | $0 | $91,641 | $148,917 | $114,551 | $0 | $0 | $355,109 |
| 9 | Detailed engineering | $0 | $172,561 | $64,711 | $0 | $0 | $0 | $237,272 |
| 10 | Construction | $0 | $0 | $437,081 | $393,373 | $0 | $0 | $830,454 |
| 11 | Equipment installation | $0 | $0 | $0 | $105,454 | $131,818 | $0 | $237,272 |
| 12 | Commissioning & closeout | $0 | $0 | $0 | $0 | $118,636 | $0 | $118,636 |
| 13 | Finish | $0 | $0 | $0 | $0 | $0 | $0 | $0 |
| 14 | Project management | $45,410 | $45,410 | $45,410 | $45,410 | $45,410 | $3,493 | $230,545 |
| 15 | Contingency reserve | $74,927 | $74,927 | $74,927 | $74,927 | $74,927 | $5,764 | $380,399 |
| | **Total Quarterly Costs** | $259,883 | $726,354 | $789,124 | $746,461 | $383,536 | $10,237 | $2,915,595 |
| | **Cumulative Costs** | $259,883 | $986,236 | $1,775,361 | $2,521,822 | $2,905,358 | $2,915,595 | $2,915,595 |

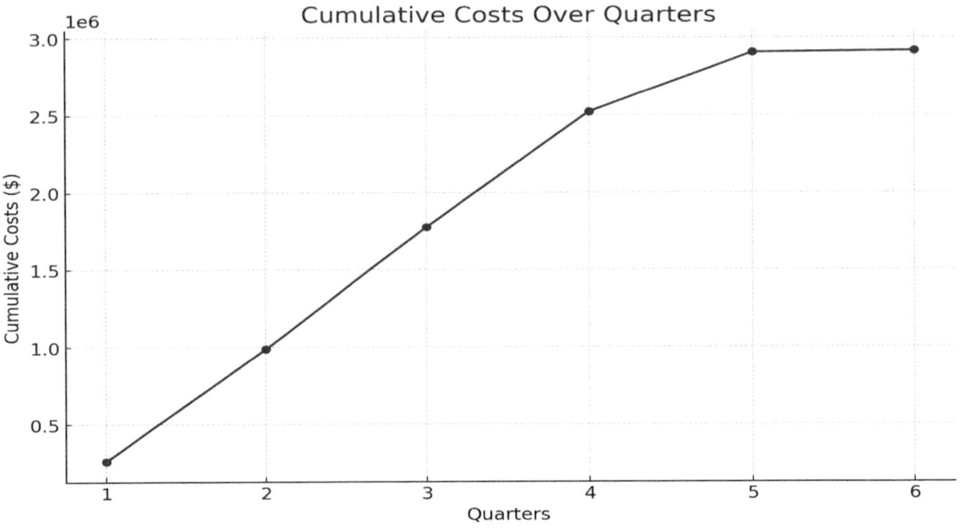


* Table 10.3 and Table 10.6

## 7. RISK REGISTER

A risk register is a vital tool in project management, designed to document, track, and manage risks throughout the life cycle of a project. The register should include both threats and opportunities, where the former would have potentially negative and the latter positive impacts on project objectives if they materialize. The basic process for managing both threats and opportunities is the same.

The following sections will explore the structure, benefits, and implementation of a risk register, highlighting its importance in effective project management.

### Structure of a Risk Register

A risk register typically includes several key components that provide comprehensive information about each risk. These components include:

- *Risk ID*: A unique identifier for each risk to facilitate tracking and reference
- *Risk description*: A clear and concise description of the risk, outlining what could go wrong
- *Risk category*: Classification of the risk based on its nature, such as technical, financial, operational, or external
- *Likelihood*: An assessment of the probability that the risk will occur, often rated on a scale from low to high
- *Impact*: An evaluation of the potential consequences if the risk materializes, also rated on a scale from low to high
- *Risk score*: A combined measure of likelihood and impact, used to prioritize risks (often calculated as likelihood × impact)
- *Risk response*: The planned strategy to address the risk, including actions to mitigate, transfer, avoid, or accept the risk
- *Risk owner*: The person or team responsible for managing the risk and implementing the response strategy
- *Status*: The current status of the risk, such as open, in progress, or closed
- *Date identified*: The date when the risk was first identified
- *Comments/notes*: Additional information or updates regarding the risk

### Benefits of a Risk Register

- *Enhanced risk management*: A risk register provides a structured approach to risk management, ensuring that all potential risks are identified, assessed, and managed systematically
- *Improved decision making*: By prioritizing risks based on their likelihood and impact, project managers can make informed decisions on where to allocate resources and focus efforts
- *Increased transparency*: Documenting risks in a centralized register enhances transparency, making it easier for stakeholders to understand the risk landscape and the measures in place to address them
- *Proactive risk mitigation*: A risk register enables proactive risk management by allowing project teams to plan and implement response strategies before risks materialize
- *Continuous monitoring*: The risk register facilitates ongoing monitoring and control of risks, ensuring that new risks are identified and existing risks are re-evaluated as the project progresses

## Implementing a Risk Register

1. *Risk identification*: Begin by identifying potential risks with the project team and stakeholders. Use techniques such as brainstorming, expert interviews, and historical data review to identify a comprehensive list of risks.
2. *Risk analysis*: Evaluate the likelihood and impact of each identified risk. Use qualitative and, wherever applicable, quantitative methods to prioritize risks based on their risk level.
3. *Risk response planning*: Develop response actions for each risk aligning with each one of the commonly used strategies discussed later in this chapter.
4. *Assign risk owners*: Assign a risk owner to each risk, ensuring that someone is accountable for managing the risk and executing the response plan. Risk owners should have the authority and resources needed to address the risk effectively.
5. *Document in the risk register*: Enter all relevant information about each risk into the risk register. Ensure that the register is comprehensive and up-to-date, capturing the risk ID, description, category, likelihood, impact, risk score, response, owner, status, date identified, and comments.
6. *Monitoring and review*: Regularly review and update the risk register as the project progresses. Conduct periodic risk assessments to identify new risks, re-evaluate existing risks, and update response plans as needed.

## Use Case for a Risk Register

Gen AI proves to be a highly effective tool for generating comprehensive risk registers, encompassing both threats and opportunities on projects. The versatility of ChatGPT allows for the creation of risk lists at various levels of detail, depending on the project's needs. Whether at a high level for the entire project or at a more granular level for individual tasks, ChatGPT can be utilized to identify potential risks systematically.

To generate these risk lists, you can provide ChatGPT with an overall project work scope. The model can then analyze this scope to identify potential threats and opportunities that may impact the project. Furthermore, ChatGPT can perform detailed analyses of the identified risks, assessing their probability of occurrence and potential impact. It can also rank the risks based on the analysis, giving the project managers a broad perspective on the risk landscape of their projects.

In our illustration, we developed risk registers for Project Pinot threats and opportunities. We supplied ChatGPT with detailed input data, including the project background information and scope of work. This ensured the LLM had all the necessary context to generate accurate and relevant risk assessments. We arbitrarily requested 20 threat statements. To keep it simple, we only asked for five opportunity statements.

The results of this process are presented in two tables: Table 10.9 for threats and Table 10.10 for opportunities. These tables showcase the prompts we used to instruct ChatGPT, the input data provided, and the resulting risk registers. This approach demonstrates the practical application of Gen AI in enhancing risk management practices in project management.

**Table 10.9** Use case for the threat register

| Prompt |
|---|
| Attached are two files. One* describes the organization where Project Pinot is initiated and gives background information on the project, and the other** provides a work breakdown structure for the entire project. As a project risk management expert, can you please create a risk register with 20 threats? Write the threat statements using "if, then, leading to" format; for example, if the project scope is not clearly defined, then scope creep could occur, leading to delays and cost overruns. Analyze each threat for its probability as well as impact on a scale of very low, low, average, high, and very high. Show the risk level (combination of probability and impact) using the same scale. Rank the threats based on the risk level. Explain your ranking when multiple threats have the same risk level. |
| **Response** |

**Threat Register**

| ID | Risk Description | Probability | Impact | Risk Level | Rank |
|---|---|---|---|---|---|
| 1 | If there is a delay in obtaining the environmental permit, then the project timeline will be extended, leading to overall project delays and potential cost overruns. | High | Very High | Very High | 1 |
| 2 | If the OmniTreat technology fails during the feasibility study, then the project will need to find an alternative solution, leading to significant delays and increased costs. | High | Very High | Very High | 2 |
| 3 | If unforeseen expenses arise, then the project costs will increase, leading to potential budget overruns and financial strain. | High | Very High | Very High | 3 |
| 4 | If there are supply chain disruptions affecting procurement, then the necessary materials and equipment will be delayed, leading to delays in project execution. | High | Very High | Very High | 4 |
| 5 | If there are delays in the FEED phase, then subsequent project phases will be delayed, leading to overall project timeline extension. | High | Very High | Very High | 5 |
| 6 | If there are regulatory changes impacting project requirements, then the project will need to adjust to new regulations, leading to potential delays and additional costs. | Medium | High | High | 6 |
| 7 | If adverse weather conditions occur during construction, then construction activities will be halted or delayed, leading to extended project timelines and increased costs. | Medium | High | High | 7 |
| 8 | If key engineering resources are unavailable, then the project will lack the necessary expertise, leading to potential delays and quality issues. | Medium | High | High | 8 |
| 9 | If the construction contractor underperforms, then the project quality and timeline will be compromised, leading to delays and potential rework. | Medium | High | High | 9 |
| 10 | If the OmniTreat technology becomes obsolete, then the project will need to invest in new technology, leading to increased costs and potential delays. | Medium | High | High | 10 |

*Continued*

**Table 10.9** *continued*

| ID | Risk Description | Probability | Impact | Risk Level | Rank |
|---|---|---|---|---|---|
| 11 | If there are issues with customized pumps procurement, then the installation schedule will be delayed, leading to potential project timeline extensions. | Medium | Average | Average | 11 |
| 12 | If stakeholders resist project changes, then implementation of necessary changes will be delayed, leading to potential project setbacks. | Medium | Average | Average | 12 |
| 13 | If the project funding is inadequate, then the project will face financial shortfalls, leading to potential project halts or scaled-back scope. | Low | High | Average | 13 |
| 14 | If there are legal challenges in technology licensing, then the project will face legal delays and additional costs, leading to potential project delays. | Low | High | Average | 14 |
| 15 | If there are data security breaches during the project, then sensitive project information will be compromised, leading to potential project setbacks and reputational damage. | Low | Average | Low | 15 |
| 16 | If there is a misalignment between R&D and engineering teams, then project coordination will be poor, leading to delays and potential quality issues. | Low | Average | Low | 16 |
| 17 | If the cost estimates are inaccurate, then the project budget will be insufficient, leading to financial overruns and potential project delays. | Low | Average | Low | 17 |
| 18 | If there is poor communication among project stakeholders, then misunderstandings and misalignments will occur, leading to project inefficiencies. | Low | Average | Low | 18 |
| 19 | If the project deadlines are not met, then the project timeline will be extended, leading to potential financial penalties and stakeholder dissatisfaction. | Low | Average | Low | 19 |
| 20 | If there are health and safety incidents on-site, then project activities will be halted, leading to delays and potential legal issues. | Low | Average | Low | 20 |

**Explanation of Ranking**

When multiple threats have the same risk level, the following criteria are used to determine their rank:

1. Impact score: Threats with higher impact are ranked higher.
2. Probability score: If the impact score is the same, threats with higher probability are ranked higher.
3. Order of listing: When both impact and probability scores are the same, the threats are ranked based on the order they were initially listed during the risk identification process. This means that the threat identified first is given a higher rank.

* Table 9.1

** The entire WBS of the project is available at www.pmaihandbook.com

**Table 10.10** Use case for the opportunity register

**Prompt**

Attached are two files.* One describes the organization where Project Pinot is initiated and gives background information on the project, and the other provides a work breakdown structure for the entire project. As a project risk management expert, can you please create a risk register with five opportunities? Write the opportunity statement using "if, then, leading to" format. Analyze each opportunity for its probability as well as impact on a scale of very low, low, average, high, and very high. Show the risk level (combination of probability and impact) using the same scale. Rank the opportunities based on the risk level. Explain your ranking when multiple opportunities have the same risk level.

**Response**

**Opportunity Register**

| ID | Opportunity Description | Probability | Impact | Risk Level | Rank |
|---|---|---|---|---|---|
| 1 | If advanced wastewater treatment technology is implemented, then efficiency will be improved, leading to cost savings and higher performance. | High | Very High | Very High | 1 |
| 2 | If innovative procurement strategies are used, then material costs can be reduced, leading to overall project cost savings. | High | High | High | 2 |
| 3 | If strong stakeholder engagement is maintained, then support and cooperation will be enhanced, leading to smoother project execution and fewer disruptions. | High | High | High | 3 |
| 4 | If effective risk management practices are applied, then potential issues can be mitigated early, leading to a more predictable and controlled project outcome. | High | High | High | 4 |
| 5 | If the project is completed ahead of schedule, then additional resources can be allocated to other projects, leading to increased productivity and potential financial bonuses. | Medium | High | High | 5 |

**Explanation of Ranking:**

When the opportunity level is the same for more than one opportunity, the ranking is determined by:

1. Impact score: Higher impact opportunities are ranked higher.
2. Probability score: If the impact is the same, higher probability opportunities are ranked higher.
3. Order of listing: For opportunities with identical impact and probability scores, the order of listing in the original assessment is used. This means that the opportunity identified first is given a higher rank.

* Table 9.1

** The entire WBS of the project is available at www.pmaihandbook.com

## 8. RISK RESPONSE PLANNING

A critical process in project risk management, risk response planning ensures that proactive and reactive measures are in place to manage potential negative impacts and capitalize on positive risks, thereby improving the likelihood of project success. The approach involves leveraging established risk response strategies tailored to the nature of the risks involved.

Risk response planning begins with delineating specific response actions for each risk identified, corresponding to common risk response strategies (see Table 10.11). Once potential actions are identified, it is essential to evaluate their pros and cons, considering factors such as feasibility, cost, and potential impact. This evaluation helps rank the actions in order of preference, enabling informed decision making.

**Table 10.11** Common risk response strategies

**A. Threats**

| Strategy | Description |
|---|---|
| Avoidance | Eliminating the threat by changing the project plan or approach to avoid the risk entirely. |
| Mitigation (minimize probability) | Reducing the likelihood of the risk occurring by implementing preventive measures. |
| Mitigation (minimize impact) | Reducing the impact of the risk if it does occur by implementing contingency plans. |
| Transfer | Shifting the impact of the risk to a third party, such as through insurance or outsourcing. |
| Active acceptance | Acknowledging the risk and developing a contingency reserve or plan to address it if it occurs. |
| Passive acceptance | Acknowledging the risk and deciding to deal with it as it occurs without a proactive plan. |
| Escalation | Referring the risk to a higher authority or level within the organization for resolution. |

**B. Opportunities**

| Strategy | Description |
|---|---|
| Exploit | Taking actions to ensure that the opportunity is realized, increasing the probability of the opportunity occurring. |
| Enhance (increase probability) | Increasing the likelihood of the opportunity occurring by reinforcing its drivers. |
| Enhance (increase impact) | Increasing the positive impact of the opportunity if it occurs by maximizing its benefits. |
| Transfer | Sharing the opportunity with a third party who can help to achieve or maximize the opportunity, such as through partnerships or joint ventures. |
| Active acceptance | Recognizing the opportunity and creating plans to capitalize on it if it occurs. |
| Passive acceptance | Recognizing the opportunity and choosing to benefit from it as it occurs without proactive measures. |
| Escalation | Referring the opportunity to a higher authority or level within the organization for further action. |

## Best Practices in Risk Response Planning

Effective risk response planning is built on a foundation of proven best practices that ensure risks are addressed systematically and comprehensively. Some of these practices include:

1. *Prioritization of risks*: Focus on high-priority risks that have the most significant impact on project objectives. This ensures that resources are allocated effectively to address the most critical threats and opportunities.
2. *Integration with project baselines*: Ensure that selected risk response actions are reflected in the project's scope, schedule, and cost baselines. This alignment avoids surprises and keeps the project on track.
3. *Collaboration with stakeholders*: Engage key stakeholders and project team members in the planning process. Their insights and expertise can help identify realistic and effective response actions while fostering alignment.
4. *Proactive and preventive measures*: Emphasize proactive strategies that address risks early, minimizing their potential impact before they escalate into issues.
5. *Flexibility and adaptability*: Recognize that risks evolve throughout the project life cycle. Continuously revisit the risk response plan to update strategies as new risks emerge or conditions change.
6. *Clear documentation and communication*: Clearly document risk response actions, roles, and responsibilities to ensure all team members and stakeholders understand their roles in risk management. Effective communication is critical to maintaining alignment and accountability.
7. *Evaluation and ranking of responses*: Carefully assess the feasibility, cost, and potential impact of each response action to prioritize the most effective solutions.
8. *Balancing threats and opportunities*: Treat opportunities with the same level of rigor as threats. Proactively enhancing or exploiting opportunities can generate additional value for the project.

## Use Case for Risk Response Planning

For our illustration, we utilized ChatGPT to develop risk response plans for the number one *threat* and the number one *opportunity* from the respective ranked listings from Tables 10.9 and 10.10. We provided ChatGPT with prompts requesting actions for each response strategy. Even though you can request multiple alternative actions for a given strategy, for the sake of simplicity, we asked for only one action per strategy.

Table 10.12 displays the prompt we used to address the number one threat, along with the results generated by ChatGPT. This table includes the proposed actions, their evaluations, and the final ranking of the actions based on their overall effectiveness. Similarly, Table 10.13 presents the prompt and results for responding to the number one opportunity following the same structured approach. The LLM generally ranks the threat strategies in the order of avoidance, mitigation, transfer, acceptance, and escalation. It will also rank opportunity strategies in a similar fashion. But if it is given more specific information on the project's scope, schedule, cost, and other constraints, it will make better ranking recommendations by performing a more effective evaluation of each strategy.

**Table 10.12** Use case for threat response actions

**Prompt**

You're a project risk management expert. For the no. 1 ranked threat for Project Pinot (see Table 10.9), please identify one action aligning with each one of the response strategies: avoidance, mitigation by minimizing probability, mitigation by minimizing impact, transfer, active acceptance, passive acceptance, and escalation. For each identified action, present one pro and one con. Rank the response action in order of preference. Present the results in a tabular format with the columns labeled: Strategy, Action, Pro, Con, and Rank.

**Response**

| Strategy | Action | Pro | Con | Rank |
|---|---|---|---|---|
| **Avoidance** | Discharge into local sewer by paying surcharges instead of building a treatment plant | Completely avoids the need for an environmental permit | Potentially high and ongoing costs due to surcharges | 1 |
| **Mitigation by minimizing probability** | Engage early with environmental regulatory bodies | Reduces likelihood of permit delays | Requires ongoing communication and resource allocation | 2 |
| **Mitigation by minimizing impact** | Develop a contingency plan to discharge into local sewers temporarily if delays occur | Ensures continued operations despite permit delays | Potentially high temporary costs due to surcharges | 3 |
| **Transfer** | Hire a specialized consultancy to handle permit acquisition | Expertise of consultants can expedite permit process | Additional costs for consultancy services | 4 |
| **Active acceptance** | Allocate buffer time in the project schedule for permit delays | Directly addresses potential delays within the project timeline | Increases overall project duration | 5 |
| **Passive acceptance** | Do nothing specific, monitor, and react if delays occur | No immediate additional costs | High risk of significant project delays | 6 |
| **Escalation** | Escalate the issue to senior management for additional support | Ensures higher-level attention and resources | May not guarantee faster permit acquisition | 7 |

**Explanation:**

1. Avoidance: Choosing to discharge into the local sewer and pay surcharges avoids the permit issue entirely but could result in high, ongoing costs.
2. Mitigation by minimizing probability: Engaging with regulatory bodies early can reduce the probability of delays, but requires sustained effort and resource commitment.
3. Mitigation by minimizing impact: Developing a contingency plan to discharge into local sewers if delays occur minimizes the impact on operations, but could incur high temporary costs.
4. Transfer: Hiring a consultancy transfers the risk to experts, potentially expediting the process at an additional cost.
5. Active acceptance: Adding buffer time directly addresses potential delays but lengthens the project timeline.
6. Passive acceptance: Monitoring and reacting are cost-effective initially, but carry a high risk if delays occur.
7. Escalation: Escalating to senior management can bring more resources to bear, but doesn't ensure faster results.

**Table 10.13** Use case for opportunity response actions

**Prompt**

You're a project risk management expert. For the no. 1 ranked opportunity for Project Pinot (see Table 10.10), please identify one action aligning with each one of the response strategies: enhance, exploit by increasing probability, exploit by increasing impact, transfer, active acceptance, passive acceptance, and escalation. For each identified action, present one pro and one con. Rank the response action in order of preference. Present the results in a tabular format with the columns labeled: Strategy, Action, Pro, Con, and Rank.

**Response**

| Strategy | Action | Pro | Con | Rank |
|---|---|---|---|---|
| Enhance | Conduct additional R&D to further improve OmniTreat technology | Increases the likelihood of successful implementation | Additional costs and time required | 1 |
| Exploit by increasing probability | Partner with a technology expert to co-develop and validate OmniTreat technology | Leverages expertise to ensure success | Potential sharing of intellectual property and profits | 2 |
| Exploit by increasing impact | Scale up the implementation of OmniTreat technology to other projects | Maximizes the impact by expanding successful use | Requires additional resources and may increase complexity | 3 |
| Transfer | Form a strategic alliance with Omni, Inc. to share risks and benefits | Distributes risks and benefits between parties | Dependence on partner and potential conflicts | 4 |
| Active acceptance | Allocate additional resources to support OmniTreat implementation | Directly addresses resource needs for successful implementation | Increases overall project budget | 5 |
| Passive acceptance | Monitor the progress and provide support as needed | Minimal initial cost and effort | High risk of missing out on maximizing the opportunity | 6 |
| Escalation | Escalate to senior management to ensure top-level support and resources | Ensures high-level commitment and resources | May lead to resource reallocation from other critical areas | 7 |

**Explanation:**

1. Enhance: Conducting additional R&D can improve the technology, increasing the chance of success, though it requires more investment.
2. Exploit by increasing probability: Partnering with a technology expert ensures the technology's success but involves potential profit sharing.
3. Exploit by increasing impact: Scaling up the technology to other projects maximizes its impact but requires more resources and may complicate project management.
4. Transfer: Forming a strategic alliance with Omni, Inc. distributes the risks and benefits, but creates dependency on the partner.
5. Active acceptance: Allocating more resources supports the implementation directly, but increases the project budget.
6. Passive acceptance: Monitoring and providing support as needed is cost-effective initially, but risks not fully capitalizing on the opportunity.
7. Escalation: Escalating to senior management ensures top-level support but might divert resources from other critical areas.

You can use LLM models to manage risks, starting at the project level and then drilling down to the phase and task levels. You can go through the process of identifying, analyzing, and prioritizing response actions for every one of the risks on your risk register and decide on the actions you would take to treat the risks. Remember to go back and revise the scope, schedule, and cost baselines in accordance with any up-front proactive risk treatment actions you have decided to take. If you added proactive measures for some of the threats, thereby minimizing the overall project risk, you may not need as much contingency reserve as before. Accordingly, you may lower the contingency reserve.

To further refine the process, project managers can conduct collaborative review sessions with stakeholders and the project team to address gaps in AI-generated outputs. These sessions ensure that the selected actions are realistic, strategically aligned, and agreed upon by all relevant parties. Moreover, as risks evolve over the project life cycle, LLMs can assist in revising the risk register and updating response plans. This iterative process helps maintain alignment with project progress and reduces the likelihood of unanticipated disruptions.

This methodical integration of AI into risk response planning equips project managers with the tools to manage uncertainties more effectively, ensuring both threats and opportunities are addressed in a manner that enhances overall project performance.

## IN CONCLUSION

As we have explored throughout this chapter, the application of AI in project planning can significantly enhance the efficiency of developing and managing the three fundamental baselines: scope, schedule, and cost. Integrating AI into project planning processes, especially including risk management, offers a transformative approach that not only improves decision making but also enhances overall project performance.

In the next chapter, we will shift our focus to AI use cases in the project execution phase. This will include exploring how AI can assist in tracking project progress, forecasting future performance, resolving team conflicts, etc. By delving into these aspects, we will gain a comprehensive understanding of how AI can support the entire project life cycle, from planning through execution and completion.

# 11

# AI USE CASES IN PROJECT EXECUTION

Project execution is the phase where plans are implemented and the project deliverables are created and completed. It is a critical stage in project management because it involves coordinating people and resources, managing stakeholder expectations, and ensuring that project objectives are achieved on time and within budget. In this chapter, we will explore how artificial intelligence (AI) can assist project execution by enhancing various key processes and activities.

AI can provide significant benefits in project execution by offering real-time insights, automating repetitive tasks, and facilitating better decision making. Integrating AI tools into project execution processes can increase efficiency, reduce errors, and improve project outcomes. In Chapter 2, Tables 2.3 through 2.5 identified numerous tactical, operational, and strategic use cases of AI in project management, respectively. Many of these use cases are applicable in project execution, including brainstorming, task automation, resource allocation, change management, conflict management, progress evaluation, forecasting, report generation, PowerPoint slides preparation, and many more. Out of the numerous possible use cases, we selected a few key cases for illustration in this chapter:

1. *Conflict resolution*: Conflicts are inevitable in any project and resolving them effectively is essential for maintaining team cohesion and project success. AI can facilitate conflict resolution by analyzing communication patterns, identifying potential conflicts early, and suggesting appropriate resolution strategies. This helps maintain a positive project environment and ensures smooth project execution.
2. *Earned value management (EVM) for cost performance*: EVM is a standard project management technique for measuring project performance and progress. By using EVM, project managers can objectively assess the project's cost performance trends and make informed decisions to keep the project on track with the budget. EVM provides early warning signals for potential issues, allowing for timely corrective actions. Whereas EVM is typically used for evaluating both cost and schedule performance, in this book, we illustrate a use case for cost only because of the limitations of EVM with schedule evaluation. Instead, we will use a different approach for schedule performance as explained later.
3. *Earned time management (ETM) for schedule performance*: ETM—analogous to EVM but specifically adapted to scheduling—is a powerful technique for measuring schedule performance and tracking progress. It helps to identify variances from the project plan and take corrective actions promptly. (We previously introduced rudiments of EVM and ETM while illustrating the use case of data analysis for the kitchen renovation project in Chapter 5.)

4. *Change control form (CCF)*: Managing changes during project execution is crucial to ensure project objectives are met without compromising quality or exceeding budget. AI can assist in the creation and management of CCFs by automating the process of documenting, reviewing, and approving changes. This ensures all changes are properly tracked and evaluated for their impact on the project.
5. *Project progress report*: AI can streamline the process of generating project progress reports by automatically collecting and analyzing data from various sources. This allows project managers to quickly assess the project's status, identify potential issues, and make informed decisions to keep the project on track.

As we explore these use cases, we will continue using the Project Pinot case study introduced in Chapter 9. This ongoing example will maintain continuity and provide a cohesive narrative, making it easier for you to understand the practical application of AI in project execution. By following Project Pinot in various scenarios of execution, we aim to provide relatable insights into how AI can enhance project execution.

By the end of this chapter, you should have a comprehensive understanding of how generative AI (Gen AI) can be applied to various aspects of project execution. Integration of these tools will improve execution efficiency and contribute to the overall success of the project.

## 1. CONFLICT RESOLUTION

Conflict resolution is a key component of project management since conflicts, if left unresolved, can derail even the most meticulously planned projects. Conflicts can arise from a variety of sources within a project, including differing stakeholder goals, miscommunications, resource allocations, and technical disagreements. Effective conflict resolution involves understanding the underlying causes of the conflict, addressing concerns constructively, and finding a path that aligns with the project's objectives.

### Understanding Conflict in Projects

The first step in managing conflict is recognizing it early and understanding its nature. Conflicts can typically be categorized as task-, process-, or relationship-related. Task-related conflicts arise from disagreements on the work, such as different interpretations of project specifications or the quality standards required. Process-related conflicts concern how the project is managed, including resource distribution and task assignments, while relationship-related conflicts stem from personal dynamics among team members.

### Strategies for Conflict Resolution

Effective conflict resolution strategies are essential for maintaining team harmony and ensuring project success. Common strategies include:

- *Mediation*: Involving a neutral third party to facilitate a resolution that respects the interests of all parties involved
- *Arbitration*: Agreeing to accept the decision made by an external arbitrator after all parties present their viewpoints

- *Compromise*: Finding a middle ground where concessions are made by all parties to reach a mutually acceptable solution
- *Collaboration*: Working together to come up with a solution that satisfies all parties, often leading to a win-win scenario
- *Avoidance*: Deliberately ignoring the conflict or postponing its resolution, which might be strategic in situations where the conflict is minor

## Best Practices in Conflict Resolution

- *Encourage open communication*: Encourage open and honest dialogue among team members to express concerns without fear of retribution
- *Focus on interests, not positions*: Focus on the needs and interests driving individuals' positions rather than on the positions themselves
- *Emphasize common goals*: Remind everyone of the project's overall goals, which can help realign conflicting parties
- *Foster an inclusive environment*: Promote an inclusive culture where diverse viewpoints are expected and valued to enhance decision making and problem-solving

## AI in Conflict Resolution

Gen AI can play a transformative role in conflict resolution within project management by facilitating communication, analyzing sentiments, and proposing equitable solutions. Here are some ways Gen AI can aid with conflict resolution:

- *Proactive conflict detection*: By continuously analyzing project data, Gen AI can proactively detect and alert project managers to potential conflicts before they escalate, allowing for timely interventions
- *Automated mediation*: AI can analyze the context of a conflict and suggest personalized mediation strategies, ensuring all parties feel heard and valued
- *Scenario simulation*: AI can simulate the outcomes of various conflict resolution strategies, helping project managers choose the most effective approach based on predicted outcomes
- *Enhanced communication*: AI-driven platforms can assist in maintaining clear and continuous communication among project teams, reducing the chances of misunderstandings and miscommunications

## Win-Win Solutions and Their Importance

Conflicts can result in a range of outcomes, including lose-lose, win-lose, lose-win, and the ideal win-win, where all parties benefit. Gen AI can help by suggesting strategies that promote win-win solutions, fostering a cooperative rather than competitive atmosphere, which is crucial for the long-term success of any project. By ensuring that solutions benefit all involved, AI helps in aligning the project outcomes with the interests of all stakeholders, thereby enhancing overall project success.

The integration of AI into conflict resolution processes represents a cutting-edge frontier in project management, transforming challenges into opportunities for growth and innovation. This approach identifies and resolves conflicts more efficiently and maintains a harmonious project environment conducive to achieving project goals.

## Use Case for Conflict Resolution

Transitioning from theory to practice, we present a practical use case from Project Pinot, illustrating conflict resolution within a project setting. This specific instance details a significant dispute between the engineering and R&D teams at Acme, centered around the adoption of a new technology for Project Pinot.

Table 11.1 outlines the conflict, capturing the core disagreements and perspectives of the parties involved. To address this issue, we engaged ChatGPT to propose and evaluate strategies for resolution. The interactions and outcomes are detailed in Table 11.2. Our prompt to ChatGPT was simple and specific, and the suggested solutions were practical and common in the industry.

**Table 11. 1** Project Pinot—conflict between engineering and R&D

**Background**

As Project Pinot approached the conclusion of its initiation phase, Acme's leadership made a significant decision to implement OmniTreat, an innovative technology developed by Omni B.V. in the Netherlands, for their wastewater treatment operations. To mitigate the risks associated with deploying this advanced technology on a full scale, the project includes a preliminary pilot feasibility study. A budget of $100,000 has been allocated for this 12-week study, which is crucial since any delays could impact the overall project timeline, given its placement on the critical path.

The selection of OmniTreat sparked some controversy within the project team, primarily composed of engineers who favored tried-and-tested, conventional technologies known for their reliability and effectiveness. Their reservations were multifold: they questioned the effectiveness of the new technology, highlighted the additional costs and time implications of the feasibility study, and expressed concerns that Acme's push for innovation in wastewater treatment might divert focus from its core chemical manufacturing operations. These factors collectively underscored the internal debate over balancing innovation with operational stability and efficiency.

**The Conflict**

With the progression of Project Pinot into the execution phase, the reservations held by the project team regarding OmniTreat only deepened. Doubts were exacerbated following initial meetings with engineers from Omni B.V., leading to increased concerns over the technology's feasibility and efficiency. The team feared that continued reliance on OmniTreat might result in significant project delays and substantial financial losses if the technology failed to perform as expected. Consequently, they strongly urged the leadership to reconsider and switch to a more traditional approach.

Contrastingly, the R&D department was steadfast in their support for OmniTreat, motivated by a commitment to innovation and a firm belief in the technology's potential. This stance resulted in a pronounced divide within the project: the engineering team advocated for a cautious approach, while the R&D team pushed for pioneering and potentially groundbreaking advancements.

**The Decision Maker**

Caught in the midst of this escalating conflict was Jean Peterson Minelli, the project sponsor. She was tasked with making a crucial decision—whether to side with the engineering team's conservative, risk-averse strategy or to back the R&D team's push for innovation and novel solutions. Her choice would significantly shape the project's path forward, balancing the practical concerns of the present with the ambitious vision of the future.

**Table 11.2** Use case for conflict resolution

| Prompt |
|---|
| The attached document* describes a conflict that arose between engineering and R&D teams on Project Pinot. You are an expert at resolving conflicts on projects. Please suggest two win-win solutions and describe them in detail. Also, identify one of each win-lose, lose-win, and lose-lose solutions. Please prepare a short table showing one pro and one con of all the above solutions. |

**Response**

**Detailed Win-Win Solutions**

**1. Pilot Testing with Parallel Development:**

- **Description:** Initiate a pilot phase for OmniTreat within a controlled environment of the project while continuing development with conventional technology. This dual-path strategy ensures that if OmniTreat underperforms, the project can swiftly pivot without significant time loss or financial impact.
- **Benefits:** This approach mitigates the risks associated with fully committing to a new, untested technology by providing a fallback option that maintains project momentum.
- **Challenges:** Requires careful resource management to handle two simultaneous tracks which could increase the project budget and complexity.

**2. Incremental Integration:**

- **Description:** Start with conventional technology and gradually introduce OmniTreat components where feasible. Use performance data to decide subsequent phases of integration, adjusting the approach based on real-time results and feedback from both technologies.
- **Benefits:** Reduces the initial risk by allowing the team to gather data on OmniTreat's performance and make informed decisions on its wider application throughout the project life cycle.
- **Challenges:** May delay the full benefits expected from the innovative technology and requires a robust monitoring and evaluation mechanism to assess technology performance continuously.

These strategies aim to balance the innovative drive of the R&D team with the practical and risk-averse approach of the engineering team, providing a roadmap that could satisfy both parties and ensure the project's success.

**Conflict Resolution Strategies for Project Pinot**

| Solution Type | Suggested Solution | Pro | Con |
|---|---|---|---|
| Win-Win | Pilot testing with parallel development | Allows actual testing of OmniTreat while keeping conventional tech as backup | Increases project complexity and may require more resources |
| | Incremental integration | Gradually integrates OmniTreat, adjusting based on performance and feedback | Slower rollout may delay final project benefits |
| Win-Lose | Full implementation of OmniTreat | Maximizes R&D's innovation agenda | High risk of failure, which could derail the project |
| Lose-Win | Revert completely to conventional technology | Ensures project stability and reliability | Kills innovation and may demoralize the R&D team |
| Lose-Lose | Halt project pending further review | Temporarily avoids making a hard decision | Delays can escalate costs and decrease project viability |

* Table 11.1

The use of ChatGPT in this conflict resolution scenario underscored several strengths and limitations of employing AI in project management. The AI's ability to quickly analyze the conflict and propose multiple resolution strategies, aligned with industry practices, provided a range of outcomes, including win-win, win-lose, and lose-lose. This comprehensive approach would enable the project team to evaluate different strategies and select the most suitable one for this situation.

However, the exercise also revealed some limitations. For example, ChatGPT's understanding of the conflict was limited to the details explicitly mentioned, which may have excluded nuances such as the historical dynamics between the engineering and R&D teams or the individual personalities and motivations of key stakeholders. This highlights the importance of providing comprehensive and accurate input when utilizing AI tools for decision making. Additionally, while the solutions proposed were viable, they did not fully account for the long-term implications on the organization's culture and future projects, suggesting the need for human oversight.

Overall, the use of ChatGPT in this conflict resolution scenario demonstrated the potential of Gen AI to enhance decision-making processes in project management. By providing quick and practical solutions, AI can help project teams navigate complex conflicts and identify mutually beneficial outcomes.

## 2. EARNED VALUE MANAGEMENT FOR COST PERFORMANCE

EVM is a powerful project management technique used to measure project performance and progress. It integrates project scope, schedule, and cost variables to provide a comprehensive view of project status and performance. By using EVM, project managers can objectively assess the project's health, predict future performance trends, and make informed decisions to keep the project on track. EVM is particularly valuable because it provides early warning signals for potential issues, allowing for timely corrective actions. Its ability to combine scope, schedule, and cost performance into a single integrated system makes it an essential tool for managing complex projects.

### Building Blocks of EVM

The fundamental components of EVM are:

- *Planned value (PV)*: As the budgeted cost of work scheduled, PV represents the approved budget for the work to be completed by a specific date. It is the baseline against which actual performance is measured. PV provides a benchmark for evaluating project progress.
- *Earned value (EV)*: As the budgeted cost of work performed, EV measures the value of work actually completed by a specific date, expressed in terms of the approved budget. EV provides a quantifiable measure of project progress and helps in assessing how much of the planned work has been accomplished.
- *Actual cost (AC)*: As the actual cost of work performed, AC represents the actual expenditure incurred for the work completed by a specific date. It includes all costs associated with the work performed, such as labor, materials, and overhead. AC provides a clear picture of the financial investment made in the project so far.
- *Budget at completion (BAC)*: The BAC is the total budget allocated for the entire project. It represents the planned total expenditure required to complete the project. The BAC is a reference point for comparing actual and projected costs throughout the project life cycle.

## Performance Indicators

EVM uses different key indicators to evaluate project cost performance and to predict future trends:

- *Cost variance (CV)*: CV is the difference between EV and AC (CV = EV – AC). It indicates whether the project is under or over budget. A positive CV means the project is under budget, while a negative CV indicates a cost overrun.
- *Cost performance index (CPI)*: CPI is the ratio of EV to AC (CPI = EV/AC). It measures cost efficiency, indicating how effectively the project is using its budget. A CPI greater than 1 indicates efficient use of resources (under cost), while a CPI less than 1 suggests inefficiency (cost overrun).
- *Estimate at completion (EAC)*: EAC is a forecast of the expected total cost of the project at any given time. If the cost efficiency for the remainder of the project is assumed to continue at the current CPI, it is calculated using the formula, EAC = BAC/CPI.
- *Estimate to complete (ETC)*: ETC is the estimated budget required to complete the remaining work. It is calculated using the formula ETC = EAC – AC, helping project managers plan future budget needs.
- *Variance at completion (VAC)*: VAC is the difference between BAC and EAC (VAC = BAC – EAC). It indicates whether the project is expected to be on, under, or over budget at completion. A positive VAC suggests potential cost savings, while a negative VAC indicates potential cost overruns.

As mentioned in the introduction to this chapter, we are not discussing schedule performance using the standard EVM formulas because of their limitations.

## AI in Earned Value Management

AI is poised to transform EVM. By integrating AI, the complex data analysis required for EVM can be streamlined, enhancing accuracy and efficiency. AI algorithms can automatically process vast amounts of project data to identify discrepancies between planned and actual progress, suggest corrective actions as necessary, and forecast future performance trends. This proactive approach helps project managers anticipate issues and make informed decisions swiftly.

Moreover, AI can facilitate the continuous monitoring of project variables, enabling real-time updates to earned value metrics. This capability ensures that project stakeholders have up-to-date information, leading to better strategic planning and resource allocation. It also assists in automating the calculation of critical EVM metrics such as CPI, reducing the potential for human error and allowing project teams to focus on higher-level strategic tasks.

## Use Case for EVM for Cost Performance

Automating the generation of EVM reports for real-time or to-date project cost performance is feasible when the necessary input data is available. However, for many organizations, generating this input data is a challenge, even though the EVM metrics, formulas, and calculations themselves are universally straightforward.

For our use case illustration, we prepared Table 11.3. It details task completion percentages and actual task costs, along with other project progress information, for Project Pinot following the completion of front-end engineering and design. We used this data to direct ChatGPT to generate EVM results. Notably, we excluded any percentage of completion for project management because

**Table 11.3** Project Pinot progress highlights

**Acme Internal Memorandum**

**Date:** Today
**From:** Emily Carter, Project Pinot Project Manager
**To:** Jean Minelli, Project Pinot Sponsor
**Subject:** Progress Highlights

Hi Jean,

As you know, Project Pinot embarked on its execution phase on schedule. This phase was launched with an alignment between the project team and leadership on several preemptive risk mitigation strategies, which have been diligently implemented. Since we entered the execution phase, 23 weeks (115 workdays) have elapsed, and we have just completed front-end engineering and design (FEED). Here, I just wanted to provide you with progress highlights, many of which you are already familiar with.

**Risk Mitigation and Implementation Details**

The initial controversy regarding OmniTreat vs. conventional technology was resolved by evaluating both concurrently in the feasibility study. No budget or schedule modifications were made for this task, adhering to the allocated $100,000 and a timeline of 60 days. In case of cost overruns, the leadership believed that there was enough contingency reserve in the budget. Ultimately, the feasibility study with the innovative OmniTreat technology failed. So, we adopted conventional technology for the wastewater treatment plant (WWTP) design.

To streamline the process concerning environmental and construction permits, CRS Consultants LLC was engaged, offering their specialized expertise to expedite the permitting process. Just yesterday, they raised a red flag pointing out that the required standard of wastewater treatment would be more rigorous than we believed, therefore, necessitating an additional treatment step (sand filter) in our process design.

Recognizing the potential delays in acquiring customized pumps, a critical component for the project, the leadership authorized the pumps as long-lead items and approved the budget for preliminary engineering and procurement. This forward-thinking decision facilitated the early engagement of a pump supplier and initiation of its design process along with the feasibility study.

**Contingency Plans**

The leadership has also strategized for unforeseen delays in the WWTP's readiness. Should the WWTP not be operational by the time the new production unit is ready, Acme will continue discharging wastewater into the local sewer system, albeit at an additional surcharge. Conversely, if the WWTP is operational ahead of the production unit, it will begin processing existing operations' wastewater, potentially saving surcharges by avoiding discharge into the local sewer.

**Project Task Status**

| ID | Task Name | Task Cost | % Completion | Actual Cost | Comments |
|---|---|---|---|---|---|
| 1 | Start | $0 | 100% | $0 | |
| 2 | Feasibility study | $100,000 | 100% | $120,000 | OmniTreat was proven ineffective. The project has pivoted to conventional technology based on which the WWTP design was developed. |
| 3 | Project definition | $118,636 | 100% | $100,000 | Delays were caused due to the unavailability of a key engineer. |
| 4 | Project sanction | $47,454 | 100% | $30,000 | |

*Continued*

**Table 11.3** *continued*

| ID | Task Name | Task Cost | % Completion | Actual Cost | Comments |
|---|---|---|---|---|---|
| 5 | Environmental permit | $50,000 | 10% | $13,000 | Higher effluent standards are required, so the WWTP design needs to include an additional unit process (sand filter). This is a scope change that requires leadership approval. |
| 6 | Construction permits | $20,000 | 30% | $15,000 | Initial work has begun, and the permits are expected to be obtained on time. |
| 7 | FEED | $189,818 | 100% | $210,000 | Once the scope change is authorized, the FEED needs to be revisited to include the new unit process (sand filter). |
| 8 | Procurement | $355,909 | 10% | $35,000 | A pump supplier was hired. The initial pump design has been completed. |
| 9 | Detailed engineering | $237,272 | | | |
| 10 | Construction | $830,454 | | | |
| 11 | Equipment installation | $237,272 | | | |
| 12 | Commissioning & closeout | $118,636 | | | |
| | Project management | $230,545 | | | % Completion is excluded because this task is categorized as "level of effort." So, its cost is expected to accrue uniformly over the project's baseline duration, thereby making its % completion the same as % time passed. |
| | Contingency reserve | $464,003 | | | |
| | **Total Project Cost** | **$3,000,000** | | **$523,000** | |

it is categorized as a *level-of-effort* task. Consequently, project management costs are expected to accrue uniformly over time, precluding any cost variance for this task. Similarly, we opted not to include the contingency reserve in the EVM calculations, allowing for its strategic utilization as needed. This approach enhances our understanding of the project tasks' cost performance through the EVM method. Table 11.4 presents the prompt we used for ChatGPT to calculate the project's EVM cost metrics and the results we received. Table 11.5, on the other hand, focuses on our prompt and ChatGPT's response related to forecasting the future budget needs as represented by EAC and ETC under two different potential project scenarios.

**Table 11.4** Use case for EVM calculations—cost performance

| Prompt |
|---|
| The attached table* provides total budgeted cost, actual cost, and % completion (to-date) of the completed and ongoing tasks of Project Pinot. As a cost engineering expert, please perform the earned value management (EVM) calculations for each task and display them in a tabular form with the following columns: ID, Name, Task Cost, % Completion, Actual Cost (AC), Earned Value (EV), Cost Variance (CV), and Cost Performance Index (CPI). Also, calculate EV, AC, CV, and CPI for the entire project. If there is a cost overrun, apply it to the contingency reserve and calculate the remaining reserve. |

**Response**

**Project Pinot EVM Analysis**

| ID | Name | Task Cost | % Completion | Actual Cost (AC) | Earned Value (EV) | Cost Variance (CV) | Cost Performance Index (CPI) |
|---|---|---|---|---|---|---|---|
| 1 | Start | $0 | 100% | $0 | $0 | $0 | N/A |
| 2 | Feasibility study | $100,000 | 100% | $120,000 | $100,000 | -$20,000 | 0.83 |
| 3 | Project definition | $118,636 | 100% | $100,000 | $118,636 | $18,636 | 1.19 |
| 4 | Project sanction | $47,454 | 100% | $30,000 | $47,454 | $17,454 | 1.58 |
| 5 | Environmental permit | $50,000 | 10% | $13,000 | $5,000 | –$8,000 | 0.38 |
| 6 | Construction permits | $20,000 | 30% | $15,000 | $6,000 | –$9,000 | 0.40 |
| 7 | FEED | $189,818 | 100% | $210,000 | $189,818 | –$20,182 | 0.90 |
| 8 | Procurement | $355,909 | 10% | $35,000 | $35,591 | $591 | 1.02 |
| 9 | Detailed engineering | $237,272 | 0% | $0 | $0 | $0 | N/A |
| 10 | Construction | $830,454 | 0% | $0 | $0 | $0 | N/A |
| 11 | Equipment installation | $237,272 | 0% | $0 | $0 | $0 | N/A |
| 12 | Commissioning & closeout | $118,636 | 0% | $0 | $0 | $0 | N/A |
| | **Project Total** | **$2,305,451** | **N/A** | **$523,000** | **$502,499** | **–$20,501** | **0.96** |

**Summary:**

- Total earned value (EV): $502,499
- Total actual cost (AC): $523,000
- Total cost variance (CV): –$20,501
- Total cost performance index (CPI): 0.96

**Contingency Reserve Status:**

- Contingency reserve = $464,003
- Remaining reserve = $464,003 – $20,501 = $443,502

* Table 11.3

**Table 11.5** Use case for EVM calculations—budget forecasting

**Prompt**

As an expert in earned value management (EVM), please calculate the estimate at completion (EAC) and estimate to complete (ETC) for the project in the two scenarios presented below. Also, given these estimates, evaluate if there is enough budget available. If a cost overrun or underrun is projected, how much would that be in dollars and in percentage? Make sure to account for project management cost, which we ignored in the EVM calculations. In both scenarios, assume the project will finish on time, so that there will not be any additional cost (e.g., project management) because of project delay.

1. **Continued Efficiency:**
    - Assume that the remaining work will continue at the current cost performance index (CPI).
    - This includes the work needed to complete the remainder of the ongoing tasks and the work required to complete the tasks that have not yet started.
2. **Baseline Adherence:**
    - Consider the project's current cost performance for the work completed so far, whether it is under budget, on budget, or over budget.
    - For the remaining work, assume it will adhere strictly to the original baseline cost.

**Response**

**Scenario 1: Continued Efficiency**

EAC = BAC/CPI = $3,000,000/0.96 = $3,125,000

ETC = EAC – AC = $3,125,000 – $523,000 = $2,602,000

**Scenario 2: Baseline Adherence**

EAC = AC + (BAC – EV) = $523,000 + ($3,000,000 – $502,499) = $3,020,501

ETC = EAC – AC = $3,020,501 – $502,499 = $2,497,501

**Evaluation of Budget Availability**

- Scenario 1: Continued efficiency: The EAC of $3,124,563 exceeds the BAC of $3,000,000, indicating a cost overrun of $124,563 (4.15%).
- Scenario 2: Baseline adherence: The EAC of $3,020,501 also exceeds the BAC of $3,000,000, indicating a cost overrun of $20,501 (0.68%).

In both scenarios, the project will exceed the budget, and additional funds will be needed to complete the project.

While ChatGPT successfully identified the correct formulas, obtaining accurate results required multiple iterations involving modifications to the input information. This process highlighted both the strengths and limitations of using a large language model (LLM) for complex project management tasks. Generating accurate results was particularly challenging due to the intricate calculations involved, as we discussed in the use case of *analyzing data* for the kitchen renovation project in Chapter 5. Initially, the AI made simple arithmetic errors, such as incorrectly summing a series of numbers. For example, it miscalculated the project's actual cost by inaccurately adding up the individual task costs. To address this and other issues, we had to refine our prompts and ensure that the input data was both comprehensive and clearly presented. This iterative process underscored the importance of specificity and clarity when structuring prompts for AI.

Additionally, we had to be meticulous in describing the two forecasting scenarios, especially because of the nuances involved in the calculations. For example, calculating EAC and ETC requires understanding how the CPI is applied, how level-of-effort tasks like project management are accounted for, and how the contingency reserve is managed. It is crucial to clearly describe these scenarios in the prompt so the LLM can understand and accurately process the information to generate correct results. Despite these challenges, the experience demonstrated the potential of AI to assist in complex project management tasks, provided that the prompts are well-structured and include detailed input data.

## 3. EARNED TIME MANAGEMENT FOR SCHEDULE PERFORMANCE

Despite its comprehensive nature, EVM has severe limitations in its applicability to schedule performance. These limitations are largely due to how the schedule metrics, schedule variance (SV) and schedule performance index (SPI), are conceptualized and reported. For instance, SV is typically expressed in monetary units, which can be hard to understand when assessing time-based performance discrepancies. More critically, the SPI, which aims to reflect the efficiency of time usage against the planned schedule, approaches a value of 1.0 as tasks or projects conclude. This normalization to 1.0 occurs regardless of whether the tasks were completed on time. Therefore, a project could finish late but still report an SPI of 1.0, misleadingly suggesting it was on schedule. To overcome some of these challenges, Lipke (2009) introduced *earned schedule*, which is conceptually similar to earned value, but is still expressed in monetary units, which is confusing to many.

In response to these shortcomings, Kodukula (2020) proposed an alternative approach called *earned time management* (ETM) that adapts the principles of EVM to more accurately reflect schedule performance. This method involves calculating the earned time for each project task in terms of time units, such as days, weeks, and months, instead of monetary units as proposed by Lipke (2009). Earned time is determined by multiplying the task's baseline duration by its percent of completion—just like earned value is calculated by multiplying the task's baseline cost by its percent of completion. This approach shifts the focus from financial to time-based metrics, providing a clearer picture of actual schedule performance. The calculations are as follows:

- *Earned time (ET)*: For each task, ET is computed as the product of the task's baseline duration and its percentage of completion to date. This figure represents the amount of scheduled work effectively completed to date, expressed in time units (e.g., days).
- *Schedule variance*: SV is calculated as the difference between the earned time and the actual time spent to date on the task. The SV of the ETM method is expressed in time units. (The SV of the EVM method is measured and expressed in monetary units, e.g., dollars.) This variance provides a direct measure of whether the task is ahead of, on, or behind schedule compared to its baseline duration.
- *Schedule performance index*: SPI is the ratio of earned time to actual time spent on a task. It offers a measure of time efficiency, with values greater than 1.0 indicating better-than-planned performance, and values less than 1.0 indicating delays.

Additionally, for an overarching view:

- *Project SPI*: This is determined by dividing the sum of earned times of individual tasks by the sum of actual times spent on those tasks. This provides a consolidated measure of the project's overall schedule efficiency.
- *Critical path SPI*: This is calculated in the same fashion as the project SPI. It focuses solely on critical tasks instead of all the tasks, offering insight into the performance of the project's most sensitive components that directly impact the project's finish date.

The AI's ability to interpret complex project data and calculate SPI underscores its capability to support project managers in real-time decision making. The SPI can be used to gauge the current schedule performance and can also be applied to predict future performance. For example, if the current performance level is expected to stay the same for the remainder of the project, the critical path SPI can offer a predictive insight into the project's end date.

This use case serves as a compelling example of how Gen AI can be applied to ETM, providing a robust tool for project managers to:

- *Forecast completion dates*: By analyzing current performance trends and applying them to future tasks, project managers can obtain a more dynamic and potentially accurate forecast of project timelines.
- *Enhance real-time adjustments*: With AI-driven insights, managers can make informed decisions about resource allocation, deadline adjustments, and proactive interventions to steer the project back on course if deviations occur.
- *Scale across projects*: The methodology demonstrated with Project Pinot is not limited to a single project type or industry but can be adapted to various other projects, enhancing the universality and utility of ETM when combined with AI capabilities.

ETM holds greater potential for broader application in managing schedule performance compared to EVM. The integration of Gen AI with ETM offers significant transformative potential. Despite EVM's successful application in the defense sector, its adoption in other industries has been extremely limited. Most organizations do not possess the comprehensive infrastructure required for effective EVM implementation, and the responsibility for cost monitoring and control often does not fall to project managers. Conversely, schedules are universally monitored and of interest to all stakeholders. Therefore, ETM emerges as a more practical and widely applicable tool. Furthermore, given that most project managers regularly track schedules, ETM aligns more seamlessly with their existing workflows.

## Use Case for Earned Time Management

To demonstrate the practical utility of Gen AI using ETM, we employed ChatGPT to perform a real-world evaluation of Project Pinot's schedule performance. The input data (see Table 11.6) for this purpose contains critical information such as the baseline durations of tasks, actual times spent, percent of completions, and indicators of whether the tasks were on the critical path. Responding to our prompt displayed in Table 11.7, ChatGPT provided insights into the project's current schedule status, as shown in the same table. Additionally, Table 11.8 presents the prompt and the results from the language model for forecasting the future schedule of Project Pinot under different scenarios.

The challenges we faced with the ETM use case were similar to those with EVM. Obtaining accurate results required several iterations of prompt refinement. Another challenge specific to ETM is the use of formulas. ETM is a methodology introduced by Kodukula (2020), and due to the limited information available in the public domain, the language models are probably not yet trained for this application. This lack of widespread knowledge necessitated being very specific about the formulas in our prompts. Therefore, in Table 11.8, we provided the formulas explicitly. For forecasting, we again needed to be specific, ensuring the AI had all the necessary information to perform accurate calculations.

While AI tools like ChatGPT can significantly enhance project management processes, human oversight remains essential to ensure accuracy, especially in use cases where calculations are

**Table 11.6** Project Pinot schedule progress information*

| ID | Name | Baseline Duration, Weeks | Predecessor Task | Critical Task? Yes/No | Actual Time, Weeks | % Completion |
|---|---|---|---|---|---|---|
| 1 | Start | 0 | | Yes | 0 | 100% |
| 2 | Feasibility study | 12 | 1 | Yes | 15 | 100% |
| 3 | Project definition | 2 | 2 | Yes | 3 | 100% |
| 4 | Project sanction | 1 | 3 | Yes | 1 | 100% |
| 5 | Environmental permit | 50 | 4 | Yes | 4 | 10% |
| 6 | Construction permits | 14 | 4 | No | 4 | 30% |
| 7 | FEED | 3 | 4 | No | 4 | 100% |
| 8 | Procurement | 30 | 7 | No | 4 | 10% |
| 9 | Detailed engineering | 10 | 7 | No | | 0% |
| 10 | Construction | 18 | 6, 9 | No | | 0% |
| 11 | Equipment installation | 8 | 8, 10 | No | | 0% |
| 12 | Commissioning & closeout | 4 | 11 | No | | 0% |
| 13 | Finish | 0 | 5, 12 | Yes | | 0% |

* Tasks 9 through 12 have not yet started.

**Table 11.7** Use case for ETM calculations—schedule performance

**Prompt**

The attached table* provides you with the schedule progress on Project Pinot.

1) Please calculate the following:

a. Earned time (ET) for each task = duration × % completion
b. Task schedule variance (SV) = earned time − actual time
c. Task schedule performance index (SPI) = earned time/actual time
d. Project SPI = total earned time/total actual time
e. Total earned time for critical tasks
f. Total actual time for critical tasks
g. Critical path SPI = Total earned time for critical tasks/total actual time for critical tasks
h. Critical path SV = Total of SV for critical tasks

2) Prepare a table with the following columns: ID, Name, Duration (weeks), Critical Task? (Yes/No), Actual Time (weeks), % Completion, Earned Time (weeks), Task SPI (weeks), Task SV (weeks)

**Response**

**Task Details and Calculations**

**Calculations:**

1. Earned time (ET) for each task: *duration × % completion*

2. Task schedule variance (SV): *ET − actual time*

*Continued*

**Table 11.7** *continued*

3. Task schedule performance index (SPI): $\frac{ET}{actual\ time}$

4. Project SPI: $\frac{total\ earned\ time}{total\ actual\ time}$

5. Critical path SPI: $\frac{total\ earned\ time\ for\ critical\ tasks}{total\ actual\ time\ for\ critical\ tasks}$

6. Critical path SV: *total of SV for critical tasks*

**Earned Schedule Management Table**

| ID | Name | Duration (Weeks) | Critical Task? (Yes/No) | Actual Time (weeks) | % Completion | Earned Time (Weeks) | Task SPI (Weeks) | Task SV (Weeks) |
|---|---|---|---|---|---|---|---|---|
| 1 | Start | 0 | Yes | 0 | 100% | 0 | N/A | 0 |
| 2 | Feasibility study | 12 | Yes | 15 | 100% | 12 | 0.80 | –3 |
| 3 | Project definition | 2 | Yes | 3 | 100% | 2 | 0.67 | –1 |
| 4 | Project sanction | 1 | Yes | 1 | 100% | 1 | 1.00 | 0 |
| 5 | Environmental permit | 50 | Yes | 4 | 10% | 5 | 1.25 | 1 |
| 6 | Construction permits | 14 | No | 4 | 30% | 4.2 | 1.05 | 0.2 |
| 7 | FEED | 3 | No | 4 | 100% | 3 | 0.75 | –1 |
| 8 | Procurement | 30 | No | 4 | 10% | 3 | 0.75 | –1 |
| 9 | Detailed engineering | 10 | No | 0 | 0% | 0 | N/A | 0 |
| 10 | Construction | 18 | No | 0 | 0% | 0 | N/A | 0 |
| 11 | Equipment installation | 8 | No | 0 | 0% | 0 | N/A | 0 |
| 12 | Commissioning & closeout | 4 | No | 0 | 0% | 0 | N/A | 0 |
| 13 | Finish | 0 | Yes | 0 | 0% | 0 | N/A | 0 |

**Project Metrics**

- Total earned time for all tasks: 30.2 weeks
- Total actual time for all tasks: 35 weeks
- Project SPI: 0.86
- Critical tasks earned time: 20 weeks (for tasks 1, 2, 3, 4, 5)
- Critical tasks actual time: 23 weeks
- Critical path SPI: 0.87
- Critical path SV: –3 weeks

* Table 11.6

**Table 11.8** Use case for ETM calculations—schedule forecasting

**Prompt**

The actual time lapsed on Project Pinot to date is 23 weeks. As an expert in earned value management, calculate the estimate at completion for the schedule (EAC-S) in the two scenarios presented below. If a schedule delay or an early completion is projected, how much would that be in weeks and in percentage?

1) **Continued efficiency:** Assume that the remaining work on the critical path will maintain the current schedule performance index (SPI) of the critical tasks and no new critical paths are introduced. The remaining work includes:
    a. Critical tasks that have not yet started
    b. Critical tasks that are still ongoing

   To calculate the remaining duration to perform the remaining work:
    a. First, calculate the earned time (ET) of the critical tasks by multiplying the actual time lapsed by the SPI of the critical tasks.
    b. Next, determine the remaining duration (baseline) by subtracting the above earned time from the baseline total duration.
    c. Finally, adjust the remaining duration considering the SPI of the critical tasks by dividing the remaining duration (baseline) by the SPI of the critical tasks.
2) **Baseline adherence:** Accept the project's current schedule performance—early, on time, or late. For the remaining duration required to complete the remaining work (as in Scenario 1), assume it will be completed according to the original baseline durations and no new critical paths are introduced.

**Response**

**Continued Efficiency**

1. **Calculate earned time (ET):**
    - Actual Time Lapsed = 23 weeks
    - SPI of critical tasks = 0.87
    - ET = actual time Lapsed * SPI = 23 weeks * 0.87 = 20 weeks
2. **Determine the remaining duration (baseline):**
    - Baseline total duration = 65 weeks
    - Remaining duration (baseline) = baseline total duration – ET = 65 weeks – 20 weeks = 45 weeks
3. **Adjust the remaining duration considering the SPI:**
    - Adjusted remaining duration = remaining duration (baseline) / SPI = 45 weeks / 0.87 ≈ 51.72 weeks
4. **Calculate the estimate at completion for schedule (EAC-S):**
    - EAC-S = actual time lapsed + adjusted remaining duration = 23 weeks + 51.72 weeks = 74.72 weeks

**Baseline Adherence**

1. **Accept the current schedule performance:**
    - The project is late as of now (23 weeks of actual time lapsed with ET of 20 weeks).
2. **Assume remaining work will adhere to the original baseline durations:**
    - Remaining duration (baseline) = 45 weeks (as calculated earlier)
3. **Calculate the estimate at completion for schedule (EAC-S):**
    - EAC-S = actual time lapsed + remaining duration (baseline) = 23 weeks + 45 weeks = 68 weeks

*Continued*

**Table 11.8** *continued*

**Schedule Delay or Early Completion Analysis**

1. **Continued efficiency:**
    - Projected EAC-S = 74.72 weeks
    - Baseline duration = 65 weeks
    - Delay = 74.72 weeks – 65 weeks = 9.72 weeks
    - Delay percentage = (9.72 weeks / 65 weeks) * 100 ≈ 14.95%
2. **Baseline adherence:**
    - Projected EAC-S = 68 weeks
    - Baseline duration = 65 weeks
    - Delay = 68 weeks – 65 weeks = 3 weeks
    - Delay percentage = (3 weeks / 65 weeks) * 100 ≈ 4.62%

involved. The need for multiple iterations and careful prompt structuring highlights the current limitations of AI and the importance of a collaborative approach. By combining the strengths of AI with human expertise, project teams can leverage technology to achieve more accurate and efficient outcomes.

## 4. CHANGE CONTROL FORM

In project management, change is inevitable. Projects often encounter modifications due to evolving requirements, unforeseen obstacles, regulatory changes, technology evolution, or stakeholder demands, among many other reasons. To manage these changes effectively, a structured approach is essential. This is where the CCF comes into play. It is a crucial tool that helps project managers to document, review, and approve changes systematically, ensuring that the project remains aligned with its objectives while adapting to necessary adjustments.

The primary purpose of a CCF is to provide a formal process for requesting, assessing, and implementing changes within a project. It serves as a record of all change requests and decisions, facilitating transparency and accountability. The CCF helps in:

- *Documenting change requests*: Captures detailed information about the requested change, including its origin, nature, and rationale
- *Evaluating impact*: Assesses the potential impact of the change on the project's scope, schedule, budget, and quality
- *Approving or rejecting changes*: Provides a structured process for stakeholders to review and decide on the change requests
- *Implementing approved changes*: Ensures that approved changes are communicated and executed effectively

### Key Components of a Change Control Form

A comprehensive CCF typically includes the following sections:

- *Project information*: Basic details about the project, such as project name, manager, and identification number

- *Change request details*: Information about the change, including a description, the reason for the change, and who is requesting it
- *Impact analysis*: An assessment of how the change will affect the project's scope, schedule, budget, quality, and resources
- *Risk assessment*: An evaluation of the risks associated with implementing the change
- *Approval section*: Signatures or approvals from relevant stakeholders, such as the project manager, sponsor, and steering committee
- *Implementation plan*: A plan for how the change will be implemented, including tasks, responsibilities, and timelines

## Best Practices for Change Control

To ensure the effectiveness of the change control process, consider the following best practices:

- *Establish clear procedures*: Define a clear and consistent process for submitting, reviewing, and approving change requests. Ensure that all team members and stakeholders understand the process.
- *Perform thorough impact analysis*: Evaluate the potential impact of the change on all aspects of the project. Consider not only immediate effects but also long-term implications.
- *Maintain transparency*: Keep all stakeholders informed about change requests and decisions. Transparency builds trust and ensures that everyone understands the reasons behind changes.
- *Document everything*: Record all change requests, impact analyses, decisions, and implementation plans. This documentation provides a historical record and helps in future audits or reviews.
- *Monitor and review changes*: Regularly review the status of approved changes and monitor their implementation. Ensure that changes are executed as planned and address any issues that arise promptly.
- *Update project plans*: Ensure that the project baselines (scope, time, cost) are promptly updated reflecting the approved changes.

## AI in Change Control

AI can significantly enhance the change control process. By automating data collection and analysis, it can streamline the creation of CCFs and ensure that all necessary information is captured accurately. Generation of CCFs, logging them into a change log, and tracking them on a regular basis can be automated using the correct AI tools if the required project input data is available. AI can also assist in impact analysis by predicting the potential effects of changes based on historical data and current project conditions.

Moreover, AI can facilitate faster decision making by providing real-time insights and recommendations. For example, AI algorithms can analyze the project's current status, identify potential risks associated with the change, and suggest mitigation strategies. This allows project managers and stakeholders to make informed decisions quickly.

Additionally, AI-powered dashboards can provide a comprehensive view of all change requests along with their statuses and their impacts. These dashboards can be customized to display information at the project, program, or portfolio level, helping organizations manage changes across multiple projects effectively.

## Use Case for Change Control Form

The use case we selected for the CCF involves a requested scope change in Project Pinot as outlined in Table 11.9. This particular use case exemplifies the procedural aspects of project change management, highlighting the essential steps required to document and authorize changes within a project. The prompt we utilized for ChatGPT to simulate this scenario and the resulting output are presented in Table 11.10, showcasing the practical application of AI in streamlining administrative tasks.

This example demonstrates a straightforward yet crucial aspect of project management that ensures all changes are systematically recorded and approved, maintaining the integrity of the project's scope. Unlike more complex use cases that require intricate calculations and data analysis, this scenario focuses on the procedural accuracy and thorough documentation necessary for effective change management. By leveraging tools like ChatGPT, project managers can enhance their efficiency in handling routine tasks, allowing them to focus on more strategic elements of project execution.

In this scenario, ChatGPT showed remarkable proficiency in generating a comprehensive CCF. It effectively identified and organized the necessary components, ensuring that all critical information was captured. This capability significantly reduces the administrative burden on project managers.

However, one limitation we observed was the AI's occasional struggle with nuanced project-specific details that require contextual understanding. For example, the AI might not fully grasp the implications of changing a project's scope in relation to stakeholder expectations or the potential

**Table 11.9** Project Pinot internal memorandum—change request

**Acme Internal Memorandum**

| | |
|---|---|
| **Date:** | Today |
| **From:** | Emily Carter, Project Pinot Project Manager |
| **To:** | Jean Minelli, Project Pinot Sponsor |
| **Subject:** | Risk Management |

Hi Jean,

I wanted to follow up on our discussion from the other day. Our permitting consultant, CRS, has concluded that the environmental standards for treating Acme's process wastewater will be stricter than we initially assumed. We had thought the standards would be as if the treated effluent was discharged directly into the Mississippi River. However, our plan is to discharge it into a nearby small stream that eventually flows into the Mississippi.

Since the stream has a relatively small flow and a sensitive ecosystem, the effluent standards will be more rigorous. Based on CRS's analysis, we need to add an additional treatment process, specifically a sand filter, to the overall treatment train. This causes a scope change that must be approved by you, the project sponsor.

We are currently at the end of the FEED phase, so we expect the schedule and cost impact to be relatively small. The team has estimated that the overall cost for this addition (including FEED, detailed engineering, procurement, construction, equipment installation, etc.) will be around $150,000. We anticipate it will add 15 days to the critical path.

Attached is the change control form for your authorization of the scope change. Your prompt action on this would be greatly appreciated.

Thank you,

**Table 11.10** Use case for change control form

| Prompt |
|---|
| The attached document* contains the basic information about a change that has been requested on Project Pinot. Based on the information in this document, as an experienced project manager, please prepare a change control form. |
| **Response** |
| **Project name:** Project Pinot<br>**Change request number:** CR-001<br>**Date of request:** Today<br>**Requester name:** Emily Carter<br>**Change description:** Addition of sand filter to the treatment process.<br>**Reason for change:** Environmental standards for treated effluent are stricter due to discharge into a small stream with a sensitive ecosystem.<br>**Impact on scope:** Additional treatment process (sand filter) to be added to the overall treatment train.<br>**Impact on schedule:** Adds 15 days to the critical path.<br>**Impact on budget:** Estimated additional cost of $150,000.<br>**Risk assessment:** Relatively small impact on schedule and cost due to early engineering phase.<br>**Approval status:** Pending<br>**Approver name:** Jean Minelli<br>**Approval date:** |

* Table 11.9

impact on the project's critical path. While ChatGPT can handle standard procedural tasks effectively, it may require further fine-tuning and human intervention to address unique project circumstances or to interpret subjective elements of the change request. Overall, this use case underscores the potential of Gen AI in optimizing administrative processes in project management.

## 5. PROJECT PROGRESS REPORT

A project progress report is an essential tool in project management, providing a snapshot of the current status of a project. It serves multiple purposes, such as informing stakeholders about progress, identifying potential issues, and ensuring that the project stays on track. Effective progress reporting helps maintain transparency, foster accountability, and facilitate informed decision making.

The primary reason for generating project progress reports is to communicate the project's status to stakeholders. Progress reports ensure everyone is on the same page regarding the project's timeline, budget, and scope. The reports help in identifying deviations from the plan early, allowing for timely corrective actions. Additionally, these reports can boost team morale by highlighting achievements and progress made.

A comprehensive project progress report typically includes:

- *Project overview*: A summary of the project, its objectives, and its current phase
- *Status summary*: A high-level view of the project's progress, often using a red, yellow, and green traffic light system to indicate overall health

- *Key milestones*: Information on the completion status of major milestones and deliverables
- *Budget overview*: An update on the financial status, including actual expenditure versus planned budget
- *Schedule update*: Information on task completion, delays, and any changes to the project timeline
- *Risks and issues*: A summary of identified risks, issues, and mitigation strategies

Table 11.11 lists the general *dos and don'ts* of progress reports. To create an effective project progress report, consider the following best practices:

- *Keep it high-level*: Focus on the big picture and avoid getting bogged down in too many details. Stakeholders typically prefer concise and to-the-point reports.
- *Be consistent*: Use a consistent format and reporting schedule to ensure comparability over time.
- *Highlight key information*: Emphasize critical updates, significant achievements, and areas requiring attention.
- *Be honest*: Provide an accurate and honest assessment of the project's status, including any challenges or setbacks.
- *Use visuals*: Incorporate charts, graphs, and traffic light indicators to make the report easier to understand. One of the most common techniques used for progress reporting today in the project management industry is the traffic light system, involving the red, yellow, and green indicators:
    - **Green**—the project is on track, meeting its objectives, and no major issues exist
    - **Yellow**—there are some concerns or minor issues that could potentially impact the project if not addressed
    - **Red**—significant problems exist that are jeopardizing the project's success

Criteria for these states can vary, but generally include schedule adherence, budget status, and risk levels.

**Table 11.11** General *dos and don'ts* of progress reports.

| Dos | Don'ts |
|---|---|
| • Do provide a clear and concise summary | • Don't overwhelm stakeholders with too much detail |
| • Do use visual aids to enhance understanding | • Don't ignore or downplay issues and risks |
| • Do keep the report focused on the most important aspects of the project | • Don't use overly technical language or jargon |
| • Do update the report regularly and consistently | • Don't provide outdated or irrelevant information |
| • Do include actionable insights and recommendations | • Don't forget to follow up on actions and recommendations from previous reports |

## AI in Progress Reports

AI can significantly enhance the process of generating project progress reports. By automating data collection and analysis, AI tools can create real-time, accurate reports with minimal manual effort. AI can also help identify patterns and predict potential issues, providing proactive insights to project managers.

Moreover, AI can create dashboards that offer a comprehensive view of project performance at the project, program, and portfolio levels. By aggregating data from individual projects, these dashboards provide a holistic view, enabling better strategic decision making and resource allocation.

## Use Case for Progress Reports

A well-crafted project progress report is an essential element of effective project management. These reports play a crucial role in providing stakeholders with clear, actionable insights that drive project success. By integrating best practices and utilizing AI, project managers can significantly enhance the quality and utility of these reports.

To demonstrate this capability, we tasked ChatGPT with generating a project progress report for Project Pinot. Our prompt (see Table 11.12) requested specific information for the report. To enable the model to produce the required information, we provided the necessary documentation, including:

- *Table 11.3*: Information on proactive risk mitigation strategies implemented at the beginning of the project execution phase, along with percentage of task completion information
- *Tables 11.4 and 11.5*: Project EVM data, detailing the current cost performance status and future performance forecasts
- *Tables 11.6 through 11.8*: Project schedule progress highlights and ETM data on schedule performance status, along with project timeline forecasts through completion
- *Tables 11.9 and 11.10*: Change request memorandum from the project manager and the CCF, with information on the requested scope change

To ensure ChatGPT produces the exact report you need, it is crucial to provide the necessary documentation. The project input folder (discussed in Chapter 4) can be extremely helpful for the LLM in capturing ongoing performance and reporting progress accurately. If your organization has a customized language model and ongoing or real-time project data availability, the model can generate standardized reports automatically at specified intervals. This capability allows for seamless integration of new information, improving the accuracy and relevance of its reports and recommendations.

Table 11.12 presents the progress report ChatGPT produced in response to our prompt. This example showcases the language model's ability to synthesize requested information from provided documentation without requiring additional calculations.

Despite the advantages mentioned earlier, AI in progress reporting faces limitations, particularly regarding data quality and completeness. The accuracy of AI-generated reports heavily depends on the quality of input data, and any inaccuracies or omissions can lead to misleading information. In illustrating the previously mentioned use case, we had to go through several iterations in providing the input data and structuring the prompts. AI may also struggle with contextual understanding and nuanced project-specific details, requiring clear and detailed prompts to guide its outputs effectively. Additionally, it cannot be overstated that human oversight is crucial to review and validate AI-generated reports, ensuring they align with project realities and stakeholder expectations.

Developing customized language models tailored to organizational needs and project management practices can improve report quality. Combining AI capabilities with human expertise through a collaborative approach ensures strategic decision making and validation of AI outputs.

**Table 11.12** Use case for progress report

| Prompt |
|---|
| Based on the attachments,* please prepare a project progress report including:<br>• Date: Today<br>• Progress period: To date<br>• Status summary: A high-level view of the project's progress, using a red, yellow, green traffic light system to indicate overall health. Green: project's cost and schedule performance is within 15% of baselines, yellow: between 15% and 20%, red: more than 20%.<br>• Key milestones: Information on the completion status of major milestones and deliverables.<br>• Budget overview: An update on the financial status, including actual expenditure versus planned budget. Forecast of future budget needs.<br>• Schedule update: Information on task completion, delays, and any changes to the project timeline. Forecast of the project's finish time.<br>• Risks and issues: A summary of identified risks, issues, and mitigation strategies.<br>• Next steps: An outline of upcoming activities and key focus areas for the next reporting period. |

**Response**

**Project Pinot Progress Report**

| Item | Details |
|---|---|
| **Date** | Today |
| **Progress Period** | To date |
| **Status Summary** | **Green:** The project's cost and schedule performance is within 15% of the baselines |
| **Key Milestones** | **Completion Status of Major Milestones and Deliverables**<br>- Start: Complete<br>- Feasibility study: Complete<br>- Project definition: Complete<br>- Project sanction: Complete<br>- Environmental permit: In progress (10% complete)<br>- Construction permits: In progress (30% complete)<br>- FEED: Complete<br>- Procurement: In progress (10% complete)<br>- Detailed engineering: Not started<br>- Construction: Not started<br>- Equipment installation: Not started<br>- Commissioning & closeout: Not started<br>- Finish: Not started |
| **Budget Overview** | **Financial Status**<br>- Planned budget: $3,000,000<br>- Actual expenditure to date: $523,000<br>- Forecasted EAC (continued efficiency): $3,124,563 (overrun of $124,563 or 4.15%)<br>- Forecasted EAC (baseline adherence): $3,020,501 (overrun of $20,501 or 0.68%) |

*Continued*

**Table 11.12** *continued*

| | |
|---|---|
| **Schedule Update** | **Task Completion and Timeline**<br>- Actual time elapsed: 23 weeks<br>- Earned time (ET): 20 weeks<br>- Current SPI (critical path): 0.87<br>- Forecasted EAC-S (continued efficiency): 74.72 weeks (delay of 9.72 weeks or 14.95%)<br>- Forecasted EAC-S (baseline adherence): 68 weeks (delay of 3 weeks or 4.62%) |
| **Risks and Issues** | **Identified Risks, Issues, and Mitigation Strategies**<br>- Regulatory approval delays: High probability, high impact, mitigation: Engage with regulatory bodies early and frequently.<br>- Customized pump procurement delays: High probability, high impact, mitigation: Authorize pumps as long lead items.<br>- Hurricane impact: Average probability, very high impact, mitigation: Develop contingency plans for weather-related delays.<br>- Project scope definition: High probability, average impact, mitigation: Ensure clear and detailed project scope documentation.<br>- Stakeholder engagement: Average probability, high impact, mitigation: Conduct regular stakeholder meetings and updates.<br>- Inaccurate WWTP design basis: Average probability, high impact, mitigation: Conduct thorough feasibility and pilot studies.<br>- Financial funding issues: Average probability, high impact, mitigation: Secure funding early and maintain financial oversight.<br>- Project manager continuity: Low probability, high impact, mitigation: Develop a succession plan.<br>- Legal regulatory challenges: Low probability, high impact, mitigation: Engage a strong legal team early. |
| **Next Steps** | **Upcoming Activities and Key Focus Areas**<br>- Environmental permit: Continue to work with CRS Consultants LLC to expedite the permitting process.<br>- Construction permits: Finalize and obtain necessary construction permits.<br>- Detailed engineering: Initiate detailed engineering phase.<br>- Procurement: Continue procurement activities for critical components.<br>- Change control: Implement the approved change for the sand filter addition.<br>- Stakeholder engagement: Conduct a project status meeting with key stakeholders.<br>- Risk management: Update the risk register and mitigation plans based on current project status. |

* Tables 11.3 through 11.10

## IN CONCLUSION

The integration of AI into the project execution phase can provide substantial value across multiple domains. From conflict resolution to EVM, ETM, CCFs, and progress reporting, this chapter has demonstrated AI's capability to enhance efficiency and accuracy. By leveraging advanced data analytics and predictive capabilities, project teams can proactively address potential conflicts, accurately forecast project costs and schedules, and streamline the change control process. These AI-driven insights ensure that projects remain on track, within budget, and aligned with strategic goals.

As we transition to Chapter 12, which focuses on AI use cases in the project closeout phase, it is essential to recognize the continuity and interdependence of project phases. The insights gained and efficiencies achieved during the execution phase set a robust foundation for a successful project closeout.

# 12

# AI USE CASES IN THE PROJECT CLOSEOUT PHASE

The closeout phase of a project is a period where the final touches are made to ensure that all project objectives have been met, deliverables are completed, and lessons learned are documented for future reference, among other key activities. In this chapter, we discuss the role of generative artificial intelligence (Gen AI) in enhancing the effectiveness and efficiency of the closeout phase within a waterfall project management environment. We explore how Gen AI can be leveraged to streamline some of the key processes associated with the closeout phase, ultimately contributing to more successful project outcomes.

Closeout does not necessarily mean the final project closeout; it can also refer to the closeout of a specific phase of a project or completion of a major deliverable. For example, in a multiphase construction project, there may be a closeout at the end of the front-end engineering and design (FEED) phase or completion of a set of process manuals. The use cases presented in this chapter are applicable to these types of closeouts as well.

To provide a comprehensive overview, we present Table 12.1, which lists several use cases of Gen AI in the project closeout phase. These use cases demonstrate the versatility and potential of Gen AI to address diverse aspects of project management, from documentation and reporting to stakeholder communication and compliance. While the structure of the prompts required for most of these use cases is relatively simple, the large language models (LLMs) demand substantial data to produce meaningful results. For example, capturing lessons learned from the entire project in the closeout phase necessitates providing relevant information from the entire project life cycle.

Given the significant data requirements and to maintain clarity and focus, we have selected only two use cases for illustration purposes in this chapter:

1. *Lessons learned*: The process of capturing and documenting lessons learned is crucial for continuous improvement. Gen AI can facilitate this by organizing sessions, prompting relevant questions, summarizing discussions, and categorizing insights for future projects.
2. *Project summary report*: Creating a comprehensive project summary report that highlights key accomplishments, milestones, and outcomes is essential for stakeholders. Gen AI can help compile information from various sources, generate clear and concise reports, and provide a detailed overview of the entire project.

To illustrate these two use cases, we apply Project Pinot because it provides a comprehensive example that seamlessly transitions from previous project phases into the closeout phase. This continuity makes it easier to build upon the existing case study, offering clear and practical insights into the application of Gen AI in capturing lessons learned and final project summary reports.

**Table 12.1** Use cases of Gen AI in the project closeout phase

| Use Case | Description |
|---|---|
| Documentation and reporting | Generate comprehensive project closeout reports, finalize documentation, and summarize project outcomes. AI can ensure that all necessary data is accurately reflected in coherent documents |
| Lessons learned | Facilitate lessons learned sessions and document insights by prompting relevant questions, summarizing discussions, and categorizing insights for future reference |
| Stakeholder communication | Draft clear and concise final communications to stakeholders, including tailored emails, presentations, and executive summaries to keep them informed and engaged |
| Knowledge transfer | Assist in the handover process by generating detailed documents and guides, ensuring critical project knowledge is transferred to operational or future project teams |
| Contract closure | Help review contract terms, ensure all contractual obligations are met, and draft necessary correspondence for contract closure, including finalizing payments and resolving issues |
| Post-project evaluation | Design and analyze surveys to gather feedback from team members and stakeholders, create survey questions, and generate reports highlighting areas of success and improvement |
| Archiving project information | Assist in organizing and archiving project documents, creating metadata and tags for easy retrieval, ensuring project information is well-organized and accessible |
| Compliance and auditing | Review compliance checklists, ensure all regulatory requirements are met, and prepare necessary documentation for audits, including generating audit reports and summaries |
| Financial reconciliation | Help reconcile project budgets, track final expenditures, and ensure all financial documentation is accurate and complete, generating financial reports to support project closure |
| Recognition and team wrap-up | Assist in organizing recognition events, drafting speeches, and creating certificates or awards for team members, as well as planning and documenting project wrap-up activities |

Through these examples, we will illustrate how Gen AI can be effectively utilized to enhance the closeout phase of projects, whether it be the final project closeout, the closeout of a specific phase, or completion of a major deliverable.

## 1. LESSONS LEARNED

Capturing lessons learned is a critical component of the project closeout phase. The primary purpose of this practice is to document both the successes and failures encountered during the project life cycle. This information serves as a valuable resource for future projects and possibly the remainder of the current project, enabling organizations to replicate successful strategies and avoid repeating past mistakes. The benefits of capturing lessons learned include:

1. *Continuous improvement*: By systematically documenting and analyzing lessons learned, organizations can continually refine their processes, methodologies, and strategies, leading to better project outcomes over time.
2. *Knowledge sharing*: Lessons learned facilitate knowledge transfer within the organization, ensuring valuable insights are shared across teams and departments. This helps in building a culture of learning and collaboration.

3. *Risk management*: Understanding what went wrong in past projects allows project managers to identify and mitigate similar risks in future projects, thereby enhancing the overall risk management strategy.
4. *Enhanced decision making*: Having a repository of lessons learned provides project managers and stakeholders with data-driven insights that can inform decision-making processes, leading to more informed and effective choices.

## Challenges in Capturing Lessons Learned

Despite the clear benefits, capturing lessons learned is not without its challenges. Some of the common obstacles include:

1. *Lack of participation*: Team members may be reluctant to participate in lessons learned sessions due to time constraints, disinterest, or fear of blame for failures. Additionally, as team members disperse toward the end of the project, many may not be available to complete the lessons learned process. These factors can result in incomplete or biased data collection.
2. *Inadequate documentation*: If lessons learned are not documented properly, the insights may be lost or misunderstood. Inconsistent or unstructured documentation can make it difficult to extract useful information.
3. *Limited accessibility*: To be useful, lessons learned must be easily accessible. Without a centralized repository or proper indexing, valuable insights can remain hidden and underutilized.
4. *Follow-through issues*: Capturing lessons learned is only the first step; the real challenge lies in ensuring that these insights are applied in future projects. Lack of follow-through can render the entire process ineffective.
5. *Cultural barriers*: An organizational culture that does not prioritize learning from mistakes or values short-term successes over long-term growth can hinder the effective capture and utilization of lessons learned.

## Best Practices for Effective Lessons Learned

To overcome these challenges and maximize the value of lessons learned, organizations should adopt the following best practices:

1. *Structured process*: Implement a structured process for capturing lessons learned. This can include standardized templates and guidelines for documentation, ensuring consistency and completeness.
2. *Inclusive participation*: Encourage participation from all team members by creating a safe and open environment where individuals feel comfortable sharing their experiences without fear of blame or retribution. This can be facilitated through anonymous surveys or moderated discussions.
3. *Centralized repository*: Maintain a centralized, searchable repository for lessons learned. This makes it easy for project managers and team members to access and reference past insights when planning and executing new projects.
4. *Integration with processes*: Integrate lessons learned into the organization's standard operating procedures and project management methodologies. This ensures that insights are systematically applied and not overlooked.

5. *Life-cycle documentation*: Capture lessons learned throughout the entire project life cycle, not just at the end. Some teams may complete their tasks early and leave, which is why it is important to gather insights as each phase concludes.
6. *Publishing insights*: If organizational confidentiality policies allow, publish the lessons learned as a case study or a story internally within your organization through newsletters or externally at conferences or professional association meetings.
7. *Positive focus*: Emphasize a positive, future-forward approach rather than focusing on past mistakes and assigning blame. Highlight successes and opportunities for improvement to foster a constructive learning environment.
8. *Continuous capture*: Encourage teams to document lessons learned continuously as the project progresses. Waiting until the end may result in losing valuable insights since some team members may have already moved on to other projects or left the organization. Regularly scheduled reflections throughout the project ensure that knowledge is retained and leveraged effectively.

By adhering to these best practices, organizations can effectively capture and utilize lessons learned, thereby fostering a culture of continuous improvement and achieving greater success in future projects. The role of Gen AI in this context cannot be overstated. Gen AI tools can automate the documentation process, facilitate structured sessions, and provide advanced analytics to identify patterns and actionable insights, making the entire process more efficient and effective.

To address the challenge of ensuring that lessons learned are actually applied in future projects, consider implementing a review process where project managers must reference past lessons during project planning stages. Additionally, incorporating lessons learned into performance evaluations and project assessments can reinforce their importance and encourage teams to leverage this valuable information actively.

## Role of AI in Capturing and Documenting Lessons Learned

Gen AI plays an impactful role in the process of capturing and documenting lessons learned, significantly enhancing efficiency and effectiveness. AI tools like ChatGPT can automate the collection and organization of feedback, ensuring valuable insights are captured. During lessons learned sessions, AI can facilitate discussions by prompting relevant questions, summarizing key points in real time, and categorizing insights for future reference. Furthermore, AI can analyze large volumes of project data to identify patterns and trends, providing actionable recommendations that might not be immediately apparent to human reviewers. This advanced analytical capability helps project teams to gain deeper insights and apply these lessons to improve future project outcomes.

## Use Case for Lessons Learned

Gen AI tools, such as ChatGPT, offer significant potential to enhance the process of capturing lessons learned. This capability is exemplified in the context of Project Pinot, as illustrated in the following tables.

Table 12.2 is an internal memorandum from the project manager highlighting key events since the completion of FEED. Using this as a supporting document in addition to all the other documents previously used by ChatGPT, we asked it to summarize the lessons learned on this project. Table 12.3 includes both the prompt applied and the results obtained. In the context of Project Pinot, ChatGPT effectively captured and documented key lessons learned.

**Table 12.2** Project Pinot internal memorandum—project closeout

**Acme Internal Memorandum**

**Date:** Today
**From:** Emily Carter, Project Pinot Project Manager
**To:** Jean Minelli, Project Pinot Sponsor
**Subject:** Risk Management

Hi Jean,

I hope this email finds you well. I am writing to provide an update on Project Pinot as we transition the fully operational wastewater treatment plant (WWTP) to our operations team. This report highlights the key events that occurred after the completion of the FEED phase, detailing how we navigated challenges and leveraged opportunities to achieve project success.

**1. Procurement delays for customized pumps:** We encountered significant delays in procuring customized pumps critical to the wastewater treatment process. Extended lead times due to global supply chain disruptions impacted our procurement schedule, delaying subsequent installation activities. The delay would have been even more significant if not for our proactive measure of procuring the pumps as long-lead items. This experience underscored the importance of proactive supplier engagement and contingency planning.

**2. Detailed engineering challenges:** During the detailed engineering phase, discrepancies were discovered between the FEED outputs and site conditions, necessitating rework and additional design efforts. These challenges affected our schedule and budget, but the engineering team successfully revised the design plans and worked closely with the construction team to mitigate further delays.

**3. Early environmental permit approval:** We successfully obtained the environmental permit from the Louisiana Department of Environmental Quality (LDEQ) earlier than anticipated. However, the commissioning and start-up tasks had just begun and required a full four weeks to complete. Although we could not capitalize on the early approval immediately, this highlighted the need for better synchronization of permitting timelines with project execution schedules. If we had known about this opportunity, we could have accelerated our construction schedule to some extent.

**4. Construction and weather impacts:** The construction phase commenced during peak hurricane season, resulting in weather-related disruptions. These interruptions led to significant schedule delays as safety protocols mandated halting construction activities. Enhanced weather monitoring and revised construction schedules incorporating potential weather-related contingencies helped manage these disruptions.

**5. Commissioning and start-up delays:** The commissioning and start-up phase started with a three-month delay but was completed within four weeks as planned. This phase was critical in validating the performance of the conventional technology that ultimately won out over the innovative OmniTreat and ensuring compliance with environmental standards.

**6. WWTP operations and new production unit integration:** With the new WWTP operational, wastewater from existing operations is no longer discharged into the local sewer system, eliminating the need to pay municipal surcharges. The new production unit started one month after the WWTP became fully operational. Two weeks were spent ensuring the WWTP was running effectively as wastewater from the new unit began treatment. The effluent from the WWTP consistently meets the standards stipulated in the environmental permit.

*Continued*

**Table 12.2** *continued*

**7. Project cost and schedule adjustments:** The project experienced a delay of three months, meaning that, compared to the plan, it took an extra three months for the WWTP to become operational and compliant. But we had to wait for another month until the new production unit came into operation, followed by a two-week additional WWTP testing period involving the new wastewater stream.
The operations department just reported that the system is operating smoothly under steady-state conditions. The final total installed cost ended up at $3,290,000, which is still within the 10% allowed cost overrun limit. Despite these adjustments, the project achieved its core objectives.

As we wrap things up, I will soon send you a lessons learned document and a final project summary report. Then, I would like to schedule a final meeting to celebrate the successful completion of the project.

Thank you.

**Table 12.3** Use case for lessons learned

| **Prompt** |
|---|
| As an expert in project management, can you please summarize key lessons learned, based on the information provided to you so far on Project Pinot. |

**Response**

**Key Lessons Learned**

**1. Proactive procurement management**

**Event:** Significant delays were encountered in procuring customized pumps due to global supply chain disruptions.

**Lesson:** Engage suppliers early and frequently to mitigate supply chain risks. Establish contingency plans for critical equipment to avoid delays in procurement and installation. Proactively identifying and managing long lead items can help mitigate potential delays.

**Recommendation:** Implement early supplier engagement strategies and maintain regular communication to anticipate and manage supply chain issues.

**2. Rigorous design review**

**Event:** Discrepancies between FEED outputs and site conditions necessitated rework and additional design efforts.

**Lesson:** Conduct thorough reviews and validations of design outputs against site conditions to prevent rework and ensure accuracy in the detailed engineering phase.

**Recommendation:** Enhance the design review process by incorporating detailed site assessments and cross-functional team reviews to identify and address potential discrepancies early.

**3. Synchronization of permits and execution**

**Event:** Obtaining the environmental permit earlier than anticipated highlighted the need for better synchronization of permitting timelines with project execution schedules.

**Lesson:** Align permitting processes with project schedules to take advantage of early approvals and streamline execution timelines.

**Recommendation:** Develop a synchronized permitting and execution schedule, and regularly review and adjust timelines based on permit acquisition progress.

*Continued*

**Table 12.3** *continued*

**4. Weather contingency planning**

**Event:** Construction commenced during peak hurricane season, leading to weather-related disruptions and schedule delays.

**Lesson:** Incorporate robust weather-related contingencies into the construction schedule, especially in regions prone to severe weather conditions.

**Recommendation:** Implement enhanced weather monitoring systems and develop flexible construction schedules that can accommodate weather-related disruptions.

**5. Thorough commissioning planning**

**Event:** The commissioning and start-up phase took longer than expected, but the additional time was used effectively to ensure all systems were tested and operational.

**Lesson:** Allocate sufficient time and resources for commissioning and start-up activities to ensure all systems are thoroughly tested and operational before project completion.

**Recommendation:** Develop detailed commissioning plans and schedules that include sufficient buffer time for testing and validation activities.

**6. Integration of WWTP and new production unit**

**Event:** The new WWTP became operational, eliminating municipal surcharges for wastewater discharge. However, the new production unit started one month later, providing an opportunity to fix any last-minute issues with the WWTP.

**Lesson:** Coordinate the integration of new facilities and systems to ensure smooth transitions and optimize operational readiness.

**Recommendation:** Develop an integration plan that aligns the start-up of new production units with the commissioning of supporting facilities, allowing time for system optimization and issue resolution.

**7. Effective cost and schedule management**

**Event:** The project experienced a three-month delay, and the final installed cost was $3,290,000, within the 10% allowed cost overrun limit.

**Lesson:** Despite delays and cost overruns, effective cost and schedule management can help achieve core project objectives.

**Recommendation:** Continuously monitor and manage project costs and schedules, implementing corrective actions as needed to stay within acceptable limits.

**8. Conflict resolution**

**Event:** A conflict arose between the engineering and R&D teams regarding the adoption of OmniTreat technology.

**Lesson:** Utilizing win-win solutions, such as pilot testing with parallel development and incremental integration, can help balance innovative and risk-averse approaches.

**Recommendation:** Foster collaboration and open communication between teams to address conflicts and reach mutually beneficial solutions.

**9. Change management**

**Event:** A change control form was issued to add a sand filter to the treatment process due to stricter environmental standards.

**Lesson:** Effective change management processes are crucial in accommodating necessary changes without significantly impacting the project scope, schedule, or budget.

**Recommendation:** Establish a robust change management system to evaluate, approve, and implement changes efficiently.

*Continued*

**Table 12.3** *continued*

| |
|---|
| **10. Earned value management (EVM)** |
| **Event:** EVM calculations revealed potential cost overruns and provided insights for budget forecasting. |
| **Lesson:** Regular EVM analysis helps in early identification of cost and schedule variances, enabling timely corrective actions. |
| **Recommendation:** Implement continuous EVM monitoring and analysis to maintain control over project costs and schedules. |

The input data we provided to ChatGPT in this use case was rather limited. Yet, by highlighting recurring issues and successful strategies, the LLM provided actionable recommendations for future projects. For instance, it helped uncover the importance of proactive procurement management and rigorous design reviews, which were crucial in mitigating delays and cost overruns in Project Pinot. By leveraging ChatGPT, Acme Chemical Corporation can now enhance its knowledge repository, ensuring that the insights gained from Project Pinot are effectively applied to improve future project outcomes.

If all the documentation and digitized communications on a project are made available to an LLM through a project input folder or some such mechanism, comprehensive lessons can be captured by the model on an ongoing basis. Furthermore, the LLM can also facilitate structured and insightful sessions to ensure that valuable knowledge is systematically gathered from all team members.

By facilitating such sessions, the LLMs encourage participation from all stakeholders, ensuring diverse perspectives are captured. Additionally, the tools ensure consistency and standardization in the documentation, enhancing the quality and usability of the knowledge captured for future projects.

Despite its strengths, ChatGPT's effectiveness is highly dependent on the quality of the input data provided by the project team. Incomplete or biased data can lead to gaps in the documentation. While the model can analyze and summarize data effectively, it may lack the contextual understanding that human reviewers possess, potentially missing subtleties in project experiences. Additionally, the tool may not fully grasp emotional and interpersonal dynamics that influence project outcomes, which human reviewers can provide insights into. Finally, ensuring data security and privacy is crucial when using AI tools like ChatGPT since they handle sensitive project data. Robust measures must be implemented to protect proprietary and confidential information.

## 2. PROJECT SUMMARY REPORT

The project summary report is an essential document created during the closeout phase of a project, providing a comprehensive overview of the project's life cycle from initiation to completion. The primary purpose of this report is to document the project's key accomplishments, milestones, challenges, and outcomes. This serves several critical functions:

1. *Stakeholder communication*: The project summary report ensures that all stakeholders, including sponsors, team members, and clients, are informed about the project's results and how they align with the initial objectives. It provides transparency and accountability, demonstrating that the project has met its goals and justifying the resources invested.
2. *Performance evaluation*: By detailing the project's adherence to scope, schedule, budget, and quality standards, the report provides a basis for evaluating the project's performance.

This evaluation helps stakeholders understand what went well and what could be improved, offering insights for future projects.

3. *Knowledge sharing*: The report is a formal record, preserving valuable information for future reference. It captures lessons learned, successful strategies, and areas for improvement, contributing to organizational learning and continuous improvement.
4. *Documentation*: The project summary report serves as an official record of important decisions, changes, and outcomes. This documentation is crucial for legal and compliance purposes, ensuring that all aspects of the project are properly recorded.

## Major Items to Be Included in the Project Summary Report

A comprehensive project summary report typically includes several key components:

1. *Project overview*: This section provides basic information about the project, including the project name, manager, start and end dates, budget, and sponsor. It sets the context for the rest of the report.
2. *Project objectives*: Clearly defined goals and objectives at the outset of the project, and how these objectives were met during the project life cycle. This section aligns the project outcomes with the initial goals.
3. *Scope*: Details of the initial scope and any changes that occurred during the project. It includes the final deliverables and any additional features or tasks completed beyond the original plan.
4. *Timeline*: A comparison between the planned timeline with key milestones and the actual timeline, noting any deviations and reasons for changes. This section helps understand how well the project adhered to its schedule.
5. *Budget summary*: A comparison between the initial budget and the final costs, along with an explanation of any cost overruns or savings. This section provides insights into the financial performance of the project.
6. *Key accomplishments*: Major achievements and milestones reached during the project. It highlights the significant deliverables and their impact on the project's success.
7. *Challenges and mitigation*: Key challenges faced during the project and the strategies and actions taken to mitigate these challenges. This section offers lessons for managing similar issues in future projects.
8. *Lessons learned*: Insights gained from the project experience, including what worked well and what could be improved. Based on these lessons, recommendations for future projects can be made.
9. *Stakeholder feedback*: A summary of feedback from key stakeholders, including their perceptions of the project's success and areas for improvement.
10. *Next steps*: Follow-up actions or recommendations for ongoing support and any future work or phases related to the project.

## Role of AI in Project Summary Reports

Gen AI can significantly streamline the creation of project summary reports by automating the collection and organization of data from various project documents. AI tools can generate clear and concise summaries, reducing the manual effort required from project managers. They can analyze large volumes of project data to identify patterns, correlations, and insights that might not be immediately apparent to human reviewers. This advanced analysis provides a deeper understanding of the project's performance and highlights areas for improvement. Additionally, AI can ensure consistency and accuracy in the report, making it a reliable resource for future reference. By leveraging AI, organizations can produce high-quality project summary reports more efficiently, enhancing their ability to learn from and improve upon their project management practices.

## Use Case for Project Summary Report

Table 12.4 presents the prompt we used to request ChatGPT to produce a project summary report for Project Pinot and the response received. Unlike the detailed specifications provided for the project progress report (as seen in Chapter 11, Table 11.12), we kept the prompt for the project summary report simple and straightforward. We attached numerous project documents to ensure the language model had sufficient information to synthesize and present a comprehensive and meaningful summary report.

**Table 12.4** Use case for project summary report

| Prompt | |
|---|---|
| Using the information provided in the attached documents,* please generate a final project summary report. | |
| **Response** | |
| **SECTION** | **DETAILS** |
| **Project Overview** | |
| **Project Name:** | Project Pinot |
| **Project Manager:** | Emily Carter |
| **Start Date:** | January 2, 2023 |
| **End Date:** | August 31, 2024 |
| **Budget:** | $3,290,000 |
| **Sponsor:** | Jean Peterson Minelli |
| **Project Objectives:** | The primary objectives of Project Pinot were to design and build a wastewater treatment plant (WWTP), reduce operational costs, and ensure environmental compliance. These objectives were met by successfully commissioning the WWTP, which now treats wastewater effectively, eliminating municipal surcharges and complying with environmental standards. |
| **SCOPE** | |
| **Initial Scope:** | Design and implement a wastewater treatment plant using OmniTreat technology. |
| **Final Scope:** | Included additional features for environmental compliance and enhanced performance, such as the incorporation of a sand filter to meet higher effluent standards. |
| **TIMELINE** | |
| **Planned Timeline:** | - January: Planning<br>- February–March: FEED<br>- April–May: Detailed engineering<br>- June–December: Construction<br>- January–February: Commissioning |

*Continued*

**Table 12.4** *continued*

| | |
|---|---|
| **Actual Timeline:** | - January: Planning<br>- February–April: FEED<br>- May–August: Detailed engineering<br>- September–March: Construction<br>- April–May: Commissioning<br>- June–August: Final adjustments |
| **Total Delay:** | Three months due to procurement and weather-related challenges. |
| **BUDGET SUMMARY** | |
| **Initial Budget:** | $3,000,000 |
| **Final Budget:** | $3,290,000 (within the 10% allowed cost overrun limit) |
| **KEY ACCOMPLISHMENTS** | |
| | - **Successful implementation of conventional technology:** Despite initial challenges, the project pivoted to conventional technology after proving OmniTreat ineffective during the feasibility study.<br>- **Achieved environmental compliance:** The WWTP now consistently meets the standards stipulated in the environmental permit from the Louisiana Department of Environmental Quality (LDEQ).<br>- **Eliminated municipal sewer surcharges:** With the WWTP operational, wastewater from existing operations is no longer discharged into the local sewer system.<br>- **Effective stakeholder engagement and project team collaboration:** Proactive measures, such as early engagement with suppliers and detailed design reviews, contributed to the project's success. |
| **CHALLENGES AND MITIGATION** | |
| **Procurement Delays:** | Significant delays were encountered in procuring customized pumps due to global supply chain disruptions. Proactive supplier engagement and contingency planning helped mitigate these delays to a certain extent. |
| **Design Discrepancies:** | Discrepancies between FEED outputs and site conditions required rework. Thorough design reviews and site assessments helped address these issues. |
| **Weather Impacts:** | Construction during peak hurricane season led to weather-related disruptions. Enhanced weather monitoring and flexible scheduling helped manage these disruptions. |
| **Commissioning and Start-Up Delays:** | The commissioning and start-up phase started with a three-month delay but was completed within four weeks as planned. This phase was critical in validating the performance of the conventional technology and ensuring compliance with environmental standards. |

*Continued*

**Table 12.4** *continued*

| | |
|---|---|
| **LESSONS LEARNED** | |
| | - **Proactive procurement management:** Early and frequent supplier engagement is crucial to mitigate supply chain risks.<br>- **Parallel testing in the feasibility study:** Allocate adequate time and resources for feasibility studies, including pilot testing and scenario planning, to evaluate different solutions.<br>- **Rigorous design review:** Thorough reviews and validations of design outputs against site conditions can prevent rework.<br>- **Synchronization of permits and execution:** Align permitting processes with project schedules to take advantage of early approvals and streamline execution timelines.<br>- **Weather contingency planning:** Incorporate robust weather-related contingencies in construction schedules.<br>- **Thorough commissioning planning:** Allocate sufficient time and resources for commissioning and start-up activities to ensure all systems are tested and operational before project completion.<br>- **Integration of WWTP and new production unit:** Coordinate the integration of new facilities and systems to ensure smooth transitions and optimize operational readiness.<br>- **Effective cost and schedule management:** Continuously monitor and manage project costs and schedules, implementing corrective actions as needed to stay within acceptable limits.<br>- **Conflict resolution:** Foster collaboration and open communication between teams to address conflicts and reach mutually beneficial solutions.<br>- **Change management:** Establish a robust change management system to evaluate, approve, and implement changes efficiently.<br>- **Earned value management (EVM):** Implement continuous EVM monitoring and analysis to maintain control over project costs and schedules. |
| **STAKEHOLDER FEEDBACK** | |
| | - Positive feedback on project outcomes.<br>- Suggestions for improved communication and more frequent updates. |
| **NEXT STEPS** | |
| | - Conduct post-project review meetings.<br>- Document and archive all project information.<br>- Apply lessons learned to future projects. |

* Tables 11.3, 11.12, 12.2, and 12.3

The primary strength of using ChatGPT for generating a project summary report, as demonstrated with Project Pinot, lies in its ability to efficiently process and synthesize large volumes of data. Considering the relatively meager documentation we provided, ChatGPT performed an effective job in summarizing the project. The resulting summary was comprehensive and inclusive of all relevant aspects of Project Pinot. Additionally, the AI's capacity to generate a clear and concise summary enhanced the clarity and readability of the report, making it easier for stakeholders to understand the project's outcomes and implications.

Despite its strengths, there are some limitations to using ChatGPT for generating project summary reports. The effectiveness of the AI-generated reports heavily depends on the quality and completeness of the input documents provided. In Project Pinot's case, any gaps or inconsistencies in the attached documents could lead to a summary that lacked important details or context. Furthermore, while ChatGPT efficiently synthesized information, it might not fully capture the nuanced understanding of project dynamics and interpersonal factors that a human project manager could include. This was evident in the report's occasional lack of depth in addressing specific team interactions and conflict resolutions. There is also a risk of overreliance on the AI, which might lead to overlooking the importance of manual review and validation to ensure the accuracy and relevance of the report.

## IN CONCLUSION

The closeout phase of a project, as demonstrated through the use cases of Project Pinot, is a critical juncture where final validations, documentation, and knowledge transfer occur. By facilitating various project closeout activities, AI ensures that the project's outcomes are thoroughly documented and easily accessible for future reference. This not only aids in continuous improvement but also secures a solid foundation for future projects by preserving valuable insights and data.

Concluding the section on the various phases of the project life cycle—initiation, planning, execution, and closeout—highlights the transformative potential of Gen AI across the entire spectrum of project management. Each phase has unique challenges and requirements, and AI has demonstrated its capability to enhance decision making, streamline processes, and improve overall project outcomes in a structured waterfall environment. From defining project objectives and developing detailed plans to executing tasks and ensuring thorough closeout procedures, AI's integration into project management practices indicates a significant advancement in how projects are managed and executed.

SECTION 4

# *AI in an Agile Environment*

# 13

## AGILE ESSENTIALS

This chapter serves as a foundation for understanding agile frameworks in project management, setting the stage for the following chapters, where we will explore practical examples of how generative artificial intelligence (Gen AI) can enhance and streamline agile processes. Whether you are new to agile or an experienced practitioner, this chapter provides the essential building blocks to ensure a comprehensive understanding of the concepts, principles, and methods underpinning agile project management.

While Chapter 8 introduced agile as a development approach (alongside others such as waterfall and hybrid), this chapter takes a deeper dive into specific agile frameworks. We begin with an overview of the origin of agile, tracing its evolution from traditional development approaches to the creation of the Agile Manifesto—a landmark in modern project management philosophy.

Next, we introduce some of the most prominent agile frameworks, including Lean, Kanban, and Scrum, each of which offers distinct tools and techniques for achieving iterative and incremental progress. Special emphasis is placed on Scrum, the most widely adopted agile framework, with a discussion on the Scrum process and its core elements, including artifacts, ceremonies, team roles, sprints, and so on. Together, these concepts form the *flywheel* of incremental delivery—a cycle that enables teams to adapt quickly to change, deliver value in small, usable increments, and foster continuous collaboration.

Scrum artifacts and ceremonies will take center stage as key enablers of team alignment, transparency, and the delivery of consistent value. The former ensure clarity and transparency, while the latter provide opportunities for planning, alignment, and reflection. Chapters 14 and 15 will use this classification to explore these concepts in greater depth.

If you are already well-versed in agile frameworks, you may choose to simply skim this chapter as a refresher or reference guide. However, for readers new to agile, this chapter is essential for grasping the foundational principles needed to fully appreciate the AI use cases that will be explored in the chapters that follow. By building this understanding, you will be better equipped to leverage Gen AI as a powerful ally in agile project environments, enhancing your ability to plan, execute, and optimize projects with speed, precision, and creativity.

## INTRODUCTION TO AGILE

Agile has revolutionized how projects are managed. Traditional plan-driven methods no longer meet today's demands for speed, flexibility, and customer focus. Agile frameworks like Scrum, Kanban, and Lean emphasize an iterative, incremental approach with continuous customer feedback. Teams can quickly adapt to changing requirements and deliver high-priority features sooner. Agile has become critically important in the software industry, spreading its wings in recent years into other industries such as construction.

Let us begin with some foundational definitions to understand agile basics. Agile is described as a philosophy, mindset, or set of principles for managing projects and developing products. It provides a guiding set of values and principles that will be discussed in more detail later. It is an adaptive project development approach prioritizing flexibility, collaboration, and iterative progress rather than rigid adherence to predetermined plans. Several frameworks have been developed over the last three decades that offer a structure for implementing agile principles in a consistent way. Examples of such frameworks include Lean, Kanban, and Scrum (described in more detail later), which emphasize new ways of planning, development, and delivery, characterized by flexibility and a readiness to embrace change. At their core, they prioritize customer satisfaction, the early and frequent delivery of value, and adaptability to changing requirements.

If you are a project manager with experience in predictive approaches such as waterfall, you might find agile principles and practices to be a significant departure from the structured and sequential processes you are accustomed to—and that is entirely valid. Agile is not designed to replace traditional project management but to provide an alternative approach for projects where change is inevitable and the business value is not entirely clear from the outset. This approach offers a way to thrive in dynamic environments, enabling teams to adapt, iterate, and deliver incremental value.

## HISTORY AND DEVELOPMENT OF AGILE

The rise of agile project management represents a paradigm shift in how organizations approach work. Rather than following traditional, plan-driven processes, agile promotes an adaptive, incremental style of project delivery. The roots of this modern agile movement can be traced back several decades to Lean manufacturing practices that emphasized maximizing value while eliminating wasteful activities. As software development demands increased in the 1990s, teams sought new ways to deliver high-quality products faster and more responsively. This catalyzed the creation of the Agile Manifesto in 2001 that formally outlined the foundational values and principles underlying agile (Beck, et al., 2001; Ambler and Lines, 2022).

Agile evolved from various iterative and incremental software development approaches that were prominent in the early 1990s. The increasing complexity of projects and the demand for faster turnaround times led to the search for more flexible methodologies. It was common that software projects would sometimes be extended by months or years because requirements changed as the original project progressed, business rules were modified, stakeholders changed, and so on.

The traditional waterfall approach was put to the test, trying to cope with this level of volatility. The piles of documentation were suddenly obsolete, the relationship with the customer was at a very low point, and the contract clauses were used more as a threatening strategy instead of an added value tool. These were some of the frequent scenarios that project managers had to live with for quite some time—until agile philosophy permeated the organization. As you will realize from the following paragraphs, agile merges concepts from Lean manufacturing and iterative development, like rapid application development.

## The Agile Manifesto

The origin of agile started with the Agile Manifesto (see Table 13.1), an agreement formulated in February 2001 by 17 software developers, who discussed lighter, more flexible approaches to software development in response to the challenging and frequent issues faced by project managers at that time. This manifesto came as a revolutionary approach emphasizing new ways to manage projects. It was carefully developed so it did not disregard the good practices that had been developed so far. The four core values encapsulated in the Manifesto transformed the software industry and, later, the project management practice as a whole. You may say that it is how revolutions usually start.

In addition to the four core values, 12 principles were built to accompany them (see Table 13.2). They underpin the Manifesto and are designed to encourage a flexible, iterative, and collaborative approach to project management, particularly in software development. These principles guide agile teams to be more adaptable, flexible, and customer-focused in their approach to project management, allowing for better responsiveness to changing project needs and environments. It is indeed a significant change from traditional project management, where teams were basically told what to do at every step, tasks were very rigid, and changes were seen as obstacles.

**Table 13.1** Agile Manifesto

We are uncovering better ways of developing software by doing it and helping others do it. Through this work, we have come to value:

- Individuals and interactions over processes and tools
- Working software over comprehensive documentation
- Customer collaboration over contract negotiation
- Responding to change over following a plan

That is, while there is value in the items on the right, we value the items on the left more.

https://agilemanifesto.org

**Table 13.2** Agile Principles

1. Our highest priority is to satisfy the customer through early and continuous delivery of valuable software.
2. Welcome changing requirements, even late in development. Agile processes harness change for the customer's competitive advantage.
3. Deliver working software frequently, from a couple of weeks to a couple of months, with a preference for the shorter timescale.
4. Businesspeople and developers must work together daily throughout the project. Encourage daily collaboration between business stakeholders and developers.

*Continued*

**Table 13.2** *continued*

| | |
|---|---|
| 5. | Build projects around motivated individuals. Give them the environment and support they need and trust them to get the job done. |
| 6. | The most efficient and effective method of conveying information to and within a development team is face-to-face conversation. |
| 7. | Working software is the primary measure of progress. |
| 8. | Agile processes promote sustainable development. The sponsors, developers, and users should be able to maintain a constant pace indefinitely. |
| 9. | Continuous attention to technical excellence and good design enhances agility. |
| 10. | Simplicity—the art of maximizing the amount of work not done—is essential. |
| 11. | The best architectures, requirements, and designs emerge from self-organizing teams. |
| 12. | At regular intervals, the team reflects on how to become more effective, then tunes and adjusts its behavior accordingly. |

https://agilemanifesto.org/principles.html

## Origin of Agile: Lean and Kanban

Agile philosophy has its roots in the best practices of two foundational frameworks: Lean and Kanban. Both originated in the manufacturing industry, offering innovative approaches to efficiency, waste reduction, and continuous improvement, which have seamlessly transitioned into the realm of project management. Lean, with its emphasis on delivering value by eliminating waste, and Kanban, with its visual workflows and focus on managing work in progress, have significantly influenced agile thinking and practices. Together, they form a solid foundation upon which the Scrum framework is built. Scrum, while distinct in its structure and focus, incorporates the principles of adaptability, incremental and iterative delivery, and team empowerment rooted in Lean and Kanban, making it one of the most widely adopted agile frameworks today. In the following sections, we first introduce Lean and Kanban briefly and then delve deeper into Scrum, exploring its roles, ceremonies, and practical applications in modern project management.

### *Lean*

Originating from the Toyota Production System (TPS) in the mid-20th century, Lean focuses on optimizing efficiency and minimizing waste (*muda*) in manufacturing processes. It was developed by Taiichi Ohno (Ohno, 1988; Liker, 2021) and Shigeo Shingo (Shingo, 1989) among others as a response to the limitations of mass production. Lean's principles of continuous improvement, flow, innovation, and respect for people gradually found their way into other industries, including software development.

By emphasizing value creation and waste elimination, Lean evolved into a vital part of the agile movement, influencing frameworks like Kanban and Scrum. The Lean concept was later popularized in the West by Womack and his coauthors with their book, *The Machine That Changed the World* (Womack, et al., 1990; Seddon, 2023). Among the main industries that have adapted Lean are manufacturing, which was Lean's core industry, focusing on waste reduction and efficiency; healthcare, where Lean principles are applied to improve patient care efficiency and reduce waste in processes; and software development, where Lean is used to optimize the development process, eliminating unnecessary tasks and focusing on value creation.

### *Kanban*

Kanban, meaning *visual board* or *sign* in Japanese, also has its roots in TPS. It was developed in the late 1940s by Taiichi Ohno as a tool to manage work at a personal and team level. Kanban was later adapted and promoted for knowledge work as a method for managing tasks by David J. Anderson in the early 2000s (Anderson, 2010). The primary characteristic of Kanban is a board with different columns—for example, *To Do, Doing*, and *Done*—where cards below each column's title represent tasks that flow from To Do to Done. Team members are responsible for moving their cards from each state to the next and making things *flow*. The board accomplishes many objectives including transparency of work, workflow, communication, and showing potential bottlenecks in the process.

Kanban became a part of the agile framework for its ability to visualize work, limit work in progress, and maximize efficiency. Kanban's flexibility and focus on continuous delivery made it an attractive choice for teams aiming to improve their workflow and adaptability. The main industries that use Kanban are manufacturing, with main applications in inventory management and production scheduling; software development, where workflow and priorities are managed in a *visual* fashion; and service industries, like marketing agencies, operations, and HR departments, where tasks and projects are prioritized on Kanban boards.

## SCRUM

Scrum, one of the most widely recognized agile frameworks, finds its roots in the early 1990s, significantly influenced by Hirotaka Takeuchi's and Ikujiro Nonaka's groundbreaking *Harvard Business Review* article, "The New New Product Development Game" (Takeuchi and Nonaka, 1986). In this article, they likened high-performing, cross-functional teams to a rugby scrum, emphasizing collaboration and adaptability. Building on this concept, Ken Schwaber and Jeff Sutherland formalized Scrum as a framework for software development projects in the early 1990s. Scrum was introduced to the broader software community at the OOPSLA conference in 1995. This was followed by the publication of their influential article, "Agile Software Development with Scrum" (Schwaber, 1995; Schwaber and Sutherland, 2020), which played a pivotal role in defining and popularizing Scrum as a central framework in the agile landscape.

Drawing inspiration from Lean and iterative development models, Scrum introduced the concept of *sprints*—time-boxed periods where a team works to complete a set amount of work. Scrum's structure of regular meetings, roles (like the Scrum master and product owner), and artifacts (like the product backlog, sprint backlog, increment) provided a framework that was easily adaptable and emphasized team collaboration, frequent delivery of product increments, and response to change (Schwaber and Beedle, 2002; Schwaber and Sutherland, 2020).

The main industries that use Scrum are:

- *Software development*—for its high degree of flexibility; compatible with the development of complex software systems in stages
- *Product development*—where rapid prototyping and iterative design are key
- *Research and advanced technologies*—where flexibility and speed are crucial

## The Core Principles of Scrum

Scrum operates on a set of fundamental principles that guide its implementation and practices:

- *Control of the empirical process*: Scrum's processes are mainly empirical and based on experimentation and experience. Transparency, inspection, and adaptation are the three main ideas that govern this process.
- *Self-organization*: Independence and self-organization are fundamental to Scrum and the teams' daily work, as they are responsible for managing and governing their own activities.
- *Collaboration*: Scrum is a collaborative-first experience. It is based on the premise that the team will self-regulate toward the completion of the project and that without directive leadership objectives are accomplished too.
- *Value-based prioritization*: Tasks are organized and prioritized based on the value added to the client and the business. This is the north star of every Scrum team.
- *Time-boxing*: Tasks are finished in Sprints, which have a limited duration. Different ceremonies are built around them.
- *Iterative development*: The project is built iteratively during the development process.

## Scrum Process Overview

Figure 13.1 depicts a brief overview of the Scrum process, which is described briefly here. The process begins with the *product backlog*, a prioritized list of work items that reflect the project's requirements. During sprint planning, the team selects a subset of these items to include in the sprint backlog and defines the sprint goal. The team then works collaboratively within a sprint to deliver a product increment, which is a usable and potentially shippable part of the product. Daily progress is reviewed in the *daily Scrum*, a brief meeting where team members synchronize, address challenges, and adjust plans. At the end of the sprint, the team holds a *sprint review* to present the completed increment to stakeholders and gather feedback, followed by a *sprint retrospective* to reflect on the sprint process and identify improvements for future iterations. This iterative process

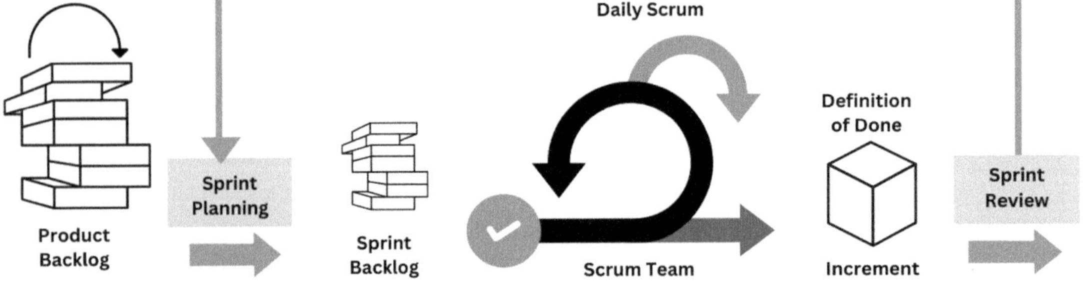


**Figure 13.1** Scrum process overview

ensures continuous progress, adaptability to changing requirements, and delivery of value to stakeholders. A more detailed description of these process steps is presented in Chapters 14 and 15.

## Core Elements of Scrum

The core elements of Scrum form the foundation of this agile framework, driving its structure and effectiveness. These include *Scrum artifacts*, which provide transparency and focus; *Scrum ceremonies*, which facilitate collaboration, planning, and continuous improvement; and *Scrum teams*, which ensure accountability and collective ownership. At the heart of Scrum are *sprints and incremental delivery*, enabling teams to achieve iterative progress while consistently delivering value to stakeholders. These core elements are discussed in more detail in the following sections.

### *Scrum Artifacts*

Scrum artifacts serve as the key deliverables and tools that provide transparency and structure to the Scrum framework, ensuring the team aligns with its goals. The product backlog is a prioritized list of features, user stories, and tasks that define the scope of the product, evolving throughout the project to reflect new requirements and feedback. The sprint backlog, derived from the product backlog, outlines the specific work the team commits to completing during a sprint, offering clarity on short-term objectives. The increment represents the sum of completed work, providing a tangible outcome that meets the *definition of done* (DoD) and demonstrates progress toward the overall product goal. These artifacts enable effective communication, support iterative development, and foster collaboration among stakeholders, ensuring that the Scrum team remains focused, adaptable, and aligned with the project vision while delivering incremental value with each sprint.

### *Scrum Ceremonies*

Scrum ceremonies are structured events that promote collaboration, transparency, and alignment within the Scrum framework. The *sprint planning meeting* kicks off each sprint, allowing the team to define the sprint goal and determine the work they will commit to completing. The daily Scrum is a brief, time-boxed meeting where team members share progress, discuss challenges, and align their efforts for the day. The sprint review takes place at the end of the sprint, providing an opportunity to showcase completed work to stakeholders, gather feedback, and assess progress toward the product goal. Finally, the sprint retrospective encourages the team to reflect on their processes, identifying opportunities for improvement to enhance future sprints. These ceremonies establish a rhythm for the team, ensuring continuous communication, regular feedback, and iterative development, all of which are essential for delivering value in an agile and collaborative manner.

### *Scrum Teams*

Scrum is designed to facilitate teamwork, communication, and iterative progress toward a clearly defined goal. Its structure is simple yet highly effective, based on the Lean and agile principles studied before. It focuses on continuous improvement and adaptability to change. Scrum teams usually have between three and seven members. This size is small enough to remain adaptive and agile, and large enough to complete significant work within a sprint. If you have a larger team, it is common to divide them into one or more teams dedicated to different activities. If a Scrum team has more than seven members, communication issues may arise, and complexity will harm the process. Central to the framework are the different roles that the team members should carry out during the different ceremonies of Scrum: the product owner, the Scrum master, and the development team. The following sections examine their descriptions and main responsibilities.

#### Product Owner

The product owner is the visionary leading the project; the one who defines the features of the product and decides on the project direction based on customer requirements and value added. This role is responsible for managing the product backlog (all the tasks related to building the project itself) and prioritizing the backlog items (user stories, features, bugs) to ensure that work focuses on those with maximum value aligned with project goals. The product owner acts as the liaison between the stakeholders and the development team, ensuring a clear understanding of expectations and providing communication to stakeholders on progress.

#### Scrum Master

The Scrum master acts as a facilitator for the Scrum team. The Scrum master's main task is to remove impediments to the team's progress and ensure Scrum practices are followed correctly. This involves scheduling and facilitating the different Scrum ceremonies, such as the sprint planning, the daily stand-up (Scrum) meeting, and retrospective sessions, among others.

The Scrum master coaches the team members in self-organization and cross-functionality while helping them to improve their technical practices and team dynamics. At the same time, they protect the team from external disruptions and distractions to keep the focus on the work during the sprint. This is a role that doesn't exist in traditional project management and is often misunderstood or seen as not required, while the reality is that it is a very significant pillar for building a high-performing team leading to project success.

#### Development Team

The development team is the group of professionals who deliver the product. Ideally, they should have a high level of cross-functional skills to perform the different tasks required to deliver the product increment, sprint by sprint. It is the responsibility of the development team to ensure the deliverables meet the necessary quality standards.

Scrum teams are self-organizing, meaning they decide internally how to turn the product backlog into an increment of potentially shippable products. This is quite different from traditional project management, where the project manager organizes everybody's work in a top-down process. This is usually one of the main showstoppers for the Scrum framework, which cannot permeate an organization due to these traditional power holders that see autonomy as a threat, instead of seeing it as a moving force. Effective Scrum teams are characterized by a high level of collaboration and open communication. They interact in several meetings, such as daily standups, sprint planning sessions, and sprint reviews. Each team member is committed to the goals set in the sprint and is accountable for their contribution toward achieving these goals. The team must be capable of adapting to changing requirements and feedback, a core principle of agile.

### *Sprints and Incremental Delivery*

A central feature of Scrum is the use of sprints—fixed-length iterations, typically lasting two to four weeks. Sprints are at the heart of the Scrum framework, providing a structured yet flexible approach to managing projects. A common practice is to start with two-week sprints, which provide a good balance between responsiveness and manageable workloads. Once a couple of sprints are completed, the team should choose the final sprint length, which should be maintained for the rest of the project. During each sprint, specific work must be completed and made ready for review. It is not recommended for sprints to last longer than four weeks as speed and commitment tend to decay. The secret is to find a frequency that maintains speed and keeps morale high.

Each sprint begins with a sprint planning session, where the team selects work from the product backlog to complete during the sprint. Each sprint aims to produce a potentially shippable product increment, building upon previously completed work. The increment should meet the DoD, a clear and concise list of criteria that must be met before a product increment is considered complete. This cadence of regular increments ensures that the product is continuously evolving and improving, providing tangible value to the customer at regular intervals.

## IN CONCLUSION

This chapter laid the groundwork for understanding agile essentials, tracing its origins to the Agile Manifesto and foundational frameworks like Lean and Kanban. While these frameworks contribute unique perspectives, the chapter emphasized the Scrum framework, renowned for its focus on flexibility, collaboration, incremental delivery, and iterative improvement. We explored Scrum's core elements: artifacts, ceremonies, roles, and sprints, illustrating how these components integrate to create a cohesive system for agile project management. By delving into these elements, this chapter highlighted Scrum's ability to foster transparency, alignment, and continuous value delivery, making it a cornerstone of modern agile practices.

Looking ahead, Chapter 14 shifts focus to Scrum artifacts, examining how AI technologies can enhance and streamline these critical tools. From refining the product backlog to optimizing sprint backlogs, AI offers innovative ways to improve workflows, boost efficiency, and support better decision making. This exploration will provide practical insights into leveraging AI to unlock the full potential of Scrum artifacts, demonstrating how cutting-edge technology can transform traditional agile practices into even more effective systems.

# 14

# AI USE CASES IN AGILE SCRUM ARTIFACTS

In the evolving landscape of project management, the integration of artificial intelligence (AI) into agile methods, particularly Scrum, is reshaping how teams approach project planning, execution, and delivery. Generative AI (Gen AI) tools, such as large language models (LLMs) like ChatGPT, present new opportunities to enhance Scrum practices by optimizing workflows, streamlining communication, and supporting informed decision making. This chapter focuses on the practical applications of ChatGPT in enhancing the effectiveness of key Scrum artifacts.

Scrum relies on defined artifacts to maintain transparency, structure, and collaboration throughout the project life cycle. These artifacts—*product backlog, epics, and user stories*—are fundamental in guiding teams toward successful outcomes. Integrating AI tools into these artifacts allows Scrum teams to improve their ability to prioritize, plan, and execute tasks efficiently. This chapter explores key use cases that demonstrate how ChatGPT can enhance the management of three Scrum artifacts. In addition, it also includes the use case of predictive analytics that can help the Scrum team with the artifacts. These use cases include:

1. *Product backlog*: In this use case, we showcase how ChatGPT can assist in creating and organizing the product backlog by prioritizing tasks, incorporating stakeholder feedback, and aligning with project goals. ChatGPT provides support by analyzing project vision and requirements to generate actionable backlog items, enabling teams to focus on delivering high-priority outcomes.
2. *Epics*: Building on the foundation of the product backlog, this use case highlights ChatGPT's ability to structure high-level epics. It demonstrates how AI can help define epics based on strategic objectives, stakeholder input, and market needs, and break them down into smaller, manageable components that provide a clear roadmap for the team.
3. *User stories*: This use case delves into the process of transforming epics into detailed user stories. ChatGPT is pivotal in ensuring these stories are well-defined, actionable, and aligned with team capacity and project priorities. The tool assists in refining user stories, facilitating prioritization, and bridging strategic goals with specific tasks.
4. *Predictive analytics*: Finally, we explore how AI-driven predictive analytics can complement Scrum artifacts by offering actionable insights. ChatGPT aids in anticipating risks, optimizing workload distribution, and enhancing sprint planning and performance, allowing teams to proactively address potential challenges and maximize efficiency.

Throughout the chapter, we will use Project Victor—an initiative to enhance the AcuTrack software at GeneMatrix (GMX), a biotechnology company—as a case study to illustrate practical applications of ChatGPT. GMX was previously introduced in Chapter 7 during discussions on AI use cases in project portfolio management. Project Victor will serve as a practical example, illustrating how AI tools like ChatGPT can enhance the management of Scrum artifacts.

By the end of this chapter, you will gain actionable insights into how AI tools can enhance Scrum practices, making them more efficient and adaptive to the demands of modern project environments.

## PROJECT VICTOR CASE STUDY

Project Victor is undertaken by GMX to enhance its flagship software, AcuTrack, designed to support advanced genetic analysis. The goal of the project is to improve the software's functionality, user experience, and scalability to better meet the needs of GMX's diverse customer base, which includes medical testing laboratories, genetic researchers, and clinicians.

Throughout this chapter, we will use Project Victor to demonstrate AI use cases for the Scrum artifacts mentioned earlier. This hypothetical project makes it an ideal backdrop for exploring how Gen AI tools like ChatGPT can be integrated into Scrum practices to drive innovation and efficiency. For a detailed overview of Project Victor and its objectives, please refer to Table 14.1. For a brief description of GMX, you may refer to Chapter 7, Table 7.2.

**Table 14.1** Project Victor case study description

| |
|---|
| GeneMatrix Inc. (GMX)* is a leading biotechnology company specializing in DNA microarrays and software solutions for genetic analysis. The company's flagship software product, "AcuTrack," is an advanced tool designed to process and analyze the vast amounts of data generated from DNA microarrays and sequencers. Initially developed for GMX's own arrays, AcuTrack has proven so successful that customers are now requesting compatibility with products from other array and DNA sequencer makers. Recognizing this demand, GMX's leadership team has decided to enhance AcuTrack's functionality to support a broader range of devices and improve its user interface and data management capabilities. |
| **The Need for AcuTrack Enhancement** |
| The decision to enhance AcuTrack stems from several strategic considerations. First, there is a growing demand from customers for a more versatile and robust software solution that can seamlessly integrate with various DNA sequencers from different manufacturers. This capability would enable GMX to strengthen its position in the market by offering a more comprehensive solution to its clients, particularly medical testing laboratories that rely heavily on diverse sequencing technologies. Second, enhancing AcuTrack aligns with GMX's strategic goals of expanding revenue streams through new product development and increasing customer satisfaction by providing innovative, user-friendly tools that meet evolving needs. |
| **The Sponsor: Chief Technology Officer (CTO)** |
| The project to enhance AcuTrack is sponsored by GMX's chief technology officer (CTO), Dr. Maria Lopez. With a background in bioinformatics and software engineering, Dr. Lopez is deeply familiar with the technical and scientific challenges associated with genetic data analysis. She is responsible for overseeing the development and implementation of new technologies at GMX, ensuring they align with the company's strategic vision. Dr. Lopez recognizes the importance of AcuTrack as a revenue-generating product and as a critical component in advancing GMX's reputation as an innovator in the biotechnology space. Her sponsorship of the AcuTrack enhancement project reflects her commitment to leveraging cutting-edge technology to meet customer needs and drive the company's growth. |

*Continued*

**Table 14.1** *continued*

**Collaboration with the Chief Information Officer (CIO) and IT Team**

To successfully execute the AcuTrack enhancement project, Dr. Lopez collaborates closely with GMX's chief information officer (CIO), John Kim. As CIO, Mr. Kim oversees the company's IT infrastructure and software development efforts, providing the necessary resources and support for technology projects. His role is crucial in coordinating the IT team's efforts to ensure that the enhanced AcuTrack software is developed efficiently and meets the highest quality standards.

Under Mr. Kim's guidance, the IT team is structured as a typical Scrum team, comprising cross-functional members with diverse expertise. The Scrum team includes a product owner, Scrum master, developers, testers, and data scientists, all of whom work collaboratively to deliver high-quality software increments. Together, Dr. Lopez and Mr. Kim align their teams around the shared goal of developing a robust, scalable, and user-friendly version of AcuTrack that caters to the diverse needs of their customer base.

As the initiative, code-named "Project Victor," gets off the ground, Dr. Lopez convenes a series of collaborative meetings with key stakeholders, including the CIO and the Scrum team. These meetings aim to gather input from various perspectives to ensure the new version of AcuTrack meets the needs of its diverse end users, including medical testing laboratories, researchers, and clinicians who rely on genetic data analysis for diagnostics, research, and personalized medicine.

During these sessions, the Scrum team, led by the product owner, facilitates discussions to identify the core functionalities and features required for the enhanced software. The team considers five key factors:

- *End-user needs and usability*: Understanding the specific needs of medical testing laboratories, genetic researchers, and clinicians, and ensuring the software is user-friendly and effective for their purposes.
- *Data integration and management*: Ensuring compatibility with various DNA sequencers and seamless integration with existing data systems to manage and process genetic data effectively.
- *Performance and scalability*: Focusing on high-performance data processing and scalability to accommodate future growth and high-throughput requirements.
- *Security and compliance*: Implementing robust security measures and ensuring the software meets all relevant regulatory standards to protect sensitive genetic information.
- *Feedback and continuous improvement*: Utilizing feedback from current users to continually refine and enhance the software to better meet user needs and respond to market changes.

By consolidating these considerations, the team maintains a clear focus on the most critical aspects of the AcuTrack enhancement, balancing technical, functional, and user experience requirements. The team uses agile methods, specifically the creation of user stories, to articulate the needs and priorities of the end users. After a series of brainstorming sessions, discussions, and prioritization exercises, the team compiles a high-level list of 15 key requirements for the AcuTrack enhancement.

**High-Level Requirements for AcuTrack Enhancement**

1. *Compatibility with multiple sequencers*: The software must support data input from various DNA sequencers, including those from third-party manufacturers, ensuring compatibility across different platforms.
2. *User-friendly interface*: A redesigned, intuitive user interface that simplifies navigation and enhances user experience for novice and expert users.
3. *Advanced data visualization*: Integration of advanced data visualization tools to help users easily interpret complex genetic data, such as heat maps, scatter plots, and bar charts.
4. *Real-time data processing*: The ability to process genetic data in real time, allowing users to receive immediate feedback and insights during experiments.

Continued

**Table 14.1** *continued*

5. *Customizable reporting*: Feature to create customizable reports that can be tailored to specific research or clinical needs, including automated generation of standard report templates.
6. *Cloud integration*: Cloud-based data storage and processing options to handle large datasets and enable remote access for users working in different locations.
7. *Data security and compliance*: Robust security features to protect sensitive genetic information, including encryption and compliance with regulatory standards such as HIPAA and GDPR.
8. *Batch processing capabilities*: Ability to handle batch processing of multiple datasets simultaneously, improving efficiency and throughput for high-volume labs.
9. *Automated quality control checks*: Built-in tools for automated quality control checks to detect and flag any issues with data integrity or sample quality before analysis.
10. *Integration with laboratory information management systems (LIMS)*: Seamless integration with existing LIMS to streamline data flow and minimize manual data entry errors.
11. *Machine learning algorithms for data analysis*: Incorporation of machine learning (ML) algorithms to enhance data analysis, enabling more accurate predictions and identification of genetic patterns.
12. *User access controls*: Advanced user management and access control features, allowing administrators to define user roles and permissions based on their responsibilities.
13. *Scalability for high-throughput data*: The software should be scalable to accommodate the increasing data loads associated with high-throughput sequencing and large-scale genetic studies.
14. *Multilingual support*: Availability of the software in multiple languages to cater to international clients and users with diverse linguistic needs.
15. *Comprehensive help and support system*: An integrated help and support system, including tutorials, FAQs, and user manuals, to assist users in navigating the software and troubleshooting issues.

Project Victor, under the joint leadership of CTO Dr. Maria Lopez and CIO John Kim, is poised to embark on the next phase of development, which involves breaking down the high-level requirements into detailed user stories and creating a prioritized product backlog. As they prepare to kick off the first sprint, the Project Victor team is focused on delivering a robust, scalable, and user-friendly version of AcuTrack that meets the evolving needs of their customers and solidifies GeneMatrix's position as a leader in the biotechnology industry. The journey ahead will test their agility, collaboration, and commitment to innovation as they strive to bring this strategic vision to life.

* Please see Table 7.2 for a profile of GMX.

# 1. PRODUCT BACKLOG: THE HUB OF AGILE DEVELOPMENT

A well-organized product backlog is the cornerstone of effective agile project management. Serving as a dynamic to-do list, it encompasses all potential work required to deliver a product. The product backlog is not static; it evolves continuously as new information, feedback, and priorities emerge throughout the product life cycle. It is the hub through which all work flows, starting from the product vision and strategy and moving through user stories, tasks, predictive analytics, risk mitigation, sprint planning, sprint backlog, development, testing, bug identification, and backlog grooming.

The product backlog is a central source of truth for the Scrum team, aligning everyone around what needs to be done and in what order. Table 14.2 summarizes the typical items that can be found in a product backlog. Each item plays a critical role in moving the project forward and ensuring the team delivers a high-quality product. User stories are often the most visible part of

**Table 14.2** Typical items in a product backlog

| No. | Item | Description |
|---|---|---|
| 1 | Epics | High-level initiatives that represent significant areas of functionality; they are broken down into smaller, manageable user stories that can be delivered incrementally |
| 2 | User stories | High-level features or functionality described from the user's perspective, outlining what the user wants to achieve |
| 3 | Features | Larger, more complex functionalities made up of multiple user stories, often requiring work across several sprints |
| 4 | Technical tasks | Specific, actionable tasks required to implement user stories or features |
| 5 | Enhancements | Improvements to existing features based on feedback or team insight |
| 6 | Bug fixes | Issues identified during testing or from user feedback that need to be addressed in future sprints |
| 7 | Refactoring | Code improvements that optimize performance or readability without changing functionality |
| 8 | Spikes | Research tasks to explore technical solutions or to investigate uncertainties before implementation |
| 9 | Technical debt | Work needed to improve or fix past shortcuts in the code or system |
| 10 | Documentation tasks | Work related to updating manuals, API documentation, or internal project documentation |
| 11 | UX/UI improvements | Design and usability improvements for a better user experience |
| 12 | Operational/infrastructure tasks | Tasks related to deployment, configuration, or scaling system infrastructure |
| 13 | Nonfunctional requirements | Performance, security, and scalability requirements that support the overall system architecture |
| 14 | Compliance or regulatory requirements | Tasks to ensure compliance with industry standards, legal, or regulatory requirements |
| 15 | Customer feedback | Suggestions from customers that drive new features or adjustments in the product |
| 16 | Innovations and experiments | Ideas or prototypes for new features or technologies that may add significant value in the future |

the product backlog. Still, a well-balanced backlog also includes bug fixes, refactoring (improving code), and tasks to address technical debt (deferred code maintenance) or operational issues. For Scrum teams to be successful, they must continuously refine and prioritize the backlog.

## Flow of Work

The flow of work in Scrum begins with the product vision and strategy, guiding the subsequent creation and refinement of the product backlog, and continues through various phases until the product increment is delivered. The following list is a detailed outline of this workflow:

1. *Product vision and strategy*: This serves as the overarching framework that drives the backlog and ensures that every item in the backlog contributes to the long-term product goals and business objectives. It represents the strategic vision for what the product is meant to achieve, aligning the team's efforts with the organization's priorities.

2. *Epics*: Epics are large, unifying user stories that represent substantial components of the product. They capture broad functionality spanning multiple sprints and serve as placeholders for complex requirements. Epics help to organize and prioritize the product backlog by grouping related user stories under broader themes.
3. *User stories*: User stories break down epics into smaller, manageable chunks of work that deliver value to the end user. Each user story is written from the user's perspective and describes a piece of functionality along with its importance. These stories form the core of the product backlog and are refined through discussions with stakeholders and the team.
4. *Tasks*: During sprint planning, user stories are further decomposed into actionable tasks that outline the specific technical work needed for completion. Tasks provide clarity and detail, guiding the development team in understanding and executing the work needed to implement user stories.
5. *Predictive analytics*: Once tasks are outlined, predictive analytics can be used to estimate the likelihood of task completion, evaluate risks, and allocate resources effectively. This step leverages historical data and team performance metrics to forecast the complexity and potential challenges of completing backlog items.
6. *Risk mitigation*: Predictive analytics helps identify potential risks in the workflow, enabling teams to develop risk mitigation strategies. This might involve adjusting priorities, introducing buffer time, or allocating additional resources to reduce the chances of delays and disruptions.
7. *Sprint planning*: The Scrum team selects the highest-priority user stories from the product backlog for the upcoming sprint. During sprint planning, these user stories are further broken down into tasks, discussed, and estimated to ensure the team's commitment is feasible. The goals for the sprint are clearly defined, and the team agrees on what can be delivered within the sprint duration.
8. *Sprint backlog*: The sprint backlog is a focused subset of the product backlog, containing the user stories and associated tasks the team has committed to completing during the sprint. This backlog serves as an actionable plan for the team, outlining the work for the current sprint. Unlike the evolving product backlog, the sprint backlog remains relatively stable during the sprint unless new, urgent priorities arise.
9. *Development*: The team begins work on the sprint backlog items, moving tasks through various stages of development. The focus is on completing user stories by executing tasks efficiently and maintaining the quality of deliverables.
10. *Testing*: After development, completed tasks undergo testing to ensure they meet the defined acceptance criteria and function as intended. Testing validates the quality of the product increment and ensures it aligns with user expectations.
11. *Bug identification*: Any issues or bugs discovered during testing are documented and added to the product backlog as bug fixes or technical debt. These items may be prioritized for future sprints based on their impact on the product's functionality and user experience.
12. *Backlog refinement or grooming*: Backlog refinement, also known as grooming, involves reviewing and updating the product backlog to ensure it remains relevant and aligned with the product vision. This process includes reprioritizing items, refining user stories, and incorporating stakeholder feedback. By maintaining a well-groomed backlog, the team ensures clarity, readiness, and effective prioritization for upcoming sprints.
13. *Product increment*: Product increment represents the sum of all completed work at the end of a sprint, delivering a tangible and potentially shippable product that adds value

to stakeholders. It includes newly developed features as well as all previously completed increments, ensuring continuous progress toward the overall project goal.

The workflow described here may appear sequential in nature, but this is far from reality. For the sake of clarity and illustration, it has been presented in a linear fashion. In practice, however, many of these activities—such as development, testing, and backlog grooming—are highly iterative and overlapping. Additionally, certain activities are performed at multiple stages of the workflow rather than confined to a single step. For instance, predictive analytics and risk mitigation are not limited to the initial planning phase; they may also occur when creating user stories, defining tasks, or even during sprint execution. Similarly, backlog grooming can take place iteratively across various sprints to ensure alignment with evolving priorities. This iterative nature is a hallmark of Scrum, allowing teams to continuously adapt and refine their processes to deliver the highest possible value.

## Characteristics of a Good Product Backlog

A well-maintained product backlog is essential for the success of any agile project. It is not just a simple list of tasks but reflects the strategic direction of the product and aligns with the long-term goals of the organization. A good product backlog is often described as DEEP:

- *Detailed*: Items at the top of the backlog are well-defined and actionable, while lower-priority items remain more abstract to allow flexibility as the project evolves.
- *Estimated*: Each backlog item has an estimated level of effort, helping the team plan effectively.
- *Emergent*: The backlog is a living document that evolves based on new information, feedback, and changing priorities.
- *Prioritized*: Items are ranked in order of priority, ensuring the team focuses on work that delivers maximum value.

Regular backlog grooming ensures the backlog remains relevant and aligned with current priorities and the larger product strategy. Items that no longer provide value are either deferred or removed.

## Guidelines for Developing a Good Product Backlog

To build an effective product backlog, consider the following guidelines:

1. *Align with product vision*: Ensure all backlog items reflect the overarching product vision and business strategy.
2. *Create comprehensive user stories*: Break down epics into smaller, actionable user stories that clearly define the needs of the user and the value they deliver.
3. *Ruthlessly prioritize*: Use prioritization methods like MoSCoW or WSJF to ensure the team works on the most important items. MoSCoW stands for *must* have, *should* have, *could* have, and *won't* have, providing a clear framework for categorizing backlog items based on their urgency and impact (Clegg and Barker, 1994; Schwaber and Sutherland, 2020). WSJF, or *weighted shortest job first*, prioritizes tasks by dividing their business value and urgency by their estimated effort, ensuring the team focuses on delivering the most value in the shortest time (Leffingwell, 2018).
4. *Estimate and involve the team*: Involve the team in estimating the level of effort required for backlog items to foster ownership and ensure realistic planning.

5. *Keep it clear and transparent*: Make sure all items are easy to understand and that the backlog is accessible to the entire team.
6. *Maintain a balanced mix*: The backlog should have a healthy mix of user stories, bug fixes, and technical tasks to keep the product competitive.
7. *Refine regularly*: Use regular backlog refinement sessions to keep the backlog updated and aligned with project progress.
8. *Engage stakeholders*: Regularly incorporate feedback from stakeholders to ensure that the backlog reflects real-world needs and priorities.

## The Role of Product Backlog in Scrum Use Cases

The product backlog itself is not a stand-alone use case; rather, it is a dynamic, living document that supports and integrates with several Scrum activities and use cases. The product backlog is the starting point for many other Scrum processes, such as breaking down epics into user stories, prioritizing the items on the backlog, performing predictive analytics, risk mitigation, sprint planning, sprint reviews, etc. Each of these processes relies on and interacts with the product backlog in some capacity. Therefore, the use case for the product backlog is like an umbrella that encompasses all these additional Scrum functions.

## AI Applications for Product Backlog

Integrating LLMs into product backlog management enhances efficiency, accuracy, and collaboration in agile project management. AI tools streamline the creation, prioritization, and refinement of backlog items while offering predictive insights for smoother project execution.

1. *Generating and refining backlog items*: LLMs can analyze unstructured data, such as user feedback and historical records, to suggest epics, user stories, or features aligned with project goals. ChatGPT can convert raw data into actionable backlog items, refine existing ones for clarity, and eliminate redundancies, ensuring they remain concise and user-centric.
2. *Prioritization of backlog items*: AI tools provide data-driven prioritization by analyzing factors like business value and dependencies. ChatGPT can recommend an optimal order for backlog items, helping product owners focus on the most impactful tasks.
3. *Automating backlog grooming sessions*: AI can streamline grooming sessions by suggesting updates or generating prompts that guide discussions. These tools enhance productivity by automating routine aspects of backlog refinement, ensuring alignment with current project priorities.
4. *Enhancing collaboration and communication*: LLMs promote better collaboration by generating clear user stories and summary reports for stakeholders. This transparency ensures alignment across all team members and reduces misunderstandings.
5. *Predictive analysis for backlog management*: AI tools anticipate risks and bottlenecks by analyzing historical sprint patterns. Predictive analysis flags potential delays or resource-intensive items, allowing teams to address issues proactively.
6. *Continuous improvement through AI insights*: Over time, AI tools like ChatGPT learn from past feedback, providing more refined suggestions for backlog management. This aligns with agile principles of adaptability and continuous improvement.

Of the various applications mentioned here, we have selected *creating epics* as an example for illustrating the AI use case in the following section. Later sections of this chapter will present use cases for user stories and predictive analytics. We will discuss use cases for ceremonies such as sprint planning and sprint reviews in Chapter 15.

## 2. EPICS

In an agile approach, the process of defining and organizing work begins with the creation of epics, which are derived from the product vision, objectives, and requirements. Epics are large, overarching user stories or requirements that encapsulate significant pieces of work within a project, often too broad to be completed in a single iteration or sprint. They are typically aligned with strategic objectives or major deliverables and help organize and prioritize work across a project timeline. To create effective epics, one begins by identifying key outcomes or features that the project aims to achieve, ensuring they align with business goals and stakeholder expectations. Collaborating with stakeholders and the product team is essential to gather insights and clarify the vision behind each epic. Next, the epic should be articulated clearly, focusing on the value it delivers to the end user or the organization.

Epics serve as the foundation for the product backlog, a prioritized list of work items that guide the development process. Once epics are established, they are broken down into smaller, more detailed user stories that describe specific functionalities or outcomes. These user stories are further divided into individual tasks, which represent actionable steps to achieve the goals outlined in the user stories. This hierarchical process mirrors the creation of a work breakdown structure (WBS) in the waterfall environment, as discussed in Chapter 10, where work is similarly decomposed into progressively smaller components. By adopting this approach, agile teams can manage work incrementally and iteratively, maintaining flexibility and focus on delivering value throughout the project life cycle.

### Use Case for Epics

To demonstrate how epics can be generated using Gen AI, we applied ChatGPT to Project Victor at GMX, introduced earlier in the chapter. The experiment aimed to highlight the role of prompt quality in shaping AI-generated results. For this purpose, we intentionally kept the prompt simple, providing ChatGPT with instructions to break down the overarching scope of Project Victor into distinct epics, as shown in Table 14.3. To support the AI's contextual understanding, two key documents from the project input folder were shared: the project description for Project Victor (Table 14.1) and the company profile of GMX (Table 7.2). Based on these inputs, ChatGPT produced a response with five epics, which are outlined in Table 14.3.

A cursory review of the LLM response indicates a lack of comprehensiveness in the generated epics, reflecting the limitations of the simplified prompt, especially considering the scale and complexity of Project Victor. The simplicity of the prompt likely contributed to the limited scope of the LLM results. A more structured and detailed approach, as demonstrated in the use case of creating a WBS (Chapter 10), can yield more exhaustive results. In that instance, the prompt was designed to be comprehensive, incorporating specific guidance and sequential refinement steps. Consequently, the results were significantly more detailed, underscoring the importance of tailoring prompts to the task at hand.

To ensure a more complete and actionable set of epics, teams should adopt a sequential prompting strategy, iteratively refining the output through follow-up prompts and incorporating additional project context. Furthermore, a collaborative review process involving key stakeholders is strongly recommended to identify and fill any gaps in the generated epics. This review enables the team to validate the AI-generated content against project objectives, ensuring alignment and completeness. By combining well-crafted prompts, iterative refinement, and collaborative review, teams can create robust, high-quality epics that provide a solid foundation for subsequent sprints and successful project execution.

**Table 14.3** Use case for epics

| Prompt |
|---|
| Attached are two documents:* one providing a profile of GeneMatrix, Inc., and the other a brief description of Project Victor. As an expert in Scrum, please generate a list of epics, which will be the baseline for the subsequent user stories that reflect the needs of the user groups and align with the goals of Project Victor. We need a table with: Epic ID, Epic Name, and Description. The list should have a maximum of five epics, and one epic could encompass more than one topic, given that it is related. |
| **Response** |
| Based on the details of GeneMatrix, Inc., and Project Victor, here is a table with five key epics for the enhancement of the AcuTrack software. These epics align with the goals and requirements of Project Victor and address the main user needs and strategic objectives. |

| Epic ID | Epic Name | Description |
|---|---|---|
| EP-001 | **Enhanced compatibility** | Expand AcuTrack's capabilities to support data input from multiple DNA sequencers, including third-party devices, ensuring seamless integration with various genetic data platforms. This epic supports GMX's strategic goal of meeting diverse client needs, particularly in medical testing laboratories. |
| EP-002 | **User interface and experience** | Redesign AcuTrack's user interface to improve usability for novice and expert users, incorporating advanced data visualization tools. This will enhance the overall user experience by making navigation more intuitive and facilitating easier interpretation of complex genetic data. |
| EP-003 | **Data management and integration** | Develop robust data management capabilities, including cloud integration, real-time data processing, and batch processing. Additionally, ensure compatibility with laboratory information management systems (LIMS) to streamline data flow and enhance the software's scalability for high-throughput environments. |
| EP-004 | **Security and compliance** | Implement advanced security measures, including encryption, user access controls, and compliance with regulations such as HIPAA and GDPR. This will protect sensitive genetic information, which is crucial for maintaining customer trust and adhering to regulatory standards. |
| EP-005 | **Machine learning and automation** | Integrate ML algorithms for more sophisticated data analysis and enable automated quality control checks. This will help users identify genetic patterns, improve accuracy in data analysis, and increase efficiency by automating quality checks on sample data. |

* Tables 7.2 and 14.1

## 3. USER STORIES

Before diving into user stories, it is important to highlight their origin—epics. While epics set the stage, user stories are the actionable elements that translate project objectives into incremental deliverables, driving development and delivering tangible value to the customer.

In agile frameworks, user stories form the foundation of project work, serving as the essential building blocks for iterative development. A user story is a concise, straightforward description of a feature or functionality from the perspective of the end user. Unlike traditional requirements that focus on technical specifications, user stories emphasize the value a feature provides to the customer. Their primary goal is to articulate the user's needs and the business objectives behind those needs in a format that is both accessible and actionable for the development team.

User stories help break down large, complex projects into manageable pieces, making it easier for teams to plan, prioritize, and execute tasks in a flexible, iterative manner. This process involves decomposing epics into smaller, actionable user stories that adhere to the INVEST criteria—independent, negotiable, valuable, estimatable, small, and testable. Regular backlog refinement sessions and collaboration with team members will further detail and estimate these stories, enabling smoother sprint planning and execution. This systematic approach ensures that teams remain focused on their objectives while staying adaptable to evolving requirements.

Additionally, user stories foster collaboration and communication across the team because they are accessible to both technical and nontechnical stakeholders. This inclusivity encourages broader participation in discussions, leading to well-rounded solutions that better address user needs and align with business goals.

User stories are typically discussed and prioritized during sprint planning meetings, refined in backlog grooming sessions, and serve as the foundation for defining acceptance criteria. Acceptance criteria are specific conditions that must be met for the story to be considered complete, ensuring that the developed feature aligns with the user's needs and expectations. This iterative approach allows agile teams to adapt to changing requirements and continuously deliver incremental value to their customers.

User stories are typically formatted in this way: "As a [type of user], I want [some goal] so that [some reason]." This structure keeps the user's needs at the forefront of the development process, ensuring the product delivers real value. Here are a couple of examples:

- "As a regular user, I want to see my past pizza orders so that I can verify when I last ordered through the app."
- "As an administrator, I want the backend to give me the option to call users using the computer so that I do not have to manually input numbers, saving time."

By using this format, teams ensure that each user story is focused on delivering a specific outcome that benefits the user, enhancing the overall user experience.

## Best Practices for Generating User Stories

Generating effective user stories involves deeply understanding your users' needs, motivations, and pain points. This can be achieved through several techniques:

- *User interviews and surveys*: Engage directly with users to gather qualitative insights into their experiences, challenges, and needs.
- *Observation and usability testing*: Observe users as they interact with your product, which can reveal gaps and opportunities that might not surface through interviews alone.
- *Workshops and brainstorming sessions*: Conduct collaborative sessions with stakeholders, including developers, product owners, and users, to ideate and refine user stories.

Once insights are gathered, they are translated into user stories using the standard format. For instance, after observing that users struggle to find items on an e-commerce site, a possible user story could be: "As an online shopper, I want to filter search results by category so that I can quickly find the product I am looking for."

Additionally, techniques like *user story mapping* can help visualize the relationship between stories and the user's journey, ensuring comprehensive coverage of user needs across all stages of interaction with the product. User story mapping allows teams to see the big picture and identify gaps or redundancies in their backlog.

When generating user stories, it is crucial to involve a diverse group of stakeholders, including users, developers, business analysts, and product owners, to ensure a comprehensive understanding of needs and potential solutions. Regularly reviewing and refining user stories is also essential to keep them aligned with evolving user needs and project goals. Utilizing tools and templates can help maintain consistency and clarity across user stories, making them more effective in guiding the development process.

Furthermore, it is beneficial to conduct regular backlog grooming sessions to review and prioritize user stories. This ensures that the backlog remains organized, relevant, and aligned with the strategic objectives of the project. By following these guidelines, teams can enhance the effectiveness of user stories in driving agile project success.

## Characteristics of a Good User Story

A well-crafted user story should meet the following criteria:

- *User-centric*: Focus on a specific user's need or problem
- *Simple and clear*: Use plain, clear language that is easy for anyone on the team to understand
- *Concise*: Be brief but include sufficient detail to convey the user's requirements clearly
- *Achievable*: Ensure the story is realistic and can be completed within a sprint
- *Testable*: Include acceptance criteria to define what success looks like, ensuring that the feature can be validated against these criteria

Using this checklist, teams can create user stories that are actionable, clear, and aligned with user needs and business goals.

## Relationship of User Stories with the Sprint Backlog

User stories are integral to agile methods and the sprint backlog. They represent the work that the team commits to completing in a sprint. Each user story contributes to the iteration's goals, driving the development of features that add value to the end user. In some cases, user stories can be complex and require multiple sprints to complete. When this happens, the story is often broken down into smaller, more manageable tasks that can be distributed across sprints, facilitating incremental progress.

The sprint backlog consists of user stories selected for development in the upcoming sprint, reflecting the team's commitment based on their capacity and the priority of the stories. This dynamic prioritization process ensures that the most valuable and impactful stories are addressed first, keeping the team focused on delivering continuous value to users.

User stories are a cornerstone of agile methods, providing a user-focused framework for planning and executing work in an iterative, flexible manner. By centering development around user needs and ensuring that stories are actionable, clear, and prioritized, teams can continuously deliver value and adapt to changes effectively. In the following sections, we will explore how Gen AI tools can assist in creating and refining user stories, enhancing their clarity, relevance, and impact.

## Use Case for User Stories

Building on the epics created earlier, the next step involves breaking them down into actionable user stories that align with the project's objectives. To demonstrate this process, we used ChatGPT to generate user stories from the epics, ensuring each was actionable and detailed. The prompt for this use case, presented in Table 14.4, includes specific instructions to estimate story points using the Fibonacci series and to define acceptance criteria for each user story. The AI-generated response, comprising a list of user stories with story point estimates and acceptance criteria, is also presented in Table 14.4.

**Table 14.4** Use case for user stories

**Prompt**

Please generate a set of 21 user stories that reflect the needs of the user groups and align with the goals of Project Victor. The user stories should be structured using the following format: As a [type of user], I want [some goal] so that [some reason].

For each user story:

- Estimate the story points for each user story using the Fibonacci series (1, 2, 3, 5, 8, 13) based on complexity and effort
- Define acceptance criteria that provide a clear understanding of what constitutes successful completion
- Please divide the 21 user stories into three groups of seven each: High-priority (detailed), Medium-priority (moderate detail), Low-priority (brief)
- Present the user stories in tabular form with the following columns: ID No., Epic ID and Name, User Story, Story Points, Acceptance Criteria

Start with high-priority stories, followed by medium-priority, and finally, low-priority stories. Present all of them in the same table.

**Response**

Here's a table with 21 user stories for Project Victor, categorized into high-, medium-, and low-priority groups. Each user story follows the requested format and includes story points and acceptance criteria.

| ID No. | Epic ID and Name | User Story | Story Points | Acceptance Criteria |
|---|---|---|---|---|
| | | **High Priority** | | |
| 1 | EP-001: Enhanced compatibility | As a lab technician, I want AcuTrack to support my existing sequencer model so that I can analyze data seamlessly without compatibility issues. | 8 | • AcuTrack can successfully import data from various sequencer models.<br>• Data integration is smooth, with no data corruption during import.<br>• Compatibility is verified with at least three different third-party sequencers. |
| 2 | EP-001: Enhanced compatibility | As a geneticist, I want AcuTrack to process large data sets from multiple sequencers so that I can analyze high-throughput genetic data efficiently. | 13 | • AcuTrack can handle batch data processing without lag.<br>• Software successfully processes data sets over 1TB.<br>• Performance benchmarks meet lab standards for high-throughput requirements. |

*Continued*

**Table 14.4** *continued*

| ID No. | Epic ID and Name | User Story | Story Points | Acceptance Criteria |
|---|---|---|---|---|
| **High Priority continued** | | | | |
| 3 | EP-002: User interface and experience | As a novice user, I want AcuTrack's interface to be intuitive so that I can easily navigate without extensive training. | 8 | • Interface design meets user experience standards.<br>• Navigation flow is consistent and simple.<br>• New users can complete core tasks within 10 minutes of onboarding. |
| 4 | EP-002: User interface and experience | As a researcher, I want customizable dashboards in AcuTrack so that I can view data in ways that support my unique workflow. | 5 | • Users can create and save at least three dashboard layouts.<br>• Dashboard configurations include key metrics and visualizations relevant to genetic research.<br>• Customizations are persistent across sessions. |
| 5 | EP-003: Data management and integration | As a bioinformatician, I want AcuTrack to integrate with our existing LIMS so that I can avoid redundant data entry and streamline our workflow. | 8 | • LIMS integration is functional and data flows automatically into AcuTrack.<br>• System allows data synchronization without conflicts.<br>• Integration reduces manual entry by at least 80%. |
| 6 | EP-004: Security and compliance | As a compliance officer, I want AcuTrack to have encryption for all sensitive data to secure patient information. | 5 | • Data encryption is enabled for all sensitive information.<br>• Encryption follows HIPAA and GDPR guidelines.<br>• System logs confirm successful encryption for each data transaction. |
| 7 | EP-004: Security and compliance | As a systems administrator, I want AcuTrack to provide customizable user access controls so that I can manage who has access to sensitive data. | 5 | • Admins can assign roles and permissions to individual users.<br>• Permissions limit access to specific data types.<br>• System tracks user access with audit logs. |

*Continued*

**Table 14.4** *continued*

| ID No. | Epic ID and Name | User Story | Story Points | Acceptance Criteria |
|---|---|---|---|---|
| | | **Medium Priority** | | |
| 8 | EP-001: Enhanced compatibility | As a project manager, I want AcuTrack to support both GMX and third-party sequencers to enhance flexibility for our lab partners. | 5 | • Successful integration with at least three third-party sequencers.<br>• Data flows accurately from each sequencer to AcuTrack without conversion errors. |
| 9 | EP-002: User interface and experience | As a clinician, I want AcuTrack to have an advanced data visualization module so that I can interpret complex genetic data easily. | 5 | • Data visualization module includes heatmaps, scatter plots, and bar charts.<br>• Visualizations update in real time.<br>• Clinicians can export visualizations for reports. |
| 10 | EP-003: Data management and integration | As a remote researcher, I want AcuTrack to provide cloud access so that I can work with data from any location. | 8 | • Cloud access is enabled with secure login.<br>• Users can access and modify data from remote locations.<br>• System ensures data integrity between cloud and local storage. |
| 11 | EP-003: Data management and integration | As a technician, I want AcuTrack to offer batch processing capabilities so that I can process multiple samples simultaneously. | 5 | • Batch processing feature can handle at least 50 samples in parallel.<br>• Process completion time meets lab standards.<br>• System generates a status report after each batch. |
| 12 | EP-004: Security and compliance | As an IT auditor, I want AcuTrack to log all data access activities so that I can review who accessed what data and when. | 3 | • Access logs track user actions in real time.<br>• Logs include timestamps and user information.<br>• Logs are tamper-proof and meet compliance standards. |
| 13 | EP-005: ML and automation | As a genetic analyst, I want AcuTrack to include ML tools to help identify genetic patterns in the data. | 8 | • ML algorithms can detect genetic patterns in data sets.<br>• System flags potential patterns and anomalies.<br>• Analysis results meet accuracy benchmarks. |

*Continued*

**Table 14.4** *continued*

| ID No. | Epic ID and Name | User Story | Story Points | Acceptance Criteria |
|---|---|---|---|---|
| | | **Medium Priority continued** | | |
| 14 | EP-005: ML and automation | As a researcher, I want AcuTrack to automate quality control checks so that I can identify data integrity issues before analysis. | 5 | • Automated QC checks run before each analysis.<br>• System flags and reports any data integrity issues.<br>• Users can view and override QC results as needed. |
| | | **Low Priority** | | |
| 15 | EP-001: Enhanced compatibility | As a developer, I want to standardize AcuTrack's API to improve integration with third-party sequencers. | 3 | • API follows industry-standard formats.<br>• Third-party devices can integrate without additional modifications.<br>• API updates do not affect existing integrations. |
| 16 | EP-002: User interface and experience | As a technician, I want to adjust the software's language to match my preferences so that I can use it comfortably. | 3 | • Users can select from at least three language options.<br>• Language settings persist across sessions.<br>• All labels and messages display in the selected language. |
| 17 | EP-003: Data management and integration | As a geneticist, I want AcuTrack to archive old data efficiently so that I can maintain a clean and organized database. | 3 | • Data older than six months is archived automatically.<br>• Archived data is easily retrievable if needed.<br>• Archive settings are customizable. |
| 18 | EP-004: Security and compliance | As a compliance officer, I want AcuTrack to provide multifactor authentication (MFA) so that user accounts are secure. | 2 | • MFA is enabled for all user accounts.<br>• Users can set up at least two types of MFA (e.g., SMS and email).<br>• Access is denied if MFA is not completed. |
| 19 | EP-005: ML and automation | As a researcher, I want AcuTrack to learn from past analyses so that it can improve its pattern detection over time. | 8 | • System uses past analysis data to refine ML models.<br>• Pattern detection accuracy improves over time.<br>• Changes in accuracy are recorded and tracked. |

*Continued*

**Table 14.4** *continued*

| ID No. | Epic ID and Name | User Story | Story Points | Acceptance Criteria |
|---|---|---|---|---|
| | | **Low Priority continued** | | |
| 20 | EP-005: ML and automation | As a geneticist, I want AcuTrack to suggest analysis settings based on past preferences so that I can save setup time. | 5 | • System saves user analysis preferences.<br>• Suggested settings align with past preferences.<br>• Suggestions reduce setup time by at least 20%. |
| 21 | EP-005: ML and automation | As an analyst, I want AcuTrack to auto-generate basic reports so that I can share initial findings quickly. | 3 | • Reports include key metrics and data summaries.<br>• Reports can be generated in under 5 minutes.<br>• Users can export reports in multiple formats (e.g., PDF, CSV). |

This table provides a comprehensive set of user stories categorized by priority, each with estimated story points and clear acceptance criteria for guiding development.

For this demonstration, we instructed ChatGPT to produce 21 user stories and organize them into three priority categories: high, medium, and low. For more comprehensive results, ChatGPT could be tasked with breaking down each epic into user stories one at a time, allowing for greater detail and specificity. Despite the constraints of this example, the results in Tables 14.3 and 14.4 highlight the potential of Gen AI to accelerate the initial stages of product backlog creation, providing teams with a strong foundation to plan and execute their work.

Using an LLM like ChatGPT to create user stories during the early planning stages offers several advantages. It can serve as a valuable brainstorming tool for product owners, helping to quickly generate initial drafts of user stories and stimulate ideas. This rapid drafting capability is particularly useful in accelerating the backlog creation process and providing a structured foundation for further refinement. ChatGPT can also assist in creating high-level release plans or forecasting, offering preliminary insights that can inform broader planning activities. However, it is crucial to emphasize that these outputs should not be treated as finalized user stories. The results often lack the nuanced understanding and context-specific details required for unique projects. Therefore, product owners and teams must invest time in reviewing, grounding, and refining the AI-generated stories to ensure alignment with project objectives and strategic priorities. The ultimate responsibility for the user stories must remain with the human team since overreliance on AI can disengage stakeholders and weaken their sense of ownership.

Moreover, while ChatGPT may suggest initial story point estimates, using these directly without team involvement could undermine the collaborative discussions that are central to agile practices. Story point estimation is a technical exercise and a team-building activity designed to foster shared understanding and encourage meaningful dialogue among developers, testers, and other team members. Relying on AI for such activities risks bypassing these critical interactions, which could harm team cohesion and the overall quality of the user stories. Instead, teams should use ChatGPT-generated outputs as a springboard for discussion, ensuring that the process remains collaborative and rooted in shared expertise.

To maximize the benefits of LLMs like ChatGPT while mitigating potential drawbacks, a structured approach is recommended. Teams can begin by crafting detailed prompts for epics and iteratively refining these into actionable user stories. Collaborative review sessions involving the development team and key stakeholders should be an integral part of this process, ensuring that the outputs are both relevant and high quality. By balancing the speed and efficiency of AI-generated results with the nuanced understanding and expertise of human input, teams can leverage ChatGPT to enhance rather than replace their creative and collaborative processes. This ensures that user stories remain actionable, clear, and well-aligned with the project's goals while preserving the collaborative spirit of agile methodologies.

## 4. PREDICTIVE ANALYTICS

In the realm of Scrum, predictive analytics has emerged as a powerful tool that empowers teams to make informed decisions, forecast outcomes, and proactively manage risks. As projects grow in complexity and the demand for real-time insights increases, the integration of predictive analytics becomes an essential practice to maintain efficiency and adaptability.

### What Is Predictive Analytics?

Predictive analytics refers to the use of data, statistical algorithms, and ML techniques to identify patterns and predict future outcomes. In the context of Scrum, predictive analytics involves analyzing historical project data, team performance metrics, and other relevant information to forecast the likelihood of completing user stories and tasks within a given time frame. This practice allows teams to anticipate potential challenges, allocate resources effectively, and adjust plans proactively to achieve optimal results.

### Why Do We Need Predictive Analytics?

The dynamic nature of Scrum necessitates a level of foresight that predictive analytics provides. The main reasons for incorporating predictive analytics into Scrum include:

- *Enhanced risk management*: By forecasting potential bottlenecks and delays, predictive analytics enable teams to identify and mitigate risks before they affect project timelines.
- *Resource allocation*: It assists in distributing the workload more evenly across the team by analyzing historical performance data and predicting task completion times.
- *Better sprint planning*: Predictive insights help in estimating story points more accurately and determining whether the planned workload fits the sprint's capacity.
- *Continuous improvement*: Teams can use predictive data to assess past sprints, learn from them, and implement process improvements that enhance future performance.
- *Stakeholder communication*: Providing stakeholders with data-backed forecasts fosters trust and transparency, strengthening their confidence in the project's progress.

### When to Develop Predictive Analytics

Predictive analytics should be integrated at various stages of the Scrum process:

1. *During sprint planning*: Analytics can inform the team about the feasibility of completing user stories within the sprint by analyzing past data and team velocity.

2. *After task breakdown*: Once user stories are broken down into tasks, predictive analytics can help identify potential risks and forecast the likelihood of task completion.
3. *Throughout the sprint*: Real-time predictive monitoring allows the team to make adjustments if issues arise, ensuring the sprint stays on track.
4. *Post-sprint reviews and retrospectives*: Teams can review predictive data to evaluate their performance and refine processes for future sprints.

## Best Practices for Implementing Predictive Analytics

Adopting predictive analytics in Scrum requires a thoughtful approach to ensure it adds value to the project. Here are some best practices:

- *Leverage accurate and comprehensive data*: Ensure that the data used for analysis is up-to-date, relevant, and comprehensive. Historical sprint data, team velocity, and task completion times should be included for more accurate predictions.
- *Involve the entire team*: Collaborative input from team members during the data analysis phase ensures that the predictive models consider practical insights and team dynamics.
- *Regularly update predictive models*: As the project evolves, so should your predictive analytics. Continuously refine and update models to reflect changes in team performance, project scope, and resource availability.
- *Integrate predictive insights into planning and review*: Use the insights derived from predictive analytics to inform sprint planning and retrospective discussions, creating a feedback loop that drives continuous improvement.
- *Prioritize transparency*: Make predictive data and insights accessible to all team members to promote a culture of informed decision making and collaborative problem-solving.

## AI Applications for Predictive Analytics

Gen AI and ML models, such as ChatGPT and other LLMs, bring significant advantages to predictive analytics in Scrum:

- *Automated data analysis*: AI tools can quickly sift through historical data and generate insights on team velocity, task completion rates, and sprint outcomes. This automation saves time and reduces human error.
- *Predictive forecasts for sprint planning*: AI can provide data-driven projections on the feasibility of sprint goals, highlighting the likelihood of meeting deadlines and completing tasks based on past performance metrics.
- *Risk identification and mitigation strategies*: LLMs can analyze data and flag potential risks, suggesting mitigation actions such as resource reallocation or schedule adjustments.
- *Workload balancing*: In plan-driven environments, AI optimizes task distribution by analyzing workloads and preventing overloading. In agile settings, while tasks are self-assigned, AI can provide insights into workload trends, helping teams collaboratively manage capacity and maintain balance.
- *Scenario simulation*: Gen AI can run "what-if" scenarios, allowing teams to simulate different sprint plans and assess their potential impact on project timelines and outcomes.
- *Natural language processing for reports*: LLMs can generate easy-to-understand predictive reports, converting complex data into actionable insights and recommendations for the team.

Integrating predictive analytics into the Scrum process can significantly enhance the team's ability to plan, adapt, and deliver projects effectively. By leveraging Gen AI tools, Scrum teams can automate the analysis, make data-driven decisions, and create more accurate forecasts, ultimately leading to a more predictable and successful project life cycle. In the following section, we will illustrate these concepts using the Project Victor case study at GMX, showcasing practical applications and lessons learned.

## AI Use Case for Predictive Analytics

To illustrate the practical application of predictive analytics in Scrum, we again turn to Project Victor as our case study. Table 14.5 presents the prompt used to guide ChatGPT in performing predictive analytics for Project Victor. The task included generating insights such as completion probability, potential bottlenecks, risk analysis with mitigation strategies, workload distribution, estimated task completion times, and the impact of blockers.

Table 14.5 also illustrates the response generated by ChatGPT, which provides significant value to the Scrum team. The response offers a comprehensive breakdown that can assist teams in assessing the feasibility of their sprint goals, preparing for potential delays, and managing workloads effectively. By using data-driven predictions, the Scrum team can anticipate challenges and preemptively take actions that enhance its likelihood of meeting sprint objectives. Additionally, the analysis aids in balancing the workload, ensuring that tasks are distributed in a manner that aligns with team capacity and expertise, while also mitigating risks highlighted by the predictive insights.

**Table 14.5** Use case for predictive analytics

| Prompt |
|---|
| Based on the 21 user stories identified previously for Project Victor, please prepare a predictive analysis report focused on the high-priority user stories only:<br>• *Completion probability*: Assess the likelihood that each task will be completed within the two-week sprint, considering task complexity, team capacity, and past performance metrics.<br>• *Potential bottlenecks*: Identify any tasks that could potentially delay the sprint, highlighting key dependencies, resource constraints, or areas where team expertise may be lacking.<br>• *Risk analysis*: Predict any risks associated with task completion, such as resource availability, technical challenges, or external dependencies. Suggest risk mitigation strategies.<br>• *Workload distribution*: Analyze the workload distribution across the team to ensure tasks are assigned evenly, preventing team members from being overloaded or underutilized.<br>• *Estimated task completion time*: Provide a prediction for the estimated time to complete each task, using historical sprint data or task complexity as inputs.<br>• *Impact of blockers*: Forecast the potential impact of any identified blockers on sprint progress and task completion.<br>The results should help the team prioritize efforts, mitigate risks, and refine the sprint plan. Please provide your analysis in a structured report format that includes key insights, visualizations (if applicable), and recommendations for improving sprint outcomes. |

*Continued*

**Table 14.5** *continued*

| Response |
|---|
| Here is a structured predictive analysis report based on the high-priority user stories for Project Victor's upcoming sprint. This report assesses completion probability, potential bottlenecks, risk analysis, workload distribution, estimated task completion time, and the impact of blockers. |

**Predictive Analysis Report: High-Priority User Stories for Project Victor***

**1. Overview**

This report examines the top seven high-priority user stories for Project Victor, assessing their likelihood of completion within the two-week sprint period. By analyzing task complexity, team capacity, historical sprint data, and anticipated blockers, the team can prioritize tasks effectively, mitigate risks, and improve sprint outcomes.

**2. Completion probability**

Each task's probability of completion within the sprint was calculated using the complexity (story points) and past team performance on similar tasks. For this analysis:

- Tasks with story points of 5 or less are considered low-complexity.
- Tasks with story points between 5 and 8 are considered moderate-complexity.
- Tasks with story points above 8 are considered high-complexity.

| ID No. | User Story | Story Points | Completion Probability |
|---|---|---|---|
| 1 | AcuTrack compatibility with existing sequencer model | 8 | 75% |
| 2 | High-throughput data processing for multiple sequencers | 13 | 50% |
| 3 | Intuitive user interface for novice users | 8 | 80% |
| 4 | Customizable dashboards for unique workflows | 5 | 85% |
| 5 | Integration with existing LIMS to streamline workflow | 8 | 75% |
| 6 | Data encryption for all sensitive information | 5 | 90% |
| 7 | Customizable user access controls for managing sensitive data | 5 | 85% |

**3. Potential bottlenecks**

Potential bottlenecks were identified based on task dependencies, resource requirements, and team expertise.

| User Story | Potential Bottlenecks |
|---|---|
| AcuTrack compatibility with sequencer model | Dependency on external API integration with sequencers. Requires coordination with third-party providers. |
| High-throughput data processing | Significant data volume may strain processing resources. Limited capacity could delay task completion. |
| Integration with existing LIMS | Integration with LIMS may face compatibility issues and require data migration expertise. |
| Data encryption | Requires advanced security knowledge; potential lack of expertise may slow progress. |

*Continued*

**Table 14.5** *continued*

**4. Risk analysis**

Risk predictions for each task focus on resource availability, technical complexity, and dependencies.

| User Story | Predicted Risks | Risk Mitigation Strategies |
|---|---|---|
| Compatibility with existing sequencer model | Dependency on third-party sequencer providers could cause delays if API changes are required. | Engage early with external providers to validate API compatibility. |
| High-throughput data processing | Processing high data volumes may challenge the current infrastructure and lead to performance issues. | Allocate additional processing power if needed. Schedule processing in off-hours. |
| Integration with LIMS | LIMS integration could require significant data transformation and testing. | Plan for dedicated support from data engineering resources. |
| Data encryption | Advanced encryption might demand additional testing and could be time-consuming. | Engage security specialist to expedite implementation and testing. |

**5. Workload distribution**

The workload distribution analysis ensures that tasks are allocated evenly across team members with the right expertise. Each team member's capacity and expertise were considered, aiming for an even balance.

| User Story | Assigned Team Members | Projected Effort (hours) |
|---|---|---|
| Compatibility with existing sequencer model | Developer (API), bioinformatician | 40 |
| High-throughput data processing | Data engineer, bioinformatician | 50 |
| Intuitive user interface for novice users | UX designer, front-end developer | 35 |
| Customizable dashboards | UX designer, back-end developer | 30 |
| Integration with LIMS | Data engineer, integration specialist | 45 |
| Data encryption | Security specialist, developer | 30 |
| User access controls | Developer, security specialist | 25 |

**6. Estimated task completion time**

Based on team capacity and story points, we estimate completion times for each task. These estimates consider team experience with similar tasks in past sprints.

| User Story | Estimated Completion Time |
|---|---|
| Compatibility with existing sequencer model | 7 days |
| High-throughput data processing | 8 days |
| Intuitive user interface for novice users | 6 days |
| Customizable dashboards | 5 days |
| Integration with LIMS | 7 days |
| Data encryption | 5 days |
| User access controls | 4 days |

*Continued*

**Table 14.5** *continued*

**7. Impact of blockers**

Forecasting the impact of potential blockers reveals that two tasks—*compatibility with existing sequencer models* and *high-throughput data processing*—may affect the overall sprint if unresolved. These tasks depend on external resources or technical infrastructure that could hinder progress if delayed.

| User Story | Potential Blocker | Impact on Sprint |
|---|---|---|
| Compatibility with sequencer model | Dependency on third-party API integration | Moderate to high impact; delays will affect overall sprint flow |
| High-throughput data processing | Limited processing resources for handling large data volumes | High impact; may delay analysis capabilities for the sprint |

**8. Key insights and recommendations**

1. *Prioritize third-party integrations early*: To mitigate delays, prioritize tasks involving third-party API integrations early in the sprint to allow sufficient time for adjustments.
2. *Allocate additional processing resources*: To support high-throughput data processing, allocate additional processing resources temporarily or schedule processing during low-demand periods.
3. *Balance workload across team*: Workload distribution should be reviewed to ensure no team member is overloaded. Consider rotating team members with similar expertise if any unexpected delays occur.
4. *Frequent check-ins on bottlenecks*: Set up daily stand-ups or check-ins specifically for tasks facing potential bottlenecks, like third-party dependencies or high-throughput data processing, to address issues as they arise.
5. *Monitor task progress on encryption and security features*: Given the importance of encryption and access controls, ensure tasks involving security are closely monitored. Engage specialists as needed to avoid delays.

**9. Visual summary (task priority and predicted completion times)**

The following bar chart** provides a visual summary of task completion probability and estimated completion times for high-priority user stories.

This structured report provides a clear roadmap for managing high-priority user stories, with a focus on mitigating risks, managing dependencies, and optimizing team capacity for a successful sprint outcome. By addressing potential bottlenecks and distributing workloads effectively, the Project Victor team can enhance its probability of completing high-priority tasks on time and with high quality.

* Accuracy in predicting completion probability, workload distribution, project effort, and estimated task completion time can be significantly enhanced by including reference information in the project input file. Examples of such information include developers' capabilities, team maturity, project effort history, and similar metrics. This use case example demonstrates how LLMs can effectively generate an initial draft, which can then be refined and improved further.

** Omitted due to space limitations

## IN CONCLUSION

This chapter explored use cases for enhancing Scrum artifacts, focusing on the product backlog, user stories, and predictive analytics. By leveraging AI, teams can automate repetitive tasks, foresee potential challenges, and streamline user story development, leading to a more efficient workflow. The value of AI in core Scrum elements lies in breaking down work into manageable chunks, flagging risks, and offering actionable insights to improve decision making. As seen with Project Victor at GeneMatrix, these tools go beyond automation, boosting team efficiency, fostering meaningful discussions, and encouraging continuous improvement.

In Chapter 15, we will shift our attention to AI applications in Scrum ceremonies, including key processes such as sprint planning, sprint reviews, and sprint retrospectives. We will dive more deeply into how Gen AI tools can enhance these ceremonies by fostering transparency, enabling data-driven decision making, and boosting collaboration throughout each phase of the sprint cycle.

# 15

# AI USE CASES IN AGILE SCRUM CEREMONIES

Effective communication, transparency, and continuous improvement are paramount for success in agile project management. The Scrum framework incorporates these principles through a series of structured meetings known as Scrum ceremonies. These ceremonies—such as sprint planning, sprint reviews, and sprint retrospectives—are critical for ensuring team alignment, fostering collaboration, and maintaining momentum throughout the project life cycle. However, managing these ceremonies effectively can be challenging, particularly as project complexity and pace increase. This is where generative artificial intelligence (Gen AI), including tools like ChatGPT, proves invaluable.

This chapter explores how Gen AI can enhance Scrum ceremonies, showcasing its ability to streamline processes and boost team productivity. We will discuss seven use cases, grouped under three main headings: sprint planning, sprint reviews, and retrospectives. Each use case demonstrates practical applications of AI in improving efficiency, fostering collaboration, and delivering better project outcomes.

**Sprint Planning:**

1. *Creating tasks from user stories*: AI can analyze user stories and automatically generate actionable tasks, ensuring clarity and alignment with sprint goals
2. *Task estimation*: AI assists in allocating tasks, estimating effort, and organizing workflows to optimize team capacity for the upcoming sprint
3. *Sprint backlog*: AI helps create and prioritize sprint backlogs, aligning them with the product vision and team objectives

**Sprint Reviews:**

4. *Sprint assessment*: AI evaluates sprint performance by analyzing completed tasks, providing insights into achieved objectives and any deviations
5. *Burndown and burnup charts*: AI generates dynamic visualizations to track sprint progress, highlighting remaining work and trends over time
6. *Velocity charts*: AI calculates team velocity, enabling better forecasting and planning for future sprints

**Sprint Retrospectives:**

7. *Retrospectives*: AI facilitates retrospective sessions by summarizing feedback, identifying patterns, and suggesting actionable improvements for the next sprint

These use cases are illustrated through Project Victor at GeneMatrix (GMX), continuing the real-world application showcased in earlier chapters. For details on Project Victor, refer to Table 14.1, and for more on GMX, see Table 7.2.

This chapter aims to illustrate how teams can leverage AI to optimize their Scrum ceremonies, ultimately leading to better project outcomes and a more adaptive, efficient project management approach.

## SPRINT PLANNING

A sprint is a fixed period during which a development team works to complete a specific set of tasks selected from the product backlog. These tasks are chosen to achieve specific goals and deliver incremental product improvements quickly and efficiently. Sprints are a core concept in agile practices, particularly Scrum, and typically last one to four weeks (Levison, 2019). The duration is often determined by the project's complexity and length; for projects longer than three months, a two-week sprint is often ideal, while one-week sprints are more suitable for smaller projects. This cadence helps maintain transparency, visibility, and a steady pace for the project, ensuring that progress is both measurable and sustainable.

Sprint planning is a crucial ceremony in the Scrum framework that sets the tone for each sprint cycle, ensuring the development team has a clear and actionable roadmap to follow. During sprint planning, the Scrum team reviews prioritized product backlog items, estimates the effort required (if it is not already done in backlog grooming), and selects tasks that align with the sprint goals. The outcome is a detailed sprint backlog that outlines the work the team will focus on during the sprint. This planning promotes a shared understanding among all team members and aligns their efforts toward achieving the sprint goal, fostering accountability and collaboration.

Sprint planning ensures that the team commits to a realistic scope of work, balancing ambition with feasibility. It sets expectations for what can be delivered and helps the team establish a shared vision for the sprint. Effective sprint planning involves clear communication, realistic capacity planning, and an understanding of task dependencies and potential risks. When well-planned, it leads to a focused, productive sprint where progress is transparent, and teams are prepared to adapt to challenges as they arise.

Gen AI tools like ChatGPT can greatly enhance sprint planning by automating repetitive tasks, providing data-driven insights, and facilitating team discussions. These tools help teams estimate work more accurately, break down user stories into actionable tasks, and optimize the sprint backlog. By leveraging AI, Scrum teams can spend less time on manual preparation and more time on strategic discussions, ensuring a higher-quality sprint plan and ultimately, more successful project outcomes. In the following sections we explore each one of the three use cases under sprint planning.

## 1. CREATING TASKS FROM USER STORIES

Creating tasks from user stories is an essential step in sprint planning that helps transform high-level requirements into actionable work items. This process bridges the gap between strategic planning and execution, enabling the team to understand what needs to be accomplished to deliver each user story. Tasks are the specific, manageable pieces of work that need to be completed to fulfill the criteria outlined in a user story, and breaking down these stories into tasks ensures that the development team can approach the work in an organized and efficient manner. The process of creating tasks is crucial for several reasons:

1. *Clarity and focus*: Tasks provide a clear roadmap for what needs to be done, eliminating ambiguity and ensuring that team members understand their responsibilities.
2. *Effort estimation*: Tasks allow for more granular estimation, helping the team allocate time and resources effectively and ensuring that the work planned for the sprint aligns with the team's capacity.
3. *Progress tracking*: By breaking down user stories into tasks, teams can better track progress throughout the sprint. This division helps identify potential bottlenecks and areas where additional support might be needed.
4. *Accountability*: Assigning tasks to specific team members fosters ownership and accountability, ensuring that everyone knows their role in the sprint's success.

## Process for Creating Tasks from User Stories

1. *Review user stories*: Begin by thoroughly reviewing each user story in the product backlog. Ensure the user stories are well-defined, prioritized, and have clear acceptance criteria.
2. *Break down the work*: Collaboratively break down the user story into specific, manageable tasks. This step typically involves the development team working with the product owner and Scrum master to ensure all aspects of the user story are covered.
3. *Define task types*: Identify the nature of each task (e.g., development, testing, bug fix, documentation) to help with workload distribution and progress tracking.
4. *Estimate task effort*: Estimate the effort required for each task, often using story points, ideal hours, or other estimation techniques that the team is comfortable with.
5. *Assign tasks*: Assign tasks to team members or leave them unassigned for selection during the sprint, ensuring an even workload distribution and leveraging the team's strengths.
6. *Add dependencies*: Identify any dependencies between tasks and document them to prevent delays and ensure smooth progress throughout the sprint.

## Best Practices for Creating Tasks

- *Keep tasks small and manageable*: Tasks should be small enough to be completed within one sprint. This approach helps maintain momentum and makes it easier to identify issues early.
- *Involve the entire team*: Task creation should be a collaborative process to leverage the diverse expertise of the team and gain different perspectives.
- *Ensure task alignment*: Verify that tasks align with the acceptance criteria of the user story to maintain consistency and avoid scope drift.
- *Document clearly*: Write task descriptions clearly so that any team member can understand what is required, even if they are not the one who created the task.

## AI Applications for Creating Tasks from User Stories

Gen AI tools can significantly enhance the process of creating tasks from user stories by automating certain steps and providing valuable suggestions. Here are some ways in which AI can be applied:

1. *Automating task creation*: AI can analyze user stories and generate initial task breakdowns based on historical data and best practices, saving the team time and effort.
2. *Providing task descriptions*: AI can draft detailed task descriptions that include the purpose, expected outcome, and steps involved, ensuring clarity and uniformity.
3. *Identifying dependencies*: By analyzing task details, AI can suggest potential dependencies between tasks to facilitate smoother sprint execution.
4. *Suggesting effort estimates*: Using data from previous sprints, AI can suggest effort estimates for each task, helping the team plan more effectively.
5. *Continuous learning*: AI models can learn from previous sprints and refine their suggestions over time, improving the quality and relevance of task breakdowns in future planning sessions.

By integrating AI into the process of creating tasks from user stories, Scrum teams can enhance efficiency, improve accuracy, and focus on higher-value activities like strategic discussions and problem-solving. It should be reiterated that the responses from the large language models (LLMs) should be treated as initial drafts to be discussed and refined by the Scrum team. The following section will demonstrate how Project Victor at GeneMatrix benefited from this AI-driven approach, showcasing a real-world application of these principles.

## AI Use Case for Creating Tasks from User Stories

In Chapter 14, we illustrated how user stories for Project Victor could be developed from the scope of work. Building on that, this section focuses on breaking down those user stories into actionable tasks, a crucial step for efficient sprint planning and execution. For this use case, we selected the top three high-priority user stories identified for Project Victor (Table 14.4), which are likely candidates for development in the first sprint.

Using the structured prompt shown in Table 15.1, we tasked ChatGPT to break down these user stories into detailed tasks. Each task was accompanied by a description and a categorization to identify its nature (e.g., new feature, technical task, or improvement). Table 15.1 also displays the results generated by ChatGPT, illustrating the model's ability to decompose complex user stories into manageable components.

The use of Gen AI to break down user stories into tasks provides several advantages while also presenting certain limitations. On the strengths side, AI significantly enhances efficiency by automating a time-intensive process, enabling the development team to focus on refining and validating tasks instead of starting from scratch. The model also ensures consistency in how tasks are described and categorized, which can streamline sprint planning. However, the AI's outputs may lack contextual depth, as they are not tailored to project-specific or domain-specific nuances. Additionally, the granularity of tasks can vary—some outputs may be too broad or overly detailed—and dependencies between tasks may not be fully captured, requiring manual refinement.

**Table 15.1** Use case for breaking down user stories into tasks

| Prompt |
|---|
| From the seven high-priority user stories in the attached table,* please choose three, refine them if necessary, and provide a detailed task breakdown for each. Limit the number of tasks to five per story. Present the results using a tabular format with the following columns: User Story ID, User Story, Task ID, Task Description, and the Task Type (e.g., a new feature, improvement, technical task, or bug fix). |

*Continued*

**Table 15.1** *continued*

**Response**

| User Story ID | User Story | Task ID | Task Description | Task Type |
|---|---|---|---|---|
| US-01 | As a geneticist, I want the AcuTrack software to integrate data from multiple DNA sequencers so that I can run analyses on diverse sequencing platforms seamlessly. | T-01 | Design the data integration framework for handling multiple DNA sequencers | New feature |
| | | T-02 | Develop connectors for different DNA sequencers | Technical task |
| | | T-03 | Implement a data transformation layer to standardize sequencing data | Improvement |
| | | T-04 | Create automated tests to ensure seamless integration with new sequencers | Technical task |
| | | T-05 | Test integration with existing and new sequencing platforms | Technical task |
| US-02 | As an IT administrator, I want robust security features in AcuTrack, including encryption and access control, so that sensitive genetic data is protected. | T-06 | Design and implement encryption protocols for genetic data storage | New feature |
| | | T-07 | Set up user roles and access control based on security requirements | Improvement |
| | | T-08 | Implement two-factor authentication for user logins | New feature |
| | | T-09 | Test security measures for vulnerability and compliance | Technical task |
| | | T-10 | Perform penetration testing on security features | Technical task |
| US-03 | As a research scientist, I want real-time data processing so that I can receive immediate feedback during experiments and adjust protocols on the fly. | T-11 | Design real-time data processing architecture for AcuTrack | New feature |
| | | T-12 | Implement a data streaming engine for real-time analytics | New feature |
| | | T-13 | Integrate real-time feedback into the user interface | Improvement |
| | | T-14 | Create automated alerts for real-time data anomalies | Technical task |
| | | T-15 | Test real-time processing features under different experimental conditions | Technical task |

* Table 14.4

To address these challenges and maximize the benefits, teams should use AI outputs as a starting point, refining them collaboratively during planning sessions. Structuring prompts hierarchically can help generate high-level tasks initially and then drill down into sub-tasks, maintaining depth and consistency. Utilizing iterative feedback loops and combining AI-generated outputs with the team's technical expertise further enhance the quality of the task list. By blending AI capabilities with human judgment, teams can create well-defined and actionable tasks that effectively drive sprint execution and continuous improvement.

## 2. TASK ESTIMATION

Task estimation is an essential, iterative Scrum process that establishes the foundation for each sprint by defining the work to be done and aligning the team on sprint goals. As part of this cyclical process, the Scrum team reviews prioritized items from the product backlog, estimates the required effort, and selects the most valuable tasks to include in the sprint backlog. The aim is to create a practical, achievable plan that matches the team's capacity and the overarching project objectives.

This continuous cycle involves several key activities: reviewing the product backlog, defining specific sprint goals, estimating tasks, and finalizing the sprint backlog. It also requires effective communication and collaboration among the product owner, Scrum master, and development team to ensure a shared commitment to the sprint's outcomes and to maintain alignment with the project's progression.

### Key Components of Task Estimation

1. *Reviewing the product backlog*: The product owner presents the top-priority items from the product backlog, which have been refined and are ready for consideration. These items usually include user stories, tasks, and bugs that align with the project's goals. The development team collaborates with the product owner to ensure a shared understanding of the requirements and objectives. This review connects to the previous step of breaking down user stories into tasks, as discussed in the prior use case section.
2. *Defining the sprint goal*: The sprint goal is a concise statement that captures the intended outcome of the sprint. It provides focus and direction for the team, ensuring that all work completed during the sprint contributes to achieving this goal. The sprint goal is collaboratively defined by the development team, with input from the product owner to ensure it aligns with the broader project objectives and stakeholder expectations.
3. *Task estimation and effort analysis*: The development team estimates the effort required for each task or user story using techniques like story points, planning poker, or T-shirt sizing (Rubin, 2012). Accurate estimation is essential for creating a realistic sprint backlog and preventing overcommitment. This step also involves discussing potential risks, dependencies, and uncertainties that could impact the sprint.
4. *Creating the sprint backlog*: Based on the prioritized backlog items and estimated effort, the development team selects the tasks they believe they can complete within the sprint duration. These selected items form the sprint backlog, a detailed plan that guides the team's work throughout the sprint. This process connects to the subsequent section, where we delve into the use case of preparing the sprint backlog in more detail.
5. *Definition of done (DoD)*: The *definition of done* is a crucial component that ensures the quality and completeness of work. It is a checklist or set of criteria that each task, user story,

or product increment must meet to be considered complete. The DoD is collaboratively created by the development team, product owner, and Scrum master to align with the project's objectives and quality standards. This ensures consistency in the work delivered and helps maintain a high level of quality across the project. The DoD can apply at different levels, such as tasks, user stories, or product increments, ensuring that the work meets agreed-upon standards at various stages of development.

6. *Commitment to the plan*: At the end of the sprint planning session, the team commits to the sprint plan, including the sprint goal and the sprint backlog. This commitment fosters a sense of ownership, accountability, and motivation to achieve the sprint objectives and ensure that everyone is aligned on what will be accomplished during the sprint.

## Guidelines for Effective Sprint Cycle Planning

- *Time-boxing*: Maintain a fixed time frame for the sprint planning meeting to ensure discussions stay focused and efficient.
- *Capacity planning*: Accurately account for team availability, including factors like holidays and other commitments, to create a feasible sprint plan.
- *Prioritization*: Work with the product owner to prioritize items that deliver the most value and align with sprint goals.
- *Decomposition*: Break complex tasks into manageable pieces for more straightforward tracking and execution.
- *Definition of done*: Ensure clarity about what constitutes task completion to maintain consistency and quality.

## AI Applications in Sprint Cycle Planning

AI tools can greatly enhance the sprint planning process by automating repetitive tasks, generating insights from data, and fostering improved collaboration. The following list explains how Gen AI, such as ChatGPT, can contribute:

1. *Facilitating task estimation and effort analysis*: One of the most time-consuming aspects of sprint planning is estimating the effort required for each task. LLMs such as ChatGPT can streamline this process by analyzing historical project data, including previous sprint velocities, task completion times, and team performance metrics. By leveraging this data, LLMs can provide initial estimates that account for task complexity, effort, and uncertainty, helping teams make informed decisions during planning sessions.
2. *Enhancing task prioritization and selection*: Selecting tasks for the sprint cycle is essential for maximizing value delivery. AI-driven insights can help identify high-priority tasks by analyzing their dependencies, business impact, and customer value. This helps the team maintain alignment with the sprint goals and prioritize work that contributes most to the project's objectives.
3. *Generating and validating sprint goals*: AI can assist teams in drafting sprint goals by analyzing the selected backlog items and extracting common themes or strategic objectives. ChatGPT, for instance, can suggest preliminary sprint goals that the team can refine collaboratively. This ensures that the sprint goal is clear, aligns with the overall project direction, and provides the team with a focused path forward.
4. *Supporting the DoD*: The DoD is a key element in ensuring consistency and quality across sprint tasks and user stories. AI tools can facilitate the creation of a comprehensive DoD

by analyzing project requirements, industry standards, and past project data. By providing AI-generated templates and suggestions, ChatGPT can assist teams in defining clear, practical criteria for completion that are aligned with the project's quality standards and team objectives. The DoD is collaboratively created by the development team, product owner, and Scrum master to align with project objectives and ensure quality deliverables.

5. *Automating documentation and routine tasks*: Generating documents, updating sprint plans, and keeping track of meeting outcomes can be labor-intensive. ChatGPT can automate these activities, creating records of discussions, task lists, and sprint plans, thereby freeing up team members to focus on strategic aspects of planning.
6. *Continuous feedback and improvement*: AI tools such as ChatGPT can aid in continuous improvement by learning from prior sprints and providing refined suggestions for task estimation, prioritization, and workload balancing. Over time, these tools can become more tailored to the specific needs of the team, further streamlining sprint planning and execution.

By integrating AI into planning the sprint cycle, agile teams can gain efficiency, consistency, and enhanced decision-making capabilities. This sets the stage for the next phase of preparation—creating the sprint backlog, where the selected tasks and defined criteria guide the team through the actual development work during the sprint. We must reiterate the importance of the Scrum team treating AI-generated results as initial drafts, using them as a starting point before refining and aligning them with project-specific goals.

## Use Cases for Task Estimation

To illustrate how AI can support sprint planning, Table 15.2 showcases the prompt used to guide ChatGPT in developing a comprehensive sprint plan for the first cycle of Project Victor. This prompt was designed to extract valuable insights from ChatGPT by asking it to generate sprint goals, create a task list, identify risks along with mitigation strategies, estimate workloads and potential blockers, and describe the DoD for key tasks. The detailed response from ChatGPT is also presented in Table 15.2, providing an actionable starting point for creating a sprint backlog. This response ensures that all significant activities are aligned with the sprint objectives and are ready to be transferred into the sprint backlog for team execution.

The AI-generated sprint plan offers valuable benefits while also presenting some challenges that teams must address. By analyzing historical data and task complexity, AI tools like ChatGPT provide initial workload estimates, enabling teams to align their sprint plans with capacity and improve efficiency. These tools also help identify risks, such as resource constraints or task dependencies, early in the process, allowing teams to take proactive measures. Additionally, automating routine planning tasks, such as generating initial estimates and sprint goals, streamlines the process and frees up time for teams to focus on strategic discussions and collaboration.

However, AI-generated outputs are not without limitations. They may lack project-specific context and require refinement to align with the unique needs of each team. While AI can flag common risks, its depth of analysis for complex scenarios is often limited, making human expertise essential for robust risk management. Similarly, AI-generated DoDs often default to general criteria, necessitating careful review to ensure they align with project goals and quality standards.

To maximize the value of AI, teams should treat AI outputs as a foundation for further refinement, using them to spark deeper team discussions during sprint planning sessions. Regular feedback loops, incorporating lessons from past sprints, can help align AI suggestions with team expectations over time. By combining AI-driven insights with human expertise, teams can create comprehensive plans, address risks effectively, and optimize sprint performance.

**Table 15.2** Use case for sprint planning

| Prompt |
|---|
| Please review the prioritized user stories and task breakdowns provided for Project Victor.* Based on this information, create a comprehensive sprint plan for the first sprint, which will be two weeks in duration. The team's estimated capacity for this sprint is 25–30 story points. Your sprint plan should include:<br>• Sprint goals: Clearly outline the objectives for the sprint based on the highest-priority user stories<br>• Task breakdown: Incorporate task-level details for each user story, ensuring they align with the sprint capacity<br>• Risk and mitigation: Identify potential risks related to task completion and propose mitigation strategies<br>• Estimation of workload: Ensure the sprint workload aligns with the estimated capacity of 25–30 story points<br>• Dependencies: Address any task dependencies or potential blockers that may impact the sprint's progress<br><br>The output of this sprint planning process will be used to develop the sprint backlog, ensuring all key activities are captured and aligned with the sprint objectives. |

| Response |
|---|
| **Sprint goals:**<br>1. Integration of DNA sequencer data: Ensure that the AcuTrack software can integrate data from multiple DNA sequencers<br>2. Robust security implementation: Implement enhanced security features, including encryption and access control, to protect sensitive genetic data<br>3. Real-time data processing: Develop the capability for real-time data processing to provide researchers with immediate feedback during experiments<br><br>**Task breakdown:**<br>**User story 1:**<br>*As a geneticist, I want the AcuTrack software to integrate data from multiple DNA sequencers so that I can run analyses on diverse sequencing platforms seamlessly.*<br>• Task 1.1: Design the data integration framework for handling multiple DNA sequencers<br>Type: New feature<br>Story points: 5<br>• Task 1.2: Develop connectors for different DNA sequencers<br>Type: New feature<br>Story points: 8<br>• Task 1.3: Implement a data transformation layer to standardize sequencing data<br>Type: Technical task<br>Story points: 5<br>• Task 1.4: Create automated tests to ensure seamless integration with new sequencers<br>Type: Testing<br>Story points: 3<br>• Task 1.5: Test integration with existing and new sequencing platforms<br>Type: Testing<br>Story points: 3<br>Total story points for user story 1: 24 |

*Continued*

**Table 15.2** *continued*

**User story 2:**

*As an IT administrator, I want robust security features in AcuTrack, including encryption and access control, so that sensitive genetic data is protected.*

- Task 2.1: Implement data encryption for sensitive genetic information

  Type: New feature

  Story points: 5
- Task 2.2: Develop role-based access control for different user groups

  Type: Improvement

  Story points: 5
- Task 2.3: Test encryption and access control mechanisms

  Type: Testing

  Story points: 3

Total story points for user story 2: 13

**User story 3:**

*As a research scientist, I want real-time data processing so that I can receive immediate feedback during experiments and adjust protocols on the fly.*

- Task 3.1: Design a real-time processing engine to handle incoming experimental data

  Type: New feature

  Story points: 5
- Task 3.2: Implement the real-time data processing functionality in AcuTrack

  Type: New feature

  Story points: 8
- Task 3.3: Test real-time data processing accuracy and performance

  Type: Testing

  Story points: 3

Total story points for user story 3: 16

**Risk and mitigation:**

1. Risk: Delay in developing data connectors for multiple DNA sequencers
2. Mitigation: Prioritize development for the most critical sequencing platforms and leave lesser-used platforms for future sprints
3. Risk: Potential performance issues with real-time data processing due to large datasets
4. Mitigation: Conduct early performance benchmarking and use optimized algorithms for real-time data processing
5. Risk: Security vulnerabilities in the encryption and access control implementation
6. Mitigation: Include additional security testing and involve external experts for a security review

**Estimation of workload:**

- User story 1 (integration of DNA sequencers): 24 story points
- User story 2 (security features): 13 story points
- User story 3 (real-time processing): 16 story points
- Total story points: 53 (this exceeds the 25–30 story point capacity, so adjustments will be made in the sprint backlog)

*Continued*

**Table 15.2** *continued*

**Dependencies:**

- Task 1.3 (data transformation layer) depends on task 1.1 (integration framework) being completed
- Task 1.5 (integration testing) depends on the completion of task 1.2 (develop connectors)
- Task 2.3 (security testing) depends on the completion of task 2.1 (encryption) and task 2.2 (access control)
- Task 3.3 (real-time data testing) depends on tasks 3.1 and 3.2 (design and implementation)

**Next steps:**

- Based on this plan, we will need to refine the sprint backlog to fit within the 25–30 story point limit, prioritizing high-impact tasks and possibly moving some tasks to the next sprint
- Develop the sprint backlog from the sprint plan, removing or adjusting tasks that exceed the current capacity

* Table 15.1

# 3. SPRINT BACKLOG

The sprint backlog is a subset of the product backlog items selected for a specific sprint, along with a detailed delivery plan. It includes user stories, tasks, bugs, and any other work that the team has committed to completing within the sprint. Unlike the product backlog, which is broad and evolving, the sprint backlog is more focused and time bound. It is a dynamic entity, allowing for adjustments and re-prioritization while maintaining a clear focus on achieving the sprint goals. The sprint backlog serves as a roadmap for the team during the sprint, outlining what needs to be done and helping to monitor progress.

## Characteristics of a Good Sprint Backlog

A well-crafted sprint backlog is characterized by several key attributes:

- *Well-defined tasks*: Each task or work item in the sprint backlog should be clearly defined with specific goals, detailed descriptions, and acceptance criteria. These items are typically selected from the top portion of the product backlog, where they have already been refined and are ready for execution.
- *Prioritized*: Tasks are ordered by their importance and urgency, ensuring that the team focuses on high-priority items first. This prioritization helps maintain momentum and ensures that the most valuable work is completed within the sprint.
- *Realistic*: The workload should be feasible within the sprint's time frame, considering the team's capacity and velocity. A good sprint backlog balances ambition with realism, ensuring the team can achieve the expected goals without overcommitting.
- *Flexible*: While the sprint backlog is focused, it also allows for adjustments in response to unforeseen challenges or changes in project scope. This flexibility is crucial for accommodating minor shifts in priorities without derailing the sprint.
- *Transparent*: All team members should have access to the sprint backlog and understand what needs to be done and what remains. This transparency promotes accountability, collaboration, and a shared sense of purpose.

AI tools like ChatGPT can enhance these characteristics by aiding in task definition, prioritization, and transparent communication among team members.

## Sprint Backlog vs. Product Backlog: Key Differences

Understanding the distinction between a sprint backlog and a product backlog is essential for effectively managing agile projects:

- *Scope and focus*: The product backlog is a comprehensive list of all potential work for the product, including new features, enhancements, bug fixes, technical debt, and research activities. It reflects the broader vision and strategic goals of the project. In contrast, the sprint backlog is a narrower, more focused subset of the product backlog, containing only the items that the team commits to completing during a specific sprint. It is aligned with the sprint goal and is designed to provide a clear work plan for a short, fixed period.
- *Dynamic nature*: Both the product backlog and sprint backlog are dynamic, but they differ in how they evolve. The product backlog is continually updated and reprioritized based on new insights, stakeholder feedback, and changes in market conditions. The sprint backlog, however, is more stable once the sprint begins. While minor adjustments may be made during the sprint, the team aims to avoid significant changes to maintain focus and achieve the sprint goal.
- *Ownership and management*: The product backlog is managed by the product owner, who is responsible for prioritizing items based on their value and alignment with project goals. On the other hand, the sprint backlog is managed by the Scrum team, which decides how to achieve the sprint goals and which tasks to include. This distinction reflects the shift from a strategic focus (product backlog) to a tactical, execution-focused approach (sprint backlog).

By understanding these differences, teams can better manage their work and ensure that both backlogs serve their intended purposes, supporting a balanced and effective agile workflow. Integrating AI can make the transition from product backlog to sprint backlog smoother by analyzing task dependencies and suggesting optimal selections.

## Estimation of Tasks in Sprint Backlogs

An accurate estimation of tasks in the sprint backlog is critical for effective sprint planning and execution. Several methods can be used to estimate tasks:

- *Story points*: This method assigns points to each backlog item based on complexity, effort, and uncertainty rather than specific time estimates. Story points provide a flexible and abstract measure of effort, often using the Fibonacci sequence (e.g., 1, 2, 3, 5, 8, 13) to categorize tasks by size. This approach allows teams to gauge the relative size of tasks without committing to specific time frames, which can be helpful in maintaining flexibility.
- *Planning poker*: A consensus-based estimation technique where team members independently estimate tasks using numbered cards, then discuss differences to reach an agreement. This method encourages open discussion and helps identify any misunderstandings or knowledge gaps within the team.
- *T-Shirt sizes*: Assigning relative sizes (e.g., XS, S, M, L, XL) to tasks as a preliminary measure of effort, which can later be refined into more precise estimates. This method is particularly useful for teams that are new to agile or are transitioning from traditional estimation methods.
- *Ideal days*: Estimating the number of ideal workdays required to complete a task, assuming no interruptions or distractions. While this can provide a useful baseline, it often needs adjustment to account for real-world conditions and unforeseen events.

By choosing the most appropriate estimation method and involving the entire team in the process, Scrum teams can create a realistic and achievable sprint backlog that supports effective execution and continuous improvement. AI-powered tools like ChatGPT can streamline estimation by leveraging historical data to suggest accurate task effort, enhancing consistency and reducing biases.

## Guidelines to Create Sprint Backlogs

Guidelines for creating an effective sprint backlog involve several key steps:

- *Review the product backlog*: Start with a prioritized product backlog to select items that align with the sprint's goals. Ensure the selected items are ready for development and have well-defined user stories and acceptance criteria.
- *Sprint planning*: Engage the entire Scrum team in sprint planning to discuss and commit to achievable tasks within the sprint. Ensure everyone understands the sprint goals and the tasks needed to achieve them.
- *Set clear sprint goals*: Clearly define what the team aims to achieve by the end of the sprint. This provides focus and direction and helps align the team's efforts with the overall project objectives.
- *Define tasks clearly*: Break down user stories and backlog items into specific tasks, ensuring each task is manageable and clearly defined. This clarity helps team members understand what is expected and facilitates smoother execution.
- *Estimate accurately*: Use appropriate estimation techniques, such as story points or planning poker, to gauge the effort required for each task. Accurate estimates help in creating a realistic sprint backlog and prevent overcommitment.
- *Prioritize tasks*: Rank tasks by their importance and urgency to focus the team's efforts on delivering the most valuable outcomes first.
- *Ensure team agreement*: Confirm that all team members understand and agree with the sprint backlog's scope and commitments. This alignment is crucial for fostering collaboration and ensuring everyone is on the same page.
- *Account for potential deviations*: If there is a known risk of changes or interruptions, include these as potential scenarios in the sprint planning. Make sure stakeholders are aware and that the team is prepared to pivot if necessary.

## AI Applications in Sprint Backlogs

Integrating AI tools into the management of sprint backlogs can significantly enhance the efficiency and effectiveness of agile teams. The sprint backlog is a critical component of Scrum since it defines the work the team commits to completing within a sprint. Managing this backlog efficiently involves several activities, including task estimation, prioritization, monitoring progress, and adapting to changes. AI can streamline these processes, provide valuable insights, and automate routine tasks, allowing teams to focus more on delivering value. The following list examines several ways AI can be applied to improve sprint backlog management:

1. *Automating task estimation and effort analysis*: Estimating tasks accurately is one of the most challenging aspects of sprint planning. LLMs like ChatGPT can assist in this process by analyzing historical project data, including past sprint velocities, task completion times, and team performance metrics. By leveraging this data, LLMs can provide initial task estimates that consider complexity, effort, and uncertainty. For example, ChatGPT can analyze the attributes of similar tasks completed in previous sprints and suggest estimated

story points for new tasks in the sprint backlog. This data-driven approach helps reduce estimation biases, enhances accuracy, and ensures the workload is manageable within the sprint time frame.

2. *Enhancing backlog prioritization*: Prioritizing tasks within the sprint backlog is crucial for ensuring that the team focuses on the most valuable ones first. ChatGPT can help streamline this process by providing recommendations based on various factors, such as task dependencies, business value, customer impact, and potential risks. Using natural language processing capabilities, ChatGPT can analyze the descriptions and details of each task, identify critical dependencies, and suggest an optimal sequence of work. This helps teams avoid bottlenecks, reduce rework, and maintain a steady flow of progress throughout the sprint. Additionally, AI can highlight tasks that may have been overlooked or suggest reprioritizations based on changing project dynamics or external factors.
3. *Facilitating backlog refinement sessions*: Backlog refinement (or grooming) sessions are essential for keeping the sprint backlog organized, relevant, and actionable. AI tools can enhance these sessions by automatically generating prompts or questions to guide the team through the refinement process. For example, ChatGPT can suggest questions such as, "Are there any new dependencies for this task?" or "Have we considered potential blockers for this user story?" Moreover, the language model can assist in refining task descriptions, ensuring all tasks are well-defined with clear acceptance criteria. This automation reduces the time and effort required for backlog refinement, allowing teams to focus on strategic discussions and decision making.
4. *Improving communication and collaboration*: Effective communication and collaboration are critical for managing the sprint backlog and ensuring that all team members are aligned on sprint goals. ChatGPT can serve as a collaborative assistant by providing consistent, AI-driven feedback on backlog items and facilitating discussions among team members. For instance, during sprint planning or daily stand-ups, ChatGPT can generate summaries of backlog items or highlight changes made since the last meeting, keeping everyone current. Additionally, the language model can help document decisions made during backlog discussions and ensure that all team members, including remote or asynchronous participants, have access to the same information. This transparency fosters a collaborative environment and ensures that the team remains focused on shared objectives.
5. *Supporting continuous monitoring and adaptation*: Sprint backlogs are dynamic, and teams often need to adapt their plans in response to unforeseen challenges or changing priorities. AI tools can support continuous monitoring of sprint progress by analyzing real-time data from project management tools and generating insights or alerts about potential issues. For example, if the team falls behind on a critical task or if new risks are identified, an LLM can provide early warnings and suggest possible mitigation strategies. This proactive approach helps teams stay agile and make informed decisions to keep the sprint on track.
6. *Generating and analyzing performance reports*: AI can also enhance the generation and analysis of performance reports related to the sprint backlog. ChatGPT can automatically generate burndown, burnup, and velocity charts based on real-time sprint data, providing teams with valuable insights into their performance. These reports, discussed in more detail later in the chapter, help teams understand their progress, identify areas for improvement, and make data-driven decisions for future sprints. Additionally, ChatGPT can analyze historical sprint data to identify trends or patterns in team performance, such as consistently overestimated tasks or recurring blockers. By providing these insights, AI

helps teams refine their backlog management practices and continuously improve their processes. AI tools offer significant potential for enhancing sprint backlog management by automating routine tasks, providing data-driven insights, and facilitating better communication and collaboration. By integrating AI into their sprint backlog processes, agile teams can improve their estimation accuracy, optimize task prioritization, and maintain a steady focus on delivering value. In the next section, we will illustrate a use case with a practical example from Project Victor, demonstrating how ChatGPT can help sprint backlog management in a real-world scenario.

While integrating AI tools into sprint backlog management offers numerous advantages, it is critical to approach their use thoughtfully and consider several important caveats. Most publicly available LLMs like ChatGPT are trained on publicly accessible data, which limits their ability to provide outputs that are specific and directly applicable to your project. These results should be treated as initial drafts that require thorough review and refinement to align with your project's unique goals and requirements.

One way to mitigate this limitation, particularly when using a public LLM, is by creating a project input folder (PIF), which we introduced in Chapter 4. A well-maintained PIF containing comprehensive project-specific data—such as resource skills, availability, ongoing project reports, and historical performance data—provides critical context for the AI, enabling it to generate more accurate and actionable outputs. For example, detailed data in the PIF allows the AI to better estimate tasks, prioritize backlog items, and recommend adjustments. Without this contextual information, the AI's outputs may be generic and less aligned with the team's actual needs.

Furthermore, custom-built LLMs trained on organizational data offer a more tailored solution compared to publicly available models. However, even custom LLMs require project-specific inputs to provide valuable insights. Integrating an AI system with project libraries, including emails, chats, databases, and historical records, can enhance its ability to deliver more precise recommendations. The iterative process of building a PIF as the project evolves ensures that the AI remains informed about the project's changing dynamics and requirements.

Another critical consideration is the collaborative role of the team. While AI can streamline certain tasks, it is essential to ensure that its use does not disengage the team or diminish collaboration. For example, story point estimation is a key activity in agile processes, fostering discussion and consensus among team members. Relying solely on AI for such activities may undermine this collaborative spirit, impacting team engagement and understanding. Teams should therefore balance AI's efficiency with the need for human interaction and collaboration.

Finally, data security and confidentiality are vital, particularly when using a public LLM. Sensitive project data should be anonymized to protect organizational information. Configuring appropriate privacy settings and enabling restricted access ensures your project data remains confidential. By using a robust PIF in conjunction with privacy measures and a structured review process, organizations can fully leverage the potential of AI tools in sprint backlog management while minimizing risks and maintaining the quality of their project outcomes.

## Use Cases for Sprint Backlog

To illustrate how Gen AI tools can be applied to create a sprint backlog, we examine Project Victor's first sprint cycle. Table 15.3 presents the specific prompt used to instruct ChatGPT to translate the selected tasks for this sprint into a comprehensive sprint backlog. This prompt outlines key details, such as user story IDs and names, task IDs and names, assigned teams, levels of effort, and story points, ensuring the generated response includes essential planning components.

**Table 15.3** Use case for sprint backlog

**Prompt**

As an experienced agile practitioner, please translate the user stories from the attached table* into executable tasks for the upcoming sprint. Generate a sprint backlog table at the task level, including the following columns: User Story ID, User Story, Task Description, Team Assigned, Story Points, Priority, and Comments. Ensure the total story points for the sprint remain between 25 and 30.

**Response**

Based on the goals and constraints provided, here's a refined sprint backlog with tasks selected to stay within the 25–30 story point range. Tasks have been prioritized based on impact and dependencies. Some lower-priority tasks will be deferred to the next sprint.

| User Story ID | User Story | Task Description | Team Assigned | Story Points | Priority | Comments |
|---|---|---|---|---|---|---|
| US-1 | As a geneticist, I want the AcuTrack software to integrate data from multiple DNA sequencers so that I can run analyses on diverse sequencing platforms seamlessly. | 1.1 Design the data integration framework | Data Engineering | 5 | High | Foundation for subsequent integration tasks |
| | | 1.3 Implement a data transformation layer to standardize sequencing data | Backend/ DevOps | 5 | High | Depends on Task 1.1 |
| | | 1.4 Create automated tests to ensure seamless integration with new sequencers | QA/ Automation | 3 | Medium | Enables regression testing pipeline |
| US-2 | As an IT administrator, I want robust security features in AcuTrack, including encryption and access control, so that sensitive genetic data is protected. | 2.1 Implement data encryption for sensitive genetic information | Security/ Backend | 5 | High | Ensures data protection compliance |
| | | 2.2 Develop role-based access control for different user groups | Security/ Backend | 5 | High | Supports fine-grained authorization |
| | | 2.3 Test encryption and access control mechanisms | QA/Security | 3 | Medium | Depends on 2.1 and 2.2; validate implementation |

*Continued*

**Table 15.3** *continued*

| User Story ID | User Story | Task Description | Team Assigned | Story Points | Priority | Comments |
|---|---|---|---|---|---|---|
| US-3 | As a research scientist, I want real-time data processing so that I can receive immediate feedback during experiments and adjust protocols on the fly. | 3.3 Test real-time data processing accuracy and performance | QA/Data Science | 2 | Medium | Early validation of incoming pipeline; implementation follows in next sprint |

**Tasks Moved to Next Sprint**

| Task ID | Description | Reason for Deferment |
|---|---|---|
| 1.2 | Develop connectors for different DNA sequencers | High effort (8 SP); integration framework must come first |
| 1.5 | Test integration with new sequencing platforms | Depends on 1.2 |
| 3.1 | Design a real-time processing engine | Postponed to balance capacity and ensure foundational work first |
| 3.2 | Implement the real-time data processing functionality in AcuTrack | Depends on 3.1 |

**Summary**

- Total Story Points: 28
- Sprint Goals Covered: All three (Integration, Security, Real-Time)
- Risk-Driven: Highest-impact and dependency-unblocking tasks selected
- Balanced Workload across Engineering, QA, and Security teams

* Table 15.2

The response generated by ChatGPT, shown in Table 15.3, demonstrates how AI can effectively support sprint backlog creation by providing structured data and enhancing clarity for team assignments and workload distribution.

ChatGPT significantly enhances the sprint backlog process by swiftly compiling details, ensuring all fields, like user story IDs, task names, and effort levels, are consistently documented. This provides teams a clear view of workload distribution and priorities, streamlining alignment and planning. The AI's adaptability allows for quick updates when project requirements or task details change, while its ability to organize interdependent tasks supports efficient handling of complex sprints. However, limitations remain, such as gaps in understanding specific project contexts or nuanced team dynamics, and challenges in capturing intricate task dependencies.

Teams must avoid overreliance on AI outputs and ensure they critically review results to validate practical applicability. Effective use involves supplementing AI-generated outputs with human insights, refining prompts for specificity, and encouraging cross-functional collaboration.

By maintaining a balance between automation and human oversight, Scrum teams can leverage ChatGPT to enhance sprint backlog creation while preserving control over strategic decisions.

## SPRINT REVIEWS

In the agile framework of Scrum, sprint reviews are a fundamental aspect that supports the iterative development cycle by promoting transparency, collaboration, and continuous improvement. They are essential Scrum ceremonies held at the end of each sprint to inspect the increment and adapt the product backlog based on stakeholder feedback. The primary purpose of the sprint review is to ensure transparency, validate the product increment, and align the product development with stakeholder expectations. It provides an opportunity for the team to showcase their work, celebrate achievements, and gather insights that inform the next steps.

### Understanding Sprint Reviews in Scrum

A sprint review typically includes the following activities:

- *Demonstration of completed work*: The Scrum team presents the work that has been completed during the sprint. This often involves live demonstrations of new features, bug fixes, or enhancements added to the product.
- *Stakeholder feedback*: Stakeholders, including customers, users, and business representatives, provide feedback on the completed work. This feedback is crucial for ensuring the product meets user needs and aligns with business objectives.
- *Discussion of next steps*: Based on the feedback received, the team discusses potential adjustments to the product backlog and priorities for the next sprint. This may involve adding new items, reprioritizing existing ones, or refining the acceptance criteria for upcoming tasks.

### Tools for Conducting Sprint Reviews

Several tools (Overeem, 2021) can facilitate effective sprint reviews by supporting demonstration, feedback collection, and backlog management. Here is a sample of such tools:

- *Jira*: Provides functionalities for showcasing completed work and gathering stakeholder feedback directly within the platform, ensuring seamless integration with the product backlog
- *Miro or MURAL*: Digital whiteboarding tools that enable real-time collaboration and visualization during sprint reviews, helping teams present work and gather feedback effectively
- *Zoom or Microsoft Teams*: Video conferencing tools that allow remote teams to conduct sprint reviews, share screens for live demos, and facilitate interactive discussions with stakeholders
- *Confluence*: A documentation tool that integrates with Jira, allowing teams to document feedback, decisions, and action items from sprint reviews in a centralized location

The following sections of the chapter will focus on the use cases that illustrate how Gen AI can enhance sprint reviews. Specifically, we will discuss three use cases: sprint assessment, burndown/burnup charts, and velocity charts. Each of these use cases serves a distinct purpose in evaluating progress, maintaining alignment, and planning for future sprints, thereby ensuring that the project remains on track and aligned with stakeholder expectations.

## 4. SPRINT ASSESSMENT

A sprint assessment is not defined as a *formal* Scrum ceremony but is part of the overall sprint review process. It serves as a critical step in the Scrum process, conducted at the end of each sprint to evaluate the work completed, gather feedback, and align with stakeholders on future actions. This process goes beyond a simple demonstration of the completed increment; it facilitates a thorough examination of the team's work, its alignment with the product vision, and the identification of potential areas for improvement. By engaging the Scrum team and stakeholders, sprint assessments support continuous improvement and ensure that the product development process remains dynamic and responsive.

### Guidelines for Conducting an Effective Sprint Assessment

To maximize the value derived from sprint assessments, Scrum teams should adhere to several best practices:

1. *Prepare a demonstration*: Ensure that completed work is showcased through live demonstrations. This approach provides stakeholders with tangible insight into progress and fosters more meaningful feedback.
2. *Invite stakeholders*: Engage relevant stakeholders to attend and contribute to the sprint assessment. Their input is vital for validating progress and ensuring the product aligns with user needs and business objectives.
3. *Encourage feedback*: Create a welcoming environment that encourages stakeholders to provide honest and constructive feedback. This input helps identify opportunities for improvement and validates key decisions.
4. *Update the product backlog*: Act on the feedback received by updating the product backlog. This could involve reprioritizing tasks, refining acceptance criteria, or adding new items based on discussions.
5. *Maintain an informal tone*: Keep the session structured but informal, fostering open dialogue and building a collaborative partnership between the Scrum team and stakeholders.

### AI Applications for Sprint Assessments

AI, particularly tools like ChatGPT, can significantly enhance the effectiveness of sprint assessments by automating documentation, summarizing feedback, and improving communication. Here is how AI can be leveraged for this purpose:

1. *Automating feedback summaries*: AI can generate concise summaries of feedback from sprint assessments, capturing critical points and suggested improvements, saving time for the Scrum team.
2. *Facilitating real-time Q&A*: AI can provide quick answers to common questions during assessments, streamlining discussions and ensuring stakeholders' queries are addressed efficiently.
3. *Providing insights on feedback trends*: AI can analyze feedback across multiple sprints to identify recurring themes and guide the team in refining future sprint goals and backlog items.
4. *Generating actionable backlog updates*: AI can suggest updates or additions to the product backlog based on assessment feedback, aiding the product owner in promptly identifying priorities.

5. *Enhancing communication*: AI can tailor communication to different stakeholders, ensuring that relevant information is shared, maintaining alignment, and fostering collaborative decision making.
6. *Simulating* what-if *scenarios*: AI can model the impact of proposed changes based on sprint assessment feedback, providing a clearer picture of how adjustments might influence upcoming sprints.

## Use Case for Sprint Assessments

Assessing sprint performance as part of the sprint review is an essential activity at the conclusion of each sprint. It aims to demonstrate the completed work, gather stakeholder feedback, and align on the next steps to refine the product backlog. For the purposes of this use case, we will illustrate how Gen AI tools like ChatGPT can be leveraged to produce a comprehensive sprint review report that synthesizes all relevant project information.

In this simulation for Project Victor, the team utilizes Jira as their primary tool for managing the product vision, product backlog, sprint planning, and progress tracking. Although Jira effectively organizes key project data, it does not consolidate related information such as email correspondence, meeting minutes, and related project documentation (e.g., project charter, risk documentation, epics, user stories, tasks). However, a thorough sprint review relies on integrating all these elements to achieve the goals of assessing completed work, gathering stakeholder feedback, and outlining next steps.

Given access to these diverse sources of project data, Gen AI tools can generate a more complete and insightful sprint review report. To simulate this process, we have used two data sources: an output report from Jira capturing key project updates from the first sprint of Project Victor and an email from the development team to the Scrum master summarizing key project activities.

Table 15.4 presents the report extracted from Jira, showcasing data related to the work completed, user stories addressed, and tasks performed during the sprint. Table 15.5 shows an illustrative email from the development team detailing project activities, challenges encountered, and solutions applied.

**Table 15.4** Jira output*

| Issue Type | Summary | Description | Story Point Estimate | Priority | Status |
|---|---|---|---|---|---|
| Task | Reference frameworks for AcuTrack | 1.1 Design the data integration frameworks for AcuTrack | 5 | Medium | Done |
| Task | Data transformation layer | 1.3 Implement a data transformation layer to standardize sequencing data | 5 | Medium | Done |
| Task | Automated tests for integration | 1.4 Create automated tests to ensure seamless integration with new sequencers | 3 | Medium | In Progress |

*Continued*

**Table 15.4** *continued*

| Issue Type | Summary | Description | Story Point Estimate | Priority | Status |
|---|---|---|---|---|---|
| Task | Develop connectors for sequencers | 2.1 Implement data encryption for sensitive genetic information | 5 | Medium | Done |
| Task | Design encryption protocols | 2.2 Develop role-based access control for different user groups | 5 | Medium | In Progress |
| Task | Test security measures | 2.3 Test encryption and access control mechanisms | 3 | Medium | Done |
| Task | Test real-time processing features | 3.3 Test real-time data processing features under different experimental conditions | 2 | Medium | In progress |
| Story | Integrate data from DNA sequencers into AcuTrack | As a geneticist, I want the AcuTrack software to integrate data from multiple DNA sequencers so that I can run analyses on diverse sequencing platforms seamlessly. | 11 | High | To do |
| Story | Security features, encryption, and access control | As an IT administrator, I want robust security features in AcuTrack, including encryption and access control, so that sensitive genetic data is protected. | 0 | High | To do |
| Story | Real-time data processing | As a research scientist, I want real-time data processing so that I can receive immediate feedback during experiments and adjust protocols on the fly. | 14 | High | In progress |

*This table was generated from Jira with its "Issues Filtering View" using the filter: "Sprint=1" and "Type=Issue Type Story"

**Table 15.5** Email: sprint progress report

**Date:** Today
**To:** Robin Khan, Scrum Master, Project Victor
**From:** The Development Team, Project Victor
**Subject:** Sprint 1

As sprint 1 for Project Victor concludes, we wish to highlight the challenges, achievements, and areas for potential improvement that may not be fully captured by the Jira report. The following list describes the key reflections and observations based on our experience throughout the sprint:

1. **Task dependencies and communication gaps:** While working to set up user roles and access control, we experienced delays due to unclear communication regarding dependencies with the UX team. This led to a bottleneck that affected task completion timelines. Future coordination sessions or a designated liaison for cross-functional teams could help streamline communication and ensure alignment.
2. **Morale and workload balance:** Several team members felt the sprint workload was unevenly distributed, resulting in some individuals experiencing significant pressure to meet their deadlines. This imbalance affected team morale and overall productivity. We suggest a mid-sprint workload check-in to identify and redistribute work as needed.
3. **Unforeseen technical challenges:** The task related to real-time data processing posed more complexities than anticipated, requiring additional hours for troubleshooting and technical research. This issue not only delayed our progress but also revealed a need for a deeper technical review during sprint planning to better estimate the level of effort required.
4. **Successes and team collaboration:** Despite the previously mentioned challenges, our team demonstrated strong collaboration during daily stand-ups and was proactive in seeking solutions. Notably, the completion of the data transformation layer was a team highlight, showcasing our adaptability and teamwork.
5. **External feedback and revisions:** Toward the end of the sprint, feedback from stakeholders prompted last-minute revisions, leading to rushed adjustments that impacted other scheduled tasks. Incorporating more structured feedback loops earlier in the sprint could prevent these reactive changes and promote better time management.
6. **Learning and continuous improvement:** Team members voiced appreciation for the learning opportunities gained, especially in working with new tools and methodologies introduced in this sprint. However, there was consensus on needing additional training sessions for tools that were less familiar to the team.

These points serve as the basis for our collective learning and growth, and we look forward to discussing these insights in greater depth during the upcoming sprint retrospective.

Using the data from these two tables as input, we tasked ChatGPT to create a detailed sprint review report that simulates what might be generated during an actual sprint review session. Table 15.6 displays the prompt provided to ChatGPT and its response, illustrating how AI can process and synthesize the diverse project information into a coherent report. The generated report serves as an example of how AI can streamline the preparation for sprint reviews by gathering all relevant data, summarizing project activities, and highlighting key findings and feedback. This approach can save teams significant time and effort, allowing them to focus more on analysis and decision making during the review session.

This exploration of how AI can be utilized for sprint review sessions, as illustrated by Project Victor, provides a clear understanding of its potential applications and practical outcomes. To deepen our perspective, the following sections will examine the specific strengths and limitations of this approach and offer tailored recommendations to enhance its value for Scrum teams.

Gen AI tools like ChatGPT are exceptionally adept at aggregating data from various sources, such as Jira reports and email correspondence, to create detailed and cohesive sprint review reports. This capability streamlines the reporting process, ensuring that Scrum teams have a complete picture of their progress, challenges, and outcomes without having to manually compile information. The automation of such tasks significantly reduces the time spent on administrative work, allowing team members to focus on analyzing feedback and planning next steps. Additionally, AI

**Table 15.6** Use case for sprint review

| Prompt |
|---|
| Act as an experienced Scrum master. Attached are files* obtained from Jira with the results of the first sprint and a memorandum sent from the development team to the Scrum master. Please prepare a sprint review document to be used by the team. Include main risks, prediction of potential tasks that could be late, and what the team's main focus should be. |
| **Response** |

**Sprint Review Format: Project Victor—Sprint 1**

**Date:** [Insert Date]

**Facilitator:** Robin Khan, Scrum Master

**Attendees:** Development Team, Product Owner, Stakeholders

**1. Sprint Goals and Achievements**

- Sprint goal: [Define the primary goal or focus of sprint 1]
- Achievements:
    - Completed tasks: Data transformation layer, develop connectors for sequencers, design data integration framework
    - Highlights: Strong team collaboration and completion of critical data transformation tasks

**2. Key Risks Identified**

- Task dependencies:
    - Bottlenecks due to misaligned dependencies with the UX team impacted the progress of security features
- Workload distribution:
    - Imbalanced workload created productivity and morale challenges
- Unforeseen technical challenges:
    - Tasks like real-time data processing exceeded initial complexity estimates
- Stakeholder feedback:
    - Late-stage feedback caused rushed revisions, impacting task schedules

**3. Prediction of Potential Delays**

- Tasks at risk:
    - Security features: Dependencies and additional complexity may cause delays
    - Real-time processing features: Likely to require more troubleshooting and adjustments
    - AcuTrack integration with DNA sequencers: Involves significant coordination and technical challenges
- Dependencies to monitor:
    - Cross-functional team coordination (e.g., UX and development)

*Continued*

**Table 15.6** *continued*

**4. Main Focus for Upcoming Sprint**

- Communication improvements:
  - Set up cross-functional alignment sessions or appoint liaisons to manage dependencies effectively
- Workload balancing:
  - Implement mid-sprint check-ins to monitor workload and redistribute tasks as needed
- Estimation refinement:
  - Conduct technical deep dives during sprint planning to improve effort estimation
- Stakeholder Management:
  - Introduce structured feedback loops earlier in the sprint to mitigate last-minute changes

**5. Task Status Overview**

| Task | Status | Priority | Story Points | Next Actions |
|---|---|---|---|---|
| Reference frameworks for AcuTrack | In progress | Medium | 5 | Continue development |
| Test real-time processing features | To do | Medium | 5 | Address unforeseen technical challenges |
| Security features, encryption | In progress | High | 8 | Align dependencies with UX |
| Integrate data from DNA sequencers into AcuTrack | To do | High | 8 | Plan integration with sequencers |

**6. Retrospective Highlights**

- Strengths:
  - Collaborative teamwork during daily stand-ups
  - Successful completion of key tasks despite challenges
- Improvements needed:
  - Addressing uneven workload distribution and technical training gaps

**7. Next Steps**

1. Conduct a retrospective meeting to delve into key challenges and solutions
2. Plan the next sprint with improved focus on dependencies and workload balancing
3. Ensure team members receive training on unfamiliar tools

* Tables 15.4 and 15.5

can process large volumes of data quickly to uncover recurring themes in stakeholder feedback or highlight patterns in project progress, supporting more informed decision making.

However, the effectiveness of AI-generated reports relies heavily on the quality and completeness of input data. Inconsistent or incomplete data from sources like Jira can lead to subpar outputs, and while AI excels at summarizing and synthesizing information, it may miss nuances or project-specific contexts that a human reviewer would naturally identify. This creates a potential risk of overreliance on automation, which could diminish the critical analysis performed by the Scrum team. Furthermore, AI tools, while efficient, may not offer the depth of interpretative feedback or recommendations that experienced team members can provide.

To address these challenges and optimize the use of AI in sprint reviews, teams should ensure all relevant project data is accurate and comprehensive before inputting it into AI tools. AI-generated reports should serve as a starting point, with Scrum masters and team members reviewing them critically to incorporate project-specific nuances and insights. Training team members on how to effectively use AI tools and their limitations can also enhance the balance between automation and human judgment. Regular validation of AI outputs through cross-referencing with team observations and stakeholder feedback is essential to maintain accuracy and trust. Over time, teams can refine their use of AI tools by iterating on prompts and input strategies, tailoring the outputs to better fit their unique workflows and project needs. This balanced approach leverages AI's strengths while ensuring that the human element remains central to decision making and strategic planning.

## 5. BURNDOWN AND BURNUP CHARTS

Burndown and burnup charts are essential visualization tools in Scrum for tracking progress during a sprint or project. While both charts provide insights into a team's advancement, they highlight different aspects of progress: a burndown chart focuses on the remaining work, whereas a burnup chart shows the work completed in relation to the total scope. Using these tools together offers a comprehensive understanding of team performance, scope adjustments, and pace.

### Understanding Burndown and Burnup Charts

These charts include:

- ***Burndown chart***: Displays the amount of work left over time.
    - *Ideal burndown line*: Represents a consistent pace toward completing all tasks.
    - *Actual burndown line*: Tracks real progress and fluctuates based on team performance.
- ***Burnup chart***: Shows progress over time.
    - *Total work line*: Reflects the total effort needed, which can change with scope alterations.
    - *Work completed line*: Indicates the cumulative effort completed, rising as work progresses.

These visual aids help teams monitor real-time status, anticipate deviations, and adjust plans accordingly. A burndown chart warns if the team is behind schedule, while a burnup chart clarifies progress alongside scope changes.

### Guidelines for Effective Chart Creation

- *Regular updates*: Keep charts current with daily updates for accuracy
- *Clear differentiation*: Ensure visual clarity between the actual and ideal lines in burndown charts and between total work and completed work lines in burnup charts
- *Reflect scope changes*: Burnup charts should account for changes in scope, providing a transparent view of any added or removed tasks
- *Visual indicators*: Highlight milestones or significant scope adjustments for quick comprehension

## Tools for Chart Generation

- *Jira*: Offers built-in velocity chart functionalities, allowing teams to track their sprint-by-sprint performance and make data-driven adjustments
- *Trello*: With power-ups that provide velocity tracking, teams can visualize their output effectively
- *VersionOne*: Provides comprehensive agile reporting tools, including velocity charts, that help teams optimize their workload and performance
- *Microsoft Excel or Google Sheets*: For more customizable needs, these tools can be adapted to create tailored velocity charts

## AI Applications for Burndown and Burnup Charts

Gen AI tools, such as ChatGPT, can enhance the use of these charts:

1. *Automating chart updates*: Reduces manual input by pulling real-time data from project tools
2. *Analyzing data trends*: AI identifies patterns and advises on team performance improvements
3. *Highlighting milestones*: AI emphasizes significant progress or scope changes
4. What-if *scenarios*: Models potential impacts of scope changes for better planning
5. *Enhanced communication*: Tailors chart summaries for different stakeholder needs
6. *Continuous improvement*: Reviews past data for actionable recommendations on team strategy

By combining burndown and burnup charts, teams gain a clearer picture of their progress and can make more informed, agile decisions.

## Use Case for Burndown and Burnup Charts

To illustrate the use case for utilizing AI to enhance burndown and burnup charts, we turn to Project Victor again as an example. Here, we demonstrate how Gen AI can leverage project data to automate and optimize chart generation, enabling teams to better monitor progress and adjust their plans. (For simplicity, we focus only on burndown charts, but the prompt and process presented later would be similar for burnup charts.)

The input for this use case involves data gathered from two key sources: a Jira report summarizing the progress of the first sprint (Table 15.4) and a progress report memo from the development team to the Scrum master (Table 15.5). These inputs provide the foundational data on tasks completed, ongoing work, and any noted blockers or challenges encountered during the sprint. Using these sources, we constructed a comprehensive prompt, outlined in Table 15.7, directing ChatGPT to create a burndown chart. The response generated by ChatGPT, also displayed in Table 15.7, showcases its capability to parse the input data, generate visual progress tools, and provide analysis and insights based on the chart trends. ChatGPT divided the story points to be completed evenly across the 10 days of the sprint (7.5 points per day for a total of 75 points). Based on the results from the Jira report, the LLM showed progress in completing the points on the actual burndown line.

ChatGPT enhances sprint management by automating the creation and analysis of burndown and burnup charts, integrating data directly from project management tools to reduce human error and increase efficiency. Its ability to identify trends, flag potential risks, and model *what-if* scenarios provides valuable foresight, while tailored reporting ensures that both the development team and stakeholders receive relevant insights. However, the effectiveness of these AI-generated

**Table 15.7** Use case for burndown chart

**Prompt**

Please generate a burndown chart for Project Victor based on the information provided in the attached table,* which presents a Jira summary report for the first sprint that has just been completed. The planned velocity for this chart was 75 story points. Generate the graphic, using a dashed gray line as the burndown baseline and a solid line as the actual burndown. Make sure both lines start from the same point in the graphic.

Below the graphic, add a list of tasks done and tasks in progress. Make it compact.

**Response**

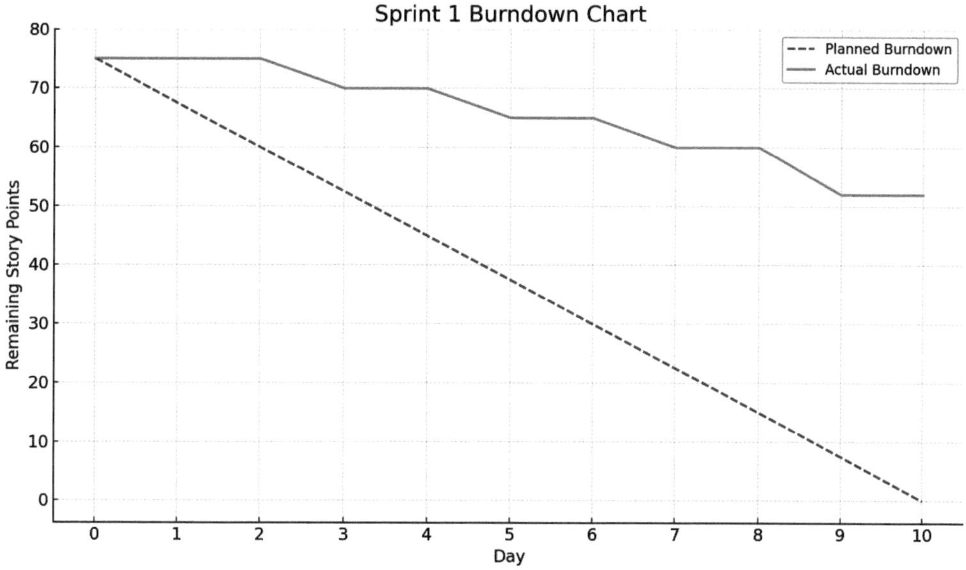


**Tasks done:**

- Real-time data processing (5 story points)
- Data transformation layer (5 story points)
- Develop connectors for sequencers (8 story points)
- Design data integration framework (5 story points)

**Tasks in progress:**

- Reference frameworks for AcuTrack (5 story points)
- Set up user roles and access control (5 story points)
- Real-time data processing story (5 story points)
- Security features (8 story points)

* Table 15.4

charts depends on the quality and completeness of the input data, and their interpretation often requires human expertise to understand unexpected trends or nuances. Major or frequent changes in project scope can also challenge the AI's ability to represent data accurately.

To maximize the benefits of AI in chart generation, teams should validate input data regularly, combine AI-generated insights with human oversight, and standardize data formats for smoother integration. Incorporating these charts into sprint reviews can guide discussions, pinpoint bottlenecks, and inform adjustments for future sprints. As demonstrated with Project Victor, this approach shows how Gen AI can streamline sprint planning while maintaining a balance between automation and human judgment.

## 6. VELOCITY CHARTS

Velocity charts are crucial tools in Scrum that help visualize a team's capacity and the work completed during each sprint. This type of chart tracks how many story points, hours, or tasks a team completes over multiple sprints, providing a clear historical record of team performance. By analyzing this data, teams can forecast their capacity for future sprints and set realistic goals, enhancing planning accuracy and decision making.

### Understanding Velocity Charts

Like the burndown and burnup charts discussed earlier, velocity charts are essential for tracking progress but with a focus on completed work over time. The main components of a velocity chart include:

- *Completed work bar*: Represents the total number of story points or other units completed in each sprint, visually demonstrating the team's output
- *Trend line*: Shows the pattern or trajectory of the team's work over time, allowing teams to identify whether their velocity is stable, increasing, or decreasing

Velocity charts provide insights into trends that help teams optimize future sprints, set achievable targets, and improve their workflow. Initially, velocity might be more volatile, especially during the early sprints of a project as teams find their rhythm. By the third or fourth sprint, velocity tends to stabilize, offering a clearer capacity forecast for future iterations.

### Guidelines for Building an Effective Chart

A well-constructed velocity chart can be an effective visual display—sometimes referred to as an *information radiator*—of project information, providing the team with quick and actionable insights into their performance. Here are some guidelines for creating an effective team velocity chart:

1. *Visual accessibility*: Ensure the velocity chart is prominently displayed for all team members. Whether on a physical board in the workspace or an online project management tool, the chart should be easy to access and view, promoting transparency and alignment within the team.
2. *Simplicity and clarity*: Keep the chart straightforward and intuitive. Use consistent scales and labels that clearly indicate story points or completed work units. Avoid excessive detail that could distract from the core insights, ensuring the chart provides quick, digestible information at a glance.
3. *Regular updates*: Update the velocity chart at the end of each sprint to maintain an accurate representation of team performance. Timely updates enable teams to make real-time decisions and plan their future sprints more effectively.
4. *Include contextual annotations*: Provide brief notes for any significant changes or anomalies, such as unexpected scope increases, team member absences, or major challenges encountered during the sprint. This context helps the team understand fluctuations in velocity and make more informed planning adjustments.

5. *Review and reflect*: Use the velocity chart during sprint retrospectives to evaluate past performances and identify areas for improvement. Encourage the team to review velocity trends and provide feedback on enhancing the chart's usefulness or accuracy for future sprints.
6. *Highlight trend lines*: Incorporate a trend line to show the general trajectory of the team's velocity over time. This helps identify patterns, such as gradual increases in capacity as the team gains efficiency or dips that signal potential issues needing attention.

By following these guidelines, teams can build an effective velocity chart that functions as an information radiator, keeping everyone informed and promoting data-driven decision making.

## Tools for Generating Velocity Charts

The tools for generating velocity charts are often the same as those used for burndown and burnup charts mentioned in an earlier section, since they are integral to most agile project management software. They include Jira, Trello, VersionOne, etc.

## AI Applications for Velocity Charts

As with burndown and burnup charts, Gen AI tools can enhance the use and interpretation of velocity charts in several ways:

1. *Automating chart updates*: AI can automate data collection and chart updates at the end of each sprint, ensuring accuracy and reducing manual workload.
2. *Predictive insights*: ChatGPT can analyze historical velocity data to forecast future team performance, accounting for factors such as team changes and upcoming sprint complexities.
3. *Identifying anomalies*: AI can detect deviations in performance and provide explanations, noting potential causes like unexpected technical challenges or team member absences.
4. *Facilitating communication*: AI can create targeted summaries of velocity chart data for different audiences, simplifying updates for executives and in-depth analyses for team members.
5. *Simulating planning scenarios*: AI can model hypothetical scenarios based on velocity data, aiding teams in exploring how changes to their sprint plan or resources might impact their velocity and overall sprint goals.
6. *Providing continuous improvement suggestions*: AI can analyze past sprint data and recommend strategies to optimize future sprints, such as better workload distribution or more accurate task estimation.

## Use Case for Velocity Charts

Velocity charts provide a powerful means of understanding a team's capacity over time, helping guide realistic sprint planning and strategic decision making. To illustrate this use case with Project Victor, we utilized ChatGPT to create and analyze a velocity chart based on input data. For this example, we gathered sprint performance data from the first sprint, which is shown in a Jira progress report (Table 15.4). This report, combined with a sprint update memo from the Scrum master (Table 15.5), provided comprehensive context on the team's sprint outcomes and key activities. The prompt shown in Table 15.8 tasked the model with generating a velocity chart that visualizes the amount of work completed during the sprint, indicating story points completed and capturing the trends. Table 15.8 also shows the resulting velocity chart and analysis generated by the LLM. This output offers valuable insights into team capacity, past performance trends, and potential areas for future improvements.

**Table 15.8** Use case for velocity chart

| Prompt |
|---|
| Attached are tables* summarizing the results from Project Victor's first sprint and key observations of the development team.<br><br>Please build a velocity chart that predicts the velocity ranges for the next 4 sprints (sprints 2, 3, 4, and 5), considering that there is a learning curve happening in the team, that trust is setting, and that the team is working better. We have still more than 200 story points to go in our backlog. A few insights to be included in the graphic:<br>- Sprint 2 seems like it will not have a lot of complexity<br>- Sprints 3 and 4 need a lot of dependencies<br>- Sprint 5 would have the same level of complexity as sprint 2<br><br>Generate a line chart showing the historical velocity and the predicted ranges. Each sprint should have 3 values: a mean of the predicted velocity and minimum and maximum values for the range. |
| **Response** |
| 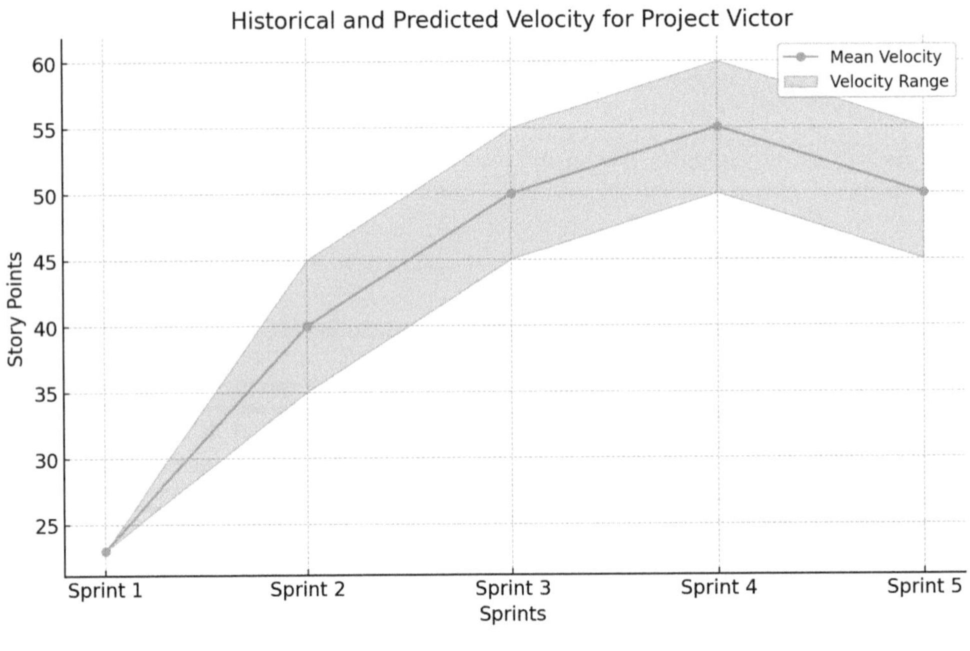 |
| Here is the chart showing the historical and predicted velocity for the next 4 sprints (sprints 2 to 5).<br>• Sprint 1 reflects the actual velocity achieved<br>• The shaded region represents the predicted velocity range (minimum to maximum) for the upcoming sprints, while the line marks the mean predicted velocity<br>• Sprint 2 anticipates a gradual improvement, with lower complexity<br>• Sprints 3 and 4 account for higher dependencies and complexity<br>• Sprint 5 mirrors sprint 2's simpler nature.<br><br>This visualization can help align team expectations and track progress as the team evolves. |



* Tables 15.4 and 15.5

AI tools simplify the creation of velocity charts by automating data visualization and identifying trends, helping teams adjust sprint plans based on performance trajectories. These tools save time and provide detailed explanations for deviations, such as outliers caused by team absences or unforeseen complexities. However, while AI can process data efficiently, it may lack the contextual awareness to interpret nuanced changes, such as interpersonal dynamics or qualitative factors. Its recommendations might be technically sound, but impractical without human validation.

To enhance the effectiveness of AI in velocity chart management, teams should supplement AI outputs with expert insights, ensure comprehensive data inputs, and validate results regularly. Integrating retrospective feedback into AI prompts can also help balance quantitative analysis with qualitative insights. Additionally, training AI with project-specific data can improve its adaptability and relevance to unique team environments.

## SPRINT RETROSPECTIVES

Sprint retrospectives are a key Scrum ceremony focused on reflecting on the sprint that just ended and identifying opportunities for improvement. Unlike sprint reviews, which focus on product and stakeholder feedback, sprint retrospectives are inward-looking meetings aimed at enhancing the Scrum team's processes, collaboration, and overall effectiveness. By fostering a culture of continuous improvement, retrospectives help agile teams refine their workflows, address challenges, and build a stronger, more cohesive team environment.

### Differences Between Sprint Reviews and Sprint Retrospectives

While both sprint reviews and sprint retrospectives occur at the end of a sprint, they serve different purposes and focus on different aspects:

- ***Focus:***
  - *Sprint review*: Focuses on the product and the increment delivered. The goal is to showcase completed work and gather feedback from stakeholders to align on future product direction.
  - *Sprint retrospective*: Focuses on the process and the team. The goal is to reflect on the team's workflow, collaboration, and overall effectiveness to identify improvements.
- ***Participants:***
  - *Sprint review*: Involves the Scrum team and external stakeholders (customers, users, business representatives) who provide feedback on the product.
  - *Sprint retrospective*: Involves only the Scrum team (product owner, Scrum master, and development team). It is a closed meeting to foster open and honest discussions about internal processes and team dynamics.
- ***Outcome:***
  - *Sprint review*: Results in an updated product backlog reflecting new insights and priorities based on stakeholder feedback.
  - *Sprint retrospective*: Results in a set of actionable improvement items or tasks aimed at enhancing team performance and processes in the next sprint.

# 7. RETROSPECTIVES

The following sections take a deeper dive into sprint retrospectives leading to the AI use case illustration using Project Victor.

## Understanding Sprint Retrospectives

A sprint retrospective typically involves the following activities:

- *Reflection on the sprint*: The Scrum team discusses what went well during the sprint, what didn't go well, and what could be improved. This reflection helps team members understand their strengths and identify areas where they can make adjustments.
- *Identifying improvement actions*: The team collaboratively identifies specific actions they can take to improve processes, collaboration, or practices in the next sprint. These actions are often captured as improvement stories or tasks to be added to the next sprint backlog.
- *Building team cohesion*: Retrospectives provide a safe space for team members to share their thoughts and feelings, helping to build trust, improve communication, and enhance team dynamics.

The primary purpose of a sprint retrospective is to facilitate continuous improvement by fostering an open dialogue among team members. This meeting focuses on learning from the sprint's experiences and making actionable changes to enhance future performance.

## Guidelines for Conducting an Effective Sprint Retrospective

To maximize the effectiveness of sprint retrospectives, Scrum teams should follow these best practices (Derby and Larsen, 2006):

1. *Create a safe environment*: Encourage open and honest communication by fostering a safe space where team members feel comfortable sharing their thoughts without fear of judgment or repercussions.
2. *Structure the discussion*: Use a structured format to guide the discussion, such as "Start, Stop, Continue," "4Ls (Liked, Learned, Lacked, Longed For)," or "What Went Well, What Didn't, What Can We Improve?" This structure helps ensure all aspects of the sprint are covered and all voices are heard.
3. *Focus on actionable outcomes*: Ensure that the retrospective results in concrete, actionable items that the team can implement in the next sprint. This focus on tangible outcomes drives continuous improvement and helps the team make incremental changes to their processes.
4. *Review previous actions*: Start the retrospective by reviewing the actions agreed upon in the last retrospective. This helps the team assess whether they successfully implemented those actions and what impact they had, reinforcing the importance of continuous improvement.
5. *Encourage participation*: Use facilitation techniques to encourage active participation from all team members. This could include round-robin discussions, silent brainstorming, or using digital tools for anonymous input. Ensuring everyone's voice is heard enriches the discussion and fosters team cohesion.

## Tools for Conducting Sprint Retrospectives

Several tools can facilitate effective sprint retrospectives by supporting structured discussions, capturing feedback, and tracking improvement actions:

- *Miro or MURAL*: Digital whiteboarding tools that enable interactive and collaborative retrospectives, allowing teams to visualize feedback and ideas in real time.
- *FunRetro*: A dedicated retrospective tool that provides various templates and formats for conducting retrospectives, enabling teams to collect feedback and vote on improvement ideas.
- *Retrium*: A comprehensive tool designed specifically for retrospectives, offering built-in facilitation techniques and formats to foster team engagement and capture actionable outcomes.
- *Microsoft Teams or Zoom*: Video conferencing tools that allow remote teams to conduct retrospectives, share screens for collaborative brainstorming, and facilitate open discussions.

## AI Applications for Sprint Retrospectives

AI tools like ChatGPT can significantly enhance the effectiveness of sprint retrospectives by automating data collection, providing insights, and facilitating more focused discussions. The following list examines how AI can be applied to optimize sprint retrospectives:

1. *Automating retrospective summaries*: ChatGPT can automatically generate summaries of the retrospective discussions, capturing key points, identified issues, and agreed-upon action items. This automation helps ensure that all feedback is documented accurately and saves time for the Scrum team.
2. *Providing data-driven insights*: AI can analyze data from multiple retrospectives to identify recurring themes, patterns, or areas for improvement. ChatGPT can provide insights into these patterns, helping the team focus on the most critical areas for improvement based on historical data.
3. *Enhancing actionable outcomes*: AI can suggest potential improvement actions based on the feedback received during the retrospective. For example, ChatGPT can recommend specific practices or tools to address identified issues, helping the team develop more targeted improvement plans.
4. *Simulating impact of improvement actions*: ChatGPT can simulate the potential impact of proposed improvement actions, helping the team understand the potential benefits or trade-offs of different approaches. This capability supports more informed decision making and encourages experimentation.
5. *Tracking and reviewing improvement progress*: AI tools can help track the progress of actions agreed upon during previous retrospectives and provide reminders or prompts to ensure these actions are reviewed and assessed in subsequent retrospectives.

## Use Case for Sprint Retrospectives

For the sprint retrospective use case involving Project Victor, Gen AI can be utilized to facilitate reflective sessions and enhance the insights derived from sprint reviews. This section demonstrates how ChatGPT is leveraged to analyze and summarize data, providing a comprehensive retrospective report that drives continuous improvement.

To simulate a practical scenario, two input sources were used: Table 15.4, which contains a Jira report summarizing the first sprint, and Table 15.5, a memo from the development team to the

Scrum master highlighting specific challenges and achievements encountered during the sprint. Using these inputs, a prompt was crafted as shown in Table 15.9 to guide ChatGPT in generating a sprint retrospective report. The table also displays the LLM's response, offering a detailed overview of the sprint's outcomes, areas for improvement, and actionable recommendations for the next sprint cycle.

ChatGPT excels at analyzing diverse data points, generating consistent retrospective summaries, and providing actionable insights for improving sprint performance. Its efficiency saves time compared to manual report preparation while ensuring a standardized review process. However,

**Table 15.9** Use case for sprint retrospective

**Prompt**

Attached are tables* summarizing the results from the first sprint of Project Victor and key observations from the development team.

Prepare a sprint retrospective where all the elements of the sprint will be reviewed. Follow these instructions:

- Generate an agenda for the retrospective at the beginning
- List attendees
- After that, set up the typical structure of a retrospective
- The first retrospective should not take more than 30 minutes and will be on-site
- Make the format compact and easy to fill out, since you will use the output of this prompt as a template for the retrospectives of the project
- Use tables and try to fit everything on one page

**Response**

**Sprint Retrospective Template**

**Project Name:** Project Victor

**Sprint:** Sprint 1

**Date & Time:** [insert date & time]

**Location:** On-site - [insert location]

**Duration:** 30 minutes

**Agenda**

1. **Introduction and objectives** (5 min):
   - Overview of sprint goals
   - Expected outcomes of the retrospective
2. **Sprint review** (10 min):
   - Review of achievements and challenges based on Jira outputs and team memo
3. **Discussion** (10 min):
   - What went well?
   - What could be improved?
   - Actionable insights for the next sprint
4. **Closing** (5 min):
   - Summary of key takeaways
   - Assign owners for improvement actions

*Continued*

**Table 15.9** *continued*

**Participants**

| Role | Name |
|---|---|
| Scrum master | Robin Khan |
| Product owner | [insert name] |
| Development team | [insert names] |

**Structure**

| Section | Input |
|---|---|
| **What Went Well?** | [E.g., "Strong team collaboration on the data transformation layer."] |
| **What Could Be Improved?** | [E.g., "Task dependencies with UX team caused delays."] |
| **Actions to Take** | [E.g., "Set up bi-weekly coordination meetings with UX."] |

**Key Insights from Sprint 1**

- Successes: Completion of data transformation layer, strong daily stand-up collaboration
- Challenges:
  - Communication gaps with UX caused bottlenecks
  - Uneven workload balance
  - Unanticipated technical complexity in real-time data processing
- Jira highlights:
  - Completed tasks: Data transformation layer, sequencer connectors
  - Pending tasks: Testing real-time and security measures

**Action Plan**

| Action Item | Owner | Deadline | Status |
|---|---|---|---|
| Schedule cross-functional sync | Scrum master | [Date] | Pending |
| Add mid-sprint workload check-in | Scrum master | [Date] | Pending |
| Conduct a deeper technical review | Dev team lead | [Date] | Pending |

* Tables 15.4 and 15.5

the AI's output heavily relies on the quality of input data and may miss qualitative or emotional team dynamics, often critical for morale and cohesion. Customization of the AI's outputs to meet specific team needs might also require additional effort.

To maximize the benefits, teams should provide comprehensive data inputs, including qualitative feedback, and combine AI outputs with human facilitation to address contextual and emotional nuances. Iterating prompts based on feedback can further refine AI-generated summaries. Using these outputs as a foundation for focused presentations can help highlight actionable takeaways and boost team engagement, driving continuous improvement in sprint retrospective processes.

# IN CONCLUSION

This chapter has explored the critical role of AI in Scrum reporting, highlighting how advanced technologies like ChatGPT and other Gen AI tools can streamline and enhance the reporting process in agile environments. By automating the creation of key Scrum ceremonies such as sprint planning, sprint reviews, and sprint retrospectives, AI enables teams to focus more on strategic decision making and less on manual, time-consuming tasks. Furthermore, AI-driven insights and data visualizations improve transparency and communication, facilitating better alignment among team members and stakeholders. As AI continues to evolve, its integration into Scrum reporting and agile methodologies offers a powerful way to optimize project management processes, making them more efficient, adaptive, and data-driven.

As we conclude this chapter and, indeed, this book, it becomes clear that AI is not just a tool but a strategic enabler for project management in both agile and traditional environments. In Chapter 16, the final chapter, we will provide our closing reflections on the overarching theme of AI in project management. We will also discuss the future of AI in this space, considering how emerging technologies might further shape the landscape of project management and drive innovation and continuous improvement.

# 16

# FINAL THOUGHTS—EMBRACING THE FUTURE OF PROJECT MANAGEMENT WITH AI

Imagine stepping into an era where project management is no longer just about timelines, budgets, and deliverables but a seamless blend of strategic oversight and enhanced productivity, driven by the most advanced tools at our disposal—artificial intelligence (AI). This is not science fiction; it is our new reality. AI in project management is not here to replace us but to empower us. It is the tool that, like a compass, guides us through the complexities of modern projects. This chapter is our concluding note, summarizing the journey from understanding to implementing AI. It is a reflection on how AI can shape project management—and a roadmap for how to harness its full potential.

## KEY THEMES RECAP: REFLECTIONS ON OUR JOURNEY WITH AI IN PROJECT MANAGEMENT

Our intention in writing this book was to give you, the reader, a practical guide for leveraging generative AI (Gen AI) as a tool to make your day-to-day job easier and more productive as a project management professional. This book was never about what AI can do for you—it is about how you can leverage AI. We hope we fulfilled that promise.

Throughout this book, we have explored the myriad ways AI is transforming project management. From definitions and technical insights to practical applications and ethical considerations, we have laid out a comprehensive path for project professionals to engage with AI effectively.

As we bring our exploration to a close, it is essential to reflect on the critical themes and insights that have shaped our understanding of AI's role in project management. This journey has unveiled the power of Gen AI and shown how its integration into project practices can revolutionize efficiency, strategy, and leadership.

### The Power of Gen AI Engagement (GAE)

One of the foundational concepts we introduced in Chapter 4 was Gen AI engagement (GAE). We discussed how project managers should interact with Gen AI as if it were a collaborative team member. This iterative, back-and-forth communication mimics discussions with human colleagues, allowing project leaders to refine outputs, seek new perspectives, and leverage AI's unique capabilities in innovative ways. The practice of GAE enables project professionals to harness AI for more than just simple outputs—it becomes a conversation that shapes project strategy and execution.

## PRIME Methodology: A Blueprint for Effective AI Integration

Throughout the book, we presented our PRIME methodology—prepare, relay, inspect, modify, execute—as a comprehensive approach to embedding AI into project management workflows. This five-step process empowers project leaders to integrate AI with confidence and clarity. Whether developing a project timeline, analyzing cost performance, or drafting detailed stakeholder communications, PRIME ensures that AI tools are used effectively to enhance precision and productivity.

## Use Cases: Transforming Project Management with AI

Our journey through the applications of AI in project management highlighted a wide range of use cases, demonstrating the power of Gen AI in driving productivity and efficiency.

### *Routine Tasks*

One of the first areas where AI proves its value is in routine project tasks, as detailed in Chapter 5. Gen AI tools can seamlessly automate everyday activities such as drafting professional emails, creating presentations, summarizing reports, and developing project plans. By automating these repetitive yet essential tasks, project managers can redirect their focus to strategic and creative activities that require human insight. This automation extends to tasks like generating templates for project documents and performing basic data calculations and analysis in platforms like Excel, resulting in significant time savings and improved workflow efficiencies.

### *Project Portfolio Management*

A major highlight in our exploration was the use of AI in project portfolio management, as discussed in Section 2 of the book. AI tools offer unparalleled support in analyzing vast amounts of project data to delineate an organization's strategic framework, analyze the strategic fit of projects, evaluate projects for their individual merit as well as relative merit compared to the other projects in the portfolio, optimize portfolio selection, and prioritize projects. These tools not only assist in maintaining the health of the entire portfolio but also provide predictive insights that aid in foreseeing potential issues and opportunities.

### *Managing Waterfall Project Life-Cycle Phases*

The application of AI through various life-cycle phases in a waterfall environment was another significant focus of the book (Section 3). From initiation and planning to execution and closeout, we explored how AI supports project management at each phase:

- *Initiation and planning*: AI tools contribute to the development of robust project plans, identification and analysis of stakeholders, creation of accurate schedules, and building comprehensive risk registers.
- *Execution*: AI enhances the execution of project plans and the monitoring of project progress through real-time data analysis, providing metrics that support earned value management and forecasting.

- *Closeout*: AI aids in generating final reports, compiling lessons learned, and preparing comprehensive closeout documentation.

The result is a smoother, more data-informed project life cycle that helps project managers maintain control and adapt as needed.

### *Agile Project Delivery*

In the context of agile project management, the benefits of AI are even more pronounced. Section 4, dedicated to agile methodologies, illustrated how AI tools enhance different aspects of agile delivery:

- *Backlog management and sprint planning*: AI assists in identifying, refining, and prioritizing product backlogs; generating user stories; and planning sprints with better accuracy.
- *Scrum ceremonies*: Tools can facilitate daily stand-ups, produce real-time sprint reports, and generate predictive insights that help project teams make quick, informed decisions.
- *Monitoring and forecasting*: AI-generated burndown charts and velocity tracking provide project leaders with actionable data to anticipate challenges and adjust plans accordingly.

By leveraging AI, agile teams gain the ability to respond to change more effectively and deliver value continuously.

## EMBRACING THE FUTURE OF PROJECT MANAGEMENT WITH AI

The future of project management lies in a harmonious partnership between human ingenuity and AI's computational power. AI has proven its potential to elevate project outcomes by delivering real-time insights, identifying risks, and optimizing resources. However, as promising as AI is, its true impact is realized when complemented by the irreplaceable human elements of judgment, empathy, and strategic thinking. This chapter has sought to paint a vision of a future where AI not only accelerates project execution but also empowers project leaders to redefine what success looks like.

### Emerging Trends and Innovations

The future holds exciting possibilities for AI-driven project management. One of the most promising advancements is the ability to access project data in real time. Imagine AI tools that can continuously analyze and interpret data as it is generated, providing actionable decision support instantly. This capability allows project managers to pivot strategies dynamically, enhancing adaptability and resilience.

A natural progression in AI's evolution is the use of conversational interfaces, akin to Siri or Alexa, for project management. Project managers may soon be able to converse with chatbots to retrieve detailed project information, track performance metrics, and even receive updates on risks or task dependencies. This conversational AI will function as an intuitive, always-available assistant, closing the gap between data and decision making.

Taking this evolution a step further is the rise of AI agents and agentic AI, which are capable of operating autonomously in project management. These AI agents could function as *autonomous project managers*, handling routine administrative tasks, assigning resources, scheduling, and even flagging potential risks—all without direct human intervention. While this technology holds tremendous promise for increasing efficiency, it also raises questions about how these agents will collaborate with human teams, navigate ethical boundaries, and maintain transparency in decision making. The potential to have an AI agent proactively monitor project health, suggest corrective actions, and execute minor adjustments autonomously signals a transformative shift in how projects could be managed.

Organizations no longer need to rely solely on expensive large language models (LLMs) trained on vast public datasets. Instead, they can opt for smaller, tailored AI models fine-tuned with their proprietary project and organizational data. This approach ensures AI outputs are context-specific and aligned with unique organizational needs, making advanced AI tools more accessible and cost-effective, while keeping the data private at the same time.

## Leveraging Emerging Technologies

Beyond traditional AI tools, other technologies like computer vision and drones are making strides in enhancing project management practices. For instance, drones equipped with cameras and sensors can collect real-time data on project progress and site conditions in physical and infrastructure projects, offering unparalleled tracking and monitoring capabilities. This data, combined with AI's analytical prowess, creates a seamless feedback loop for project managers to make informed decisions swiftly.

Additionally, the rise of video-based tools has the potential to revolutionize communication within project teams. AI-powered platforms can enable project managers to create polished video updates, complete with simulated voiceovers, ensuring progress reports are accessible to all stakeholders at any time. These videos can serve as valuable archival resources, preserving a visual history of project milestones and decisions.

## Preparing for an AI-Augmented Future

As AI continues to evolve, project managers must evolve alongside it. Key competencies for the future include data literacy—understanding how to leverage AI insights—and expertise in change management to navigate the integration of new technologies. Emotional intelligence remains equally critical, as project managers must balance AI's capabilities with the nuanced requirements of human collaboration and stakeholder engagement.

Predictive analytics and advanced forecasting tools powered by AI will enable project managers to anticipate risks, foresee opportunities, and prepare for challenges before they arise. By analyzing historical and real-time data, these tools will offer unparalleled foresight, allowing teams to act proactively rather than reactively.

## A Call to Action

The journey toward AI-enhanced project management is not without challenges, from ensuring data integrity to addressing ethical considerations. Yet, these hurdles are not insurmountable. Organizations and project leaders must embrace a mindset of continuous learning and adaptability, preparing themselves for a future where technology and human expertise converge seamlessly.

This is a pivotal moment for project management. The tools and techniques we adopt today will shape the projects of tomorrow. By integrating AI thoughtfully and strategically, project leaders can unlock new levels of efficiency, innovation, and impact. As we close this book, let us look ahead with optimism, ready to harness the transformative power of AI to redefine what is possible in project management.

The future is not just about AI replacing tasks; it is about AI amplifying human potential. Together, human ingenuity and AI can achieve extraordinary things—not just managing projects but shaping the world around us.

### Timeless Relevance in an Evolving AI Landscape

Between the time the final manuscript for this book was completed and its release, advancements in AI, particularly in Gen AI, are inevitable. However, this does not render the content of this book irrelevant. On the contrary, the principles, frameworks, and methodologies outlined—such as GAE, the PRIME methodology, and the art of crafting effective prompts—are timeless foundations designed to adapt to evolving technologies. Alongside these, the practical use cases and case study projects presented are deeply rooted in the realities of project management, mirroring the challenges and dynamics of real-world scenarios. This ensures that you can relate to and apply these insights directly to your professional environment for many years to come.

Moreover, the chapters dedicated to the essentials of project management—covering portfolio management, waterfall methods, and agile methodologies—are presented as evergreen primers. These chapters provide foundational knowledge that transcends specific tools or technologies, remaining universally relevant regardless of future advancements. Together, these elements make the book a reflection of current AI capabilities and a forward-looking guide. It empowers project managers to integrate AI effectively into their workflows, adapt to technological progress, and maintain a strong footing in the rapidly evolving AI and project management nexus. In short, this book equips you with the mindset, skills, and strategies to thrive, no matter how AI evolves.

## RECOMMENDATIONS: NAVIGATING AI INTEGRATION

As you embark on or continue your journey with AI in project management, here are essential recommendations to guide you:

1. *Start small—incremental steps for effective adoption*: AI is powerful but can be overwhelming due to the sheer number of available tools. Just as project management can be dissected into tasks manageable by tools like Microsoft Project or Jira, so too can the adoption of AI. Begin by integrating AI into specific, time-consuming tasks like research or summarization. For example, if you are evaluating risks, tools like ChatGPT, Jasper, or Notion AI can help draft preliminary risk registers or conduct comparative analyses. Choose tools that resonate with your comfort level and align with your project needs, building your proficiency step-by-step.
2. *Embrace AI as your project assistant*: AI should be viewed as an extension of your project management arsenal. It can act as your virtual project assistant by conducting research, generating executive summaries, aiding in project planning, helping in tracking progress, forecasting future performance, or serving as a data analyst. By leveraging AI in this supportive role, you can amplify your productivity and reallocate your time to higher-level leadership activities that require your human touch.
3. *The importance of tailored inputs*: AI's effectiveness hinges on the quality of input it receives. Providing project-specific information is crucial. We emphasize creating a *Project Input Folder* (PIF), a structured repository of essential documents for *your* project. This practice ensures that AI outputs are contextual and relevant, rather than generic. The PIF could include your organization's strategic plans, your project's business case, stakeholder

communications, risk logs, status reports, and numerous other documents. Feeding the AI model project-specific data transforms it from a broad information resource into a tailored project tool.

4. *Privacy and security—addressing concerns head-on*: One question that frequently arose during our presentations on this topic over the last two years was the issue of privacy and data security. These concerns are valid, especially when handling confidential project data. While the benefits of AI are undeniable, we must stress the importance of addressing ethical and privacy considerations head-on. Integrating AI into project management comes with its share of challenges, particularly when it comes to safeguarding data and maintaining transparency. There are several practical strategies for mitigating these risks, such as using privacy-centric AI models and training proprietary AI systems. By incorporating the following strategies, project managers can engage with AI confidently, knowing that their data is protected.
    - ***Use privacy-focused AI models:*** Opt for LLMs that assure data privacy and do not retain input data, such as those provided by platforms prioritizing end-to-end encryption.
    - ***Train proprietary models:*** Organizations can invest in training their models with proprietary data, ensuring control over information security.
    - ***Retrieval-augmented generation:*** This approach allows AI to pull in data from secured, internal company databases, thus preserving confidentiality while enriching the AI's responses.
5. *A call for continuous learning*: The AI landscape is dynamic, with new tools emerging almost daily. This rapid evolution can be intimidating. However, just as we continually adapt to new project management methodologies and tools, the same approach applies to AI. Keep your eyes open, stay curious, and embrace an attitude of lifelong learning. Over time, incorporating new AI tools will become second nature, enhancing your versatility and value as a project professional.

## CONFRONTING THE FEAR: WILL AI TAKE MY JOB?

A recurrent fear in the project management community is that AI will replace project managers. The reality is more complex. AI is set to transform roles rather than eliminate them. If you ignore AI, you risk making yourself obsolete, but if you learn to leverage it, you position yourself as an invaluable leader. Your role will evolve from being a project manager who oversees processes to a project leader who inspires teams and steers strategy.

### The Shift from Management to Leadership

- *Empathy and motivation*: Leadership will increasingly be about understanding team dynamics, motivating members, and cultivating a collaborative environment.
- *Emotional intelligence*: Skills such as negotiation, conflict resolution, and active listening will become more crucial than ever. AI can assist in providing data-driven insights but cannot replace the empathetic, nuanced judgment a human leader brings.

### Emotional AI: A Glimpse into the Future

AI technologies are evolving to incorporate aspects of emotional intelligence, enabling better interaction within teams. For instance, tools that analyze the sentiment of team communications can help project leaders identify areas of concern and intervene proactively. This emotional AI augmentation fosters a stronger, more cohesive team dynamic.

### The Enduring Role of the Project Manager

Despite fears, studies show that while certain project management activities may be automated, the role will persist. Project managers will spend less time on administrative tasks and more time on leadership activities. Embrace the transition and focus on honing skills that machines cannot, yet, replicate—strategic thinking, inspiring vision, and empathetic leadership.

### The Peace Treaty: Coexisting with AI

AI is here to stay. The question is not whether it will remain but how we, as project professionals, choose to integrate it into our work. It is time to make peace with AI, using it as an ally rather than viewing it as an adversary. The more you engage, experiment, and learn, the more natural AI will feel as part of your project toolkit.

## IN CONCLUSION: THE HUMAN SPIRIT AT THE HELM

We stand at the frontier of a new era where the potential of AI is boundless, but it is the human spirit that steers its course. AI can chart a path, but it takes your vision, creativity, and leadership to navigate it. As we close this book, we leave you with this final thought: AI is a tool of immense power, but like any tool, its true value is determined by the person who wields it. Embrace it, shape it, and let it propel you toward a future where project management is not just about managing projects but leading them to success with unparalleled insight and efficiency.

The journey of project management in the age of AI is one of adaptation, growth, and reimagining. As we conclude this book, remember that while AI began as a tool, it is now evolving into a collaborative partner—its true impact still depends on how we choose to engage with it. Harness it wisely, lead courageously, and embrace the future with an open mind. This is not the end of the project management journey; it is the beginning of a new era—one where humans and AI collaborate to achieve unparalleled success. AI may chart the course, but it is the human spirit that directs the voyage. In this dynamic world of project management, embrace AI not as a rival but as an ally in your pursuit of excellence.

Let AI be your copilot, but never forget that *you* are the captain. Lead with courage, act with empathy, and drive projects with efficiency and a vision that only a human can bring.

# REFERENCES


Ambler, S.W. and M. Lines, 2022. *Choose Your WoW!: A Disciplined Agile Delivery Handbook for Optimizing Your Way of Working.* Project Management Institute, Newtown Square, Pennsylvania.

Anderson, D.J., 2010. *Kanban: Successful Evolutionary Change for Your Technology Business.* Blue Hole Press, Sequim, Washington.

AXELOS, 2017. *Managing Successful Projects with PRINCE2®*. 6th ed. The Stationery Office, London, England.

Bainey, K., 2024. *AI-Driven Project Management: Harnessing the Power of Artificial Intelligence and ChatGPT to Achieve Peak Productivity and Success.* Wiley, Hoboken, New Jersey.

Beck, K., M. Beedle, A. van Bennekum, A. Cockburn, W. Cunningham, M. Fowler, M.J. Grenning, J. Highsmith, A. Hunt, R. Jeffries, J. Kern, B. Marick, R.C. Martin, S. Mellor, K. Schwaber, J. Sutherland, and D. Thomas, 2001. *Manifesto for Agile Software Development.* https://agilemanifesto.org/ [Accessed on Jan 31, 2025].

Bory, P., S. Natale, and C. Katzenbach, 2024. *Strong and Weak AI Narratives: An Analytical Framework.* AI & Society. https://doi.org/10.1007/s00146-024-02087-8 [Accessed on Jan 31, 2025].

Bragantini, D. and D. Ferrante, 2014. *How to Shape Your Stakeholders.* Paper presented at Project Management Institute Global Congress, EMEA, Dubai, United Arab Emirates. https://www.pmi.org/learning/library/stakeholder-shape-tool-effective-communication-8706 [Accessed on Jan 31, 2025].

Brooks, R.A., 1991. *Intelligence Without Representation.* Artificial Intelligence, 47(1–3), 139–159.

Butt, A., 2018. *Project Management Through the Lens of Artificial Intelligence: A Mixed-Methods Research into How AI Systems Can Support Project Managers to Become more Efficient in their Daily Work.* Master's thesis, Chalmers University of Technology, Gothenburg, Sweden.

Clegg, D. and R. Barker, 1994. *Case Method Fast-Track: A Rad Approach (Computer Aided System Engineering).* Addison-Wesley, Wokingham, England.

Derby, E. and D. Larsen, 2006. *Agile Retrospectives: Making Good Teams Great.* Pragmatic Bookshelf, Raleigh, North Carolina.

Gardner, H., 1983. *Frames of Mind: The Theory of Multiple Intelligences.* Basic Books, New York, New York.

Goleman, D., 2020. *Emotional Intelligence: Why It Can Matter More Than IQ.* 25th anniversary ed. Bloomsbury Publishing, London, England.

Goodfellow, I., J. Pouget-Abadie, M. Mirza, B. Xu, D. Warde-Farley, S. Ozair, A. Courville, and Y. Bengio, 2014. *Generative Adversarial Nets.* In: Advances in Neural Information Processing Systems (NIPS), 27, pp. 2672–2680. https://papers.nips.cc/paper/5423-generative-adversarial-nets [Accessed on Jan 31, 2025].

Haus, M., 2013. *Are Your Communication Habits Good Enough?* ProjectManagement.com. https://www.projectmanagement.com/blog-post/18979/Are-Your-Communication-Habits-Good-Enough [Accessed on Jan 31, 2025].

Kanabar, V. and J. Wong, 2024. *The AI Revolution in Project Management: Elevating Productivity with Generative AI.* Pearson, Upper Saddle River, New Jersey.

Kerzner, H., 2022. *Project Management: A Systems Approach to Planning, Scheduling, and Controlling.* 13th ed, Wiley, Hoboken, New Jersey.

Kingma, D.P. and M. Welling, 2019. *An Introduction to Variational Autoencoders.* Foundations and Trends® in Machine Learning, 12(4), pp. 307–392.

Kodukula, P.S., 2014. *Organizational Project Portfolio Management: A Practitioner's Guide.* J. Ross Publishing, Plantation, Florida.

Kodukula, P.S. and Y. Lu, 2017. *Selecting the Right Projects for Portfolios Using Optimization and Stochastic Techniques.* Presented at Project Management Institute's Global Conference, Chicago, Illinois, October 28–30.

Kodukula, P.S., 2020. *Recovery of Troubled Projects.* Course Notes, University of Chicago.

Kodukula, P.S., 2023. *Stop Busing Project Budgets and Schedules! Apply Risk Impact Sensitivity Analysis (RISA).* Virtual Presentation at Project Control Summit, May 3–5.

Kodukula, P.S. and G. Vinueza, 2024. *Transform Your Ways of Working: Use Cases for AI in Project Management.* Presented at Project Management Institute's Global Summit, Los Angeles, California, September 19–21.

Langr, J. and V. Bok, 2019. *GANs in Action: Deep Learning with Generative Adversarial Networks.* Manning Publications, New York, New York.

Leffingwell, D., 2018. *SAFe 4.5 Reference Guide: Scaled Agile Framework for Lean Enterprises.* 2nd ed., Addison-Wesley Professional, Boston, Massachusetts.

Levison, M., 2019. *How long should a Sprint be?* Scrum.org. https://www.scrum.org/resources/blog/how-long-sprint-should-be [Accessed on Jan 31, 2025].

Levison, M., 2019. *Choosing a Scrum Sprint Length (Shorter Beats Longer).* Agile Pain Relief Consulting. https://agilepainrelief.com/blog/choosing-scrum-sprint-length.html [Accessed on Jan 31, 2025].

Liker, J.K., 2021. *The Toyota Way: 14 Management Principles from the World's Greatest Manufacturer.* 2nd ed. McGraw-Hill Education, New York, New York.

Lipke, W., 2009. *Earned Schedule.* Lulu Publishing, Raleigh, North Carolina.

Maleki, N., B. Padmanabhan, and K. Dutta, 2024. *AI Hallucinations: A Misnomer Worth Clarifying.* arXiv.org. https://doi.org/10.48550/arXiv.2401.06796 [Accessed on Jan 31, 2025].

Malone, T.W., 2018. *Superminds: The Surprising Power of People and Computers Thinking Together.* Little, Brown Spark, New York, New York.

Mariani, C. and M. Mancini, 2024. *AI's Role in Project Management: An Overview of the Literature and a Research Agenda.* Lecture Notes in Civil Engineering, Vol. 493, pp. 142–157.

McCarthy, J., M.L. Minsky, N. Rochester, and C.E. Shannon, 1955. *A Proposal for the Dartmouth Summer Research Project on Artificial Intelligence.* Unpublished Manuscript. Dartmouth College, Hanover, New Hampshire. (Cited in AI Magazine, 27(4), Winter 2006, pp. 12–14.)

McCarthy, J. 1958. *Programs with Common Sense.* In: Proceedings of the Teddington Conference on the Mechanization of Thought Processes, pp. 75–91. Her Majesty's Stationery Office, London, England.

Mollick, E. 2024. *Co-Intelligence: Living and Working with AI.* Portfolio/Penguin, New York, New York.

Nieto-Rodriguez, A. and R.V. Vargas, 2023. *How AI Will Transform Project Management.* Harvard Business Review. https://hbr.org/2023/02/how-ai-will-transform-project-management [Accessed on Jan 31, 2025].

Nieto-Rodriguez, A. and R.V. Vargas, 2023. *The Opportunities at the Intersection of AI, Sustainability, and Project Management.* Harvard Business Review. https://hbr.org/2023/10/the-opportunities-at-the-intersection-of-ai-sustainability-and-project-management [Accessed on Jan 31, 2025].

Nieto-Rodriguez, A. 2022. *Project Leaders Will Make or Break Your Sustainability Goals.* Harvard Business Review. https://hbr.org/2022/10/project-leaders-will-make-or-break-your-sustainability-goals [Accessed on Jan 31, 2025].

Nilsson, N.J., 2009. *The Quest for Artificial Intelligence: A History of Ideas and Achievements.* Cambridge University Press, Cambridge, Massachusetts.

Ohno, T., 1988. *Toyota Production System: Beyond Large-Scale Production.* Productivity Press, New York, New York.

Overeem, B., 2021. *How To Run A Sprint Review, Online?* Scrum.org. https://www.scrum.org/resources/blog/how-run-sprint-review-online [Accessed on Jan 31, 2025].

Project Management Institute, 2017. *Agile Practice Guide.* Project Management Institute, Newtown Square, Pennsylvania.

Project Management Institute, 2021. *A Guide to the Project Management Body of Knowledge (PMBOK® Guide).* 7th ed. Project Management Institute, Newtown Square, Pennsylvania.

Rubin, K.S., 2012. *Essential Scrum: A Practical Guide to the Most Popular Agile Process.* Addison-Wesley Professional, Upper Saddle River, New Jersey.

Sahoo, P., A.K. Singh, S. Saha, V. Jain, S. Mondal, and A. Chadha, 2024. *A Systematic Survey of Prompt Engineering in Large Language Models: Techniques and Applications.* arXiv.org. https://doi.org/10.48550/arXiv.2402.07927 [Accessed: Jan 2025].

Schwaber, K. 1995. *SCRUM Development Process.* In J. Sutherland, C. Casanave, J. Miller, P. Patel, and G. Hollowell (Eds.), Business Object Design and Implementation: OOPSLA '95 Workshop Proceedings. Springer, London, England. https://doi.org/10.1007/978-1-4471-0947-1_11 [Accessed on Jan 31, 2025].

Schwaber, K. and J. Sutherland, 2020. *The Scrum Guide.* Scrum.org. https://www.scrumguides.org/ [Accessed on Jan 31, 2025].

Schwaber, K. and M. Beedle, 2002. *Agile software development with Scrum.* Prentice Hall, Upper Saddle River, New Jersey.

Seddon, J., 2023. *Beyond Command and Control: A Better Way to Make Work Work.* 2nd ed. Vanguard Press, Buckingham, England.

Shingo, S., 1989. *A Study of the Toyota Production System: From an Industrial Engineering Viewpoint.* Productivity Press, New York, New York.

Simon, H.A., 1995. *Artificial Intelligence: An Empirical Science.* Artificial Intelligence, 77(1), 95–127.

Taboada, I., A. Daneshpajouh, N. Toledo, and T. de Vass, 2023. *Artificial Intelligence Enabled Project Management: A Systematic Literature Review.* Applied Sciences, 13(8), 5014.

Takeuchi, H. and I. Nonaka, 1986. *The New New Product Development Game.* Harvard Business Review, 64(1), pp. 137–146.

Tegmark, M., 2017. *Life 3.0: Being Human in the Age of Artificial Intelligence.* Alfred A. Knopf, New York, New York.

van den Oord, A., S. Dieleman, H. Zen, K. Simonyan, O. Vinyals, A. Graves, N. Kalchbrenner, A. Senior, and K. Kavukcuoglu, 2016. *WaveNet: A Generative Model for Raw Audio.* arXiv. https://doi.org/10.48550/arXiv.1609.03499 [Accessed on Jan 31, 2025].

Vaswani, A., N. Shazeer, N. Parmar, J. Uszkoreit, L. Jones, A.N. Gomez, L. Kaiser, and I. Polosukhin, 2017. *Attention Is All You Need.* In: Proceedings of the 31st International Conference on Neural Information Processing Systems (NIPS), pp. 6000–6010. https://arxiv.org/abs/1706.03762 [Accessed on Jan 31, 2025].

Womack, J.P., D.T. Jones, and D. Roos, 1990. *The Machine That Changed the World: The Story of Lean Production.* Free Press, New York, New York.

# INDEX

Note: Page numbers followed by "f" and "t" refer to figures and tables, respectively.